the
whole parenting
guide

the
whole

STRATEGIES, RESOURCES,
AND INSPIRING STORIES
FOR HOLISTIC PARENTING
AND FAMILY LIVING

parenting
guide

ALAN REDER, PHIL CATALFO, AND
STEPHANIE RENFROW HAMILTON

BROADWAY BOOKS   NEW YORK

BROADWAY

Broadway Books titles may be purchased for business or promotional use or for special
sales. For information, please write to: Special Markets Department, Random House, Inc.,
1540 Broadway, New York, New York 10036.

BROADWAY BOOKS and its logo, a letter B bisected on the diagonal, are trademarks of
Broadway Books, a division of Random House, Inc.

Visit our website at broadwaybooks.com

FIRST EDITION

Designed by Mauna Eichner

ISBN 0-7679-0133-9

99 00 01 02 03 10 9 8 7 6 5 4 3 2 1

To our parents and our children,
who have taught us far more than
they know, and especially to Gabriel Catalfo
(1983–1998), senior professor

contents

acknowledgments

OUR COLLECTIVE GRATITUDE TO:

Our agent, Laurie Fox (not only our ace representative, but also, in the case of Alan and Phil, a long-time, dear friend), for helping us "conceive" (as in, begin to gestate) this book. Linda Chester, for continuous behind-the-scenes guidance and support and just-in-time cheerleading. Our editors, Janet Goldstein and Tracy Behar, and their assistants, Betsy Thorpe, Daisy Alpert, and Angela Casey, for helping us "birth" the book.

Chris Radant and Teri Keough, for contributing excellent research and writing (in Chris' case, on family tree-planting, volunteer vacations, and vacations that immerse families in other cultures; in Teri's case, on the subject of relationships with extended family).

Lynn Willeford, Rachel Bendat, Lori Cangilose, Kat Wild, Karen O'Dougherty, Jeanine Calabria, and Laurie Hayden, for uncommon generosity during the interview phase.

The other parents and children whose family stories are told here, for opening their lives to us, sharing their hard-earned wisdom, and helping give this book heart.

Professional photographers Kurt Buser, Michael Allen Jones, Richard Murphy, Barbara Sonneborn, Kathy VanGorder, Nancy Warner, and Kati Zweig, and talented snapshooters Saadat Ahmad, Tracey Ballard-Kim, Teenah Barker, Chaka Hamilton, Marty Jacobs, Miriam Jacobs, Marcia Jarmel, Leah Mazel-Gee, Krysta Morgenthaler, Gordon Piper, Hyiah Reder, and James Weeks, for allowing their amazingly artful photographic images to grace our pages.

"Village elders" Drs. Benjamin Spock, Marianne Neifert, Grantly Dick-Read, Frederick Leboyer, and T. Berry Brazelton; Sheila Kitzinger; Penelope Leach; Joseph Chilton Pearce; Peggy O'Mara; and so many others, for igniting the spirit of Whole Parenting.

ALAN:

To: Hyiah, ultimate Whole Parent, who ran on empty for a year and a half so I wouldn't have to, and bathed me in love so I never went dry. I'm in awe.

Ariel and Ajene, who understood that Daddy wasn't available right now . . . or now . . . or now, because he was writing a parenting book, and loved me anyway.

My parents, whose souls shine through these pages.

Leonard Orr, who opened my eyes on birth trauma, Joe Pearce, whose books, lectures, and personal observations helped Hyiah and me raise magical children.

PHIL:

To: Alan and Stephanie, who made it possible for me to devote my attention and energy, for many months, entirely to my son's illness and recovery, even though it meant extra burdens on them in terms of completing this project. I wish, for many reasons, it could have been different, and I hope you realize how much you helped my family cope with our crisis.

Alan, again, for thirty years of the most valuable friendship anyone could ever hope to have.

Gabriella Heinsheimer, M.D.; Robin Dellabough; Peggy Taylor; Mary Mackey, Howard Rheingold, Reva Basch, and other writer friends from The WELL; and countless other friends, neighbors, and fellow wanderers in the parenting wilderness, for advice, encouragement, tips, referrals, and other indispensable info.

Jim Brandley and Summer Laurie, for research assistance.

My wife, Michelle Lerager, for sharing a lifetime's worth of personal and professional knowledge about childbirth, labor, and breastfeeding; for being the very model of a modern major mom; for blessing me with our children; and for loving them so well.

My parents, Dan and Fran Catalfo, for teaching me early on that everything in the world was somehow related to our family (given the size of our extended family, I thought that everyone in the world was, too); for bestowing upon me the experience of family; and for modeling the invincible love that lies at the heart of parenthood.

My children, Jessamine, Gabriel, and Peter, the three suns in my strange solar system, and the source of most of the joy I have known in this life, for revealing yourselves to me and teaching me to be a parent—not to mention tolerating my endless questions, and being lab rats for my journalistic experiments.

STEPHANIE:

To: James Weeks, beloved spouse, soulmate, and sweetie pie who will never let me take myself too seriously, and my beautiful children, Malcolm, Tulani, and Diallo, who will never let me *not.*

My father, Bobb Hamilton, writer and poet—you are no longer earthbound, but I can still feel your great wit and pride. And to the mothers in my life, Aishah Rahman, Barbara Hamilton, Joan Murray, and Eglantine Weeks.

My sister, Karimu Hamilton, who has made a fine start on the path to Whole Parenting. And to sisters Ifetayo Lawson-Freeman, Sabrina Hamilton, and Rachel Christmas-Derrick who are also newly on that good path—with or without my unsolicited advice.

Joan Edelstein, R.N., Ph.D., for her keen, consulting eye and delightful sense of humor. Ramona Gonzales, networker extraordinaire; Maria Iarillo at the WiseWoman Childbirth Collective; and Eric Alderman, who wrote the book on getting computer friendly and in doing so, helped me write a book, too.

the
whole parenting
guide

1

the whole parenting
approach to family life

Two beings join; cells unite; in time, a life begins. From that same process, driven by the irresistible urge of life itself, comes not just the individual but also the family, the tribe, the community; in other forms of life, the pack, the school, the grove; ultimately, from this simple but unfathomable process, repeated endlessly, comes the planet.

Looked at this way, we can see the birth of a child and the life of a family as John Muir did when he pondered the natural world and found that "[w]hen we try to pick out anything by itself, we find it hitched to everything else in the universe." For children aren't born and raised in a vacuum; families live in communities; they depend on the air and soil and water not just where they live but where their food is grown; every day, families make choices that affect far-off people and communities and species, just as distant decisions affect them.

In the following chapters, we promote an integrated view of the world and the family's place in it. All parents are interested in protecting the well-being of their children. But it is not always easy to recognize all the ways that the life we make with our family—including the activities we pursue, the things we consume, and the ways we spend our money—either enhance or detract from that well-being.

Not that any parents, the authors included, want to be told what they *should* be doing, no matter how virtuous. But we do assume that your interest in the parenting approaches described in this book means that you are unusually interested in what's best for your children—that in your life, kids come first.

In wanting the "highest possible good" for our kids, most of us would include the following: We want their minds to develop into rich expressions of intelligence, curiosity, and creativity. We want their bodies to be models of health and vigor. We also want our children to become good people, able to negotiate their way through the moral quagmires and cheap entertainments of modern culture without becoming cynical or violent. We want their hearts to be strong and their souls intact. We want what is *uniquely* best for each of our children, as well, rather than having them just settle for what society hands them in the way of food, education, recreation, and so on.

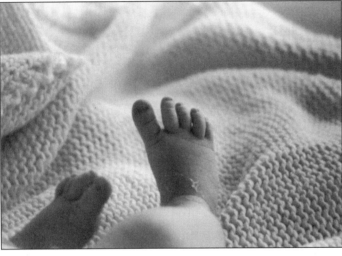

We want our children to *be* individuals, too; we know we can't insulate them from mass culture but we don't want them to disappear into it either. Finally, we want our children to realize that some of the most meaningful aspects of life—love, a sense of their place in a larger scheme—are not things they can simply purchase or possess or even put their hands on.

At the end of the day, we want to come away with a clear conscience that we did our best for our kids and the world they are inheriting. Herein, we offer you our best information on how to do just that.

We believe that a family that sees itself squarely in the grand scheme of things stands a better chance of being a happy, fulfilled family than one that doesn't. We also believe that there are many ways for you and your family to embody this outlook and that the path there is exciting and scenic. We invite you onto that path, not because we have found out everything there is to know about the landscape, but because we find the journey so rewarding.

Before we embark on that journey together, some background is in order. It took a unique combination of historical circumstances to create the predicament of the modern family. Those same circumstances prompted dramatic insights and strategies that have helped many families not only cope with this predicament but thrive in the face of it. By understanding how parenting has changed in the last few generations, you will better understand the options you face today and which of them might be a better fit both for your family and the times.

THE WHOLE PARENTING STORY

Beyond the radar of the media and an army of social critics, family life is transforming for the better for millions of American parents and children. Not that these Americans are immune from trends that stress and sometimes break apart families, but they more actively resist them. In these homes, Mom and Dad strive to be highly involved with their kids even though social and economic forces pull them in the opposite direction. They examine what mainstream society hands down as received parenting wisdom, including what their parents did with them, with a critical eye. They reject much of what corporate America and the healthcare establishment markets to them and their children. They stack their nightstands with books and articles on parenting, studying the subject as diligently as if they were back in school. They welcome the unconventional, as long as it works.

In so doing, these parents have reclaimed much of what previous generations had abandoned as primitive and unscientific—natural birthing, breast-feeding, natural healthcare, and holistic nutrition. They have challenged institutions such as public education with progressive alternatives of their own such as Waldorf schools and homeschooling. They have decried the consumerism and commercialism of American society and warn their children about its excesses. They talk about voluntary simplicity, and many of them are actually practicing it. Their efforts to transform family life don't always succeed, but many times they do, and the result is some truly remarkable kids—healthy, smart, curious, self-assured, and independent thinking.

We call this constellation of parenting approaches Whole Parenting. Ultimately, Whole Parenting is the family version of a set of values shared by a large and growing segment of the population. It encompasses holistic health, an interest in personal growth and caring relationships, a deep and more personal spirituality, a mystical appreciation of nature, environmental stewardship, a social conscience, an appreciation of different cultures, a rejection of the dominant culture's materialism, and, in its adherents' own holistic and progressive way, strong family values. Not everyone who practices Whole Parenting resides in all of these camps, but everyone who practices Whole Parenting resides in at least several of them.

As a cohesive approach to family life, Whole Parenting came together rather suddenly in the early 1970s, although threads appeared earlier. A movement without a leader or spokesperson, it encompasses millions of parents who want the best for their kids, who oppose the mainstream version of what that means, and who have enough people- and buying power to leave a large and visible stamp on the culture.

Childbirth and Infant Care—The Evolution of a Revolution

Some might guess that the roots of Whole Parenting go no deeper than the 1960s and 1970s counterculture having children of their own in their own distinctive style. But Whole Parenting is not just the imprint of a generation. Lava lamps and bell-bottoms have come and gone. The oldest boomers are now wistfully cuddling grandkids, their own child-raising years far behind them. Yet Whole Parenting remains deeply ingrained in the culture, the preferred parenting approach for vast numbers of young parents with not one nostalgic thought about John, Paul, George, Ringo, Aretha, or Jimi.

In part, Whole Parenting came about because certain pendulums in society had swung so far in one direction that there was nowhere for them to swing but back. Take, for example, the evolution of current birthing practices. Before 1900, most women gave birth at home with another woman, often a professional midwife, assisting. Midwives put their faith in nature's wisdom and waited for her to deliver the child. A fair number of women died in childbirth in those days. As a result, women dreaded giving birth, and their dread dramatically increased the pain, although the connection between fear and discomfort wasn't understood at the time.

By the turn of the century, physicians had convinced educated, upper-class women that they could make birthing faster and safer. In came a mechanized birthing procedure that featured forceps, episiotomy (surgical enlargement of the vaginal opening), and women lying on their backs for the convenience of the doctors, most of them men. Out went any attention to mother and baby's thoughts and emotions, not to mention any idea that nature's way might still have something to offer.

Doctor-assisted birthing had spread to the general population by the 1940s; most women were now having their babies in gleaming, sterile hospitals rather than their own bedrooms. Maternal and newborn death rates dropped sharply, in part from doctors' efforts and in part because improved family nutrition put mothers in better shape to give birth. Physicians also answered women's pleas to do something about the pain—with a cocktail of numbing drugs.

In infant nutrition and child care, nature was also taking a backseat to the wonders of science. Since mothers no longer trusted themselves to give birth without a doctor at hand, they began to see physicians as experts on virtually every aspect of child-rearing. They were developing a similar faith in science and technology in general, which put electric refrigerators in their kitchens, radios in their living rooms, and cars in their garages. When moms began asking their doctors the best way to feed their babies, the professionals gave them the scientific and technological answer they wanted to hear—canned baby formula. Most physicians believed formula was just as good as mother's milk and some believed it was superior.

The behavioral advice doctors were giving their patients also favored bottle-feeding. Since the turn of the century, doctors and psychologists had been suggesting putting infants on rigid feeding and sleeping schedules to prevent parents from "spoiling" the child. Women who used bottles found it easier to resist their babies' cries, both physically and emotionally, because breasts are biologically programmed to respond to baby's stress.

Science- and doctor-worship converged with other societal trends that further encouraged bottle-feeding. Freed from the binding fashions of the flapper era and reshaped by new brassieres in the 1930s and 1940s, the female breast was rediscovered as a sexual object and its natural function was ignored. Women were also now thinking about starting their own careers and otherwise cutting their ties to traditional homemaking; bottle-feeding helped make that possible. The spread of electric refrigerators helped tip the scales toward formula by making bottle-feeding easier. By 1960, 80 percent of women were bottle-feeding their babies from birth.

Ironically, the advances of medicine had prepared the ground for a new consciousness that would lessen women's dependence on their doctors. The dangers of death and disability had largely been eliminated from birthing by the 1950s, not so much because medically attended births were better than birthing at home but because doctors and midwives better understood how infections started and could rely on antibiotics to fight them. Freed from the panic that had driven them to doctors in the first place, women began to wonder whether the complete medical takeover of birthing and baby care was such a swell idea after all.

Then came the 1960s and with it a whole new way of looking at the world. A willingness to challenge authority and a distaste for materialism emerged, based in part on the defiant art and lives of the Beat poets. Suddenly, millions distrusted science and technology, which had invented the new daily terrors of atomic weapons and nuclear energy. Middle-class youths who had eaten one too many TV dinners in a tract-home kitchen began craving authenticity and the exotic. The times also saw the rise of a back-to-nature movement whose followers saw it as the path to recovering their souls.

This was also a time of a new women's consciousness. Women felt newly independent and competent, having watched their mothers fill the jobs left behind by GIs shipping out to fight World War II. Better educated now, women took a new interest in their bodies and their inner lives. They devoured the writings of Betty Friedan, Simone de Beauvoir, and, later, Gloria Steinem. Women who were ready to become mothers read the books of Fernand Lamaze, Robert Bradley, Grantly Dick-Read, and Sheila Kitzinger, who showed them how to mitigate the pain of childbirth without drugs. Good-bye, physician as guru. Birthing and child care would never be the same.

Women immersed in the counterculture and the women's movement now began demanding an array of natural options from their obstetricians. In hospital birthing, pregnant mothers stated their preferences for or against various medical procedures in "birth plans." Some women opted out of hospital births entirely, reviving the tradition of home births with a midwife. Exotic alternatives such as birthing underwater caught on with others. As dedicated moms-to-be studied the benefits of nursing, breast-feeding rates began to rise again despite the onslaught of formula advertising and free formula samples lavished on new mothers.

Having accepted the inescapable logic of women's equality, dads started taking a more active role in parenting, too, beginning as supportive partners during childbirth. The Lamaze/Bradley revolution also signaled a broader change of consciousness. Before the 1960s, most women wanted to be anesthetized during birth. Now, many wanted to be awake, an apt metaphor for a whole host of new parenting attitudes, not just birthing.

Social Consciousness, Holistic Living, and Families

The progressive political and social attitudes of the 1960s and early 1970s were also changing family life. On the ecological front, vast forestlands were being clear-cut to fuel the post-war housing boom that was still going strong in the 1960s. Mountains were being ground down to mine iron for the steel skeletons of downtown office towers and suburban shopping malls. The mass scale devastation was impossible for any nature lover to ignore, especially when it became clear that America's last old-growth tree would fall by early in the twenty-first century if present trends continued. At the same time, species the world over were becoming extinct at an alarming rate, and some of nature's most celebrated creations were in danger of joining them. When parents realized that their children might grow up in a world without forests, eagles, lions, tigers, pandas, and elephants, environmentalism became a family value.

KATHY VANGORDER

New family values were being forged out of other social movements of the era, as well. As the Civil Rights protests in the South and the violent response to them woke America up to its pathology about race, many parents decided to help the healing process by teaching more inclusive values to their children. Television brought the horrors of the Vietnam War into the family living room every night. Hundreds of thousands of Vietnamese, many of them women and children, and tens of thousands of American fathers and sons were dying there, and for goals that no one seemed able to make very clear. What did become clear to many parents was the need to show their children that peace was a better way. The peace movement also sensitized many parents to the violent themes of toys, video games, movies, and TV shows marketed to their kids, especially to boys.

The spread of the women's movement in the 1970s left its mark on family social values, too. Feminism changed the way parents thought about their daughters, from the kind of clothes they should wear, to the stories Mom and Dad should tell them, to the career guidance they should receive. If girls were to make their way in a world run by and tailored to males, their parents had to prepare them from the beginning, before society implanted its stifling ideas about their proper role.

If one idea defined the new consciousness sweeping the culture, it was the intuition that all was one. In health, this meant searching for practitioners who treated the whole person—body, mind, and spirit. It also meant seeking out natural cures that worked in mysterious ways but without the destructive side effects of regular medicine. Inside their pediatricians' offices, many mothers who had once dutifully okayed every pill, shot, and X ray were questioning the doctor's advice and asking for less harmful alternatives. Some parents even began attempting their own holistic remedies at home.

The fascination with natural health transformed family eating habits, too. Millions of parents shuddered at the thought of feeding their children the same commercial baby foods and white bread they had grown up on. Many stayed clear of conventional supermarkets entirely, helping ramshackle community natural foods stores reinvent themselves as alternative versions of the neighborhood supermarket. Doctors were getting fewer nutritional questions because many holistically oriented parents now felt they knew more about food than the M.D. did. And in many cases, they were right.

NANCY WARNER

In education, many parents looked for teachers and schools that would treat their children as feeling, curious individuals, not passive receptacles for knowledge or replacement troops for the economy. Enrollments in Waldorf and Montessori schools rose and hundreds of countercultural "free schools" sprang up around the country. Responding to the challenge, the public schools founded their own alternative programs.

For families trying to provide a spiritual home for their children, the options didn't seem nearly as obvious. Parents who embraced the new consciousness felt tugged in several different directions. For many, the religious tradition with which they were raised had stopped making sense to them, yet they felt guilty about not passing it on to their children. Millions felt the call of a spirituality deeper and more mysterious than anything their parents had talked about. It was a spirituality not easily communicated to kids, but one adults couldn't deny in themselves, so they pressed on in their search. Some began following self-anointed teachers who spoke to their experience like no minister or rabbi ever had. Some began practicing ancient religions like Hinduism and Buddhism that were more in accord with their holistic world view. Some tracked down more mystical approaches to the Christianity or Judaism their parents had practiced. Some left their hearts at home and joined traditional churches or synagogues "for the kids' sake." Some just stayed confused with few answers to offer when their children started asking about God.

The optimism, holism, and altruism of the 1960s and 1970s appeared to fade into the cynicism and materialism of the 1980s and 1990s. But a closer look at the way millions were now living suggested otherwise. For a growing number of families, birthing, infant care, social values, family healthcare, education, and spirituality were all springing from a philosophical base with its roots in more hopeful, if turbulent, times.

Whole Parenting Today

Far from being a passing fad, the consciousness that gave birth to Whole Parenting continues to deepen and mature. A pioneering 1995 survey (by market research firm American LIVES) confirmed that a huge shift in values has been taking place in the population. The vanguard group that holds these transformed values, whom the American LIVES researchers call "Cultural Creatives," is certainly not dominant in society. However, the group does constitute nearly a quarter of the adult population and is growing larger. Cultural Creatives include millions who came of age in the 1960s, but also millions who are older or younger. The very fact that the book you now hold in your hands attracted you suggests that you are someone who shares at least some of this group's values and express them in your parenting.

That being the case, you've probably run up against issues for which your values don't supply easy answers, where you have had to adapt your views to new conditions, re-examine basic premises, and otherwise accommodate the ever-changing demands of reality. These challenges, which will be more fully explored in the following chapters, include:

Commercialism. Parents who hope to instill progressive and holistic values in their kids find themselves constantly battling commercial culture. They want to feed their children healthful foods and have them play with developmentally appropriate toys. Parents also hope to teach their children to be careful, skeptical consumers once they start spending on their own. But their kids often have different ideas, seduced by relentless advertisements and influenced by peers from less resistant families. While commercialism has been a major influence on children for generations, it has dramatically expanded its reach in recent years. Advertisements now invade even the classroom and school hallways, and the deregulation of children's television, implemented by the Reagan Administration, allows companies to target children's naiveté in ways once forbidden.

Diversity. More and more parents today understand the importance of orienting their children to a more diverse world, but our culture, with its persistent blindspots on the issue, hasn't really prepared them to do it. Few parents have the background to recognize the many ways that prejudice is still structured into our institutions and day-to-day social relations, much less identify and acknowledge their own prejudices. Yet teaching children to appreciate and honor diversity depends on parents having these understandings and communicating about them to their kids.

Drugs. Parents today face a problem that rarely troubled parents before the 1960s—the likelihood that a child will try illicit drugs. Drug use spread to all sectors of American society in the 1960s for a variety of reasons. Drugs like marijuana and LSD became associated with the consciousness-raising theme of the era. America's foreign wars played a role, too—soldiers who started using marijuana during World War II or the Korean War went to college afterward on the GI Bill and helped introduce pot to middle-class students. But the society's repressive response to increased drug use has helped cement such use in place, say many experts, by making outlawed drugs seem more attractive to young people. In fact, as the war on drugs has escalated, the numbers of young people using drugs have only risen as have the numbers of drugs used. Children start taking drugs at younger ages today, and more use potentially lethal drugs such as heroin.

Education. Parents who grew up in a more liberal era still largely support public education. But public schools don't work as well as they used to. One-size-fits-all education doesn't go over well in a society where fewer people agree on values. Taxpayer revolt in many states has starved schools for resources, leading to overcrowded classes and deteriorating buildings. Absentee parenting, often forced by economic necessity, troubles children at home, creating greater behavior problems in the classroom. These factors lead many progressive families to seek alternatives such as charter schools, private schools, and homeschooling. Ironically, these approaches eat away at the strength of the public schools, making it even harder for them to satisfy the millions of progressive families who still depend upon and support them.

JAMES WEEKS

Health. Since the early 1970s, the health establishment and holistically inclined entrepreneurs have responded to massive consumer demand for natural health alternatives and more healthful foods. As a result, parents have a much easier time today finding sensitive holistic care for their children, herbal remedies for their kids' minor ills, and natural foods versions of their kids' favorite foods. But not all natural foods are made as healthily as the pastoral scenes on their packaging imply. Not all herbal products are effective or without side effects. And, inevitably, charlatans and otherwise improperly prepared practitioners now compete with trustworthy professionals in the holistic health marketplace. Today, parents who thought that natural was good enough are having to relearn what it means to be careful consumers for their families.

Sex. The rise of religious conservatives as a political force has made it more difficult than ever to get schools to do a thorough job of sexuality education, especially concerning subjects such as contraception, prevention of sexually transmitted diseases, and homosexuality. The inability of the schools to fully educate youth about sex shifts the responsibility squarely back to parents, yet few feel comfortable with the subject matter. Despite growing up in the sexually "liberated" 1960s and 1970s, today's mothers and fathers learned their sex communication "skills" from their parents, for whom sex was a hush-hush subject. So many young people still aren't getting the guidance they need, a major factor in teen pregnancy and a contributor to the high rates of AIDS and other sexually transmitted diseases in youth.

In the following pages, we endeavor to help you navigate the difficult terrain of modern parenting, not just with facts and tips of our own but with the wise counsel of other parents who share your values and who have already walked down this path. Our aim is to provide you with the guidance you seek to raise the healthy, caring, creative, *spectacular* kids you imagine. We understand, too, from our own parenting, that even the most adventurous parents will generally be less willing to experiment with their children's lives than they were with their own. We'll help you distinguish between what's known and what's not, and what's trustworthy and what's not in the new fields of knowledge on which Whole Parenting is based.

Not that we're obsessed with parenting ideas that are radically new or "alternative." Indeed, as you've undoubtedly learned, kids are kids and some of the established ways of raising them still apply. We'll help you recognize when alternative parenting ideas truly can make a difference and when they're just . . . different.

Along the way, we hope to help you find answers to questions like these:

- How can I give my child the best possible birth and welcoming to this world?

- What fun activities can I do with my child that will aid her in realizing her intellectual, physical, emotional, and social potential?

- How can I mitigate the harmful effects of the mass media on my child's mind, heart, and behavior?

- How can I set my child on a path to a long and healthy life?

- How can I feed my child in ways that not only promote his health but also the health of the planet?

- How can I best support my child's education?

- Is it possible to teach my child about the benefits of competition and striving without him growing up to be a Neanderthal?

- What can I do to encourage my child to love this planet and to support it so it will nurture her back?

- How can I best teach my child about the world outside our home— about being a part of an extended family, a neighborhood, a community, a people, and a world?

- Where can I put my money—not just investing it, but spending it—so it will both support my family and benefit society?

- How can I respond to my child's spiritual queries when I haven't found satisfying answers for myself?

---

how to use this book

The Whole Parenting Guide has been designed to help parents explore a broad range of important issues connected with a holistic or progressive approach to family life. As much as possible, we have tried to make this book a primary resource for you, offering many practical tips as well as condensing information for you that you might have to otherwise root out of several books and articles if you were researching it on your own.

Nevertheless, the very breadth of this book means that we have had to accept certain limitations. Many of the topics addressed in these pages are the sole subjects of other books. In such cases, we have introduced you to the topic and then referred you to other sources—books, organizations, Web sites, and so on—for more information. You will find these resources compiled by topic at the end of each chapter.

You may find that some of the books listed in the Resources sections are no longer available in bookstores. Many fine books go out of print quickly these days. In such cases, check your local library or used bookstore. A determined search will usually turn up what you're looking for.

2

a healthy start: conscious pregnancy, birth, and infancy

First-time parents are always amazed at how profoundly their lives, indeed their whole worldview, change with the simple addition of a third party. Taking the leap from Couple to Family reshuffles all priorities, changes the dynamic between the new parents, and gives new purpose to every thought and deed. It also means facing a host of decisions that are infinitely more important than any you had to handle before baby came along.

As we'll see in this chapter, nearly every choice we make during our child's early life bears on baby's physical, psychological, or mental development. Mom's diet and overall well-being will affect baby's size and growth. The nature and quality of the childbirth experience, as well as what happens during the postpartum period, will influence how completely mother and child bond. Whether or not mom chooses to breast-feed, and for how long, will also affect the bond, and baby's health, too. Soon after baby arrives, other important decisions must be made that involve potential risks to baby's physical or emotional well-being, e.g., whether or not to vaccinate or (in the case of boys) circumcise.

None of these is a simple, right-or-wrong issue, and caring, intelligent parents can disagree strongly about the best approach to each. In other words, we don't mean to suggest that there is only One Correct Way. Nor do we believe that parents should second-guess themselves to the point of anxiety or guilt over having "ruined" their kids or contradicted nature's plan. Fortunately for us all, children are amazingly resilient, and can withstand a fair amount of our mistakes as we try to learn what's best for them and figure out how to achieve it.

We tend to agree with the late, redoubtable Dr. Spock, who transformed the landscape of contemporary parenting more than fifty years ago by opening his landmark book, *Baby and Child Care,* with the words, "Trust yourself. You know more than you think you do." For parents have instincts, which are also part of nature's plan.

Still, your parental instincts, while they are indispensable to your success at raising a happy, healthy child, are not enough. Instincts may be natural but they aren't always correct. You also need reliable information to make informed choices. The Whole Parenting approach is an example of a parenting style that combines respect for intuition with what experts have learned about optimal child-rearing. You may or may not agree with this approach to pregnancy, birthing, infant nutrition, and other choices during this period, but we hope to make clear why many parents choose this route.

SELF-CARE DURING PREGNANCY

"Being pregnant was an honor and so magical to me. I loved what my body did in creating my children and I tried to stay out of its way as much as possible to allow it to do its work. I supported it with a healthy, relaxed, and loving attitude. I ate well, rested well, and felt happy. In return all three of my pregnancies were easy and pleasurable. I'll always cherish the memory of those flutters and rolls, and that spirit moving within me."

KAREN O'DOUGHERTY
Ashland, Oregon

Let the Nurturing Begin

For many women, like Karen, pregnancy is a time of letting nature take its course. For other women, though, the need to take charge—of their health, their stressors, their habits, and the well-being of their new child—will supersede the need to let go. Think of this chapter in terms of your own needs, whether for stories and gentle reminders or strategies and information. Simply go to where you feel most welcome on these pages.

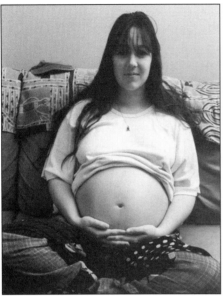

RICHARD MURPHY

If you are pregnant, the need to be-here-now is more important than ever. When you nurture yourself, you pamper and nourish the child you are carrying. Taking good care during pregnancy means paying special attention to the parts of yourself that affect your overall sense of well-being. Try to set up a rhythm, working toward a routine that embraces all areas of your daily life—the physical, the emotional, and the spiritual. The activities described below can be valuable elements in that routine.

Massage

Here's a form of prenatal pampering and therapy that helps expectant partners get in on the act. At various points during pregnancy, the temples, shoulders, back, thighs, hamstrings, calves, and feet are among the more obvious targets to massage. (Caution: If you have varicose veins in your legs, make sure that no pressure is applied directly to those veins, which are weakened from engorgement. However, massage in the general area helps treat the condition.) As long as you're not experiencing any complications—or any premature contractions—during your pregnancy, your partner's amateur approach to massage should pose no problems. But if your third trimester is plagued with aches and pains, you might want to invest in a certified or licensed massage therapist (nowadays, you may even find prenatal massage therapists; see the National Association of Pregnancy Massage Therapy listing in the Resources at the end of this chapter).

Meditation

Although the practice of meditation, or quieting the mind, can take a lifetime to perfect, the most compelling reason to attempt it during pregnancy is its ability to deepen your awareness of—and intuition about—the baby growing inside you. Meditation also helps you relax and sleep, so see if you can set aside time to do it daily.

To start, you'll want to unplug the phone and find a quiet corner or room that's free of distractions. One of the easiest meditating techniques involves the simple state of bare attention, which you attain by noticing your breath but not controlling it, and observing your thoughts but not actively thinking. Find a muscle in your abdomen that moves as you breathe. When the muscle rises, repeat silently to yourself "Rising." When it falls, repeat "Falling." "Rising . . . falling . . . rising . . . falling . . ."—like that. As you notice your breathing, thoughts will intrude and distract you. Don't suppress them or chastise yourself—that would take another thought. Just notice the thoughts as you're having them and return to observing your breathing. You are training yourself to be in the present moment rather than distracted by mental activity, so your goal is a state in which your mind is completely quiet. Don't worry about the goal during meditation either! And don't be frustrated if you don't master the technique right away. Just make the effort at first. Your meditation will improve with practice.

Meditation isn't the only way to tune in spiritually. During pregnancy, it might be just as useful to dwell on what you know, feel, or sense about the life force that is growing within. Many women feel a deep connection not only to their baby but also to a Universal Presence or some other perception of spiritual union during this time. Some even get a clear picture of what their baby looks like that turns out to be amazingly accurate. Other women take nature walks, visit sacred grounds, or engage in the simple act of praying, all of which can lead you to a sense of wholeness and peace about your upcoming role as a parent.

Rest

In the first trimester of pregnancy, your need to sleep will increase by several hours, in part because your body is forming the placenta during that time and drawing down your energy reserves to do the work. Give your body what it's asking for—by going to bed earlier, taking long naps, and little eyes-closed breaks of five or ten minutes when longer sessions aren't possible. And don't chastise yourself for being lazy! Your body is working overtime and you deserve every minute of rest you can muster.

Once you're in your fifth month of pregnancy, you'll need to avoid lying on your back or stomach. Reasons for nixing the stomach position are obvious, but lying belly up is also not recommended because it causes your uterus to compress the *vena cava,* a major vessel that carries blood back to the heart. To avoid applying any pressure on this important vein after the fifth month, the ideal lying position is on your left side. You can also approximate the supine position by first placing a pillow under your back, slightly to the right, then tucking another pillow under your right buttock so that your weight falls left, away from the vena cava, which is slightly to the right.

Having a restful pregnancy doesn't stop at putting in additional snooze time; it means embracing relaxing moments whenever possible and employing simple relaxation techniques. Take slow, deep breaths before, during, or after stressful periods during the day. This will not only help you and the baby get the oxygen you need, but will keep you grounded and mindful of what's most important.

Many women swear by the relaxation technique known as progressive muscle relaxation, especially at bedtime following a stressful or anxious day. If you are in the first five months of your pregnancy when it's still safe to lie supine, lie on your back and focus your awareness on your physical being. After a minute or so, bring your attention to your toes—flex them and tighten all muscles in them, then release this tension, imagining the toe muscles sinking into the floor or bed. Follow the exact same procedure upward, body part by body part—feet, calves, knees, thighs, hips, groin, buttocks, lower back, torso, upper back, arms, hands, fingers, shoulders, neck, and, one-by-one, all areas of the face (especially the temples, mouth, and eyes), where a great deal of tension mounts throughout the day.

Coaching Yourself

It would be marvelous if throughout your pregnancy, everyone around you were consistently encouraging and poised to help in every way. But chances are, they won't be. (For one thing, it may be months before many people even know that you are with child.) At times, even your partner may seem unattuned or be unwittingly unsupportive. So it's important to be self-nurturing, to squeeze in time to gird yourself psychically and emotionally with positive, encouraging thoughts as you move through your day. What these affirmations might be will vary according to your circumstances and temperament. But the following suggestions cover some important bases. Try repeating them to yourself whenever you find yourself disturbed by unsettling thoughts:

I am equal to the task of having this baby.

My love is stronger than my fear.

I trust my intuition.

It's okay to say what I need.

I can help my partner "see" inside me.

My body is new, yet familiar.

I love who I am and I love who you, baby, are.

Thank you, baby, for coming into my life.

I know myself, inside and out.

I am beautiful, inside and out.

Preparing the Siblings

If the baby you are carrying is not your first, you'll want to prepare your older child, soon a sibling-to-be—for your sake, as well as hers. If the older sibling is under five years old, you might want to delay breaking the news until you're showing—younger children don't really understand the concept of someone arriving seven or eight months down the line. If you plan to move your older child out of her room or crib, it's best to do so long before the birth, so she won't feel displaced. Take care to convey to your older child—through words, caresses, and special time together—that your love for her won't diminish when the new baby arrives. You might make a point of visiting more friends or relatives with infants so that your older child gets used to what babies do (not much—from a child's-eye view—beyond sleeping, watching, and crying). As another kind of rehearsal, you might start showing your soon-to-be oldest how to swaddle and cuddle using a life-size baby doll. (Water Babies, newborn-size dolls that can be filled with

TRACEY BALLARD-KIM

nearly-hot water, will be especially realistic because of their weight and warmth. They're available at many toy store chains.) If your child seems receptive, encourage her to talk to the sibling inside your belly, to listen to the fetal heartbeat.

When Phil's son Gabriel was born, he and his wife Michelle gave big sister Jessamine, then nearly four, a doll "from" her new baby brother. "It really worked to make her feel included," Phil says. "Plus," he adds, winking, "it's always amazed me that with all he had to do at the time, he could go shopping and find the perfect gift."

Remember the No-No's

Indulging even occasionally in drugs, alcohol, or cigarettes during pregnancy risks permanent harm to your baby. Caffeine—found in some teas and soft drinks as well as coffee—is best avoided or consumed in moderation (no more than three cups of coffee a day) because it can lead to calcium loss among other effects. It is also safest to steer clear of most medicines, prescription or not, unless explicitly okayed by your physician. Certain herbs should also be avoided. (See "A Family Herbal" starting on page 155.)

In some instances, taking drugs may be warranted if a disease or illness threatens the baby. For example, a fever can cause miscarriage so treating it with medication may make sense. But consult your doctor before you take any drugs, even over-the-counter ones such as aspirin.

Keep Regular

Your bowels may work less efficiently during pregnancy because your growing uterus is putting pressure on them and the increased amount of progesterone in your system is relaxing your body's smooth muscles, including the bowels. The best way to avoid constipation is to drink a minimum of eight glasses of fluids, particularly water, a day. Staying well hydrated not only helps empty the bowels, but helps flush the kidneys (squeeze lemon juice into your water for a kidney-pampering drink). However, pay attention to *when* you consume your water—make the earlier part of the day (when you're less distracted or worn out by the hustle and bustle) your peak drinking hours, and then finish most of your drinking by early evening so you won't be up for any more of those late-night jaunts to the bathroom than necessary. Try getting into the habit of consuming one or two glasses of water every morning before breakfast. Eating plenty of fruits, greens, and whole grains provides natural fiber that promotes regularity as well.

Tone the Perineum

The perineum is the small, elastic area between the vagina and the rectum. During childbirth, it undergoes a tremendous stretching (and may even tear or be cut during an episiotomy), which causes a painful, burning sensation just as the baby's head is crowning. To tone the perineal muscles before birth, many midwives recommend that moms-to-be perform Kegel exercises throughout their pregnancy. Although there's no guarantee that these exercises stretch the area enough to avoid tearing or an episiotomy, they certainly contribute to a speedy recovery after the birth. To perform Kegels, firmly contract the muscles that form a "figure 8" around your anus and vagina; hold for eight to ten seconds then slowly release the muscles and relax. These are the same muscles you use to interrupt the flow of urine, so you can get the idea of Kegels by stopping your urine a few times. Try to do this exercise as often as twenty-five times throughout the day. Some midwives also recommend that expectant mothers massage the perineum with warm olive oil while visualizing the area stretching during childbirth. There's no proof that this increases elasticity, but it does help prepare you for the burning sensations you'll be feeling as your baby's head emerges into the world.

Stay Sexual

Provided you're in a normal pregnancy and you feel physically and emotionally up for it, there is no reason to cut back on sexual intimacy. Sometimes it's difficult for one or both partners to get past the idea that they might be hurting the baby or that there are more important things that they ought to be doing as budding parents. But remember, after the baby comes, there will be more reasons to abstain than you can shake a rattle at, so there's no time like the present to enjoy some semblance of a sex life.

A Whole Pregnancy Diet

Eating well is one of the crucial building blocks of natural health for everyone, but it's more important than ever when you're pregnant.

Remember, *because a fetus is growing inside you, your body will undergo tremendous—and rapid—growth in fetal and maternal tissue, and your blood volume alone may increase up to 50 percent.* To keep up with all this growth, both you and your baby need to be fed nutritiously, at regular intervals.

In addition to eating nutritious foods, eating well means trying not to eat on the run and being aware of every bite you take, chewing carefully, and visualizing the process of nourishing your fetus as you do. And it means drinking water consciously throughout the day, to aid food metabolism and blood production. Although you'll need to boost your daily caloric intake—most pregnant women should consume about 2,400 calories a day regardless of their original weight or metabolism—you'll want to avoid getting these calories from fats, which contain far more calories per gram than carbohydrates or protein but often don't carry as many nutrients. In the information below, pay particular attention to the six important nutrients that pregnant women should take care to ingest in adequate amounts.

Supplements Are Add-Ons, Not the End-All

True, a great many of a pregnant woman's nutritional needs *can* be met without vitamin/mineral pills. But the more practical question—given today's busy lifestyles—is *will* they be met? If you were diet- and nutrition-conscious before your pregnancy, chances are you won't find it difficult to add on those extra calories of food wisely. However, keep in mind that you will need to consume more iron-rich foods to accommodate the increase in blood and tissue volume.

If you've never quite hit your stride with researching and realizing your nutritional goals, pregnancy is no time to test your dietary mettle. So don't feel that you've sold out by taking prenatal supplements. Just recognize that these pills are "add-ons," not substitutes for well-rounded meals. In fact, if you eat well-balanced meals according to the principles outlined in Chapter 5, you should already be getting most of the nutrients you need for pregnancy. In the information below, we've noted the Recommended Daily Allowance for pregnant women as well as some foods that supply the important nutrients. But you don't need a calculator to plan your meals. Just eat well while including some of the foods discussed with each nutrient. (For further discussion of the arguments for and against nutritional supplements beyond gestation, see "Vitamins and Minerals" on page 215.)

Minerals Are a Must

Three minerals in particular—calcium, iron, and zinc—are important during pregnancy. Since some of these nutrients are better absorbed either with or without other minerals, here's what you should know:

Calcium. Essential for normal blood clotting and proper muscle and nerve functioning. Helps build strong bones and teeth. Keeping up calcium stores now can help prevent osteoporosis later on.

> *Recommended Daily Allowance (RDA) for pregnant women:* 1,200 mg.

> *Nonmeat and nondairy sources (all food sources here and below are listed in descending order of content of the nutrient being discussed):* kelp, collard greens, tofu, kale, mustard greens, corn muffins, oranges, and broccoli.

> *Meat and dairy sources:* sardines (with bones), milk, yogurt, cheeses, cottage cheese, and cooked oysters. (However, getting your calcium via protein sources such as meats and dairy products can actually result in a net calcium loss to your body—see Chapter 5 for more on this.)

> *Keep in mind:* If under the direction of a nutritionist or health-care provider, you are taking large doses of calcium—say, 1,200 to 1,500 mg.—as a supplement, make sure you at least come close to consuming the 20 mg. of zinc, the RDA for pregnancy, to help your calcium absorption. Many of the same foods you should be eating anyway—leafy green vegetables, whole grains, nuts, seeds, and tofu—contain the zinc you'll need. Calcium supplements come in many forms. Calcium citrate is a good choice because it is one of the most easily assimilated and least expensive varieties. Steer clear of versions manufactured from bone meal, dolomite, or oyster shell. Pills derived from these animal sources can be laced with accumulated arsenic, lead, or mercury. Vegans in particular should take special care to get sufficient calcium.

Iron. Needed to transport oxygen to the body's tissues via the bloodstream. Helps convert food into usable energy.

RDA: 30 to 78 mg.

Nonmeat sources: kidney beans, dried peaches and figs, lima beans, prune juice, split or green peas, acorn squash.

Meat sources: cooked oysters, clams, beef, lamb.

Keep in mind: To boost absorption, eat iron-rich foods in-between meals with a beverage rich in vitamin C such as orange juice. Unless your caregiver determines that your hemoglobin level has fallen below 11 grams per deciliter of blood (which she may call "anemia"), you don't need iron supplements. In fact, high hemoglobin levels can cause your baby to have low birth weight, so only use iron supplements when needed. If you are taking an all-in-one prenatal supplement that includes iron, make sure the calcium content is no more than 250 mg. (and avoid dairy products for that period of the day), because calcium interferes with iron absorption. When using supplements, make sure you consume extra zinc, since iron has a tendency to interfere with the absorption of this mineral, thereby increasing your body's need for it.

Zinc. Regulates blood sugar levels, helps digestion, boosts the body's immune system, is essential for baby's bone formation and for promoting protein synthesis, aids the healing of wounds.

RDA: 20 mg.

Nonmeat, nondairy sources: wheat germ, brewer's yeast, walnuts, black-eyed peas, baked potato with skin, whole lima beans, green peas, whole grain cereals and pasta, watercress.

Meat and dairy sources: cooked oysters, calf's liver, beef, lamb, crabmeat, chicken, shrimp, yogurt, whitefish, milk.

Keep in mind: You'll need extra zinc if you are taking an iron supplement because iron interferes with zinc absorption.

Vitamins Are Vital

In addition to the minerals listed above, two vitamins—folic acid and B12—are essential during pregnancy, but you may have to go out of your way to include them in your diet:

Folate/folic acid. Needed for the normal development of cells and genetic material.

> *RDA:* 400 mcg. or 0.4 mg.
>
> *Nonmeat sources:* brewer's yeast, spinach, lentils, chick peas, asparagus, cantaloupe, orange juice, wheat germ, avocado, beets.
>
> *Meat sources:* chicken liver.

Vitamin B12. Aids in the growth of blood cells and is essential for nerve functioning. Because the liver can store between a three- and five-year supply of this nutrient, there is no need to consume it daily. Still, pregnant women, especially vegans, should make sure they consume B12-containing foods or supplements two or three times a week.

> *RDA:* Averages out to 3 millionths of a gram a day, though it's not essential to ingest it daily.
>
> *Nonmeat sources:* brewer's or nutritional yeast, fermented foods such as tempeh and miso.
>
> *Meat sources:* beef liver, steak.
>
> *Keep in mind:* Because the amounts of vitamin B12 in fermented foods may vary from batch to batch, these foods are not a reliable, consistent source of this vitamin, so strict vegetarians may want to invest in B12 supplements (check the label to ensure this supplement was derived from a plant or bacterial source).

Protein: Special Considerations for Both Vegetarians and Meat Eaters

Although few people in this country are in danger of experiencing a protein deficiency, conventionally trained doctors and dietitians often have a way of scaring vegans and other vegetarians, especially if they're pregnant. Why? Americans, including many in the health establishment, still haven't let go of obsolete advice (thanks in part to lobbyists for the powerful meat and dairy industries) that meat or "complete protein" should be the centerpiece of our daily meals.

Vegetarian protein sources were once thought to be inferior because they are usually deficient in one or more of the eight essential amino acids, whereas animal products such as meat contain all eight amino acids in the right amounts. As a result, vegetarians often strove to combine protein foods such as beans and rice so they would get the proper amino acid balance. This is no longer thought to be necessary—at least not during the same meal. So long as you try to eat at least two servings from two to three of these food types—grains, legumes, nuts and seeds, or meats and dairy—over the course of the day, you should be getting adequate amounts of protein.

---

daily dietary concerns

- Eat iron-rich foods along with vitamin C–rich foods to boost absorption. Good combos include kidney or lima beans (iron sources) with turnip greens or broccoli or brussels sprouts; dried peaches or figs with cantaloupe; chicken (modest portion to avoid eating too much protein) with green peppers (quite rich in vitamin C); and so forth.

- Boost your absorption of calcium (from yogurt, cow's milk, collard greens, and corn muffins, for instance) with magnesium-rich foods (such as bananas, potatoes, oatmeal, and walnuts). Kelp, by the way, is a great all-in-one source for magnesium, calcium, and other minerals. If your palate objects to the taste of this seaweed, try it in capsule form.

- Avoid calcium-rich foods, such as dairy items, when consuming iron-rich foods since calcium can inhibit iron absorption.

- When taking vitamin supplements, choose those specifically prescribed for prenatal use in order to consume nutrients in the best proportions.

Those who eat diets rich in meats and dairy products face the issue from the opposite side: They're prone to eating too much protein, which can cause problems both for pregnant women and women in general. Meat-eaters and vegetarians should both observe the following guidelines:

Proteins. Provides the body with amino acids, the building blocks of cellular growth and repair.

RDA: 60 to 74 grams. Although many natural health practitioners believe this is too high for a pregnant woman, some also believe that the World Health Organization's allowance of 44 grams for pregnant women is a bit low—especially given the recently speculated link between prenatal high blood pressure (or pre-eclampsia) and low protein intake. To be on the safe side, expectant moms would do well to follow the U.S. RDA, especially during the later months of pregnancy, when the risk of pre-eclampsia is greatest.

Nonmeat and nondairy sources: soybeans, tofu, nuts, nut butters, seeds, whole grains, beans, peas.

Meat and dairy sources: poultry (when skinless, it contains far less fat than beef or pork), beef, pork, lamb, fish, cow's milk, cheese, yogurt, eggs.

Keep in mind: Too much protein, according to recent studies, has been linked to delayed fetal growth or premature birth. Too much can also prompt the body to lose essential calcium (for more about the dangers of too much protein, see Chapter 5).

COMMUNICATING WITH YOUR UNBORN CHILD

The notion that parents can communicate with their child before birth will strike some as New Age goofiness. But others sense intuitively what most humans took for granted until this century—that babies can be reached long before they show their faces in the world. And research suggests that they're right.

In much earlier times, many peoples believed that a terrible event that occurred during a pregnancy could emotionally scar a child forever. Premodern people also believed a baby could be "improved" in utero. Pregnant mothers in Victorian England were known to frequent concerts and art museums for the sole purpose of introducing their unborn children to highbrow culture (whether baby got a discount admission is not known).

By the early 1900s, most women in industrialized countries preferred to have their babies in hospitals, and with that came a new view of who the baby was. Your unborn child, doctors convinced pregnant moms, had no thoughts and feelings. It was merely a bundle of impulses and reflexes. This view made possible the development of dehumanized, mechanical birthing procedures that were convenient for medical personnel.

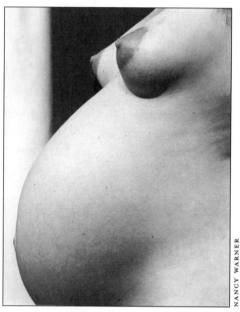
NANCY WARNER

However, it hardly represented progress from the baby's point of view, as we now know. The pioneering work of Dr. Frederick Leboyer in the 1960s and 1970s and other researchers and practitioners since then indicate that the Victorian moms were closer to the truth—unborn children do think and feel in the womb and what we do in their presence matters.

For several months before birth, babies respond to sounds and show the ability to distinguish between light and dark. We can tell by the way they move and the rate at which their heart beats, notes physician/author Niels Lauersen. These abilities only grow through the remainder of the pregnancy. Evidence also shows that, just as many of our ancestors thought, stress during pregnancy can affect a baby's physical and emotional development, and in extreme cases mark her for life. The reverse, then, would also seem to be true—that a pregnancy that is as considerate of the baby's feelings as possible will be best for its emotional and physical development.

Before talking about *how* to communicate with your baby in utero, let's look at all of the paths by which communication takes place. Biochemically, mom is sending missives to baby whether she intends to or not. Mom's emotions reach the baby via hormones that travel through her bloodstream and cross the placenta to her baby. Mom's heart rate, respiration, and muscle tension also cue the baby about how she's feeling. Babies "talk" back with their feet. For instance, babies communicate distress by kicking—that is, kicking distinct from their usual pattern, since healthy, happy babies will often dance a rumba just for the heck of it.

Parents and siblings can direct more deliberate messages to the unborn child, too—by cooing to them, caressing Mom's tummy, and so on. Similar communications take place on a more instinctual level as well. As an example, mothers the world over will reflexively rub their stomachs to transmit love and reassurance to their unborn child. This is an early manifestation of the marvelous, mysterious mother/child bond, which begins in utero.

You can also speak sentences to your baby. Your unborn child may not understand the words, but there's every indication that she will get the feelings you convey. Talking also draws parents and baby closer together, giving bonding a head start. In addition, talking with baby is a great way for dads and the baby's new siblings to involve themselves more in the pregnancy and introduce themselves to their new family member. These conversations can also take place telepathically, some feel. Project thoughts and questions to your baby and notice the answers that appear in your mind.

"I had no idea whether I would have a boy or a girl," says Rachel Bendat of Ashland, Oregon, "but I did have a sense about my baby's energy—he seemed so calm, gentle, and loving. During the last trimester I began talking to him often. When I would go on walks, I would talk out loud, describing the trees and spring flowers and asking him if he heard the birds chirping. When I did pelvic rocking exercises, I would explain to him that I was doing this to help him keep his head in the correct position for labor. At night I would say goodnight to him and throughout each day I would say hello to him. I often sat outside exposing my belly to the sunshine so that he could experience the warmth and light.

"Now my baby is six months and almost since the beginning, I've called him 'Sweet Zachariah' because he's so sweet and loving. One of his favorite things to look at are the trees and plants—I wonder if that's because I told him so much about the trees while he was in the womb?!"

Of course, the shadow side of these open communication channels is the harm that stress can cause your baby. You and your partner should do your best to avoid loud arguments and other extreme stresses, which can affect an unborn child. But let's put this in perspective. Stress is only unhealthy for the unborn when it's intense and unrelieved. Life is stressful, and many of the ups and downs of daily living can't be avoided. Remember that babies are remarkably resilient, so you needn't fret about common tensions. The last thing you should do is worry about worrying!

HOLISTIC EXERCISE FOR PRE- AND POSTNATAL MOTHERS

Let's get one thing straight at the start, moms: Exercise won't make or break your pregnancy. Your baby isn't going to refuse to come because you didn't do your Kegels. Nature gives you full permission to have a child even if the most vigorous thing you do all day is push the buttons on your TV's remote control.

What exercise will do is help you get a good night's sleep during pregnancy as well as make things easier during labor and delivery. And, of course, if you're worried about sacrificing your figure to motherhood, exercise can ease your fears. With the right workouts, you might be even more fit and shapely after pregnancy than you were before.

That said, holistic forms of exercise such as yoga, dance, and tai chi offer special benefits that few conventional programs can match. The exercise programs taught in America's aerobic dance studios and fitness centers pursue limited, easily measured goals—losing weight, burning calories, toning muscles, dropping running times, and so on. Yes, they improve health—in the case of aerobics, especially the health of the heart—and help those who do them look better on the beach or in the bedroom. But slighted in the process are such qualities as flexibility, body alignment, muscle relaxation, and grace. Holistic exercise *emphasizes* these same qualities, all of which help childbearing, both in the pre- and post-birth phases.

STEPHANIE RENFROW HAMILTON

Take flexibility. Muscles and ligaments that have been continually stretched in an exercise system such as yoga are better prepared for the contortions caused by the baby moving through the pelvis. In northern Africa, traditional cultures teach the slow, sinuous movements of belly dancing to girls entering womanhood as part of fertility rituals. When a woman gives birth, she rolls her pelvis in the same way, supported by women who a-ttend the birth and dance around her to remind her of what to do.

Learning muscle relaxation and proper breathing techniques also helps pregnant moms ease the discomfort of labor and birth. For instance, during labor, women have a tendency to react to pain by holding their breath and tightening their muscles. This is a natural response but not a helpful one because it freezes the pain in place and makes the birth more difficult. Yes, you can learn techniques to counter these reactions in Lamaze or Bradley childbirth classes, but they don't give the benefits of exercise. Learning to breathe "through" the pain and cue clenched muscles to relax is a basic part of yoga and dance training, for example.

Dance training helps mothers in other ways, too. In the recovery phase, many new moms feel compelled to exercise to get their bodies back in shape. But the demands of motherhood may be so overwhelming that the only way to exercise some days is to put on some music and dance with their baby in their arms. Dancing is not only an effective and fun way to work out but may even prove therapeutic in some cases. Lori Cangilose of Grants Pass, Oregon, a children's dance teacher, suffered a pelvic injury during the birth of her third child, Vincenzo, an exceptionally large baby. "My health therapist told me the best thing I could do to get my pelvis back in shape was dance," says Lori.

This is not to say that traditional exercises that emphasize strength and endurance aren't helpful as well. In fact, because childbirth can be its own kind of marathon, standard endurance training such as aerobics is a sensible way to prepare beforehand. Aerobic exercise also aids expectant moms' health by stimulating the heart and circulatory system, increasing the health of other organs, and building stronger connective tissue and bones.

As for strength training, pregnant moms who tone up their arms, shoulders, and upper back will be able to nurse their babies more comfortably and for longer periods without muscle fatigue and tension. Strength exercises also prep moms for carrying around the baby and the accompanying gear. For women recovering from a cesarean section, strengthening the abdominal muscles can help eliminate lower back aches and shoulder tension that can follow the operation. Dance and yoga classes may be terrific for flexibility, breathing, and relaxation but, unless performed with unusual vigor, may not do much for either endurance or strength.

Once you understand the values of holistic exercise, you can incorporate these principles into a more traditional exercise routine, avoiding the muscle injuries and rigid muscles that plague those who don't have a holistic background. Some mothers do both holistic and traditional exercise, alternating them on different days to get the benefits of each.

Of course, this being a physically precarious time for both you and baby, you should definitely observe the following precautions while exercising:

When Pregnant:

· Always check with your doctor or midwife before undertaking any exercise program.

· Only go to classes that are specially adapted for pregnancy. That goes for yoga or aerobics or anything else. (Try looking for such classes at your local YMCA or other location serving a wide variety of students.) At the same time, be wary of instructors who treat all pregnant women the same. Your instructor should assess your pre-pregnancy state of fitness before starting you on new exercises. She should also be offering different programs for different trimesters of pregnancy.

· Discontinue any movements or exercises that cause pain or straining. Avoid competitive games or even exercising competitively with others in your class. Let go of any exercise goals of your own, too. When your competitive spirit takes over, you may ignore important cues from your body. Bottom line: Don't take chances.

- If you experience dizziness, faintness, extreme pain, bleeding, shortness of breath, back and pubic pain, difficulty walking, or any other disturbing symptoms, consult a doctor. None of these symptoms are automatically something to worry about, but let a professional decide that.

- If your stomach is empty or you feel hungry, eat before exercising. Otherwise, your body may burn fat stores for energy which will produce byproducts that are harmful to your baby. Easy-to-digest, high-carbohydrate foods—especially fruits—will supply you with quick energy and be light on your system during exercise. Drink plenty of fluids after you work out.

- If you are used to a vigorous exercise program such as aerobics, you may be able to continue with it while pregnant but don't start a new program right after you conceive.

After Giving Birth:

- Consult your physician before undertaking anything strenuous.

- As with pregnancy, only do what you have the energy for. Your body has wounds that are healing and is fatigued from the whole nine-month ordeal. You also need to respect your emotional needs. You may be subject to depression and irritability, so focus on doing what you enjoy. When you enjoy the idea of exercising, that's the time to do it.

- Never ignore your baby. Her needs always come first. If she cries, find out what's the matter. If you exercise or dance with your baby, always consider her safety and comfort. Don't make any movements that would roughly jiggle or jar her.

- Don't try to regain your pre-pregnancy body too quickly. Again, focusing on fitness goals can cause you to miss important signals from your body or your baby.

For reviews of holistic and other excellent exercise books and videotapes, see Resources at the end of this chapter.

GIVING BIRTH NATURE'S WAY

When couples try to visualize the birth of their child, this is what many see: an arduous yet exhilarating labor, with soon-to-be-Mom at the helm, aware and attuned, unfettered by monitors and IVs, unaltered by drugs, untouched by a scalpel, all culminating in the birth of a healthy, alert babe. Yet despite the back-to-natural-childbirth movement, a number of cultural and medical conventions conspire against such dreams. If you are determined to give birth at home for instance, healthcare professionals, friends, and loved ones will likely deluge you with dire warnings about the risks of your choice. And even if you opt for birth in the hospital with a doctor whom you think is in sync with your "all natural" preferences, you're still likely to hear about the reasons that birth without intervention might not be possible. While these warnings are not lies, the emphasis is off-base. Dwelling on what might go wrong during childbirth can predispose you unnecessarily toward a medicated birth.

What a pity, because giving birth naturally offers a host of advantages—psychological, emotional, and physiological. When you give birth without disrupting your body's natural feedback mechanisms, you expose your baby to fewer chemicals and less physical stress, and set the stage for quicker healing and recovery after birth. Conversely, even the most seemingly harmless medical interventions during labor can create a domino effect. For example, electronic fetal monitoring requires Mom to be immobilized, which in turn can slow down contractions, eventually prompting the doctor to induce labor, which can then make contractions occur back-to-back with little time for rest in between, which in turn makes painkillers seem like a good idea after all.

In order to sidestep the conventional obstetrical outlook that views childbirth as being fraught with risk, you and your partner will need to educate yourselves and prepare to have as much control over the experience as possible. Yet herein lies the paradox: When it's time to deliver, women must also learn to *let go,* to have faith in their own body's ability and in the people they've chosen to be there for the journey.

As you aim for the most natural, low-technology birth possible, you and, ideally, your partner (if he or she is supportive and involved), will need to sort through a myriad of options. Here are some guidelines for the major decisions you face as the big event approaches:

is water birthing for you?

Birth my baby underwater? Surely you jest!, you might be thinking right around now. We can certainly understand that gut reaction. But water birthing is not as strange or risky as it sounds, and water labor can make the time between contractions more relaxing. Immersion in water gives the laboring mom a feeling of weightlessness, which in time can encourage her to relax her muscles; it also applies counter-pressure to overworked tissue, acting as a kind of total body massage. In an eight-year study of nearly 1,800 women laboring in whirlpool tubs at a birthing center in Upland, California, it was found that the women had shorter labors, less pain, and one-third the C-section rate of women laboring in hospital settings without water.

What prevents the baby, once born, from drowning? "The water temperature is kept at ninety-eight degrees, and since the water pressure and temperature feels the same as the environment in the womb, the baby doesn't have the stimulus to breathe," says Barbara Harper, a registered nurse, midwife, and director of Waterbirth International Resource and Referral Center in Portland, Oregon. "That stimulus comes when the air pressure hits the baby's face."

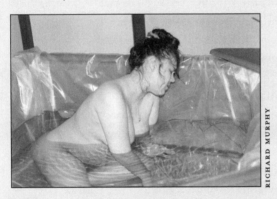

RICHARD MURPHY

Richie and Linda Murphy of San Francisco remember different aspects of their son's water birth: Linda was in the tub on all fours, having shifted and swished around in the tub to find the most comfortable birth position. Richie and Maria, their midwife, were behind her when the baby's head emerged. "His face was totally calm underneath the water, like a photo of a sleeping baby," says Richie. "When the shoulders were coming out, he turned his head from side to side. He stayed under the water about a minute or so before he was completely out. He looked so peaceful." Linda remembers the moment little Fionn came up for air: "He took a breath— 'a-hah'—he never really bawled, then Maria immersed a towel in the tub to get it warm so the baby could be covered and held to my chest."

Choosing a Childbirth Class

It's a good idea for any pregnant woman—especially a first-timer—to enroll in childbirth education classes. And right by her side should be her partner. Attending these classes together marks one of the earliest milestones of involved parenting.

Just about any childbirth course will bring couples up to speed about what the onset of labor is like, what goes on during labor's three stages, and what options they'll have regarding such procedures as fetal monitoring, episiotomies, and pain management. A good childbirth education class will also give couples hands-on techniques for handling labor pain—for instance, foot or back massages, facial muscle relaxation, changing positions, and varied breathing. Likewise, the course will instruct mothers-to-be of the importance of relaxing between contractions and offer specific ways of doing that.

Oddly enough, although most childbirth preparation instructors claim they are teaching natural childbirth methods, many—especially those affiliated with a hospital—spend so much time discussing invasive hospital procedures that their messages seem confusing or mixed, at best. Some go so far as to urge women not to fall prey to "childbirth machisma" and to accept painkillers if labor hurts. While there is nothing inherently wrong with wanting to alleviate pain, listening to this sort of thinking from a teacher who purports to prepare you for childbirth can psychologically lower your threshhold for pain *before you ever find out how much you can bear.* If a childbirth educator counsels you this way, remember, there may be politics involved: Few hospital-affiliated instructors can afford to openly criticize the medical practices of the institutions that hire them.

Therefore, we suggest you seek out childbirth classes that are independent of hospitals, preferably ones that emphasize home birth. The best people to ask about independent natural childbirth classes are midwives in private or group practice, professional labor assistants, La Leche League volunteers, or like-minded friends. As you scout, ask instructors for a course outline that gives you some indication of how much time is spent on each topic.

Marcia Jarmel and Ken Schneider of San Francisco attended both hospital-affiliated birthing classes and childbirth classes geared toward home-birthing before deciding to stick with the latter. "The local hospital classes suggested that there was always this possibility or need to treat women as bodies or machines in need of a tune-up," recalls Ken. "The midwives' collective classes offered a model of care that said 'we can educate women and their families to have the birth they want.' "

As a rule, **Lamaze classes** are best known for their system of breathing techniques, which, instructors say, should vary as labor progresses. Like many other childbirth educators, **Bradley Method** instructors, trained by the American Academy of Husband-Coached Childbirth, emphasize body awareness, labor preparation through key exercises, and the importance of the squatting position during birth. The Bradley Method also places a great emphasis on a woman's partner playing an active role as labor assistant. Bradley partners learn massage techniques and a number of verbal cues that help trigger relaxation. Many other childbirth classes offer a medley of philosophies and approaches to labor.

Although we highly recommend childbirth classes, there's no guarantee that the ones available in your area will help you to bring your full consciousness, emotions, intuition, and attunement to bear on the experience. For that, you'll need to do some reading and seek out guidance that is most in accordance with your desires and beliefs. (Your best bet for finding such guidance may be from a midwife or professional labor assistant; see "And in Whose Hands . . .", page 40, or the Resources at the end of this chapter.)

WHERE SHOULD YOU GIVE BIRTH?

Choosing a birth setting is more than just a question of venue; your decision, in fact, will affect your entire birth experience. Do you want the comfort, familiarity, and control—over external variables, at least—afforded in a home birth? Or would you prefer the sense of security that a good hospital, with all its medical expertise and equipment, can provide? Or will you opt for a setting that seems to offer both, namely a home-like birthing center?

Before exploring these options, we'd like to offer a suggestion: Throughout your pregnancy, prepare for your birth as if you were having it at home. *Why bother*, you might ask, *if I know deep down that I'm gravitating toward the expertise and equipment found in a hospital?* Answer: because your preparation and all your choices will be better informed if you've been training, rehearsing, and educating yourself for a birth in which you play an active part rather than cede responsibility to medical experts.

Home Birth

There's a lot to be said for giving birth in the comfort and familiar surroundings of home. For starters, moms-to-be tend to spend a great deal of time and psychic energy preparing a space that feels peaceful and welcoming. Similarly, their partners are also more likely to feel at ease, better able to "recharge their batteries" and less "in the way" if they are coaching or supporting the birth mother in their own homes. Without all the hustle and bustle of hospital personnel in a brightly lit, sterile, and unfamiliar setting, home birth proponents say, a woman in labor is less likely to grow tense and let fear dominate her experience.

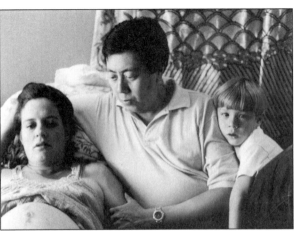

KATHY VANGORDER

Since many doctors won't perform home birth deliveries, women who choose home birth typically rule out having a birth attendant who is trained to intervene during labor. (If you'd prefer an M.D. for home birth, though, see our Resources at the end of this chapter for two orga-nizations that can refer you to such doctors.) On the other hand, in many cities and suburbs, many midwives will deliver at home, once they've screened women and ruled out certain risk factors, such as anemia, hy-pertension, and diabetes.

How does home birth compare to hos-pital birthing for mom and baby's health? In a 1976 study conducted by the Institute for Childbirth and Family Research, 1,046 women planning home births were compared with the same number of women opting for hospital births (both groups were defined as "low risk"). Dr. Lewis Mehl and his fellow researchers found that the incidence of complications were far greater in a hospital—hospitalized women were nine times more likely to have a severe perineal tear, five times more likely to develop high blood pressure, and three times more likely to experience postpartum hemorrhaging or receive a C-section. And that's just for the mother! Among the hospital babies, the incidence of fetal distress was six times higher than the children born at home, while four times as many babies developed infections or needed help to start breathing. It was the high rate of interventions, this study con-cluded, that led to the greater risk of complications to mother and child.

Despite all the compelling reasons to try childbirth at home, why do less than five percent of pregnant women in this country do so? In large part, because the medical establishment has successfully painted birth as a potentially dangerous event that must be actively managed with a full arsenal of medical technology on hand. Yet the facts don't support that conclusion—no studies of planned home births among screened women with a trained attendant have ever shown excessive risk.

Nevertheless, if you are leaning toward a home birth, you'll still need to find a satisfactory answer to the nagging question: *What if something goes wrong?* Although the risk of complications is small—they occur in about 10 to 15 percent of all births—it's a question that has to be asked. Couples should have a contingency plan that includes knowing the fastest route to a nearby hospital with an obstetrical practice that will ad-mit a home birthing woman who is having complications (typically, the midwife will make backup arrangements with the maternity unit there).

Another question you should answer before you choose home birth is, *Am I setting myself up for a great letdown if things do go wrong?* A good midwife or childbirth education class can help you come to terms with the possibility of circumstances forcing a hospital birth without scaring you half to death.

In the end, many couples base their choice on "doing what's best for the baby," and that's a perfectly natural and reasonable approach. Other women choose not to separate what's best for their babies from what's best for themselves, recognizing that the welfare of one necessarily affects the welfare of the other. And this reasoning brings a great many holistically inclined couples home, where they'll have more say in how their child is brought into the world, while taking comfort in cozier, more familiar, and more spiritually balanced surroundings.

Birthing Centers

For many couples, birthing centers represent a happy medium between giving birth at home, where no emergency facilities are available, and at a hospital with all the latest technology on hand. As long as the birth center in question is staffed with midwives, it can provide advantages from both worlds. For women whose pregnancies are normal, such centers offer the personalized yet hands-off labor services that midwives provide, along with a range of facilities to encourage natural childbirth, including a home-like environment. In many cases, birth centers also boast whirlpool baths, educational services, and access privileges to a nearby hospital with high-tech obstetrical and neonatal units. And many make available these services at roughly half the cost of a hospital birth. Most insurers will cover births at birthing centers.

Couples who want to put some distance between themselves and the hospital birthing mentality might try to seek out a freestanding, rather than hospital-based, birthing center (check with the National Association of Childbearing Centers listed in the Resources at the end of this chapter). If an in-hospital birth center is all that is available in your neck of the woods, find out if it is simply an obstetrical unit with homey decor by asking to speak to the head midwife. If there is no midwife in charge, the center is probably subject to the same regulations and routines as hospitals, even if it's staffed with progressive doctors and nurses.

Hospital Births

There's no getting around it: Once you make the decision to give birth in a hospital, you relinquish some control over the experience. We have several reasons for putting this so directly. First, hospitals—and by extension, the M.D.s who staff them—have a vested interest in following standard (i.e., interventionist) procedures that they hope will provide a defense against lawsuits should things go wrong. Doctors are also under time constraints to treat as many patients as possible and then move on. Additionally, when hospital administrators invest in high- or low-tech equipment, their purchases must be justified by constant use. A simple intravenous catheter or IV, for instance—often inserted to ensure that a mom-to-be doesn't become dehydrated or "just in case" there's an emergency—can add upwards of $100 to your bill these days.

What's more, hospitals are no less vulnerable to office politics than any other workplace. In particular, many obstetricians feel obligated to keep their anesthesiologist colleagues happy. This usually means advising women in labor not to eat or drink—in case they "need" anesthesia, which should only be administered to patients on an empty stomach. Yet if a woman's labor is long, she is going to need nourishment, especially before the cervix is fully dilated, in order to sustain the level of energy needed to finish giving birth. In teaching hospitals, OB units are set up to provide medical students with opportunities to hone their skills, an atmosphere that makes it far more likely that staffers will intervene rather than let nature take its course. In short, these institutions are set up to run efficiently, on schedule, and according to specified routines. But babies aren't born by schedules and routines, at least not naturally.

Despite the odds that intervention will take place, it *is* possible to experience natural childbirth in a hospital setting. "Living in a small artistic town that welcomes holistic philosophies, our hospital and physicians are open to alternative birth options," says Karen O'Dougherty of Ashland, Oregon. "In all three of my hospital deliveries I had the same doula [professional labor assistant] who was also a midwife. When she would give me herbs and homeopathic remedies during labor and after delivery, my physician was inquisitive about what I was receiving and why. To me, it was beautiful to see East and West work together so cooperatively to bring my babies into this world. I wanted the best of both worlds and I got it."

If you're seeking a marriage of the natural and conventional, try to find a midwife who, besides being someone you trust, has access privileges to a hospital with a decent track record in its cesarean-, episiotomy-, and electronic fetal monitoring rates (more on this later). Or shop for an obstetrician whose attitude toward labor and delivery is compatible with yours, so long as his or her track record matches this attitude. Again, this M.D. should have privileges at a hospital that has that same decent track record; you'll most likely need to interview both the doctor *and* the hospital's head maternity nurse to get a full picture of what to expect. Whichever tack you take, you and your partner must gather as much information as possible so that you can be prepared to make informed decisions about certain procedures as they come up.

. . . And in Whose Hands? (Types of Birth Attendants)

Although obstetrical care is gradually becoming less and less interventionist, it's unlikely that we have doctors' initiative to thank for this. Even today, obstetricians are trained to view childbirth as an experience fraught with risk. As some progressive OBs wryly characterize it, the obstetrician's credo is "Don't just stand there, *do* something!" whereas the midwife's motto is "Don't just do something, *stand* there." Knowing that time, training, and circumstances might prompt even the most noninterventionist of M.D.s to stop waiting for nature to take its course, you might want to consider enlisting a midwife or doula. These professionals are trained to approach labor and delivery as a natural process to be aided and abetted noninvasively. Here's a closer look at what they can offer you.

Midwives. Because a good midwife concerns herself with a woman's emotional, psychological, and nutritional well-being—not just her physical pregnancy—her approach to prenatal care and childbirth is more supportive, more personal, more holistic, and, many couples say, more gratifying. "We both felt so comfortable with our midwife immediately—it was so nice to go for a checkup and not have a doctor sort of appointment," says Linda Murphy, who had a home birth in late 1997. "We'd sit down and just talk for half an hour, about emotional and psychological stuff, and then she'd do the exam, and tell us what our options were for taking certain tests." Her husband, Richie, adds that their midwife was completely reassuring to him as well: "When it was time for the birth, my confidence was so high. I think it's due to our midwife and her classes. All my questions were answered."

The experience and training of midwives can vary. *Certified nurse-midwives* (CNMs) have gone through two years of training to become registered nurses, plus a one-year specialized education, training, and certification in midwifery. They are trained to handle a number of medical procedures, including episiotomies and sonograms; they can also administer Pitocin (a contraction-inducing drug) and sedatives. Because CNMs are required to have backup from a physician, some expectant mothers choose CNMs for their primary OB care, feeling secure in the knowledge that the OB their midwife is partnered with will attend the birth if complications arise. The downside of this, however, is that hospital-affiliated CNMs are accustomed to playing by hospital rules.

Direct-entry midwives (sometimes called *lay midwives,* although many direct-entry midwives object to the term) are commonly lumped together with unlicensed midwives—a tendency that causes them to resent the implication that they are not specially trained or licensed. Direct-entry midwives don't have nursing degrees, but they undergo three years of training and, often, apprenticeships, and have to pass a state-administered licensing exam. *Unlicensed midwives* (many of whom call themselves *lay*) have varying degrees of experience and training (some, for instance, are certified as emergency medical technicians); some even have physician backup, although this relationship is not often sanctioned legally.

If you're shopping for a midwife because you're hoping to give birth without intervention, look for midwives who work independently of hospitals (whether they're at birthing centers or at large), in a midwives' collective, or in private practice with a group of like-minded doctors and midwives. As you interview your prospects, seek out women who have experience in alternative practices, such as acupressure, massage therapy, or water labor—they may be more amenable to your desire for a low-tech birth.

Birth assistants/doulas. The *professional labor coach, labor assistant, birthing assistant, labor support person, monitrice, or labor doula* (all interchangeable terms, although *doulas* tend to emphasize their support in the days and weeks after birth) is a woman who can provide an extra pair of eyes and hands, information, and emotional support during childbirth, at home or in the hospital. To the uninitiated, birth assistance may seem like the sort of thing an expectant dad or partner should handle. But these professionals are far more experienced than most partners. Some are OB nurses or lay midwives by training, and many are hired in instances where a mother has chosen an OB as her primary care person for delivery but wants a constant, knowledgeable female presence throughout the birth. "Not all husbands can take the pressure of watching their wives in pain while reminding her to do things like drink, breathe, change positions, and so on throughout labor—and they shouldn't have to," says Phil's wife Michelle Lerager, R.N., an obstetrical nurse. "A trained coach can give them a much-needed break."

A birthing assistant may seem like a luxury, but statistics show that they can be quite a boon to the process of childbirth. In one study at Children's Hospital Medical Center of Northern California, for instance, having a birth assistant present shortened labor by 25 percent. Also, comparative studies between women who labored with trained birth assistants and those who did not showed that the mothers with help had lower rates of cesareans and forceps delivery, and the requests for epidurals dropped dramatically. For a flat fee of $250 to $1,000, depending on the duration of her hire, enlisting the aid of a professional labor assistant can be money well spent. See the Resources at the end of this chapter for help in finding one near you.

Obstetricians. For pregnant women who are in a high-risk category, or those who simply feel safer with conventional medicine—there are always obstetricians. If you require or prefer the medical expertise of an OB during birth, you'll want to shop for one who is most agreeable to the process and goals of natural childbirth. Interview candidates about their willingness to step back and wait for labor to progress naturally. But you can't afford to let your research end after your first consultation. Follow-up your inquiry by double checking with the OB nursing staff at the facility where the OB practices. You'll also want to ask about—and meet—the physician who will cover for your doctor if he or she is unavailable when you go into labor.

Interventions You Should Know About

The following procedures are commonly practiced by OBs in hospital settings. Here's what any couple planning to give birth naturally in a hospital should find out:

Cesarean rate. The average C-section rate among doctors and hospitals nationwide is about 21 percent. You should look for an institution (and practitioner) with a rate below that figure (mother-centered birth advocates advise a figure of 10 to 15 percent or less, while the American College of Obstetricians and Gynecologists recommends a rate under 16 percent). You might want to ask what were the most common reasons for C-sectioning patients. "Failure to progress," for instance, is a vague catch-all category that might include valid reasons for surgery but may also signal an unwillingness to accommodate a prolonged labor. Other reasons, such as breech babies or prolapsed umbilical cords, are harder to argue with, but they're also far more rare. See "Delivering by Cesarean" on page 46 for other options to ask about.

Birth position policy. Ask how often do laboring women at this facility squat and deliver—or, if you're interviewing a doctor, what percentage of his or her patients do so. It's fairly common knowledge now that the typical on-your-back, feet-in-stirrups position is more convenient for the doctor than it is for the mom, and it can be harmful to the baby. Yet despite this, a great many mothers in hospitals still lie back with their legs up rather than squatting. This conventional position not only fails to make the best use of gravity during contractions, but reinforces the kind of passivity that can eventually lead to a high-tech birth. Don't ever feel that you have to comply with the doctor's assumption that you'll lie back and put your feet up to give birth. Even if the hospital staff does convince you to get on the delivery table, you can still crouch (the staff won't let you fall off) or kneel on it in order to help your contractions work more effectively. Remaining upright this way helps blood and oxygen flow to the uterus and keeps weight off the vena cava.

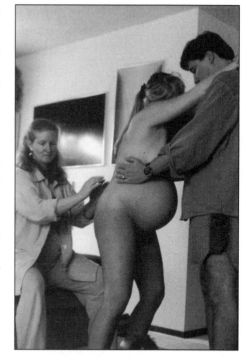

KATI ZWEIG

Episiotomies. You'll also want to know the hospital's/doctor's rate of episiotomies, or surgical incisions into the perineum. Although nearly half of all first-time mothers receive episiotomies in hospitals today, you should be looking for a rate that's less than 20 percent, according to the Coalition for Improving Maternity Services. Episiotomies were once thought to prevent severe tears and to heal better than tears, but a 1992 study of over seven hundred women (published by the American Association for the Advancement of Science) showed that mothers who were given a routine episiotomy were more than twenty-one times more likely to experience severe tearing than those who weren't cut. This study also found that those who were not cut also healed faster when they did tear and experienced less pain in postpartum months. Because of this study, most doctors and midwives are willing to accommodate your request not to cut. Just tell your practitioner that you'd rather try the alternatives: *Kegel exercises* in the months before birth, *massage* or a *heat pack* to the area during labor, *walking around or remaining upright* to make the best use of gravity as well as *coaching to push gently* until the perineum is ready to stretch.

Fetal monitoring. Find out how open the doctor/hospital is to using only intermittent fetal monitoring with a *fetal stethoscope* or a *doptone* (a hand-held ultrasound device) rather than external or internal *electronic fetal monitoring* known as EFM. Studies show that the vast majority of EFM distress signals are false alarms (often a simple shift of position to the left to relieve pressure on the vena cava will normalize signals), and that the interpretations of these signals vary widely. Research also correlates internal EFM to fetal scalp infections. Besides, watching those monitors tends to distract laboring moms from tuning in to their own bodies; EFMs also require women to lie still, tethered to the machine so that the OB staff can take accurate readings. Yet lying horizontally can slow contractions down and make them more painful, which in turn can lead to more medical interventions. Walking around, on the other hand, helps labor progress.

Induction and speeding up labor. Ask whether the hospital or doctor favors an approach to labor called "active management of labor" (AMOL) for first-time moms-to-be. If the answer is yes, your alarms should go off, no matter how progressive the term "active" sounds. Once touted as a way to reduce the rate of C-sections in Ireland, the practice of AMOL has become so adulterated here in the United States that it renders birth unnatural. The process involves checking women in early labor hourly to see if their cervix is dilating at least one centimeter per hour and, if she's not, "pitting" her with high doses of Pitocin, a synthetic form of the naturally occurring contraction-inducing hormone oxytocin. The trouble is, Pitocin-induced contractions often come on suddenly, more rapidly, and with greater intensity (which in turn makes anesthesia more likely). Again, this procedure also hampers the mom's mobility since it requires an IV and pump. "In the Dublin studies, the presence of a midwife or birthing coach—who would work with the mother to help labor along—was key to AMOL's success," says OB nurse Michelle Lerager. "But in this country, I've seen AMOL turn birth into a technical feat performed by M.D.s."

Another reason moms might want to avoid Pitocin has to do with that all-important resting time between contractions. "During my first labor I went to a place that was very deep," says Karen O'Dougherty, who might not have been able to get to such a relaxed state had her labor been chemically induced. "My husband recognized this and was immediately respectful when I went there and he made sure the rest of my birth team let me be there with little interruption. This place was familiar, comfortable, and quiet. When I was there I heard nothing and felt little. When it was time to push I would return, clear-headed, and ready to take control again."

Whether you're a first-timer about to give birth or a veteran mom, though, you'll want to ask under what circumstances the doctor/hospital prescribes Pitocin. During this discussion, you'll want to hear that the doctor/staff understands that artificially-induced contractions can cause fetal distress, overstimulation of the uterus, and other risks.

Labor policies. Again, you're looking for clues that show that your doctor and hospital will encourage or at least allow you freedom of movement during early labor, as well as such amenities as taking a warm bath, immersing yourself in a whirlpool tub, or at least taking a shower. Practitioners who suggest that you stay home as long as possible during early labor (so that you can consume high-energy, low-fat foods and beverages in preparation for the active stage of labor) are more likely to be in the less-intervention-is-better camp.

Pain management. More than half of all hospitals administer some form of medication or anesthesia to birthing women, not only because many women ask for it, but because it makes the staffers' jobs easier. Doctors and hospital support staff can be very persuasive in telling women that they shouldn't sacrifice every comfort at the altar of natural childbirth. While you can hardly blame them for wanting you to suffer less, avoiding drugs will protect your baby from potentially harmful substances and will let you stay active and alert throughout labor. Any nonregional medications administered to help mothers cope with pain will pass through the placenta to the baby, and it will take the baby quite a bit longer than you to get the medication out of its still-immature system. (And even those anesthetics that are administered regionally can wind up giving you what's known as a "spinal headache.")

Nowadays, epidurals seem to be the designer painkiller of choice. Epidurals consist of a combination of narcotics and anesthetics injected into the spinal column. They can offer a reprieve from pain from the waist down, while still allowing you to help push, say some obstetricians. However, epidurals also confine women to bed because they require an IV, a catheter connected to the bladder, and constant fetal monitoring. Besides, natural childbirth proponents point out, pushing can't be all that

delivering by cesarean

An unfortunate byproduct of the natural childbirth movement has been the devastating sense of failure that many moms can feel after having a cesarean. Though few of us expect to bring a child into the world by surgery, it's important to remember that the birth of a healthy child, by any means, is a joyous event. And a couple who has just experienced birth by C-section needs as much encouragement, admiration, and support from loved ones as anyone else.

If you wind up needing a cesarean, the following suggestions may mitigate some of your concerns and discomfort:

- Try to go into the operating room with the same birth attendants you selected when you were planning for a vaginal delivery. Their presence and support can be invaluable.

- Insist that the staff leaves one of your arms unstrapped during the procedure so that you can hold and cuddle the baby right after birth. Remind your partner to help you with this, if necessary.

- Many women experience an excruciating case of trapped gas after a C-section. If you have postsurgical gas pains, do plenty of walking or rocking. In particular, rocking in a rocking chair works the abdominal muscles in ways that help relieve the pain. Ask for a rocking chair to be sent to your room if one is available.

easy if you've lost all sensation from the waist down. If you feel completely at your wit's end and need pain relief, you might prefer an analgesic over an anesthetic because the former will relieve pain without causing numbness.

Our best advice is that you should expect labor to have some uncomfortable passages and should try to develop an arsenal of alternatives to drugs that you and your support people can use when needed. Options can include: changing position (especially shifting your weight to your left side), remaining upright, using hot or cold compacts, baths and showers, massage, acupressure, music, strategic breathing, and strategic muscle relaxation—particularly during the most painful peaks of a contraction. Ultimately, says Michelle, "Women need to know that labor is painful, but only for a certain amount of time—and not between contractions. They'll get through it."

Marcia Jarmel, whose son, Mica, was born with a midwife and her husband in attendance, believes that *transition* (the obstetrical term for that phase of labor in which the cervix is nearly fully dilated and the pushing can begin) represents a key passage in most women's threshold for pain. "I think that transition is marked by the fact that you are saying to yourself 'I can't do this anymore,' " she says. "I remember my own labor was so long I had forgotten why I was doing it on some level. But having our midwife there was instrumental—she told me to put my hand inside and feel the baby's head and that helped me to keep going. She knew just what I needed to know to get through the next bit."

In the end, it's worth remembering that pain serves a legitimate biological function during childbirth. Left unsuppressed by medicine, it can prompt you to focus on whatever it is you need to do—whether it's to sit up, push gently, or relax certain muscles—to usher your baby into the world.

Postpartum policies. You also want to know whether the baby is allowed to "room in" with you after birth; how long you'll be allowed to stay at the facility after birth; if the stay is under twenty-four to forty-eight hours, whether follow-up visits (which can help detect and treat infant jaundice and other complications) are part of the package; and whether breast-feeding consultations are offered.

A Word About Birth Plans

A birth plan is a written outline of what an expectant couple would and would not like to take place during labor and delivery. Given how often we've rallied for natural childbirth throughout this chapter, the following advice may surprise you: Don't feel like you're a failure to the cause if you don't write up a detailed birth plan.

We're just trying to be realistic here about the effectiveness of these plans. Couples who have done their homework and have found the right kind of people to attend their birth need not bother putting everything in writing. If you've chosen a midwife and/or a professional birth assistant, you'll have had many extensive talks about your concerns. So, as tempting as it may be to put the plans that you have already discussed in writing, insisting on doing so could erode the trusting relationship you spent so much time building. Better, in some instances, to clearly convey your philosophy about birth over the course of your pregnancy and look for signs that it's well received (and if it's not, keep hunting).

If your chosen OB is progressive and thinks that a written plan will protect both of you, *by all means supply one.* Some hospitals offer patients a blank standardized—albeit limited—birth plan of their own. A birth plan may also be practical if you have switched doctors or hospitals at the last minute and haven't had time to get to know everyone who will be involved in your delivery. Whenever you feel strongly that a birth plan is needed, be brief, yet warm and reader-friendly: "I'm an inventory clerk at ABC Company and the mother of a three-year-old boy. Since xyz happened at my last birth, I have some preferences about how I'd like this baby to be born. They include. . . ." As you run down the list, try to use flexible phrases like, "I'd prefer to take my chances tearing than to have an episiotomy."

after the baby: birth healing with a group

Karen O'Dougherty, mother of three in Ashland, Oregon, prefers the term "birth healing" to the more common, but negative-sounding, phrase "post-partum blues." What follows is her well-considered approach to this period of a mother's life.

"From the time a mother delivers her baby until she moves with the rhythms and flows of parenting is what I call the birth healing time. It is a magical yet confusing time, a time of great need and change physically, emotionally, and spiritually. The new mother needs to feel she can express anything in a safe and loving environment and be heard. Indeed, she should tell her birth story as often as possible so healing and growth can take place.

"To do this, a new mother might consider joining—or starting—a new mothers' support group. There, mothers can share recommendations on how to deal with specific situations; they can listen to proven suggestions from women who may have been through the exact same thing just months ago. Mothers can swap not only ideas but also clothes and other baby products.

The first place to look for prospective members is at the Childbirth Education class you've attended. If this doesn't apply, then ask your midwife if any other women are due around the same time. Often women find each other by word of mouth. But even posting a flyer inviting New Moms

(continued on next page)

. . .

There's a great body of natural childbirth literature calling upon women to take as much charge as possible to ensure that childbirth is as wonderful and unencumbered as it should be. While these books are certainly a welcome answer to the traditional point of view, it's important for all parents-to-be to put labor and delivery in perspective, if only for sanity's sake. Yes, you'll want the experience to reflect your preferences as much as possible. But ultimately, nature is in control, not you. You can take charge of the beginning location, the people who'll be present, and so forth, but you should be prepared to let go of the rest. Part of that letting go includes recognizing that childbirth is but an instant compared to the lifetime of parenting that follows.

WELCOMING YOUR NEW CHILD TO THE WORLD

In a culture that is still getting used to the idea that newborn babies are feeling beings, the notion of welcoming a child to the world can sound a bit strange. But famed French obstetrician Frederick Leboyer and other infant advocates have taught us to look at it from the baby's point of view.

For the first half of the pregnancy, the baby lives and grows in a utopian universe, all of its needs effortlessly met. But all that changes at the pregnancy's midpoint. Now the baby is growing much more rapidly than the womb and the walls begin to close in. Soon the baby is pressed up against all sides of its little room and still it continues to grow! Next comes the shock of contractions, although the baby may soon feel them as rhythmic caresses. Then the chaos and pain of birth—an invisible force that propels the baby from its former home to . . . what?

The answer to that question depends to a large degree on whether nature's "recommendations" are followed by the parents and obstetrician or midwife. Nature helps babies deal with the trauma of birth by easing the transition from womb to world. For instance, the umbilical cord is designed to continue functioning for several minutes after birth. This provides the baby with a supply of oxygen-rich blood while it is learning to breathe after birth.

Mother/child bonding also helps baby feel immediately comforted. Bonding assures the infant that someone will lov-

(continued from previous page)

to participate in a group will work. Under these circumstances, it is a good idea to meet in a community room until people get to know each other a little better. Then, you can switch to private homes if you wish.

"At the first meeting, participants can discuss the format for the group: Should it be hard-core processing with a facilitator? An orderly circle in which everyone is expected to take turns speaking? Or should it just be a casual sharing of thoughts in no particular order? Topics at this first meeting might also include a discussion of the importance of privacy, the selection of someone who will take charge of the logistics, and the best meeting time.

"At the next meeting, let the birth stories begin! This is a time of sharing that wonderful treasure each woman has that is her very own, as no two tales are alike. The telling of stories can be set up as a ritual of acceptance into a group whose members have earned their place as mothers on this planet—an initiation, if you will. The mothers can form a circle around a candle, holding their babies in their arms—or placing them on blankets on the floor (if crawling babies are present, then the candle will need to be relocated to a high, safe place). Lighting of the candle by each mother can signify the beginning of her story; as she blows it out at the end she seals her tale. Some women may not be ready to tell their story until further trust has been established, but once the stories begin, so too does the intimacy."

ingly care for it, watch out for its safety, and guide it as it feels its way around this weird, new universe. Breast-feeding, an aspect of the bonding process, supplies the baby with the perfect food that nature has "cooked up," and maintains the physical intimacy between mother and child. Before birth, the baby was part of its mother's body, in a state of constant caress. With breast-feeding, the sensation is much the same. In addition, the demands of breast-feeding ensure that the baby will have the constant company of its mother. (For more on breast-feeding, see page 53.)

So that's nature's welcoming ritual—rather well thought through, don't you think? Yet, many babies don't get the chance to experience a single aspect of it. The advent of innovative obstetricians like Leboyer and Dr. Michel Odent has caused many obstetricians and hospitals to modify their procedures in the baby's favor. But the revolution is far from complete.

For example, many obstetricians still cut the umbilical cord immediately after the baby is born, leaving the baby to establish its breathing in a state of panic with its back-up supply of oxygen cut off. In some circumstances—for example, when the cord is wrapped tightly around the baby's neck, interfering with breathing—this compromise is necessary. But most of the time, it isn't. The sedation or anesthesia used by many in birthing is hard on baby, too, because a drugged mom isn't consciously available to her infant at birth. All drugs given to pregnant moms affect the baby too, so the baby will also have some medication in her system and thus be less conscious for bonding as well. In addition, the drugged state of both Mom and baby will make it difficult to initiate breast-feeding, because the baby's sucking reflex is strongest in the twenty to thirty minutes after birth.

As if the above isn't hard enough on newborns, many babies will be separated from their mothers during most of their hospital stay, often at the suggestion of hospital staff. Other hospital procedures will separate even moms and babies who "room in" (see below)—for example, when the baby is taken away to be weighed and checked over by the on-call pediatrician. Once the baby comes home, the demands of mom's work may mean that the baby's primary contact for most of the day will be with a day care provider or other caretaker. For a variety of reasons, nearly half of all women will choose to not breast-feed.

Of course, some of these things can't be helped, and others aren't easily avoided. Economic or medical factors preclude some women from choosing natural childbirth methods. Employment and day care considerations make it impossible for some women to breast-feed. Economic circumstances force many women back to work soon after birthing, and many other women feel compelled to resume a career that is central to their feeling of self-worth.

So the following recommendations represent an ideal, best for welcoming and bonding but not always possible:

Before Birth

- *Get to know your child and begin welcoming it to the family by communicating with it in utero* (see page 27).

Choices for Birthing and Afterward

- *Choose natural childbirth procedures if you can.*

- *Minimize separation from your baby.* Full rooming-in, in which your baby stays with you after birth and at night, is best for bonding and your baby's sense of security so request it if your hospital allows it. Some hospitals require that the baby stay in the nursery at night and during visiting hours. This is called modified rooming-in. While not ideal, it's still far preferable to what's called full nursery care, in which your baby is only brought to you for feedings, although nursery care may be your only option if your child is in danger and needs constant observation. Even with full rooming-in, however, most hospitals will take your child away to be weighed, measured, tagged with a name band, washed, and examined by a pediatrician. If you protest loudly enough, you can often get the pediatrician and weighing cart brought to your room—they're just as portable as your baby. When his daughter Ariel was born, Alan insisted on going with his daughter when the nurse came for her. "I put my hand on her to reassure her and didn't remove it—except when she was weighed—until she was back with her mom. Then again," he laughs, "I'd just finished reading Salman Rushdie's novel, *Midnight's Children,* where two babies are accidentally switched in the hospital and grow up in each other's homes. I wasn't letting anybody put the wrong name tag on our kid!"

- *Breast-feed.* Your baby will be most comforted if breast-feeding starts right after birth, when the baby's sucking reflex is strongest. If this opportunity is missed, the sucking reflex won't return at full strength until the end of the baby's second day. So nature's intentions for immediate breast-feeding are clear.

- *Request parental leave from your employer if you can.* The 1993 Family Leave Act requires companies with over fifty employees to provide up to twelve weeks unpaid leave at a child's birth or adoption or to care for an ill family member, and some smaller companies will voluntarily offer this leave as well. Other companies, large and small, will offer six months of leave or more. Unfortunately, many parents can't afford to take unpaid leave even when it's available. Nevertheless, spending as much time with your baby as possible before returning to work is obviously preferable.

- *Take care of your own emotions.* Only when mom processes her own complicated emotions after giving birth can she be fully available emotionally to her child. Even if the birth took place without any unwelcome surprises, becoming a parent begins a new stage of mom's—and dad's—own emotional development and a substantial change in lifestyle. All of these circumstances can cause conflicting emotions that need to be worked through. In addition, postpartum depression, a blues that commonly strikes women for a week or two after birth, may be a factor at this time. If it lasts more than two weeks, mom might want to seek professional help to speed recovery.

- *If you can afford or otherwise arrange it, take the usual pressures off mom for a while.* Many traditional cultures encourage postnatal "lying in," in which a new mother is relieved of her regular tasks for several weeks so she can focus on her baby. You can approximate this sensible custom by asking friends and relatives for help—or by accepting help when it's offered.

- *Go easy on the welcome-home partying.* Too much celebrating or a steady stream of visitors may blow mom and baby out of the water. What's really needed is some quiet time and space to adjust to the experience of an expanded family and new life. For both of Alan and his wife Hyiah's kids, Hyiah's mother painted beautiful "Welcome" banners that greeted parents and baby when they first walked through the door together. Decorations like these set the tone perfectly, especially when that's where the partying ends!

- *Go with the flow.* Let go of any set ideas and expectations you have about the way life should or will be. Your baby's needs take precedence now and those have a way of blasting apart even your most carefully laid plans.

WHY BREAST-FEEDING MATTERS

"When I was growing up in Indiana in the seventies," recalls Rachel Bendat, "my mom was a La Leche League leader and she breast-fed each of my three younger brothers until they were four years old. When I was little, I would play 'La Leche League leader' and I would get on my play telephone to call all the moms and let them know when the next meeting would be! So I always knew that I would breast-feed my babies."

The choice may not be as obvious for you. If you still haven't made up your mind about breast-feeding, consider the following:

- *Health benefits for baby and developing child.* Breast milk transfers mom's disease-fighting antibodies as well as an army of other infection-fighting agents to her baby. It gives the baby's immune system a strong general boost as well. The liquid (called colostrum) produced before true breast milk comes in is particularly loaded with good stuff: high protein, vitamins, and infection fighters—essentially, the baby's first immunization. And all that protective power makes a difference. One recent Canadian study found that breast-fed babies had 50 percent fewer illnesses, including fewer cases of pneumonia, ear infections, blood infections, and meningitis. Others studies have shown much the same. In addition, research establishes that breast-fed infants are less likely to suffer sudden infant death syndrome (SIDS). Children who were breast-fed also seem to have denser (stronger) bones than formula-fed kids. That may be because infants absorb 67 percent of the calcium in breast milk compared to about 25 percent in cow's milk, from which most formula is made. By contrast, bottle-feeding also seems to contribute to tooth decay and malocclusion (faulty tooth alignment). Girls who were breast-fed are less likely to develop breast cancer later, suggests an early-1990s study of women aged 40 to 85; breast-fed children of both sexes are less likely to have heart disease, strokes, or high blood pressure or be obese as adults. Breast-fed children show reduced risk for insulin-dependent diabetes mellitus, multiple sclerosis, Crohn's disease, and some childhood cancers, as well. And the same goes for ordinary illnesses, too. Says Val Schultz of Ithaca, New York, "My kids just don't get sick and I attribute that entirely to long nursing and their good diet."

- *Intellectual and other developmental advantages.* On average, children who were breast-fed score higher by several points on IQ tests, according to several studies. Breast-fed kids also do a little better in school as a group, shows a National Institutes of Health study. Some experts believe the talking that moms do with their babies during breast-feeding sessions helps language development, too. Finally, switching the baby from breast to breast, a natural part of breast-feeding, enhances the baby's eye-hand coordination.

- *Advantages for preterm infants.* Preterm infants, even seriously ill ones, can usually be breast-fed as long as they're able to suckle. The infection-fighting properties of breast milk have been shown to significantly reduce infections in low-birth-weight babies. It's true that preterm babies fed formula do grow faster, but by the nine-month point breast-fed babies have made up the difference. And research shows that preterm infants who were breast-fed have an IQ (Wechsler scale) advantage of over eight points at age seven. However, mothers of preterm infants may need extra guidance from a lactation consultant (see the Resources at the end of this chapter) and their babies should be monitored by a physician.

- *Health benefits for mom.* Breast-feeding helps moms conserve iron and helps the uterus recover more rapidly from the birth. Several studies indicate that women who breast-fed their children have a significantly reduced risk of both breast cancer and bone-mineral loss in later life.

- *Economic and other practical benefits.* Breast-feeding is free, portable, hygienic, and convenient—no bottles to sterilize, wash, or fill.

Why Some Women Don't Breast-Feed

All the important medical and dietetic organizations—the American Dietetic Association (ADA), the American Academy of Pediatrics, the American College of Obstetrics and Gynecology, and the American Academy of Family Physicians—strongly recommend breast-feeding. Yet despite so much encouragement from experts, only 60 percent of American mothers were even trying breast-feeding from birth as of 1995; by the six-month point, only 22 percent of mothers were still at it.

What's wrong with this picture? Why don't more American women do what appears to be so important for their children? The problem starts in the obstetric wards. Despite the official positions of medical professional associations, surveys, such as one involving more than three thousand physicians queried by researchers at the University of North Carolina, show that few doctors and other hospital staff are well-informed enough about breast-feeding or sufficiently committed to it to offer much support to new mothers. For example, medical personnel often advise that mothers switch to formula at the first sign of breast-feeding trouble.

Healthcare economics also play a role. With short hospital stays after birth now the rule, moms have less of an opportunity to receive professional guidance, even in hospitals that support breast-feeding. Another problem is that hospital practices are generally designed more for the staff's convenience than the welfare of the baby. For example, if you don't "room-in" with your baby—i.e., your baby is kept in a nursery instead of your room—the staff may try to restrict the number and duration of feedings.

Relentless marketing by formula manufacturers may be the most negative factor of all. Companies flood hospitals, doctor's offices, public health programs, and private mailboxes with advertising, free samples, educational materials about parenting that include formula ads, and other goodies. While many hospitals and other medical facilities now prohibit such material on their premises as a matter of principle, many others do not.

Some women who fully intend to nurse give up because of problems related to going back to work. Many mothers have to return to their jobs shortly after giving birth because their employers offer only brief, if any, maternity leave. Breast-feeding by working moms is more easily managed when employers support them in expressing their milk during work hours but many do not.

Nor does the culture-at-large really encourage breast-feeding. Sexual associations with the breast make many mothers timid about breast-feeding in public, and only a few states protect mothers' civil rights to nurse publicly. Finally, unlike Rachel Bendat whom we met earlier, new moms may have few, if any, role models among their family and friends, including in many cases their mothers. In 1972, for example, only 22 percent of mothers breast-fed—about the same as today, which underscores the point. And even if support is forthcoming from other women, it may not be from the mother's partner. Some men have their own hang-ups about nursing and discourage it in their presence.

In addition, it is medically recommended that some mothers *not* nurse their babies. Doctors will generally advise—wisely, we believe—against breast-feeding if their patients use addictive or other dangerous drugs such as cocaine or PCP, drink more than the most minimal amounts of alcohol, or are receiving intense medical therapy such as chemotherapy or radiation.

How to Compensate When You Can't Breast-Feed

If you can't breast-feed because of circumstances beyond your control, you can still take several steps to close the gap, particularly in the emotional area. Here's how to form a close, psychologically nurturing relationship with your little one even when bottle-feeding:

- Nursing moms tend to touch, smile at, and rock their babies more, studies confirm. Be just as attentive and affectionate during bottle-feedings.

- Make a conscious effort to sustain eye contact with your baby, something that happens naturally with breast-feeding. Try feeding your baby in positions that are close to breast-feeding positions and switch sides like breast-feeding moms.

- Feed your baby yourself, mom, as often as you can. Passing the baby around to be fed by other family members and friends may seem democratic, but it's not the way nature designed the process. Breast-feeding moms tend to have more frequent, prolonged contact with their babies because of the feeding ritual.

- Breast-feeding sessions tend to be ended by mom and baby together in kind of an intuitive "joint decision," but moms alone tend to end bottle-feedings. Make your bottle-feedings a cooperative communication between the two of you.

- To make sure your baby enjoys her feedings, be aware of her reaction to formula. About 7.5 percent of children are allergic to or intolerant of cow's milk, which is the basis of most baby formulas. If your baby has this problem, try soy-based formula, unless your baby is also allergic to soy. Goat's milk may provide a suitable alternative because goat's milk is biochemically much closer in composition to human milk than cow's; you can buy fresh goat's milk in natural foods stores. Also, some formulas are of better quality than others; sugar content is one indicator—the less, the better.

Answers for Nursing Moms' Most Common Questions

Breast-feeding is the most natural parenting act a new mother can undertake, but most moms still need a little help in the form of information and encouragement to nurse their babies successfully. Here are answers to some of the most common questions. (Please refer to the Resources at the end of this chapter for more detailed information.)

I plan to be anesthetized during labor. Will that interfere with breast-feeding?

Anesthesia, sedation, prolonged labor, and surgical births can all lead to initial breast-feeding problems, and you can't always rely on hospital personnel to be helpful in those circumstances. Make sure you have competent, knowledgeable advice available to you from the beginning. Contact your local La Leche League representative for more guidance.

What if my body doesn't produce enough milk?

Unfortunately, the fear of not being able to produce enough milk leads many women to quit breast-feeding within the first few weeks or to begin supplementing their natural supply with formula. The fact is, says the American Dietetic Association, nearly every woman can produce enough milk for her baby. Nature makes sure of that. Close contact with your baby and the baby's frequent suckling will cue your body to produce the right amount of milk. In the meantime, your supply will match the baby's need and hunger. In any case, don't supplement with formula unless a pro—breast-feeding professional advises you to. Formula supplementation is a common cause of breast-feeding failure.

Is it safe to lose weight while I'm breast-feeding?

Yes, say most experts, if you do it in moderation and with common sense. Many women decide to bottle-feed from the beginning because they want to diet and get their bodies back in shape. That's a shame because reasonable dieting is possible while breast-feeding. In fact, because milk production burns calories, breast-feeding women tend to lose more weight than new moms who bottle-feed—about one to two pounds per month, on average—even without dieting. If you want to lose more, a University of Iowa study indicates that you can safely lose about a pound a week if you eat nutritiously while you do it. However, experts advise that you be monitored by a physician, including getting you and your baby weighed about every two weeks. What is *not* advisable, says the ADA, are severe calorie restriction (under 1,500 calories per day), liquid formula diets, and weight-loss medications, all of which may affect both your health and the quality of your breast milk.

Will my baby get enough nutrition if I'm tired and worn down?

In almost all cases, yes. The one at risk is you. If your energy and nutrient supply is depleted, your body will rob your own reserves to feed your baby, who will probably continue to do just fine. Get professional screening and guidance if you're feeling rundown and undernourished, but continue breast-feeding unless specifically told not to.

Aren't the best formulas nearly the same as breast milk?

No. Human milk is an amazing, perfect food for your baby and no manufacturer can come close to duplicating it. First, formula doesn't have the immune-system boosting and infection-fighting properties of mother's milk. Second, human milk is an amazing food that naturally changes to meet your baby's needs as he grows. Finally, breast milk is so active that it changes at different times of day, and at different stages of each feeding. Given how well babies do when breast-fed, that's probably just how nature wants it. As a matter of fact, all mammals—human or not—do better when fed the milk of their own species.

BREAST-FEEDING FOR WORKING MOTHERS

Many nursing moms assume that working again means the end of breast-feeding. Not! Yes, a job can have an impact on breast-feeding, and yes, it will take a big commitment on your part. But the myriad benefits of breast-feeding certainly justify the effort. And for working moms, there's one more advantage: Breast-feeding will reconnect you and your child like nothing else can after a long day of separation.

We want to state clearly that doing this won't necessarily be easy; in fact, it may turn out to be impossible. But here are some tips on making it more manageable:

- *Breast-feed early in the morning before you leave for work.* Allow plenty of time for this nursing session so you don't give your baby an early introduction to rush-hour stress!

- *Use a breast pump to "express" your milk before, after, and even—if you can find a private, convenient location—during work.* This can be time-consuming—you spend your lunch hour pumping away—but it will encourage your body to keep producing milk. Expressed milk can be frozen and kept for at least a month. You can get an inexpensive manual pump at any good pharmacy, but the more efficient electric pumps work best. (Learning to "let down" your milk with a pump may be a bit difficult at first. Be patient. The books reviewed in the Resources at the end of this chapter will give you more guidance on this subject.)

- *Make your environment as nursing-friendly as possible when you're away from your baby.* Some mothers have a hard time producing milk in the absence of the auditory and tactile cues—baby's hungry cry, and especially baby's sucking—which normally help prompt a nursing woman's milk to let down. You can lessen this problem by providing the right stimuli, such as reminders of your baby, and removing the wrong stimuli, such as typical workplace noise. For example, when you're pumping your milk at work find the quietest, most secluded spot possible, and bring a tape of baby sounds, a picture of your infant, and/or anything else that you find puts you in a nursing mood.

- *Nurse immediately upon returning home from work.* In fact, don't do *anything* else before you feed baby. There's time enough to change clothes, shower, or whatever, after you greet baby in this special way.

- *Nurse at night to make sure you and baby stay in the habit, and your body continues to receive milk-producing stimulation.* Then, in the hours just before rising, bring baby to bed with you and nurse once or twice before starting your day; and/or nurse after rising, before everyone else is up. Think of it as an easygoing, peaceful start of the day for each of you and the perfect way to say "Good morning!"

- *Keep the same schedule on weekends—i.e., don't nurse during the hours when you're at work on weekdays.* This can be hard, especially if baby decides not to take a bottle when you're in sight. But it could prove essential to making sure baby gets enough to eat while the two of you are apart.

- *Make nursing your top priority when you're not at work.* Cooking, cleaning, laundry, errands—they can all wait or, preferably, be done by someone else.

· *Introduce bottle-feeding—with mom's expressed milk.*

· *Train Dad or any other caregiver,* before *you return to work.* Phil learned this the hard way, when Michelle went back to work after their first child was born. Jessamine was about three months old, and had never had anything but her mother's milk, and they figured she'd be happy to take it in a bottle. Instead, she wasn't happy about *anything,* and Phil wound up having to take her to the hospital where Michelle works for some emergency nursing on Michelle's dinner break. After some weeks, Jessamine finally got comfortable with Dad bottle-feeding her, but it would have been a lot easier on all three of them if they'd gotten her accustomed to that beforehand, say Phil and Michelle today.

The best time to introduce the bottle is probably around three to four weeks of age. Any earlier, and you may inadvertently provoke "nipple confusion" in which the baby has trouble making the transition between synthetic and natural nipples. (It's easier for a baby to get milk from a synthetic nipple; she has to work harder to get it from mom's nipple.) After six weeks or so, you may wind up with a case of what we might call "nipple chauvinism," in which baby is definitely *not* confused, and wants *only* mother's breast, as Jessamine did. Incidentally, when introducing the bottle, use it at least twice a week. And if you're going to teach baby to take a bottle, mom shouldn't even be in the same room: Mom's presence will only confuse baby, who will probably turn the bottle down. (Would *you* take a bottle if Mom were at hand?)

Extra bonus bottle-feeding tip: The Playtex nipple is considered by many to be most like the human nipple, so baby's sucking action is more like that in actual breast-feeding. And no, we do not own stock in the company.

Making It Work at Work

If your employer or coworkers resist the idea of your taking time at work to express your breast milk, you may have a sizable education project on your hands. Indeed, if no one has ever attempted this at your workplace before, or if there are no facilities or other provisions for it, you may want to begin your lobbying/education efforts well before your baby arrives.

In today's economic climate, where women make up nearly half the work force (a figure that's expected to climb to over 60 percent in the next few years) and where three-fourths of working women will become pregnant during their careers, breast-feeding is increasingly becoming a workplace issue. Some companies have seen the light and adopted programs to facilitate their employees' continuing to breast-feed after returning to work. But if you don't work for such an "enlightened" outfit, the following information may help you argue your case:

- *Breast-feeding moms take less sick leave.* Moms as well as babies get health benefits from breast-feeding, and when those moms are employees, that means less work time lost to illness. The Los Angeles Department of Water and Power, which offers its employees a complete lactation program (including classes, counselors, a pump for each mother, and a lactation room), found that it saved $5 in decreased worker absenteeism and lower healthcare costs for every $1 spent on the program. Decreased absenteeism should more than make up for time spent expressing milk as well.

- *Help is available for employers interested in setting up a lactation program.* Medela, a major breast pump manufacturer (see the Resources at the end of this chapter), offers a breast-feeding supply and consultation service that will help employers get started. This outfit also provides pumps (naturally!) and lactation consultants and advises companies on setting up "pump rooms."

tips on storing expressed breast milk

You've got your pump and you've found your milk-expressing hideaway. Now here's what do you do with the milk once you've expressed it:

- *Keep expressed milk in clean plastic or glass containers and refrigerate or freeze.* Make sure the container is well sealed. Label each container with the date so you know how old the milk inside it is. Use oldest milk first. Breast milk can be refrigerated for up to forty-eight hours. It can also be stored in a refrigerator freezer. If the freezer does not have a separate door, use it within three weeks, but if the freezer has a separate door, it will keep for up to three months. If you have a "deep freezer," i.e., one whose temperature is maintained at zero degrees Fahrenheit, you can keep the milk for six months or more. *Be sure to leave extra space in the container*—the milk will expand as it freezes.

- *Separate milk into small amounts that can be used up in one feeding.* Measure two to three ounces for a newborn, four to six ounces for an older baby, so that if baby doesn't use it all, little is wasted.

- *Thaw milk slowly by holding it under tepid tap water.* Now, *very* gradually increase the temperature of the water to warm (not hot). When the bottle is ready, you can heat it further by placing it on the stove in a pan of warm water. *Do not overheat.* "Cooking" the milk can break down important nutrients, and can make it hotter than is safe for baby. And never use a microwave to thaw or heat milk. Microwaves heat unevenly, so that while the first few drops might feel "just right" to you, the milk inside may be far too hot. Microwaving milk can also break down some of the most valuable elements in your milk.

- *Don't refreeze milk.* Once thawed, refrigerated breast milk will keep for up to twenty-four hours.

- *Save unused milk.* The milk that's left over after baby's "full" light goes on can be saved for up to four hours if it's refrigerated right away, and can be used for the next feeding if it occurs in time.

• *It's the wave of the future!* Medela's employer service has attracted interest from scores of companies, and their clients include such large corporations as Amoco. Others who have set up similar programs include Dow Chemical and AT&T. "It's an idea whose time has come," says John Nicoll, director of management services for the city of Burbank, California, which has also set up an employee lactation program. "Once organizations try it, it will be as common as the existence of sick leave and medical plans." Half of the employees in Nicoll's department are women, and when several of them were breast-feeding, he realized that "I couldn't afford the price of having [them] at home." He adds: "It's appropriate and humane, and ultimately it makes good business sense."

NURSING YOUR ADOPTED BABY

No, this is not another installment of "Strange Science" or "News of the Weird." But based on the incredulous looks Alan's wife Hyiah first got from friends and family members when she nursed adopted son Ajene, we'll excuse you for wondering.

So, yes you can nurse your adopted baby, even if you've never had a child before. Obviously, adoptive nursing requires mothers (and dads) to prepare differently and deal with issues that biological parents don't have to face. But the rewards of nursing can be much the same no matter what route your baby took to arrive.

What Is Adoptive Nursing and Why Bother?

First, let's define some basic terms that come up whenever the topic of adoptive nursing is seriously discussed. **Relactation** applies to women who have given birth in the previous several months and are building back a milk supply that has fallen off or completely dried up. **Induced lactation** applies to women who either haven't given birth recently or have never been pregnant and have to coax their bodies into producing milk.

Although considerable effort may be involved on both mom's and baby's part, women who relactate will generally produce a full supply of milk. Those who attempt to induce lactation need to let go of such expectations. Most will produce some milk, and a minority will eventually produce a full supply. Others will produce none, feeding their babies either with a bottle or through special supplementing devices designed to simulate biological nursing. *However, in the adoptive nursing community, you are considered to have successfully induced lactation as long as you've established an emotionally nurturing nursing relationship, whether you produce your own milk or not.*

In fact, it's not stretching the point to say that nursing may play an even more important role in adoptive parenting. When supported by natural childbirth methods and breast-feeding, bonding to your biological child is usually instinctive and immediate. Bonding tends to occur much more gradually with adopted children, often taking a year or more. Nursing dramatically shortens the timetable for both mom and baby.

How It's Done

There are two schools of thought on how to induce lactation. The first says to use a breast pump to prepare for nursing—pumping on a schedule such as a newborn would follow may develop alveoli and ductile tissue that encourage milk production. The second says don't sweat it—you're going to have to start your baby with some form of supplementation anyway, and after several months of nursing your milk supply will be the same as if you had pumped. Who's right? In a sense, both. Studies do in fact show that there's no way to tell which adoptive mothers have pumped and which haven't after a few months. Besides, you may find pumping—which is best done with an electric machine that simulates a baby's sucking pattern—to be uncomfortable, time-consuming, and noisy, with none of the side benefits of nursing. Nor is pumping guaranteed to produce milk. But some mothers do produce either milk or colostrum while pumping, and that's an advantage in establishing a good nursing relationship, because it reinforces the baby's sucking.

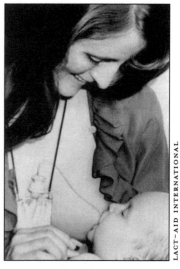

Mother using supplementer

After reading the literature, Alan's wife Hyiah chose to pump on the off-chance it might help her produce milk. It worked, and nursing was successful. But she hated every minute of the pumping, and only her fierce dedication saw her through. If you think there's any chance pumping could discourage you from nursing, forget the machine! The nipple alone will encourage the baby to suck.

What you do need is plenty of support—especially from your partner and from experienced advocates (ask your adoption agency if it can refer you to an adoptive nursing consultant)—and lots more information than we can give you here. The La Leche League guide reviewed in the Resources at the end of this chapter will answer your detailed questions about adoptive nursing. But here are some of the most commonly asked questions and their answers:

LACT-AID INTERNATIONAL

laurie hayden's story: nursing my adopted son, micah

Like most adoptive mothers, Laurie Hayden had to rely on a supplementer—a device that attaches to the breast to simulate biological breastfeeding—to nurse her son. But ultimately, she found it was the warmth and closeness of nursing that mattered to Micah, not the source of his milk:

"Among the many things that I had to let go of and accept during my infertile days of trying to get pregnant was the fact that I would not be a nursing mother. I had always pictured myself nursing my baby and now that possibility was gone, or so I thought. So when we started the adoption process and I heard that I might be able to nurse my adoptive baby, I perked right up and began to read as much as I could about inducing lactation. Since my husband and I were planning a domestic adoption, we would be receiving an infant (babies adopted internationally usually join their families at an older age). I knew that my chances for success would be better than with an older baby. I decided to go for it, all the while reminding myself that it might not work and that my flexibility would be crucial.

"My commitment was key to my success. Six weeks before our birth mother was due, I began pumping my breasts faithfully for fifteen to twenty minutes on each side, anywhere between two to four times a day. It hurt and was tedious and noisy but I persevered and after four weeks began to produce milk. The night it happened, I was alone in my house and I was screaming for joy, jumping up and down, and calling people with my news. I was astounded by my body's ability to respond to all that stimulation from the pumping and put forth the tiniest drop of milk from my breasts. It felt like

(continued on next page)

How long does it take to build up a milk supply?

Mothers inducing lactation may not produce a significant number of ounces per day for six months or full milk potential until well into the second year. Relactation is generally quicker. But there's no rule here, other than patience. Your body may plateau at several points. This commonly happens when you begin feeding your child his first solid food, for example. Your supply will probably begin building again after a while, although the experts advise you to base your goals on successful mothering, not milk quantity.

I've never been pregnant. Will that affect my ability to produce milk?

Previous nursing helps but many women who've never been pregnant successfully produce milk.

How does milk produced by induced lactation compare to milk produced in a normal pregnancy?

It's not known for sure. There are many difficulties with conducting adequate research on induced milk, not the least of which is the understandable reluctance of adoptive mothers to surrender any of their precious supply for research purposes. But as the La Leche League's Kathryn Anderson (herself an adoptive mom) writes, "what adoptive mothers who have induced significant supplies know is, their babies have thrived." And some research suggests that even a small amount of induced milk provides significant nutritional and immunological advantages over a pure formula diet.

Will all adopted babies nurse?

Most newborns will nurse immediately. With older babies, especially those past a few weeks, you'll need to be patient and persistent as they figure it out. And some adopted babies won't ever learn to nurse, no matter what you try. If that's your experience, establish the best, most loving bottle-feeding relationship you can. This isn't about getting an "A" in breast-feeding. It's about providing love and comfort for your child.

THE DISPOSABLE-DIAPER CONTROVERSY

For many years now, environmentalists have complained that the planet was being smothered under mounds of discarded Pampers, causing many a conscientious parent to reject the convenience of disposable diapers. Health-conscious moms and dads have also suspected that airtight plastic may not be the best way to pamper a tender baby bottom.

(continued from previous page)

a miracle. More and more milk surfaced in the following weeks, although never enough to really 'count' in volume.

"Once my son Micah was born, I stopped pumping and fed him his formula milk with a nursing supplementer bottle that hung around my neck and was fed to Micah through thin tubes taped to my nipples. I was very lucky with Micah, because he was a naturally 'sucky' infant and latched on immediately. The awkwardness of the supplementer didn't bother him at all.

"My milk flow was never really great, but I soon learned that this was less important to me than the fact that Micah and I had a nursing relationship. My milk ran out after three months, when Micah was only waking up once during the night; I no longer felt the commitment at that point to wake myself up to pump in order to keep up milk production. I continued to nurse him with the supplementer until he was ten months old, when he was showing a preference for his bottles of milk.

"Nursing Micah was a beautiful experience for both of us. I became very adept at 'hooking up' so that it became second nature to me. I nursed him in airplanes and in various other public places with hardly anyone noticing our unusual setup. It felt natural to me and Micah so enjoyed it that he would often times nurse for comfort only, without the supplementer attached.

"Micah is now two years old. My husband and I are beginning the adoption process for our second child and without a doubt I will attempt to nurse. If it works and the baby is receptive, great. If not, we'll go on and find our own special way to bond and feel close."

With millions of babies needing several years' worth of diapers each, the financial stakes in this debate are awesome. So, as to be expected, disposable makers and the cloth diaper service industry have battled ferociously for parents' hearts and minds and they haven't always fought fair.

Is there any way for a caring parent to make a sensible decision in this atmosphere? Let's see if we can get to the, uh, bottom of this issue.

The Planet

Disposables have long dominated the marketplace. Eighty percent of parents use them, 60 percent of those for convenience, according to one consumer survey. Many of the rest seem to have hardly considered the alternative—a testimony to how successfully disposable diaper manufacturers have marketed their product.

In the 1980s, the environmental movement began threatening the status quo by urging consumers to consider the impact of sixteen billion disposable diapers ending up in landfills every year. The disposable diaper industry counterattacked with a deep-pockets public relations blitz in which they sought not only to resell parents on their product's attributes but also convince them that disposable diapers caused no more harm to the planet than cotton diapers and diaper services. The services, they pointed out, use vast quantities of water, disinfecting chemicals, and detergents to launder their diapers. Their delivery trucks burn lots of gasoline and pollute the air. If you worry about pesticides and herbicides, cotton is one of the most heavily sprayed crops. Plus, they argued, those who wash their cloth diapers at home instead of using a service

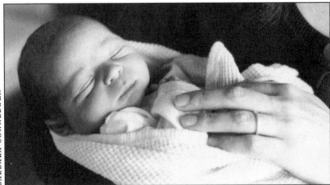

BARBARA SONNEBORN

waste water and electricity because home washers and dryers are usually far less efficient than commercial equipment.

The diaper service industry fired back with its own campaign. Ultimately, both disposable-diaper makers and the National Association of Diaper Services commissioned "scientific" studies to give their competing claims the appearance of fact. A 1990 high profile study paid for by the single largest disposable-diaper maker, Proctor & Gamble, concluded that disposables did no more damage to the planet than cloth. The diaper service industry then hired a consultant group to conduct its own study, which found disposables to be far more harmful. Of course, the studies only fed the controversy because they were so subjective. Since both sides paid the outfits that conducted their research, you might well conclude that the studies were designed from the outset to favor the client.

However, as *Mothering* magazine reports, the disposable-funded study has been widely criticized while the diaper service study has not. In fact, in the United Kingdom, the Advertising Standards Authority has ruled that Proctor & Gamble can no longer "imply that the study's conclusions are generally accepted."

The Baby

Deciding which form of diapering is best for your baby isn't nearly so complicated. From a sheer comfort standpoint, many mothers would rather put cotton than plastic against their baby's skin. As Alan's wife Hyiah says, this is a no-brainer for women who've spent a few sweltering days in pantyhose.

For many mothers, health concerns matter even more than comfort, and here cotton wins hands down (unless your child spends time in day care—see below). Because disposables hold moisture so well and keep it away from the baby's skin, parents tend to change them far less frequently than cloth. In fact, ultra-absorbent diapers are generally only changed after four hours or more. This leads to more frequent irritation—diaper rash—because the bacteria that causes it begins to grow within minutes after the baby urinates. The *amount* of moisture has nothing to do with it.

If your child spends time in day care, however, you may be smart to choose disposables for those hours. Studies show that diarrhea has a tendency to be spread in day care centers because of sloppy hygiene by caretakers. Hypothetically, then, diapers that leak less will be more hygienic. An intriguing study conducted by the Kimberly-Clark Corporation indicates that disposables do in fact leak significantly less stool than do cloth diapers covered by vinyl pants. Another part of the study showed that even freshly washed vinyl diaper coverings usually contained potentially disease-causing bacteria. Yes, Kimberly-Clark is a disposable-diaper maker with a big vested interest in its results. But nobody seems to be questioning the researchers' methods. Furthermore, many day care centers require disposables, which ends the discussion right there.

Diapering Tips—The Real vs. the Ideal

It isn't just advertising that makes disposable diapers more popular. They truly are far more convenient, so much so that even if you just use some in a pinch, you may find yourself hooked. Keeping this in mind, we offer the following tips:

Occasional disposable use. Many well-intentioned, nature-loving parents have found that in certain situations, it's hard to resist using disposables. Confining disposable use to special circumstances and using cloth the rest of the time still beats exclusive disposable use by miles. Many parents keep their babies in disposables when traveling and in day care, and stick with cloth at home. Some also use disposables, which are more absorbent, at bedtime and put cloth on in the morning.

Rachel Bendat nearly talked herself into a switch after temporarily diapering son Zachariah in disposables during a long trip to Indiana to see family: "It's really easy to think, 'What will it matter? Since so many people use disposables, how can we really make a difference?' The problem is, too many people think this way! So for now we'll continue to offer our small bit of help to the environment by using mostly cloth diapers."

Diaper services. These companies make cloth diapering as convenient as possible by delivering clean diapers and picking up dirty ones. The manner in which they dispose of the human waste is monitored by municipal health boards, a big improvement over the uncontrolled way in which consumers get rid of used disposables. Cost-wise, all the parents we've talked to find diaper services considerably cheaper than disposables, despite disposable makers' claims about their products. Self-laundering is far cheaper than both, but much more work. You'll find diaper services in your local Yellow Pages unless you live in a small town or rural area that isn't served by one.

Diaper covers. Cloth diapers don't absorb as much moisture as disposables, so you'll have to change them more frequently and use diaper covers to protect baby, her clothing, and everything else she touches. Our favorite brand of covers is Nikky, a Japanese brand available through the Natural Baby Catalog (see the Resources at the end of this chapter). Their top-of-the-line wool version is best, but the cotton model is fine and about $5 less. Two problems with Nikkys: They cost more than other brands, and if you mistakenly wash them in hot water, you destroy the waterproofing and therefore the cover itself. Another good diaper cover brand is Gerber, found in supermarkets. As a general rule, select natural fibers over synthetic for "breathability" and wool over cotton if you can afford it. Test Velcro strength on cheaper brands. And note that some brands may fit your baby better than others, so don't buy a full supply until you've found what works. Many parents prefer Kushies and Bumkins all-in-one diapers, which eliminate the need for separate covers. Obtain them from Ecobaby (see the Resources at the end of this chapter).

THE CIRCUMCISION ISSUE

Ben and Sara Greene remembered when going to a *bris*—the circumcision ceremony for eight-day-old Jewish boys—just meant dressing up, meeting a relative or friend's new baby, eating too much food, and mingling with other dressed-up folks stuffing their faces. But Daniel's bris promised to be a more trying experience, for they were attending it with new eyes. They were planning to have children of their own soon so they had discussed how they would handle the circumcision issue in their family. They knew that doctors no longer considered the procedure medically necessary and that many people now considered it barbaric, an opinion they had come to share. They also knew that as Jews, most of their relatives would vigorously disagree. Still, they weren't looking forward to what they viewed as an afternoon of "celebrating" Daniel's agony.

That day, Daniel might have sided with them if he'd had the choice. Although the *mohel* (Jewish circumcision specialist) gave him a few sips of wine to dull the pain, Daniel howled with the first slice of the scalpel. The howling continued after the procedure was completed and Daniel was taken briefly from the room to be cleaned up (he had defecated on himself, a common occurrence after circumcision.) It continued still after he was handed to his mother and beaming papa and grandpa began accepting congratulations from their scores of guests. Everyone sang and clapped—that is, besides Ben and Sara, who were quietly horrified, and Daniel, who appeared to them to be in a state of abject terror.

Daniel's circumcision is just another battle scene in a cultural tussle still far from settled. (Though, reportedly, not all circumcisions are traumatic. See "Rachel and Zachariah's Story: A Circumcision of the Heart," page 72 for example.) Updated medical information has led many Americans to decline circumcision for their sons, particularly in the face of the pain it can cause. Concerns by some that it may also cause long-term emotional harm have led still more couples to pass. Because of the body part involved, sex inevitably enters the discussion, too.

However, circumcision plays a crucial symbolic role in many religions and cultures. Its defenders cite medical advantages that, while slight, do exist. And on occasion, when performed by a skilled and sensitive practitioner (mohels have a strong reputation in this regard), circumcisions appear to cause no substantial pain, physical or otherwise.

How can you make a calm, reasoned choice in the midst of this cultural firefight? We can't turn down the heat but we can lay out a few facts that will help you make a more informed decision.

Culture and History

Circumcision isn't mentioned in the Koran, but most Muslims have the procedure performed on their infant sons. Many African and South American cultures also circumcise male children, although often not until puberty. Jews the world over have been circumcising their male children since the days of Abraham, as a sign of God's covenant with the Jewish people. To most Jews, it is unthinkable not to circumcise a son, although some younger, progressive Jewish parents are defecting on this issue.

Circumcision for nonreligious reasons has never been something that set "civilized" people apart, contrary to popular belief. In the industrialized world, it only took root in English-speaking countries such as Britain, the U.S., and Canada, and it is fast in decline in some of those (the rate has fallen to 1 percent in England and 40 percent in Canada). It has never been popular in most of Europe, Asia, Central America, or South America. Worldwide, only about 20 to 24 percent of men have been circumcised.

When circumcision did take hold in the English-speaking world, it was partly for reasons that are now discredited. American doctors began advising the practice in the late nineteenth century because they believed it would stop masturbation and the insanity that masturbation supposedly caused, as well as cut down on unconventional sex. Other English-speaking countries soon followed the Americans' lead. The medical world eventually adopted a more modern attitude towards sexuality, but found other reasons to continue recommending circumcision, especially after studies appeared suggesting a link between uncircumcised males and penile and cervical cancer. But the evidence was too inconclusive to convince many research experts. England's National Health Service stopped paying for circumcision after World War II.

Meanwhile, American doctors kept recommending circumcision for every baby boy until 1971, when the American Academy of Pediatrics (AAP) declared that the procedure was completely devoid of medical benefits. The AAP has modified its views since then, but only slightly. It now asserts that the potential advantages of circumcision are so small that parents, not doctors, should choose. As a result, circumcision rates have dropped from about 90 percent a generation ago to about 60 percent today.

The Medical Issues

When everyone with an opinion is waving their studies in your face, it's easy to feel confused. Keep in mind that the medical arguments both for and against circumcision remain so weak that most doctors throughout the industrialized world consider it optional, cosmetic surgery.

For example, a study by a prominent physician advocate for circumcision suggests that the operation may provide some protection against urinary tract infection (UTI) in the first year of life. But UTI occurs in only 1 percent of boys. Is that reason enough to circumcise all males, especially when good hygiene by itself may prevent UTI? Most doctors would say no.

Circumcision was once thought to offer protection against AIDS and other sexually transmitted diseases. However, the medical community as a whole has not been convinced by the evidence and other researchers have concluded that circumcision provides no protection at all.

Despite early doubts, circumcision has proved to protect against penile cancer. But this disease is exceedingly rare—about 1 case in 100,000 men—and also occurs in some circumcised males. Besides, penile cancer can be prevented in uncircumcised men with good hygiene.

The old prejudice that a circumcised penis is a cleaner penis persists to this day, but it doesn't wash, so to speak. In fact, nature appears to have designed the foreskin largely to keep the penis more hygienic—that is, shielded from urine and feces as well as other sources of irritation. Infection of the urinary opening (called *meatitus*) and scarring of the opening (called *meatal stenosis*) don't occur often but when they do, they almost always strike circumcised males. At any rate, soap and water will clean an uncircumcised penis just as thoroughly as a circumcised one. Fervent anti-circumcision activist Marilyn Milos, a registered nurse, notes that "the foreskin is the only part of the body we cut off so that our children won't have to learn how to clean it."

Doctors may recommend circumcision when the foreskin is too tight to draw back for easy cleaning. But this can't be determined until the child is several years old because the foreskin doesn't fully retract until at least age three.

On the pro-circumcision side of the argument, the medical risks of circumcision—excessive bleeding, blood infections, scarring, and surgical accidents—occur only on rare occasions, although in a few cases, little boys have lost their penis to a bungled procedure. The circumcision procedure does cause pain but this can be reduced with a local anesthetic. However, Milos points out that once the drug wears off, the baby will be left with a raw, sore wound that will take a week or more to heal.

Because most doctors no longer consider circumcision necessary, more and more American health plans are dropping it from coverage,

rachel and zachariah's story: a circumcision of the heart

Does circumcision have to hurt and terrify the baby? Not according to Rachel Bendat of Ashland, Oregon, who describes her son Zachariah's bris. If you hope to create an event for your son like the beautiful, caring ceremony Rachel describes, note that the use of a local anesthetic is a relatively new practice not yet adopted by all physicians and mohels. Nor does the anesthetic necessarily eliminate the pain for all babies.

"During my pregnancy, our midwife had lent my husband Ken and I videos and articles on circumcision. We couldn't make up our minds on whether to circumcise so we decided to wait and see if we had a boy. Sweet Zachariah, our beautiful son, was born July 7, 1997. We wouldn't be circumcising until the eighth day anyway—as is the custom in Judaism—so after we took our baby home, we discussed whether or not to go through with it.

"On the fifth day, our rabbi came to visit us. He sat at the foot of our bed in reverence of our sacred space, and while I held our sleeping boy in my arms he spoke quietly with us about the significance of circumcision in the Jewish tradition. We also talked about the medical aspects and he told us that both personally and as a rabbi he does not necessarily advise circumcision for a non-Jewish boy. He recommends circumcision for Jewish boys because of the spiritual bond it creates between them, their ancestors, and God.

"Rabbi David's words resonated somewhere within me. I felt that circumcision would be the right decision for this baby and we scheduled an appointment with the recommended pediatrician. (Our town is too small to support a mohel, but this doctor cooperates with Jewish circumcision methods.) Thirty minutes before the bris, we gathered in the pediatrician's waiting room with five relatives and three friends. Rabbi David played guitar and led us in songs and prayers to prepare Zachariah for the bris. It was during those prayers that we first announced his name, in keeping with the Jewish tradition of naming a boy on the eighth day.

(continued on next page)

so you may have to pay out of pocket for it. Fees range from about seventy-five to several hundred dollars.

The Psychological and Sexual Debate

Some claim that circumcision leaves males with emotional scars—sadness and anger from the loss of a body part, a sense of being unprotected in a sensitive area of the body, and the remembered pain and trauma of the procedure itself. With more and more men exploring their feelings and memories in personal growth workshops, this idea has picked up steam. One researcher, Ron Goldman of the Circumcision Resource Center, claims that surveys he has conducted of circumcised men show evidence of psychological harm. Others contend that babies soon forget the pain and can't possibly form an attitude about it. Maybe someday we'll be able to plug our brains into our computers and get a printout but until then, there's no way to know which side is correct.

That seems less the case for another common argument—that little boys will be upset if they don't look like Daddy "down there." Phil remembers the moment of discovery for his oldest, and uncircumcised, son. "Gabe, then five and a half, was taking a bath when I went into the bathroom to pee," Phil recalls. "He watched quietly and then asked, 'Daddy, what's that thing on the end of your penis?' I explained to him that it was just the tip of my penis and he had the same thing, only it was covered by skin. I even showed him the line in his foreskin it caused. I very matter-of-factly explained that when I was a little boy most doctors and mommies and daddies thought it was the best thing to do for a baby boy to have that skin taken off, but that today many doctors and mommies and daddies don't think it's such a good idea, although many do, and that except for the skin his penis and mine were just the same. He thought about it for a minute, digested it, said 'Oh,' and went back to his bath."

Phil's story validates the advice of Lewis Lipsett, director of the Child Study Center of Brown University. Lipsett suggests that as long as parents deal with the issue candidly and comfortably, everything will be just fine. Besides, we'll add, dads and sons can differ in many other big ways—suppose Dad is dark and swarthy and Billy fair, red-haired, and freckled? Growing up should include learning how to accept differences in people, including family. As for the related concern that uncircumcised boys will be made fun of in the junior high locker room, doesn't that seem unlikely with a circumcision rate of only 60 percent?

(continued from previous page)

"The doctor applied a local anesthetic, and the ten of us gathered around her in a tiny room. Rabbi David led us in a prayerful song and then he said a prayer which the doctor repeated before she began the circumcision. Each of us also spoke our intentions to Zachariah, and I told my son, 'I hope that you will always remember that you are an angel and that you came straight from God.'

"During the procedure, which took about one minute, we all continued singing and Zachariah sucked avidly on his papa's little finger, which we chose over a pacifier. He looked in his papa's eyes the entire time and did not cry at all. Afterward, while we continued singing, we gave him a few drops of sweet wine, and then we returned to the waiting room for a little celebration. Rabbi David played guitar again and we all sang and I danced with Zachariah in my arms. He looked around at everyone—he was very alert and liked the music and singing.

"While our small gathering enjoyed some fruit and wine, I sat down and nursed Zachariah. He cried some (when the music stopped!), but once he began nursing he calmed and looked in my eyes. The circumcision did not affect our nursing relationship, nor did it affect his sleep or his personality. In fact, just a week later he began smiling broadly at us!

"Zachariah's circumcision was a religious ritual with prayers, music, wine, and lots of love. He was surrounded by those who love him, he was told that the circumcision would connect him with all of his Jewish ancestors in keeping with Abraham's covenant to God, and his papa was right there by his side.

"If Zachariah was not Jewish, our circumcision decision would have been much more difficult. But while I certainly agree that the issue is complex, I feel that circumcision performed in the context of a religious ritual is spiritual and celebratory. Zachariah's bris was a positive experience for us because it was loving and thoughtful. It was not just a medical circumcision procedure—it was also a circumcision of the heart.'"

On the matter of sexuality, sex researchers Masters and Johnson say that circumcision, again, is irrelevant. However, some anti–circumcision spokespeople point to the fact that the foreskin is designed to keep the head of the penis, or glans, warm and moist and shielded from the weather and irritation. Without it, they insist, the skin becomes harder and thicker, and thus, less sensitive during sex.

The Final Decision: Up to You

With no compelling health reason to circumcise your son, you'll have to make up your own mind on the other factors. We know how Daniel, whom we met at the start of this section, would have voted the afternoon of his circumcision. But not today. And if Daniel, who is being raised as an Orthodox Jew, should one day father a boy. . . . ?

CHILDHOOD IMMUNIZATIONS

Time was when the pediatrician said "Jump" and parents asked "How high?" No more. Today's parents regard their family doctors' recommendations far more skeptically. They recognize that many medications and other treatments routinely advised by medical professionals are overprescribed, and that doctors have not always given side effects the consideration they should. Many physicians overlook—or are completely ignorant about—safer, natural methods.

Unfortunately, the public's distrust of modern medicine may have backfired in the case of childhood immunizations. In particular, fear about the risks of vaccines has led many parents to decide against having their children immunized against some dangerous childhood diseases. They have made this difficult choice because of the small but terrifying chance that the vaccine itself can have serious side effects, sometimes even causing the disease for which it is supposed to provide protection. The increasing number of parents making this decision has actually made it more likely that nonimmunized children, including their children, will get the diseases they dread.

As of the mid-1990s, only 67 percent of American two-year-olds— one of the lowest percentages in the Western world—had received the full set of immunizations widely recommended for that age group, even though children may be most vulnerable in the preschool years. Doubts about medical wisdom contribute to this low rate, but ignorance plays at least as big a part. A 1993 Gallup poll of parents of young children showed that almost half didn't realize that polio was contagious. Thirty-six percent had no idea that measles could be fatal.

Ignorance and fear aren't the only reasons that parents choose not to immunize their children. Some parents decide against immunizations, or at least delay them, with all the facts before them, knowing that vaccines do not provide perfect protection, are ill-advised in some cases, and are perhaps given too early in life, when the risks are greater.

The authors of this book and their spouses all chose, after much wrenching discussion, to have their children receive the vaccinations recommended by their pediatricians. In our opinion, childhood immunizations are an appropriate and prudent use of medical knowledge, despite the very real risks. But the decision to immunize remains a highly personal one that should involve the careful consideration of both parents.

The Background

Most pediatricians recommend that children be immunized against diphtheria, pertussis (whooping cough), polio, tetanus, mumps, regular measles, and rubella (German measles) in their first year of life. Your doctor may also advise protection against Haemophilus influenza type b (Hib) and Hepatitis B (for both infants and adolescents) as well. Doctors don't give this advice lightly. All diseases for which immunizations are routinely recommended can cause permanent disability. Some can kill.

Complications occur only rarely with childhood immunizations. But on those rare occasions, they can be catastrophic, as your doctor will inform you—either verbally or in writing or both—before administering them. The dangers of immunizations have to do with the nature of vaccines. Vaccines introduce a small amount of the disease-causing bacteria or virus (or a related protein) into your child's body in order to stimulate the body's immune system to produce antibodies against the disease. But some vaccines have the potential to cause severe reactions including the full-on disease in unusual cases. For example, the live Sabin polio vaccine commonly given to children has in a very few instances—about once in several million doses—caused polio.

In addition, as vaccination opponents are quick to point out, the vaccines do not provide 100 percent immunity—for example, about 5 percent of vaccinated children don't develop sufficient antibodies and will still come down with measles if exposed to it. Vaccinated children are far less likely than unvaccinated kids to get a disease they are exposed to, but most vaccine-preventible diseases aren't common anymore, so the risks are small in either case. Some experts also feel that several of the riskier vaccines are given too early in infancy, before the baby's immune system has had a chance to mature.

The Numbers Game—Risks Versus Benefits

Pediatricians only recommend that you expose your precious ones to these risks because the odds are so heavily weighted in your favor, and because the diseases themselves are so potentially devastating. Public health officials continually track the incidences of both the diseases and complications from vaccinations against them. When enough people in a population have been immunized against a disease, it may virtually disappear from existence. At that point, doctors will usually stop recommending the vaccine except in extraordinary situations because the risk is no longer worth taking.

In fact, that's exactly what happened with smallpox. Until the late 1960s, infants were routinely given smallpox vaccine, which was repeated at regular intervals during childhood. Then researchers noted that twenty years had passed without a single case of smallpox being reported. Yet a small number of children were still dying every year from the vaccine. In other words, the risks exceeded the benefits. That's why the U.S. Public Health Service, along with the World Health Organization and the American Society of Pediatrics, now advise *against* routine smallpox vaccination.

Even if you have complete faith in your physician, you should always do your homework before agreeing to any vaccine. Your pediatrician should ask if your child has had a moderate or serious illness recently or if she or another family member has had an unusual reaction to an immunization in the past. Responsible physicians will only advise the minimal vaccinations necessary to protect against severe illness, ask precautionary questions such as the ones just mentioned, and know if the time has come when a procedure may no longer be advisable. Keep in mind also that each vaccine and childhood disease is different and should be considered separately. A sympathetic pediatrician will take great care to answer your questions and give you space to draw your own conclusions. If you aren't satisfied with your physician's behavior in any of these areas, you should consider switching doctors.

The Social Side of Routine Vaccinations and What It Means for Your Children

Doctors have another concern in mind besides their own patients' health when they recommend vaccinations. If the percentage of people vaccinated against a disease is high enough, the disease may eventually be eradicated. On the other hand, if too few people receive the vaccination, then the disease-causing "bugs" stay alive in the population, putting all unvaccinated children at risk. So, if you decide not to vaccinate your child and a number of parents in your area are making similar decisions, then your child may be at greater risk than you imagine. For example, the series of measles epidemics that occurred in 1989–91 and killed 130 children has been directly tied to the low vaccination rate.

No conscientious parent decides to subject their child to the dangers of vaccinations without a great deal of thought and research. For more information, including useful reports on each vaccine, read *Mothering* magazine's superb *Vaccination: The Issue of Our Times* (see Resources below).

CHAPTER 2 RESOURCES

General

Journal of Family Life: A Quarterly for Empowering Families, 22 Elm Street, Albany, NY 12202, (518) 471–9532
website: www.lowmedia.com/AltEdFreeSchool
    This homegrown holistic family magazine is provocative and refreshingly uncommercial.
Mothering magazine, P.O. Box 1690, Santa Fe, NM 87504, (800) 984–8116
website: www.mothering.com
    Mothering is the pre-eminent Whole Parenting magazine.
TheWell Baby Book by Mike Samuels, M.D., and Nancy H. Samuels (New York, NY: Summit Books, 1991).
    Holistically oriented general guide to infant and children's health.

Self-Care During Pregnancy

BOOKS
Creating a Joyful Birth Experience by Lucia Capacchione, Ph.D., and Sandra Bardsley, R.N. (Fireside, 1994).
    A mind-body approach to carrying baby to term and giving birth. Her suggestions for self-realization include journal work, body-image work, inner-child exploration, and more. Includes a good section on welcoming the baby.
Mother Massage by Elaine Stillerman (Delta/Dell, 1994).
    A guide to massage for general relaxation, enjoyment, and stress relief as well as specific conditions during pregnancy and after birth. It includes information on infant massage, herbal aids, reflexology, and more. For use either alone or with a partner.

The Pregnant Woman's Comfort Guide by Sherry Jimenez, R.N. (Garden City Park, NY: Avery, 1992).

> Holistic and natural health approaches to discomforts during pregnancy such as swollen feet, nausea, insomnia, joint pains, hemorrhoids, and headaches.

ORGANIZATIONS

National Association of Pregnancy Massage Therapy, (888) 451–4945.

> Call for a licensed or certified prenatal massage therapist nearest you.

A Whole Pregnancy Diet

The Pregnancy Cookbook by Marsha Hudnall and Donna Shields (Berkley, 1995).

> Appealing recipes that nourish mother and baby while paying special attention to the food pyramid.

Vegetarian Pregnancy by Sharon Yntema (Ithaca, NY: McBooks, 1994).

> Offers thorough descriptions of nutrients needed during pregnancy, including how they help the body, how to detect deficiencies, nonmeat protein sources, and best food combinations.

See also *The Well Baby Book,* reviewed on p. 77.

Communicating with Your Unborn Child

The Secret Life of the Unborn Child by Thomas Verny, M.D., with John Kelly (Dell, 1981).

> Verny and Kelly discuss how your relationship with your baby before birth can affect his emotional and physical well-being.

Holistic Exercise for Pre- and Postnatal Mothers

Baby Dance by Elysa Markowitz and Howard Brainen (Prentice Hall, 1980).

> Offers instructions on improvisatory dance-like movements for both moms and pops to engage in with their baby.

Jane Fonda's New Pregnancy Workout and Total Birth Program by Femmy Delyser (Simon & Schuster, 1991).

> This book and its associated exercise videotape contain much valuable, holistically oriented information on breathing, diet, calming, meditation, and pregnancy and birth in general. The exercises combine some dance moves and yogic-type stretches with gentle aerobics.

Positive Parenting Fitness by Sylvia Klein Olkin (Garden City Park, NY: Avery, 1992).

> Postnatal follow-up to the author's *Positive Pregnancy Fitness* (reviewed below). Includes exercises for both parents with baby as well as exercises for new moms. Many of the exercises are classic yoga postures under other names.

Positive Pregnancy Fitness by Sylvia Klein Olkin (Garden City Park, NY: Avery, 1987).

> Although few classic yoga exercises are taught here, a yogic perspective pervades this book, including attention to flexibility and spiritual aspects of pregnancy.

Giving Birth Nature's Way

BOOKS

The Complete Book of Pregnancy and Childbirth by Sheila Kitzinger (Dorling Kindersley, 1996).

> This prominent childbirth educator offers hands-on advice from labor breathing techniques to water-birthing positions to breast-feeding tips.

Homebirth by Sheila Kitzinger (Dorling Kindersley, 1991).

A superior guide to giving birth outside of a hospital is by a leading authority on pregnancy and childbirth. She provides excellent general information on birthing as well.

Sense and Sensibility in Childbirth by Judith Herzfeld, Ph.D. (Norton, 1985).

A short (132 pages) and insightful look at why hospitals practice obstetrics the way they do and how you can still give birth naturally in such settings.

ORGANIZATIONS—GENERAL

Most of these groups will refer you to a practitioner (or institution) in your area or provide you with a regional list.

American College of Nurse Midwives, 818 Connecticut Avenue, NW, Suite 900, Washington, DC 20006, (888) 643–9433
website: www.midwife.org

Good source for locating hospital-affiliated CNMs in your area.

Biofeedback Certification Institute of America, 10200 West 44th Avenue, Suite 304, Wheat Ridge, CO 80033, (303) 420–1706

For information about relieving labor pain, send an S.A.S.E.

Doulas of North America, 1100 23rd Avenue East, Seattle, WA 98112, (206) 324–5440.
website: www.dona.com

This organization can refer you to doulas or birth assistants and can send informational brochures.

Association of Labor Assistants and Childbirth Educators, P.O. Box 382724, Cambridge, MA 02238, (888) 222–5223
website: www.alace.org

This group will locate birth assistants in your area. They can also provide names of labor assistants-in-training (low cost or free) in certain areas.

The National Association of Childbearing Centers, 3123 Gottschall Road, Perkiomenville, PA 18074, (215) 234–8068
website: www.birthcenters.org

This association can help you find a birthing center in your area. NACC prefers written requests for referrals, plus a $1.00 donation.

Waterbirth International Resources and Referral Service, (800) 641–BABY
website: www.geocities.com/hotsprings/2840

This resource and educational organization offers referrals to doctors, midwives, and hospitals that practice water labor and water birth. They also sell all manner of waterbirthing supplies, including waterproof stethoscopes, plus every book ever published on the subject. Call for a free information packet.

CHILDBIRTH EDUCATION CLASSES

American Academy of Husband-Coached Childbirth, P.O. Box 5224, Sherman Oaks, CA 91413, (800) 4–A–BIRTH

This organization will send an information packet on the Bradley Method of childbirth preparation. They also offer film rentals.

International Childbirth Education Association (ICEA), P.O. Box 20048, Minneapolis, MN 55420, (612) 854–8660
website: www.icea.org

ICEA can refer you to classes that combine techniques by birth educators such as Lamaze, Bradley, and Kitzinger.

Lamaze Birth Without Pain Education Association (also known as Childbirth Without Pain Education Association), 20134 Snowden, Detroit, MI 48235–1170, (313) 341–3816, e-mail: eatflora@juno.com

> Members of this organization consider themselves Lamaze purists. For a brochure on the original Lamaze methods, and to locate a Lamaze instructor in your area, mention *The Whole Parenting Guide* and send an S.A.S.E.

Lamaze International (formerly ASPO-Lamaze), 1200 19th Street, NW, Washington, DC 20036, (800) 368–4404
website: www.lamaze-childbirth.com

> Offers referrals to Lamaze teachers in your area.

HOME BIRTH

American College of Home Obstetrics, 2821 Rose Street, Franklin Park, IL 60131, (847) 455–2030

> For referrals to M.D.s who will deliver at home in your area, leave a brief, detailed message for Dr. William White.

Informed Homebirth and Informed Parenting, P.O. Box 1733, Fair Oaks, CA 95628, (916) 961–6923

> This organization is the brainchild of renowned midwife, author, and Waldorf educator, Rahima Baldwin. It offers information and resources on home birth, homeschooling, Waldorf schools, and raising a "magical child."

Midwives Alliance of North America, P.O. Box 175, Newton, KS 67114, (888) 923–6262
website: www.mana.org

> Call for a brochure or referrals to midwives who will deliver at home.

POSTPARTUM

Depression After Delivery, (800) 944–4773

> Offers an information packet about postpartum depression itself, treatment options, and a list of volunteers who have gone through it themselves and have volunteered to offer phone support to any new mother who needs it. They will send you a packet for a $5 donation.

Welcoming Your New Child to the World

Birth Without Violence by Frederick Leboyer (Knopf, 1976).

> Leboyer helped open the eyes of the modern world to the fact that infants are conscious beings and that birth practices insensitive to their psychological needs could scar their psyches. Gripping photos tell almost the entire story on their own.

Infant Massage by Vimala Schneider McClure (Bantam, 1989).

> A gift of love from you to your baby. Includes sections on premature babies and infants with special needs.

Why Breast-Feeding Matters

BOOKS

Breastfeeding and the Active Woman by Lillian A. Pfluke (Waco, TX: WRS Publishing, 1995).

> At last—a comprehensive how-to nursing book small enough to fit in your hand, packed with logistical suggestions (for milk storage, expressing on the job, commuting, and working with child-care providers) that show you exactly how to nurse for as long as possible.

The Nursing Mother's Companion, by Kathleen Huggins (Roxbury, MA: Harvard Common Press, 1986).

Phil's wife Michelle, an R.N. who breast-fed three kids herself and has helped many new moms learn to nurse, considers this *the* book on breast-feeding.

The Womanly Art of Breastfeeding by La Leche League International (Plume).

For three decades, LLLI has been putting out revised editions of this how-to classic. See also *The Well Baby Book* reviewed on p. 77.

ORGANIZATIONS

International Lactation Consultant Association, 4101 Lake Boone Trail, Suite 201, Raleigh, NC 27607, (919) 787–5181
website: www.ilca.com

ILCA provides referrals to professional lactation consultants.

La Leche League International, 1400 N. Meacham Road, P.O. Box 4079, Schaumburg, IL 60173–4048, headquarters: (847) 519–7730, hotline: (800) LALECHE
website:www.lalecheleague.org

With over three thousand chapters in sixty countries worldwide, LLLI is the mother of all breast-feeding-advice-and-advocacy outfits. They sponsor support groups and lactation support volunteers across the country. Their hotline answers questions about nursing and can refer you to local LLL leaders, Monday to Friday, 9 A.M. to 3 P.M. (CST). Call their non-toll-free-number to reach a "graveyard shift" volunteer for nursing emergencies.

SUPPLIES

Motherwear, 320 Riverside Drive, Northampton, MA 01062, (800) 950–2500
website: www.Motherwear.com

A conscientious company offering attractive nursing fashions and complete nursing supplies including breast pumps. Catalogs include an attached magazine with articles about nursing and parenting. A true Whole Parenting business.

Breast-Feeding for Working Mothers

BOOKS

See *Breastfeeding and the Active Woman* and *The Nursing Mother's Companion,* reviewed on p. 80.

ORGANIZATIONS

See La Leche League International listing above.

BREAST PUMP MANUFACTURERS

The best, most efficient electric breast pumps, such as those found in hospitals, can sell for $700 to $1,500, which makes them unaffordable for most people. But pumps can be bought for significantly less. The Nursing Mothers Council now sells an affordably-priced (in the $200–$300 range) pump; call 650–591–6688. You can also call two of the leading pump manufacturers for information on the purchase or rental "station" nearest you: Medela, Inc., (800) 835–5968; Ameda Egnell, (800) 323–8750. See also the Motherwear listing above.

Nursing Your Adopted Baby

See the La Leche League listing above and ask for booklet no. 55, *Nursing Your Adopted Baby.*
Lact-Aid supplementer, Lact-Aid International, P.O. Box 1066, Athens, TN 37371–1066, (423) 744–9090

website: www.lact-aid.com

Alan's wife Hyiah preferred this system, but says her preference is personal; others might like the Medela unit better. Hyiah felt the Lact-aid was softer and warmer for the baby and far less cumbersome.

Medela supplementer, Medela, P.O. Box 660, McHenry, IL 60050, (800) 435–8316

website: www.medela.com

This supplementer is also available from La Leche League (see p.81).

The Disposable-Diaper Controversy

CLOTH DIAPERING SUPPLIES

Biobottoms, c/o Genesis Direct, 100 Plaza Drive, Secaucus, NJ 07094–3613, (800) 766–1254

website: www.biobottoms.com

Offers mail-order cotton diapering supplies including diaper covers.

Ecobaby, 9319 Northview Terrace, Santee, CA 92071, (800) 596–7450

website: www.ecobaby.com

Ecobaby offers mail-order cloth diapering supplies, plus organic, natural fiber bedding and clothing.

The Natural Baby Catalog, 7835–3 Freedom Avenue, NW, Suite 2, North Canton, OH 44720–6907, (800) 388–BABY

e-mail: nbaby@cannet.com

Carries cloth diapering supplies, including Nikky diaper covers and other alternative products for children and parents.

INFORMATION

See *Mothering* magazine listing on p. 77. This magazine is a good information source for keeping up on the latest on cloth diapering methods and products. They are strong advocates of cloth over disposables.

The Circumcision Issue

Circumcision: The Rest of the Story, edited by Peggy O'Mara (Santa Fe, NM: *Mothering* magazine, 1997).

A short book available from *Mothering* magazine, a passionate opponent of circumcision, this provides an excellent anti-circumcision list including information on foreskin restoration. It is available in some bookstores or through *Mothering* (1–888–984–8116).

Childhood Immunizations

Vaccination: The Issue of Our Times, edited by Peggy O'Mara (Santa Fe, NM: *Mothering* Magazine Resource Publication, 1997).

This is a short book presenting detailed, balanced discussions by experts on pros and cons of childhood immunizations. It is available in some bookstores or through *Mothering* (1–888–984–8116).

3

beginning the weave: raising children with holistic family values

With most kid's tricycles, wagons, and other large toys today, "some assembly is required." How well we parents follow the toymaker's instructions will affect whether it meets the manufacturer's, and our, expectations.

"Some assembly" is also required with our kids. But kids are also far more complex than "put-together" toys because no matter how thoroughly nature's plan is carried out, it won't protect children against misperception, cultural bias, and human or societal error. A child may be provided the gentlest, most loving birth, but if he is exposed to a steady diet of violent entertainment, with little alternative fare, he will think that the world is as mean a place as it appears on TV. Children aren't born with racial bias, but if their parents model insensitive attitudes, or simply fail to correct the attitudes their children absorb from their peers and society, young ones will learn prejudice. Children *are* born with fundamental intellectual, emotional, physical, and social capacities but the development of those capacities is not inevitable. Who our children become will have at least as much to do with the environment in which they grow up—particularly at home—as it will the quality of their "basic equipment."

We parents may feel intimidated about the fact that we have such a massive impact on our children. But the flipside of this daunting responsibility is the opportunity to make a difference in so many ways. If our kids turn out great, it's only because we had a great deal to do with it.

It takes information, lots of it, to parent in a way that enables our kids to maximize their potential. Parenting is not a big science experiment to discover something about which little is already known. People who have devoted their careers to studying parenting do know what works in many areas. If we parents have that information at hand, we have a head start to doing the job right.

In this chapter, we do our best to make some of that knowledge available to you: The benefits of reading to your children. The types of books and playthings most likely to convey appropriate values and stimulate them in positive ways. How to teach kids to appreciate the diverse people and cultures that make up their society. How to disarm the repellent images and content that bombard children via the mass media and advertising. The most reliable way to raise kids who care about others and behave responsibly in the world.

We call this collection of concerns "holistic family values."

READING TO YOUR CHILD—WHY IT MATTERS

When adults read, they not only absorb the ideas of the author but also the way he uses language. If they read good writing, they learn to use language well. They also learn how to think, because good, clear writing is synonymous with good, clear thinking.

If reading affects grown-ups so powerfully, just imagine what it does for those whose brains are still developing and who are still learning to frame their thoughts in words. "My six-year-old, Rebecca, taught herself to write and my four-year-old, Sam, is starting now," says Lori Patch of Grants Pass, Oregon. "This is through osmosis—we don't do drills. I attribute it to the early exposure to books. We read aloud almost every night."

The Benefits of Reading Aloud

Nearly all experts—from teachers to reading specialists to learning researchers—believe in the value of reading to your children. Making your child an eager, lifelong reader and articulate speaker are just two of several ways reading aloud prepares your child for success in life. And the emotional payoffs for everyone involved would justify the time spent even if these other advantages didn't exist. Specifically, the list of benefits include:

- *Emotional nurturing.* When you take the time to read to your child, you send a message that she matters to you. Cozy storytimes strengthen your bond with your child, and build a storehouse of warm, special memories—for both of you.

- *Language development.* Babies learn language by listening to the language used around them. The stories you read to your baby become a major influence on her ability to speak.

- *Information "loading."* By age two, children are working full-time at their "job" of gathering all the information they can about the world. Books make much more of the world available to children than they would encounter in their everyday lives. The information gathered from books gives kids a head start in their schooling, too.

- *Orientation to the world of books.* During storytime, children learn how books work and how to take care of them. They learn to turn pages and hold the book right side up. They also learn the important habit of looking to books for pleasure and information. "My son is very interested in animals," says Lori Patch. "He'll ask me questions I don't know the answers to. But I can say, 'If you remind me, we'll get a book on how the blood moves in the body or why the snake slithers in the grass' or whatever the question is."

- *Appropriate modeling.* Shelve your own books, magazines, and newspapers in places where the whole family spends time together. This shows your children the importance you place on the printed word. Along with reading aloud and reading on your own, it also shows your kids how you turn to books for pleasure and information.

- *Preparation for critical thinking and responsible citizenship.* Your child is growing up in a world where the media is increasingly concentrated in a few huge corporate hands, where mainstream journalists fail to put material in context, and where sound bites take the place of real content. Avid readers are better equipped to separate the facts from the fluff, to know where to find more thoughtful sources of information, and to develop critical thinking habits that will help them make informed choices in society. Put another way, reading liberates, writes reading specialist Bernice Cullinan, who notes that American slaves weren't allowed to read because they were easier to control when uneducated.

- *Topical discussion and education.* No matter how provocative a TV program is, few families will interrupt it to have a discussion. But with books, you can pause any time to talk about issues raised by the reading. Alan and Hyiah read Mildred Taylor's Newbery award—winning *Roll of Thunder, Hear My Cry* and its sequel *Let the Circle Be Unbroken* to Ariel when she was seven. These poignant and often tense stories, about African-American sharecropping families in the Depression-era South, inspired almost nightly conversations about the causes and effects of racism, the history of the Civil Rights movement, and the values of having relationships with diverse people.

- *Development of attention spans.* Educators suspect that television shortens attention spans. They *know* that reading expands them.

- *Nurturing of the imagination.* Unlike television, which cuts short imaginative thinking (see page 109), reading to children continuously exercises this developmentally vital function. Listening to stories requires children to use their imaginations to "see and hear" the characters and settings and to feel the emotions of the characters and scene. Reading aloud also spurs imaginative play. "We've been reading a lot of flower fairy books," says Viviana Padilla, who lives near Wimer, Oregon, with her husband and two daughters. "We live out in the woods, so that's been a wonderful jumping off place for making little flower fairy homes and dishes, and just the sheer joy of pretending."

- *Vocabulary building.* Children hear words in stories and poems that they don't hear in conversations. And it's as natural for children to add new words to their language as it is for them to collect shells or stones in a shoebox.

- *Empathy building.* Reading to your children helps them see life from other points of view—that of their favorite characters, the author, and so on.

- *Versatile parenting aid.* Once you've established a reading tradition with your kids, you've got a powerful calming device at your fingertips, whether your child is sick, frightened, too restless to sleep, or just in need of attention. And older children may pick up your cue and use it to assist you in your parenting. "My children have taken the example of me reading to them and read to each other," says Kathy Dean of Rogue River, Oregon. "My middle child, Rebekah, says that the oldest, Aimee, even helped her to read."

How to Pick Good Books for Your Children

Keep in mind that most of the above advantages only apply to the right, age-appropriate children's books. Start by selecting books that are richly imagined and written, with strong characters to identify with, memorable and flowing language, vivid images, and exciting stories to ponder. Finding such treasures is easy if you know where to "shop"—generally, libraries and quality bookstores with strong children's sections and staff who can guide you to good selections.

Be wary of most mainstream toy stores, chain stores, and supermarkets—they tend to carry mainly mass-market glitz that offer little or nothing in the way of vivid writing, characters, and stories. Most books carried in such outlets are strictly "product" designed by corporate marketing departments. In many cases, they are connected with popular children's TV programs or movies that themselves are produced strictly as a marketing vehicle for "low-calorie" toys and books (see pp. 90–91). (An exception to the above would be a book superstore with substantial quality selections.) Also be wary of book clubs. Buying books sight unseen is always risky, and the quality of books marketed by mail will vary widely—although if you know what you're buying, you can find bargains through better clubs such as the Children's Book of the Month Club.

With very young children, you'll of course want to consider your child's age and stage of development (not always the same thing). But consult the age range printed on the book's cover as only a general guide, because your child may be developing at a different rate than her peers.

In that same vein, be careful not to expose your children to the rougher stories before they're ready. For instance, the horrid characters and events in some magical literature may give your children nightmares before a certain age. Kids' fears of monsters, witches, and the like increase about age four. Around six (earlier for some kids, later for others), children are starting to realize the difference between the imaginary situations in a book or television show and reality at home. But for a couple of years afterward, they may still find people-eating monsters and mutilated heroes too much to take.

In children's picture books, the quality of the illustrations counts, too. Your child will enjoy richly illustrated books more than blandly drawn ones, particularly during repeated readings. And artfully designed and illustrated books may help your child develop a taste for fine art later in life.

Very young children also enjoy predictability because they like to chime in when you read. Counting books, alphabet books, books with pictures only, and books with repeated phrases or sentence structures help them to do that. Predictability works for grade-schoolers, too; they'll often enjoy books in a series. Research also shows that having some idea of what to expect from the characters and action helps kids learn to read.

Kids aren't little adults so when choosing books, look at them through your children's eyes. For instance, some humor books may have your child rolling on the floor with laughter when the only part of you that's rolling is your eyes. Above all, pick books that reflect your child's interests, tastes, and feelings.

It's tempting for parents to use storytime to advance an agenda—not a good idea. Reading aloud should be about fostering a love of books and reading and nurturing your relationship with your child. Pushing ideas or material at them that they don't want violates that spirit. It's important that children be able to choose the stories that are read to them. And that may mean tolerating some substandard reading material at times. Trust that if you surround your children with good quality literature, they'll eventually gravitate to the better stuff on their own.

When Can Reading Aloud Start, and When Should It Stop?

Most infants are ready for their first reading experience by nine or ten months old. You can make your first attempt when baby is comfortable sitting up. But don't forget that storytime should be a fun time. If you and your baby aren't enjoying the session, back off and try again later—children at this age develop so rapidly that dramatic changes can occur within weeks. Should your baby spend much of the day in someone else's care, make sure that reading aloud is a big part of the routine once baby is ready for it.

Many parents assume that reading aloud should stop as soon as their children begin learning to read in school. Not at all. First reading books are generally primitive and dull, so reading aloud gives beginning readers enjoyment and stimulation that they may not get any other way. And remember that learning to read is a tough job. Your children may get frustrated at times. When you read them a book they really enjoy, they'll be reminded of why they're bothering to go through the effort, and the payoff can be tremendous.

Reading to grade-schoolers also helps them build their vocabularies. Beginning readers are likely to skip over words they don't know. You can fill the gap by reading books to your kids that are beyond their reading level, and explaining words they don't understand.

Research confirms the value of these measures. In studies of grade-school children, reading comprehension, vocabulary, and decoding skills improved significantly for kids who were read to regularly over a several-month span. Studies also show that reading aloud broadens children's tastes and interests. Once they begin reading independently, many children will stick to a single author or type of book. That's less likely to happen with children who were read to at home.

how to read to your children

Any reading aloud you do with your children, as long as you're reading good quality books, enhances both your relationship with them and their development. But the following tips will maximize the benefits:

- *Immerse your children in books.* Reading experts note that children who are surrounded by books at home are more likely to do well when they begin reading on their own. It needn't cost much to build or expand a home library—paperbacks are cheap, used books are cheaper, and library cards are free. As you build your supply of children's books, keep them in your child's room, out where she can always see them.

- *Make reading times special.* Bedtimes are traditional storytimes, and rightly so, because reading soothes a child before sleep. But don't stop there. Carry books with you to read in the pediatrician's waiting room, at the park, even while waiting in line at stores. When you want to show your children a little extra love, do it with an extra storytime.

- *Throw yourself into the experience.* If the humor is goofy, use a goofy voice. If a serious story is reaching a climax, use a dramatic voice.

- *Involve both parents.* Reading shouldn't be just Mom's thing or Daddy's thing.

- *Discuss what you're reading.* You won't find a better time for discussions than storytime. The Padillas regularly use reading aloud to provoke conversation, which Viviana says helps immeasurably in dealing with the children's issues: "We still come across the same problems that other families have, but we're able to communicate about them better."

Ultimately, reading aloud need never stop. Many adult couples enjoy reading poetry, short stories, or chapters of novels to each other at night. And, of course, the market for audio books has exploded in recent years as millions of American adults have transformed boring commutes into cherished read-aloud sessions with their favorite authors.

What If I Don't Like to Read?

Admittedly, all of the above will be much easier for parents who are book lovers. But don't deny your child just because reading isn't your thing. See if you can awaken in yourself a new or renewed appreciation of reading—remember that it's important for your child to see that you value reading and utilize it to solve problems.

If you don't read because you have trouble with it—and about 20 percent of the population does—explain your problem to your child and do your best to compensate. As you know better than most, there's a place in the world for people who don't read much, but it's not a very big place and it's getting smaller and less comfortable all the time.

If you're not a regular reader, you may not feel comfortable following some of the above suggestions. For example, you may not feel confident that you can recognize appropriate books for your kids. Librarians are a wonderful and eager antidote to this problem. Many libraries also offer weekly story sessions where your child can listen to well-selected books in the company of other enthralled kids—a good way of making reading aloud special if for any reason you're not able to do it at home.

THE "RIGHT" TOYS—PLAYTHINGS THAT REFLECT YOUR VALUES AND HELP YOUR CHILDREN REALIZE THEIR POTENTIAL

The best kids' toys do double duty. A toy that isn't fun will sit neglected in the corner, but there's more to a good toy than "playability." For children, play is their full-time job because it is the primary way they learn about the world. Only through appropriate forms of play can they get the most out of their developmental possibilities—intellectually, physically, emotionally, and socially. For example, intellectual development occurs as young brains grow new structures in response to mental stimulation. Without stimulating play, brain development may fall far short of its potential. The upshot is that children's toys, as well as the ways children play with them, really count.

Unfortunately, the toys that are most heavily marketed to kids today—and consequently the ones that they most want—are often questionable in the values they promote and the types of development they foster. You can still find excellent playthings that are both fun-packed and developmentally appropriate if you know where to look. However, large toy manufacturers and retailers so dominate the marketplace that you aren't likely to encounter these kinds of toys unless you go out of your way to seek them. The following guidelines will help you understand what's at stake, how you can provide the right toys for your child, and how to neutralize the negative effects of the mass-market toys that will inevitably invade your children's lives.

Selecting Toys that Encourage Healthy Play

Toys help children play but they aren't necessary. Alan and Hyiah's daughter Ariel was surrounded by toys but for years showed little interest in them. She preferred to play with smooth stones and other found objects, pretending they were the little dogs or horses that populated her imagination. Since about age six, she has been building a sizable indoor herd of plastic horses to go with her outdoor horse, Pepper. However, most of her other toys sit abandoned in her room or have been passed on to other kids.

Not that Ariel's way is better, but it does underscore the purpose of "good" toys, which is to encourage healthy play. Experts widely agree that children learn and grow the most when they exercise their imaginations; mimic adult life; participate actively instead of passively; direct their own play instead of having their play style dictated by a toy's design or by a parent; experiment and explore new options; make decisions and solve problems; do things that match their skills and interests; and have fun (if it's not fun, it's not play).

The kinds of toys that promote these qualities in play can often be found as easily around the house as in conventional toy stores. Here's what to consider when looking for toys for your kids:

- *Make sure to include "open-ended" toys—i.e., toys that can be played with in many ways.* Blocks are the perfect child's toy in this respect. Their shapes and colors are essentially random, so everything is left to the child's imagination and creativity. Notice that younger children especially will often gravitate to this type of play—that's why the box that houses expensive, highly detailed toys is often far more interesting to them than the toy itself.

- *Children should be able to interact with and manipulate their toys, not just watch or listen to them.* By interact, we mean something far more active than pressing a button that makes everything happen. Notice how quickly kids tend to lose interest in simple windup toys. Windup toys do only one thing, one way, and kids have little control over them. (Control is a crucial element of play because kids have so little control over everything else in their lives.)

- *Provide toys that match your child's skills.* We know one three-year-old who, athough extremely bright, just doesn't "get" puzzles yet. Her frustration drove her to tears until her parents realized the problem and stopped trying to guide her in something she wasn't ready to do. The best way to understand your children's interests and skill level is to spend time playing with them.

- *Variety, up to a point, teaches your children about decision-making in the process of choosing a toy for play.* Variety also leads children to decide *how* to play. For example, if the toy box includes some social toys, your children must decide whether to play alone or with a friend or sibling. The toy selection should also enable your children to choose between vigorous play such as with balls and quiet play with, say, blocks. But avoid overwhelming them with too many toys and thus too many choices, or they may walk away from the whole confusing mess.

- *Avoid gender stereotypes.* Girls tend to out perform boys on tests of verbal ability. They tend to trail boys in tests of visual-spatial and math abilities. But obviously, plenty of men write and speak well and plenty of women star in math, the sciences, and business, so these abilities may well have more to do with how kids are raised than biology.

The bottom line to all of the above is choice. Toys can only stimulate intellectual growth if they enable children to make choices about how to play with them. The box on pages 94–95 will help you stock your child's room with playthings that follow this and the other principles just mentioned.

What's Wrong with Toys Today

Few toys found in mass-market toy stores or chain-store toy departments meet the criteria discussed above and it's not too hard to figure out why. For one thing, toys such as blocks, easels, and Legos stand up to lots of abuse and don't go out of fashion, so they can be handed down in good shape from family to family and sibling to sibling. Plus, once a child has a set of blocks, he probably won't crave more. That's healthy for kids and family budgets, but not for corporate profits.

It's far better, from the manufacturers' perspective, to put out items like Barbie and GI Joe. Barbie and Joe are essentially addictive hooks to endless lines of clothing, accessories, and other toys pushed at kids through advertising during popular children's TV shows and in brochures enclosed with packaging. Children never have enough Barbie and GI Joe stuff—manufacturers make sure of that by always developing and advertising new "must have" items.

These marketing ploys might be easier to take if the toys themselves were developmentally appropriate playthings. But most experts feel that the overwhelming majority of mass-market toys fall far short of that standard. In fact, the most popular toys also tend to be the most developmentally empty ones, and that's no coincidence. Thanks to the deregulation of children's television (see page 109), the bestselling toys are almost always connected to children's television shows or are tie-ins to mega-hit movies because the shows are virtually nonstop commercials for the toys. When children engage in dramatic play using those toys, they aren't imagining so much as replaying scenes they've seen on the screen.

In most cases, those shows provide only low-grade, action entertainment, most of that violent in the case of shows aimed at boys. Add to this the fact that so many show-related toys are also highly detailed and not particularly interactive, and you end up with the worst of all possible worlds—children's play with few opportunities for creativity and thus little if any learning or mental development.

Toy manufacturers also tend to segregate their marketing by gender, or rather by gender stereotype. Their commercials and toy-associated shows push boys to identify with the stereotypically aggressive, violent

a whole parenting basic toy box

The following toys pass the test for developmentally appropriate toys that also reflect positive values:

- *Blocks.* This is the ultimate open-ended toy.

- *Legos® and other building toys.* Not quite as open-ended as blocks, but they still allow for plenty of creative play, particularly if you don't urge your child to copy the perfect buildings shown on the box!

- *So-called nesting and stacking toys (e.g., cups, objects of graduated sizes that stack or fit together, etc.) along with containers for dumping and pouring.* These open-ended toys teach children important concepts about physical relationships of objects—top, middle, bottom; small, big, bigger, biggest; and so on—which help them grasp basic math ideas later on. Containers for dumping and pouring water or mud teach vital concepts about volume, such as the physics axiom that a quart of water poured into a pint container always gets a lively reaction from your parents.

- *Paints, clay, sand, Play-Doh®, fingerpaints, water, construction paper, glue, and mud.* These materials encourage messy but highly beneficial creative play.

(continued on next page)

male heroes the shows feature. They then sell them enough toy firepower and violent action figures to start their own war. Using the same techniques but different themes, toymakers push girls to identify with stereotypical female traits and qualities—domestic roles, supportive work roles, glamour, and obsession with the latest fashions and hairstyles. The toys they create for girls—Barbie being just the most obvious example—reinforce these stereotypes.

Such marketing techniques work even better with kids than adults, because kids tend to believe what they're told—the original reason that advertising aimed at children was regulated. Just as insidiously, the TV-toy link trains kids to be unthinking consumers in later life.

Toy advertising affects the way girls and boys interact with each other, too. Girls and boys today are much less likely to play together than their parents were when they were children. This is due in large part to gender-stereotyped marketing that directs boys to play with war toys and violent action figures while girls play "My Little Pony, Barbie, dress-up, and house," note education professors Nancy Carlsson-Paige and Diane E. Levin in their book *Who's Calling the Shots?* "The trends of the sixties and seventies toward helping children expand their gender roles . . . in play, toys, and child-rearing practices," they add, ". . . have been replaced by a toy and play culture that is more gender-specific than ever. . . ."

When play locks children into stereotypical gender roles, they don't get to practice the strengths of the opposite gender. Boys don't practice cooperation and caring, and girls don't practice assertiveness and leadership. This can lead to consequences in both school and career choices, limiting both genders to unsatisfying life roles that are well beneath their original potential.

What to Do If You Can't Avoid Mass-Market Toys from Invading Your Home

Despite your best intentions, you won't be able to keep all offensive toys out of your kids' lives. You can ban junk children's TV shows in your home, but your children will still hear about the programs, characters, and products from their friends, and they'll want the toys just as badly. Besides, mass-market toys will leak in as birthday gifts or as discards from friends. Toss out the gifts and your kids will just secretly play with similar toys at their friends' homes. Fortunately, conscientious parents still retain lots of good options even as mass-market toys steadily creep into their children's lives:

(continued from previous page)

JAMES WEEKS

- *Child-scale furniture, easels, chalkboards, and so on.* Child-size objects help give children the sense of control that they crave.

- *Social toys, i.e., toys that can be played with by two or more children such as sandboxes and large sets of blocks.* These help develop social skills—taking turns, cooperation, idea exchanges, group planning, and so on.

- *Mechanical toys and manipulative toys—for example, Legos®—in general.* These toys, along with large blocks, sand, clay, and containers, help develop spatial skills that help build later math performance.

- *Consider a quality-only television/video policy (see page 112) and expose your kids to high-quality literature and playthings.* If exposed to something better, your children may find conventional toys and marketing insulting to their intelligence. Lori Patch's children watch little TV and usually watch PBS shows when they do view television. She notes, "generally, when someone gives a gift that they haven't asked you about and the child unwraps it, it's very hard to just remove it. But I've found that the things I wouldn't buy for my children, they usually haven't liked a lot . . . they haven't seen the commercials. They don't know they're supposed to drool over Barbie." For more on this subject, see page 109.

- *Encourage children to mix open-ended play with their commercial toys.* The Padilla children don't watch television at home, so "they haven't been as influenced in their play, even with commercial toys," says mother Viviana. "Our Barbies trek to the North Pole and go on safaris. They dive. [My daughters] made their own interesting Barbie house from wood scraps. They make clothes for Barbie and Ken from scraps of material [instead of buying manufactured outfits]. Even though these aren't the kinds of toys you order out of catalogs like HearthSong [Waldorf-inspired toys—see the Resources at the end of the chapter], they still do some pretty creative things with them."

- *Make play conscious.* If your little boy likes war play, talk about real wars— why they happen, who gets hurt, and the importance of peace and cooperation. If he likes playing with violent space toys, read him books about outer space and visit the local aerospace museum with him, suggest Carlsson-Paige and Levin. If your little girl is obsessed with being beautiful "like Barbie," talk about expanded, nonstereotypical roles for women. Don't act as if your children's play is wrong, just use it as an opportunity to discuss values and ideas with them.

- *Play and interact with your children in ways that avoid gender stereotypes and model nonstereotypical behavior.* Dad can show little Dawn how to use carpentry tools to build a birdhouse. Mom can build a Lego tower with little Ben. Dad can do the dishes or diaper the baby with Ben's help while Mom and Dawn carry out the trash.

- *Let children control their play.* You may not like what you see, but as long as no one is being physically hurt, it may do more damage to interfere or dictate options.

toys for children with disabilities

You don't necessarily need special toys if your child has a disability, points out Deena Maria Amato in the magazine *Independent Living*. In many cases, toys for able-bodied kids can be used by children with disabilities as well. Still, for some children toys specific to their disabilities provide undeniable and unique benefits. Toys for children with disabilities are called *adaptive toys*. In most cases, able-bodied kids will enjoy these toys as well. As always, select adaptive toys with your child's interests and abilities uppermost in your mind.

Among the more intriguing companies, products, and information sources are:

Innovative Products, 830 South 48th St., Grand Forks, ND 58201, (800) 950–5185.
website: www.iphope.com

This company manufactures electric-powered toy cars and jeeps that teach the basics of using a motorized wheelchair and develop various coordination skills. Children press a big red button on the electric dashboard and presto! they're in motion. The dashboard also includes working turn signals and a joystick. And don't worry, a remote control for parents and therapists overrides any poor decisions made by the driver. The vehicles will set you back $2,000–4,000, depending on the options and model, but they can be customized for any disability.

Sportime Abilitations, One Sportime Way, Atlanta, GA 30340, (404) 344–4364

(continued on next page)

BRINGING DIVERSITY HOME

Ever hear of the elephant in the living room? The image of a pachyderm careening in the parlor amidst all the vases and china may not be new, but it takes on different meaning when relayed by Morris Jeff, a therapist and former president of the National Association of Black Social Workers. "There's this elephant standing in the middle of America's living room floor and we don't want to acknowledge it," says Jeff. "The elephant—I call it white patriarchal racism—shifts its position occasionally, but we just keep walking around it, taking blows from it as if it weren't there."

The people who are suffering the blows are people of color, people with disabilities, the poor, foreigners, people whose accents aren't Standard American English, gays and lesbians, and girls and women of every color. Parents who prefer to remain silent about prejudice have their reasons. As protectors and providers, many feel compelled to shield their young from the ugliness of the world. Why bring up the issues of racial differences and discrimination, some figure, when our kids might not be old enough to understand? Here's why: Children are aware of race and other differences and the values or prejudices assigned to them much earlier than we might imagine. Research shows that kids as young as two become aware of racial and gender differences. So we don't do our young any favors by sidestepping these matters. They will find out soon enough. And when they do, they will think the status quo is okay with us if we have never said anything to the contrary.

The first step parents might consider taking to bring diversity home is an internal one. It has to do with admitting there's an elephant in our living room. It is also worth acknowledging that most of us still harbor some prejudices toward people who are different from us—no

---

(continued from previous page)

Sportime Abilitations produces educational games, many based on athletics, that teach coordination and cognitive skills. Among the products for visually challenged children is Feel and Count, a braille counting game. Children with visual, mental, or physical disabilities may enjoy Feel and Twist, a Twister-like game.

Passy-Muir, Inc., 4521 Campus Drive, Suite 273, Irvine, CA 92612
(800) 634–5397
website: www.passy-muir.com

Passy-Muir markets a speaking valve that allows young tracheostomy patients to talk instead of relying on sign language. They also distribute Toby Tracheasorus, a stuffed dinosaur puppet that has a tracheostomy tube in its neck for children who have undergone this surgery. With Toby, kids get a preview of their therapy in a way that's easier on their psyche than unadorned explanations from an adult. Also available: an exhalation therapy kit and other Toby items.

Toy Manufacturers of America, 1115 Broadway, Suite 400, New York, NY 10010, (212) 675–1141, or
American Foundation for the Blind, 11 Pennsylvania Plaza, Suite 300, New York, NY 10001, (212) 502–7600.

Contact either of these organizations for *The Guide for Children Who Are Blind or Visually Impaired*, a catalog that shows parents how to select and use conventional toys for their visually impaired children. The catalog is available in both print and audiocassette versions.

matter how enlightened we imagine ourselves to be. We get these views from our parents, from television and other media, and from our peers and colleagues and bosses—some of whom allow us entry into desirable cliques only if we "buy into" (or at least refrain from disputing) their biased views. The subtle and not-so-subtle messages we're exposed to are so pervasive that we sometimes unwittingly adopt them as our own.

Once we finish holding up the mirror to our own views and assumptions, fighting the good fight becomes a little easier.

Talking to Your Children About Diversity

Here are some suggestions for discussing diversity issues effectively with your kids:

Discuss race and ethnicity casually—and early. If parents never mention the fact that people come in all varieties, children may begin to think that the subject is taboo or that people of other races are inherently abnormal or bad. It's easier, naturally, to discuss these matters in passing when

there really *are* people who look different in your children's lives—at preschool, in a playgroup, at the supermarket, next door, or visiting your home, for instance. But even if your present life circumstances do not expose your kids to diversity, there will be ample opportunities to discuss differences via the books you choose to buy or television shows you allow your kids to watch.

Make positive observations out loud. We make casual and complimentary comments about people all the time, so why not make similar observations about people who don't look like us? The occasional positive remark about someone else's character, looks, or deeds can go a long way in countering the kind of xenophobia that seems so contagious in the media these days.

Don't let biased comments from children or other adults go by. A great many statements that children make about people of another race or ethnicity are said in innocence, at least initially. It's not unusual, for instance, for a preschooler to describe an Asian classmate's eyes as "funny-looking" or an African-American as "too dark" or a person with a foreign accent as "talking funny." These comments, experts say, display a kind of pre-prejudice that, if left unchecked, can become full-fledged. When kids make such statements, it's important to explain that eye shapes and accents and skin complexions are merely different, not bad or funny, and that calling them bad or funny is hurtful and that's not the way we want to be.

At the same time, it's important for parents to keep their tone rather matter-of-fact about this. Harsh reprimanding or censure can erode children's self-esteem and give these comments more weight than they deserve.

Talk to your kids about inspirational or accomplished people outside of white, male norms. Try brushing up on your knowledge of farm labor organizer Cesar Chavez, First Lady Eleanor Roosevelt, activist and singer/actor Paul Robeson, journalist and antilynching activist Ida B. Wells, film-maker Lee Mun Wah, scientist Stephen Hawking, and others. You need not memorize entire biographies—a few snippets about what they achieved and the adversity they faced will do.

Avoid saying "we're all the same." Unless you follow this up with specific examples of what you mean, such sweeping statements deny differences and only serve to imply that being different is wrong.

Be willing to say that you're not sure. A great many well-intentioned parents fall silent when a question about race, sexuality, or disability makes them feel uncomfortable. In these cases, it's better to say "I don't know, I need to think about that." Then come back later after you've thought or looked it up. The Anti-Bias Curriculum listed in the Resources at the end of the chapter is a handy, eye-opening guide for parents and teachers who are serious about combating prejudice.

Practicing What You Preach

Cultivate diverse relationships in your own life. Our children are always watching us. So if we don't have diversity in our own lives, all of our "we are the world"–style pronouncements are uttered in vain. If you don't already have friends of other races, try establishing some sort of comfort level talking to diverse acquaintances, coworkers, and neighbors. As with any casual discussions, you'll want to find common ground: raising kids, dealing with tough bosses, neighborhood problems, food, music, etc.

Place your child in multiethnic or otherwise diverse settings. Seek out child care, schools, after-school and enrichment programs, places of worship, and summer camps that really have diversity, not just one or two "others." Consider programs that are diverse in terms of economic class as well.

Expose your children to multicultural events. Street fairs, performances, exhibits, cultural storytelling hours, and author readings are all good opportunities to introduce your children to other cultures. And when you go, leave your tourist hat at home and allow yourself and your kids to plunge yourselves into the spirit of the event.

Hire and consult with diversity in mind. Many parents have no problem hiring gardeners, housekeepers, or child-care providers of color. Our culture and economy support this. But how often do we seek out doctors or dentists or lawyers or tutors or therapists of color? Many will tell themselves that they just choose the best expert for the job, regardless of color. But if the "best" never turns out to be Latino or black, for example, it's important to recognize that unconscious bias may be at work. Choosing to actively seek out professionals of color helps us all combat the stereotype of minority inferiority that is so pervasive in our society. Doing so also demonstrates to our children that we can place our trust in—and spend our money with—people of other races.

In the end, as tempting as it may be to feel passive about prejudice, Whole Parents can't afford to view it as something so low in the hierarchy of social issues that we let someone else tackle it. To truly fend off bias, we have to see it as a foe worth fighting, both inside and outside our homes.

MULTICULTURAL BOOKS, TOYS, AND OTHER RESOURCES

Children's books, toys, and films reflect the era in which they were made, and it's not always a flattering view. For example, the Disney cartoon feature *Dumbo* is one of the most beloved children's movies of all time, but it is unfortunately marred by racial stereotypes. In its black crow scene, the birds are used to evoke African-Americans and they are depicted as happy-go-lucky low-lifers. In Robert McCloskey's classic children's book, *Make Way for Ducklings,* all the faces that can be made out in McCloskey's Boston are white. Many people are quick to forgive such things because *Dumbo* and *Ducklings* were both released in 1941. Most people realize that was a less enlightened time. We know better now.

But it's not that simple because these items aren't quaint museum pieces. Both remain in heavy circulation among children in current but unrevised editions. How is an African-American child supposed to feel about those crows or about a Boston that hides her from "the mainstream"? What messages do these images send to other children? And if society as a whole is so willing to overlook these things, are we really as enlightened as we think we are?

Why It Matters

Clearly, many things have changed since Dumbo and the ducklings were in diapers. But parents must still go out of their way to create a cultural world at home for their kids that truly represents the world outside. Despite vast improvements overall, some of the same problems evident in children's toys, books, and movies from generations ago persist today. Women and minorities' contributions to society are still underrepresented in children's books and playthings. Too many books and toys still present only white faces and reflect only a whitewashed cultural frame of reference. When adult women and minorities appear at all, they often do so only in subordinate roles as maids, secretaries, full-time moms, nurses, gardeners, factory workers, and so on. This is not only disrespectful but inaccurate and it poorly prepares children for the world in which they live.

Diversity in our population is a fact of life not only statistically but in most children's daily experiences. One of every three children in public schools is a minority. What's more, the U.S. Census Bureau predicts that by the year 2050—that is, within the lifetime of most children born today—minorities will comprise nearly 50 percent of the population.

Multicultural books and toys help foster better relationships between diverse people in many important ways. For instance, multicultural stories, fables, and folktales teach your children that kids with different backgrounds may have different points of view, traditions, and daily habits from their own. Playing with dolls and action figures of different skin colors and ethnicity aid your children in rehearsing appropriate relationships. In contrast, if all the people—at least, all the "good" people—in the stories and toys you provide your children have the same skin color or ethnicity as your family, you send your child a message that these are the only people who meet your standards.

Not that there isn't a place for *Dumbo* and *Make Way for Ducklings* in a multicultural world. The fact that both works have insensitive aspects by today's more evolved criteria hardly disqualifies them as children's classics. There's no reason a child growing up in a conscientious home can't still enjoy *Dumbo*'s endearing images and story if you take care to educate her about the stereotypes in the movie. And *Make Way for Ducklings* still makes delightful and harmless bedtime reading for little ones when they are surrounded with enough other multicultural material during their day to convey an impression of rich human diversity.

It's more powerful still to reinforce with your own behavior what you're teaching through books and toys. Do your best to put your child in settings where she will have the opportunity to mix and form friendships with children of different backgrounds. And if your own relationships lack diversity, take note that this sends an unhealthy message to your kids, too, and do what you can to expand yourself in this area.

Creating a Multicultural Environment for Your Child

Supplying your children with multicultural resources such as those reviewed at the end of this chapter is just a first step in providing a culturally fair environment. The following steps rank high as well:

- *Decode old TV shows.* As we've already noted, many old cartoons and shows will contain cultural stereotypes and other racist messages typical of the era in which they were made. You can never really protect your children from these shows. If they don't see them at home, they'll eventually see them somewhere else—at a friend's house, for example. As with *Dumbo,* it is better to sit down with your children as they're watching and "decode" the inappropriate and outdated messages for them. This simple but crucial act turns flawed entertainment into educational material.

- *Decode current media, too.* Although better than in past decades, the television shows and movies of today are hardly enlightened on multicultural issues. Whites are still cast in most of the positive roles—the heroes and heroines, the supervisors, the doctors, the good parents. People of color play far more than their share of villains, crooks, unwed parents, homeless people, and drug users, reinforcing the beliefs of many whites but not necessarily reflecting social reality. For example, most drug users in America are white, a conclusion one would never draw from television and the movies. Again, it's far more beneficial to help your children analyze and criticize misleading images than attempt to wipe them from their lives.

- *Lobby for diversity in day care.* If your child spends time in day care or preschool, check to see that multicultural playthings are available. If not, suggest to those responsible that they provide some. If they're not receptive to your suggestions, consider if your child is in the hands of inappropriate role models.

- *"Convert" nondiverse books.* Dismayed by the fact that most of the strong, heroic characters in children's books were white, male, and of European descent, Viviana Padilla, a second-generation Mexican-American, changed genders and interjected names from other cultures in stories she read to her daughters. "I wanted them to see themselves and their families and their people reflected in what was being read," she says, "so they wouldn't be like ghosts, a group of people that didn't exist except at home or when you visited Grandma and Grandpa."

- *Know what's influencing your child.* Despite your best efforts, children's books and toys dominated by white faces or insensitive stereotypes will enter your children's lives as birthday gifts, as borrowed items from school libraries with old collections, and as attractive items at friends' homes. The multicultural alternatives you provide in your own home will help blunt the impact of these images but they won't completely counter them. Always be aware of what your child is reading or playing with and give her the mental tools to disarm any potentially damaging impressions.

FOLK AND WISDOM TALES

One way to measure how much the world has changed since you were a child is to scan the magical literature in a library or the children's section of a quality bookstore. There among the usual fairy tales and such, you'll find delectable volumes like Virginia Hamilton's two collections of African-American folktales, *The People Could Fly* and *Her Stories;* Amy Tan's *The Moon Lady,* a children's story in the style of a traditional Chinese folktale; Margaret Mayo's retold *Magical Tales from Many Lands,* an international folktale collection with aboriginal Australian, African-American, Arabic, Caribbean, Chinese, French, Indian, Japanese, Jewish, North American Indian, Peruvian, Russian, Scottish, and South African among the cultures represented; and many more myths, legends, and folktales from around the world.

Seeing these enticing books may awaken your own memories of enjoying myths and legends. But chances are, most of the stories you remember came from a far more limited geographical and cultural range—ancient Greece and Rome and medieval Europe. We agree with experts that ancient myths, legends, and traditional stories hold a unique power for children. But we also believe that society has come too far to offer the same old stories in the same old way.

Western Myths, Legends, and Folktales: The Upside

Before we examine the drawbacks of Western myths, legends, and folktales, let's review their strengths as children's literature. First, some terms:

Myths, legends, folktales, fairy tales, and fables all rose out of the beliefs of ordinary people or anonymous storytellers and were passed down orally. Although they may have been written down and published at various times, they have no final form. Beyond this shared trait, they differ in a few significant ways.

Myths are cosmic dramas that usually feature supernatural forces driving the action. Some offer explanations for natural phenomena such as the change of seasons, and "answer" other great human questions such as: What happens when we die? How does evil enter the world? And so on. Others are simply great adventure stories. Examples of myths include the classic tales featuring the Greek and Roman gods and goddesses.

Legends, like myths, make up part of the great traditional literature of a culture. But legends generally grow out of historical fact and depend less on supernatural elements. Examples include the stories of King Arthur and Robin Hood. Both men are historical figures but their legends stray far from actual events.

Folktales, fairy tales, and fables are usually shorter and smaller in scope than myths and legends but, like them, take place in a magical world.

They often teach simple moral lessons or illustrate a quirk of human behavior. The usual fable is quite brief and has animals as the main characters.

Because many of these traditional story types teach important lessons, they are often referred to collectively as folk and wisdom tales. This body of literature has been passed down lovingly for hundreds and, in some cases, thousands of years because it serves many powerful functions for children. For one thing, folk and wisdom tales help children find meaning in their often bewildering lives. Fairy tales may not have much to say about the unique predicaments of modern life, but they do show how humans have addressed timeless and universal problems. And they do it in ways that speak directly to kids. Children's minds don't draw distinctions between ordinary reality and the magical universe of their imaginations, so they know the world of these tales intimately.

Magical stories describe a moral and behavioral universe that children understand as well. Justice in these stories is usually swift and sure. Evil is punished, often violently, and good rewarded, often lavishly. Characters' motivations are usually clear and uncomplicated—there are good people and there are bad people. It's not always quite that simple— for instance, good people like Daedelus may have fatal flaws—but the fate that befalls characters is always a direct consequence of their actions.

Myths, legends, folktales, fairy tales, and fables also form a common cultural heritage that is passed down from generation to generation through the important ritual of storytelling. Furthermore, the magical elements of these stories can whet children's appetites for more mature fantastic literature later on such as the Arthurian legends or the "magical realism" of authors such as Gabriel Garcia Marquez. Magical literature gives children a sense of the mysterious aspects of life, too.

Potential Problems with Western Folk Literature and How to Deal with Them

Despite the wonderful advantages to Western folk literature discussed above, many parents have deep reservations about exposing their children to these stories. In fact, folk and wisdom tales are at the center of three distinct controversies:

1. Some conservative Christian leaders and parents believe their children should be shielded from all notions of the supernatural other than the supernatural elements in the Bible, which are ac-

cepted as absolute truth. Devout followers of other faiths may feel similarly protective of their own religious stories.

2. For entirely secular reasons, some parents feel that it is unhealthy to encourage children to fantasize. They fear that fantasy will interfere with their children's ability to appreciate science and logic later on, so they read only modern, "reality-based" stories to their kids and even try to disillusion them about Santa Claus, Elijah (the biblical prophet who plays a mythic part in the Jewish Passover service), the Easter Bunny, and the Tooth Fairy.

3. Experts and parents sensitive to cultural biases feel that many of the traditional Western stories contain inappropriate, damaging images and implications. For example, psychologists Darlene and Derek Hopson note that in most popular fairy tales, the good characters tend to have light skin and wear light- or bright colors while their evil opponents often have dark skin or clothes. Some dismiss these problems as simply reflecting the prejudices of the era in which these stories originated or were collected. Nevertheless, the Hopsons and others feel that, in our eagerness to impart the positive aspects of these stories to our children, we may be unintentionally conveying to them subtle negative messages about other cultures or ethnicities.

We won't address the first issue here because those who are troubled by it aren't likely to appreciate attempts to dissuade them. However, the other two issues are complex and of particular concern to many readers of this book.

Regarding children's fantasies, it is perfectly natural, and beneficial, for young children to believe in the Easter Bunny, the living Elijah, Santa, and the Tooth Fairy, not to mention the characters in magical stories. Through about age six, children believe firmly in fantasy creations, notes psychologist Bruno Bettelheim (a controversial figure in recent years but still revered for his writing on children's magical literature). For another couple of years, they'll be uncertain but still inclined to accept imaginary people and worlds. After age eight or so, they will probably know better but enjoy pretending that fantasy worlds are real. Disillusion them and you rob them of some of the greatest fun of their childhood.

Plunging children into a totally logical universe not only isn't fair, it's also unhealthy. Children begin to grasp important concepts in their "transactions" with fantasy characters. For instance, Bettelheim writes that the Tooth Fairy who leaves money for a lost tooth "symbolizes the goodwill of a world that does not want a child to lose anything without effort at compensation." Trying to teach children the same lesson via logic would be developmentally questionable to say the least. Rationality comes at a later stage of childhood. Emphasizing it too early is out of step with how morality and other abstractions naturally develop. Besides, parents needn't worry about their child's ability to separate fantasy and reality. Kids outgrow magical thinking even if their folks do nothing to discourage it.

In other words, a child's imaginings serve a vital developmental function. Children before a certain age haven't yet developed the full capacity to reason. Magical thinking helps them make sense of the world. For example, the Tooth Fairy, Bettleheim points out, helps children deal with the otherwise scary experience of losing a body part. In this light, you can only draw one conclusion about reading your child quality magical literature: the more, the better.

Ethnic prejudice in Western folk literature is a much touchier issue. You might try a couple of antidotes. As the Hopsons suggest, drop out all references to color when reading fairy tales or other traditional stories to your child. If the story doesn't deliver its same moral message in that form, stop using it.

Another option is to apply the lessons of media literacy to your child's fairy stories. Television is rife with ethnic and gender stereotypes, but parents can disarm them and even use them as a tool for awareness by discussing them with their children as they're watching (see page 102). The same goes for reading. You can remove all the biased books, videos, and television programs you want from your children's lives and they'll still be exposed to them at school, at friends' homes, and so on. Better to transform an unfortunate situation into an educational opportunity. However, be sure to consider the age of your child if you take this tack. Is he or she mature enough to understand your explanations? If not, it may be better to screen what you expose them to until you can discuss the stories and have your explanations stick.

Another way to counter stereotypes, of course, is to broaden your child's perspective with traditional literature from other cultures. Many of the books reviewed in the Resources at the end of this chapter will guide you to excellent sources of myths, legends, and folktales from around the world and from minority American cultures as well. To help counter the prejudices your child will encounter outside the home, reinforce positive images of dark-skinned and other ethnic characters you meet in these books. ("Isn't that princess courageous?" "Isn't the farmer's son handsome?")

Indeed, you may discover that once you adopt a more multicultural approach to traditional literature, some of the classics no longer wash with your kids. For instance, Viviana Padilla's daughters took exception to how the wolf was portrayed in Little Red Riding Hood: "They said, 'That's a very white view of wolves' because we've read a lot of Indian myths that counteract the Western European view of the world and nature. We have this love for wolves."

TV OR NOT TV?

The huge role that TV plays in most children's lives makes what your children watch and the time they spend watching it two of the most significant issues facing parents today. But you wouldn't know that from the scant attention TV viewing receives from experts. Surprisingly little research has been done on the effects of extensive TV watching on developing brains and lives.

What an odd state of affairs considering that television is the leading leisure activity of childhood. According to Victor Strasburger, M.D., of the American Academy of Pediatrics (AAP), children are watching roughly 27–28 hours per week by preschool age, the critical years for language and cognitive development. Between the ages of 6 and 11, the years when reading is learned and developed, children watch between 23 and 24 hours per week. By the time they graduate high school, teenagers will have spent 15,000 to 18,000 hours in front of the television compared to the 12,000 hours they've spent in school.

Of course, the most telling statistic may be the fact that the television is on about 7.5 hours per day, or about half of waking hours, in the average American household. If we parents, experts included, haven't handled our own TV addiction, no wonder society has been slow to address television's impact on children. And that impact could be profound. While research on the harmful effects of television is scarce, enough is known to warrant concern, particularly when you fill in the information gaps with common sense.

What's Wrong with TV

Victor Strasburger, coauthor of the AAP's brochure *Television and the Family*, captures the essence of the problem: "Children need to learn to read, be physically and socially active, explore a broad range of play, and develop good nutritional habits. Too much TV time can impede progress in all these areas." Here are the details behind that statement:

- *Kids watching TV aren't interacting with their families (or we with them, when we watch).* Family conversation helps the child develop language and listening skills. Families converse less than they used to, and TV is often to blame.

- *TV watching also reduces the opportunities for creative play, which is crucial for cognitive development (essentially, the ability to learn).* Creative play and reading stimulate the imagination. Television delivers story, pictures, and sound in one complete package, leaving the imagination nothing to do. Effectively, it rewards total passivity, which may be the key to its addictive power.

- *TV not only displaces reading but may well build a bias against it.* TV watching is much easier than reading. It requires little if any thinking and doesn't challenge viewers to look up new words and background information the way reading does.

- *Studies associate viewing of more than four hours per day with poor school performance.* Conversely, kids who do better in school watch less TV.

- *TV commercials aimed at children promote avid consumerism.* Prior to the 1980s, the Federal Communications Commission (FCC) regulations forbade producers of children's TV from using a show's content to market products and limited the number of commercials. The Reagan-era FCC relaxed those and other regulations designed to ensure quality programming for kids. That effectively invited toy manufacturers to enter the program production business, and they nearly trampled each other in the ensuing stampede. By the end of 1985, most of the top ten bestselling toys were all tied-in to programs. Within two more years, toy manufacturers were producing 80 percent of all children's television. And the toys they were advertising on their programs were generally as suspect from a developmental and values standpoint as the programs themselves—for instance, they created an unceasing stream of war toys and violent action figures for little boys.

- *TV commercials promote poor nutrition and poor health.* Given that the fat and sugar contents of many foods advertised on TV are high and the nutritional levels low, it's not surprising that many experts suspect a strong relationship between the amount of TV watched and poor eating habits. Heavy TV watching also correlates with poor physical fitness—again, not surprising when leisure hours are spent reclining on the couch.

- *The sexual and violent content of television may be upsetting to children or cause other harmful effects.* You don't have to be a bluenose to be wary of exposing your children to the way sex is presented on TV. Sex is used to attract and hold audiences so it is usually filmed to titillate, not to reflect real human relationships. On screen, people tumble into bed quickly and couple with intense heat and passion, and nearly everyone is a great lover. Bodies are spectacular, contraception isn't discussed, AIDS doesn't exist, and love has nothing to do with it. No wonder teenagers feel pressured by these images and storylines, as some surveys of teens have reported. (We address violent TV and video games in separate sections on pages 114 and 118.)

- *Television tends to reflect rather than correct the ethnic and other cultural stereotypes that plague American society.* Increasingly rare are the serious dramas that challenge viewers to think about prejudice and other important social issues. In addition, as University of Michigan professor and children's media critic Susan Douglas argues, TV treats the status quo as "natural," which lowers our regard for other options. The problem is made worse by a profusion of cable channels showing old cartoons, sitcoms, and dramas produced in decades when biases were even worse than they are today.

Even the celebrated *Sesame Street* must be faulted in some ways. For instance, to win kids over from competitors' shows in the same time slot, *Sesame Street's* creators employ similar fast-paced techniques, although their program does have compensating advantages such as positive images of diverse cultures and people, and treatment of emotional issues such as death. Clearly, not even the producers of supposed noncommercial programming have been able to overcome the problems created by the competitive and barely regulated environment in which children's television exists.

What Happens When Playtime Becomes TV Time

As parents, we should be asking what skills and abilities television watching develops, since the average child spends so much time doing it. What many experts say on the subject is not comforting, for they fear that most of what is practiced—as well as *not* practiced—when watching TV has a negative effect on later learning and living or at best, no positive value at all. For example, veteran teachers often complain that children today don't have the attention spans of previous generations. Many blame the production style of television, which is based on a series of brief segments—many only seconds long. Children who watch TV incessantly instead of reading, the theory goes, never develop their powers of concentration.

Many experienced teachers also believe children today as a group aren't nearly as adept at complicated forms of reasoning, reading comprehension, written expression, disciplined thinking, task perseverance, and planning as children were decades ago. Prolonged TV viewing—which does nothing to develop any of these capacities—is widely suspected to be a culprit here, too.

As childhood education specialist Jane Healy, Ph.D., points out, experts in neuropsychology know that using the brain helps build new brain connections and lack of use weakens them. Kids who spend most of their spare time slouching before the set aren't practicing skill-building activities that come naturally with more traditional forms of play. "Young brains need broad horizons," she writes in her book *Endangered Minds,* "not overbuilt neural pathways in one specific area."

Again, the lack of sufficient research on the damaging effects of TV means that we can only make educated guesses about many of the problems with excessive watching. But parents shouldn't be fooled when TV defenders say there is little evidence to show that TV viewing causes harm. As Healy says, "the primary reason there is 'little evidence' is that there has been little research!" The truth is that the reliable studies that have been done point to exactly the type of problems described above.

Not Entirely a Wasteland

Some TV watching does offer some benefits to children and teenagers. Educational programming can teach children about nature, the environment, politics, science, music, art, literature, and positive behaviors. For example, in Nickelodeon's *The Secret World of Alex Mack,* children see the main character deal with school and dating pressures successfully. Responsible programs and videos can help kids accept a new brother or sister and learn to cope with their parents' divorce or other difficult issues.

In fact, in some instances, shows convey information that books can't—consider the visuals in a nature show, notes Berkeley, California, parent and avid reader Jeremy Sherman: "There's no question that a lot of stuff is more easily learned through multimedia than through books. And there's no question that my kids are more drawn to multimedia than to books—by far." Jeremy tries to limit his children's watching to educational fare such as The Discovery Channel and Animal Planet.

Although quality programs are rare on commercial stations (Nickelodeon being a conspicuous exception), your library may stock a strong collection of educational videos, chosen with care by librarians. Many of the programs on public television also do a good job of teaching school readiness skills and encouraging reading (although *Sesame Street* has been criticized for pushing kids to read too soon). When used this selectively, television can be a valuable adjunct to school and can enhance mental development.

For all of television's problems, there are other reasons not to eliminate it from your child's life. First and foremost, media literacy is an important contemporary survival skill and you can't be media literate if you don't watch at least a little TV. Media literacy includes learning how camera movements, plot structures, stereotypes, and other devices are used to manipulate viewers' attitudes. It also means understanding the purpose and methods of advertisers. Teaching your children to become media literate lessens TV's power over their minds and transforms viewing into a learning experience. (Sources that promote media literacy are reviewed in the Resources section at the end of the chapter).

Second, TV introduces your children to the zeitgeist, or the spirit of the times. People who are successful in such fields as entertainment, politics, or marketing commercial products generally have great command of the zeitgeist. In fact, your children will experience limitations in almost any social arena, whether at school, work, or play, if they don't watch some television because TV puts them on a cultural wavelength with their peers, obnoxious as that culture may be.

Devising a Sensible TV Policy for Your Home

You can't eliminate TV from children's lives. Ban it from their home and they'll still see it at friends' houses and learn about all the crucial shows and video games from their school pals. It's far better, we believe, to equip your kids with the critical tools needed to understand what they're watching and to institute controls so they don't spend too many hours in front of the set. The following guidelines are in step with this moderate approach:

- *Place firm limits on the amount of TV watched per day.* One to two hours is a reasonable amount. Limiting viewing time also encourages kids to be more selective about what they watch. In addition to daily time limits, Susan Marchionna and Lee Jacobson of Berkeley, California, have also imposed occasional "No-TV Weeks" with their three children: "The kids start looking through their closets and drawers for gifts from Christmas and birthdays that never got attention before," says Susan. "Or we linger over dinner conversation longer, play music, read more, or play games together. They always want to turn the TV back on when the time is up, but it isn't a negative experience."

- *Help your kids decode what they see.* Watch TV with your child so you can discuss the messages delivered by programs and commercials, answer questions about what they don't understand, clarify misconceptions, help them understand audience manipulations, and reinforce positive messages and images. Lori Patch's daughter watches mainly PBS shows so her mother was surprised when she asked for some special shampoo that she'd seen advertised on TV: "I told her 'That was a commercial and they're trying to get you to buy their shampoo, not necessarily because it's better but because they want to sell as many bottles as they can.' That was a whole new idea to her."

- *If using TV as a baby-sitter, do it sparingly and conscientiously.* Using TV to distract your kids for a little while isn't such a terrible compromise—especially if you've disarmed TV's impact by raising media-literate children and limit their viewing to quality programming.

- *Emphasize developmentally appropriate videotapes over commercial TV.* Content quality is far higher and you can choose what is watched.

- *Be a good role model by limiting your own viewing.*

- *Protect preschool-age children from inappropriate or disturbing viewing.* Kids this age have little ability to control their impulses or separate fantasy from reality. You should not only carefully control what they watch alone but also what others watch when little ones are in the room.

- *Use TV as a bridge to books.* For instance, if your child notices a seeing-eye dog in a show, get books from the library on the training of these dogs, anecdotes about great guide dogs, and so on. Your child will soon understand that books contain far more information than any program can cover.

- *Make sure baby-sitters and other caregivers understand your family television policy.*

Or as a simpler, more progressive alternative to the above list, try the following: Allow your kids to watch as much educational television as they want along with occasional high-quality dramatic shows and movies. Increase their program choices by taping, purchasing, or checking out from the library quality programming such as nature shows, *Reading Rainbow,* and so on. Forbid commercial television, with the exception of select programs on quality-conscious channels like Nickelodeon. You may soon find that, having been exposed to a higher grade of TV programming, your children will not be attracted to the low-quality fare offered by most commercial stations.

A surprising number of families we interviewed do in fact "ban the box" in their homes, but that need not preclude teaching media literacy. Jim and Beverly Fety's three kids do their TV watching when the family travels. "When we're at a motel, it's another something to explore," says Beverly. "If the same motel has a pool, they're in it. They're also at the ice machine and bouncing on the beds and making the hot chocolate. But what they see about the TV is that we get the clicker and go round and round and round and there's nothing to watch."

SHOULD I LET MY CHILD WATCH VIOLENT TV PROGRAMS?

The television industry always claims that it just gives the people what they want, but sometimes you have to wonder, especially where children's programming is concerned. A 1994 Gallup poll found that 83 percent of American adults believe that TV violence contributes directly to violent behavior in children. If anything, the poll understates the issue: The Center for Media and Public Affairs has noted that "By far the most violence [occurs] during time periods aimed at young viewers"—twenty to twenty-five acts per hour.

Public outcry against violence on TV reached another in a series of climaxes in 1993 when a five-year-old Ohio boy, apparently inspired by

MTV's *Beavis and Butthead*, set his house ablaze, killing his two-year-old sister. Within days, Attorney General Janet Reno told a Senate committee that the regulation of televised violence would be "constitutionally permissible" and recommended prompt legislative action if the broadcast industry didn't clean up its act. Reno was hardly the first high administration official to issue such a stern warning. More than twenty years earlier, a task force commissioned by the surgeon general to study the link between TV violence and violent behavior found enough evidence establishing a causal relationship to "warrant immediate remedial action."

No such action was taken, of course. In fact, the last several decades have seen a repeated cycle of government calls for regulation followed by industry heads declaring renewed commitment to quality programming—followed by more bad and even dangerous programming, new government threats, and so on. And since that 1972 report, the evidence of the harmful effects of TV violence has piled even higher.

Among scholars and healthcare professionals today, it is axiomatic that heavy TV viewing (defined as four or more hours per day) can lead to aggressive behavior in children. Such viewing "is a predictor of aggressive behavior," says developmental psychologist Jerome Singer, codirector of Yale's Family Television Research and Consultation Center. "Not just *assertive* behavior, but pushing other children, knocking down blocks, hitting other kids."

Moreover, the American Psychological Association's landmark 1992 report, *Big World, Small Screen: The Role of Television in American Society,* warned that "children and adults who watch a large number of aggressive programs also tend to hold attitudes and values that favor the use of aggression to resolve conflict." One study in particular paints a grim portrait of TV's unique power to foster violence. Researchers assessed the behavior of the children in a Canadian town which could not receive television signals until 1973. Two years after TV first became available to them, the rate of aggressive behavior among these children increased by 160 percent.

And researchers have identified two other significant negative effects: "desensitization" and what some scholars call "mean world syndrome." The former makes young viewers more willing to tolerate violence in the world around them. Kids afflicted with mean world syndrome begin to believe that the world is as mean and dangerous as it appears on TV—an understandable but profound error, given that violence occurs much more frequently on TV than it does in real life.

These findings make a kind of gruesome sense when we consider the amount of time our kids watch TV and the number of violent incidents to which young viewers are exposed. By the time the average American child graduates from elementary school, he or she will have witnessed a total of 100,000 acts of televised violence, including some 8,000 murders. Again, the worst offenders are children's shows: A 1994 study by the Center for Media and Public Affairs showed that, including product commercials, those programs contained an average of 36.7 violent events per hour—more than one every half minute.

Nor should parents dismiss cartoon violence just because it's, well, cartoony. Experts note that in a way, cartoon violence is all the more pernicious *because* it is supposed to be funny. "At the very least, cartoons teach young children to laugh at violence," says Deborah Prothrow-Stith, M.D., assistant dean at the Harvard University School of Public Health and author of *Deadly Consequences.* "At worst, they show children that violent behavior may be a cartoon hero's first recourse when solving problems."

Not that we should be terribly surprised by any of this. From infancy, children are programmed by nature to mimic adult behavior—indeed, their development, their very survival, depends on it. In the modern world, this includes the behavior they see on the small screen, and kids can copy from televised role models as easily as from real-life ones. Research by the University of Washington's Andrew Meltzoff has shown that this mimicry can take place in babies as young as fourteen months.

However, while the urge to imitate is instinctive, the ability to know what *ought* to be imitated is not. When the acts being portrayed are violent, the mimicry isn't likely to be healthful either for the individual or society, especially when those indiscriminate mimics grow up.

How to Regulate Violent TV in Your Home

As noted in our section, "TV or Not TV?" (see page 108), there are plenty of reasons to limit the amount of TV viewing your children do, regardless of whether they're watching violent programs or not. Let's keep this in perspective. It's not likely that watching *Beavis and Butthead* will lead your youngsters to burn your house down. But there are usually better ways they could be spending their time! To mitigate the harmful effects of violent TV programming, we recommend the following steps:

- *Don't view to choose, choose to view.* Discourage the indiscriminate viewing that comes with remote control "channel surfing," which even a five-year-old can learn to do. Channel-surfing inevitably means exposure to more television violence. Instead, consult your local paper's TV listings and select programs for your child to choose from.

- *Let kids choose, too.* Although parents want to limit their kids' exposure to programming they find distasteful, it's important to give them a chance to participate in the selection process. But it's not too much to ask that they justify their choices. Says Howard Rheingold of Mill Valley, California: "[My daughter Mamie and I] fought every battle about television ruling. She would figure out loopholes or just wear me down until I didn't pay attention to the rules anymore. Finally, I said, 'You can watch anything you want at any time, but you have to write a report on each program and hand it to me immediately after the program. And it has to pass inspection as a decently written report that shows some thought about what you watched.' She did about twenty reports, then stopped watching television almost entirely."

- *Set an appropriate example.* Make sure your own viewing is just as selective as what you demand of your children.

- *Teach nonviolence.* As Aimee Dorr, professor of education at UCLA, points out, children in families that emphasize nonaggressive behavior are much less likely to exhibit aggressiveness, even if they watch it on TV.

- *Be sure to let your kids know when you disapprove of something being shown on the small screen.* Says Carolyn Umphries of Children's Television Workshop (CTW), producers of *Sesame Street:* "If everyone in the free world watched *Power Rangers* and my kid wanted to, I'd watch with him. And when someone got punched or blasted, I'd ask, 'Would you do that? Would you poke a playmate with a crayon because you're angry?' It's important to talk through a situation with children, so they know that what happens on a TV show isn't appropriate in real life." Media critic Jon Katz agrees: "Parents need to understand the culture of their young children. They should watch *X-Men* and *Mighty Morphin Power Rangers* with their kids and point out what they find offensive. Values are transmitted by the family, not by the TV."

Finally, get your kids to understand that violence does a lot more damage in real life than is shown on TV. For example, bullets can tear huge, gaping holes in their victims. As a policeman we know once said, "If TV showed what really happens when somebody gets shot, nobody would want to see it again."

SHOULD I LET MY CHILD PLAY WITH WAR TOYS OR VIOLENT VIDEO GAMES?

Television isn't the only medium in which kids encounter seemingly incessant violence. Take a brief stroll down the aisles of the average toy superstore, and you'll pass by enough firepower to rival that of the combined armed forces.

At first blush, this may seem like a big So What? After all, many of us played violent games, and happily used toy guns and soldier figures as children. But violence in today's toys and games is more detailed, more likely to be amoral, and far more widespread, just as it is on TV and in the movies. Many parents understandably fear that violent play will precipitate violent behavior and contribute to the violence in our everyday lives.

How much, if any, such play should we allow our children? Let's examine what experts have learned about how this kind of play affects behavior and social attitudes:

Do war toys and violent video games encourage aggressive or violent behavior?
Research results on this question have been mixed. In the mid-1980s, following video games' emergence as a major new form of recreation, several studies examined their psychosocial impact. Some researchers found an increase in aggression among children between the ages of four and seven after playing video games. One study of fourth and fifth graders, interestingly, found an increase *among girls* but the games had no effect on aggression in boys.

Yet other studies have found no increase, and one, of eleven-to-fourteen-year-olds, found that violent videos actually have a *calming* effect. One research team that had found an increase in aggressive behavior among four-to-six-year-olds also found a *reduction* among children who played video games in pairs.

Despite the lack of clearcut evidence linking violent video games with violent behavior, many parents and critics remain concerned. James Oppenheim, technology editor of the *Oppenheim Toy Portfolio,* a guide to children's media, frets about the prevalence of violent themes. "There's this constant chipping away at decency," he told *Business Week* in December 1996. "What kind of a future are we making?"

It may well be that, since much of the existing research on the effects of violent video games was done in the early years of the medium, those studies are now obsolete as games become more visually realistic, and thus more graphic and bloody. As sociologist Akira Sakamoto, of Ochanomizu Women's College in Tokyo, told *Business Week,* "All the old violence studies need to be redone."

Aren't war toys and video games inherently sexist?

Not *all* video games are, certainly, but "aggressive fantasy" games do appeal more to boys than to girls. One study found that adding more aggressive elements to a game increased its popularity among boys but lessened it among girls. Because kids often enter the computer world through games, the fact that most games are keyed to boys' tastes has implications for girls' later success in the work world.

The problem of sex stereotyping and gender division in play is even worse with war toys, which are marketed almost exclusively to boys. For more on gender division in childhood play, see "The 'Right' Toys—Playthings That Reflect Your Values and Help Your Children Realize Their Potential," page 90.

Do kids get any benefits from playing with war toys and violent video games?

You mean, besides having fun? Despite many parents' revulsion to the content and nature of so many popular video games, it's clear that kids love them. One reason they do, of course, is that the games provide unceasing action, something kids generally cannot get enough of.

Although education professors Nancy Carlsson-Paige and Diane E. Levin criticize some facets of today's war toys, they point out in their book *Who's Calling the Shots?* that war play offers many of the same advantages as what we think of as more constructive play. It allows children to feel powerful, a rare and welcome occurrence in their lives; build social skills when they play with other children; exercise their imagination as they create dramas and carry them out; and otherwise express themselves creatively and conceptually.

In a similar vein, violent video games also offer enough side benefits that parents should think twice before condemning them as worthless. For instance, even an explicitly violent video game such as boxing can have a tonic effect by providing youngsters an innocuous way to vent aggression. For benefits of video game playing in general, see page 120.

If "managing" war play and limiting violent video games still doesn't go far enough for your taste, we understand entirely. Watching your little innocents gleefully lay waste to armies of friends is not a comforting sight. But as parent Susan Marchionna points out, you may not have another

the upside of video games

The hours your child whiles away in front of the tube may not all be lost ones, especially the ones spent playing video games. The disadvantages of television don't universally apply to video games. Clearly, many of the action games are questionable in content, as discussed on page 118. Nevertheless, research and observation are starting to turn up some real advantages to this form of kid recreation:

- *Career preparation.* No one knows exactly what the work world of the future will look like, but it is clear that advanced computer skills will be in high demand. Today's game fiends will enter the workplace already partially trained because of their earlier experiences with 3-D graphics and other aspects of sophisticated games. Video games also teach kids how to respond quickly and flexibly to complex, fast-changing technology, an ability highly valued by employers.

- *Special learning skills.* For example, some research indicates that certain video games such as *Tetris* are particularly effective in teaching spatial skills such as the ability to rotate an object mentally.

- *Conditioning children to increasingly tougher challenges.* Many games are designed with increasing levels of difficulty. As soon as a player masters one level, the software encourages him to select a more challenging version of the game.

- *Social play.* Although most games can be played alone, many allow for two or more players.

option: "We didn't have too many rules about guns, because it became apparent very early on that a kid was always carrying a gun in his index finger—in fact, two of them. And sticks work just fine as guns too."

Jeremy Sherman, a peace activist of long standing, decided from the beginning that he wouldn't start a war over violent play: "I avoided making [war toys and violent video games] seem like a big deal. Some of that I did by sending it up, by making fun of the characters. But I didn't want [my kids] to think it was a big deal for me. And so I think they got whatever use they needed out of [the toys and games], and it never became a big issue."

Forcing his will on his children in this area also violates Jeremy's sense of what's good for young minds: "Yes, I believe it's important to express my opinions, but I also think it's great to let them know that it's absolutely fine for them to have opinions that are different from mine. I want to respect their opinions, too."

RAISING A MORAL CHILD

For at least 2,700 years, adults have griped that the younger generation is an unruly, morally bankrupt mob. Kids today "have bad manners and contempt for authority. They show disrespect for their elders," wrote Aristotle, born in the third century B.C.E. No doubt Fred and Wilma Flintstone made the same complaint about Pebbles and her friends once they hit puberty.

The grumbling about kids in the current era sounds especially cranky because it arises from yet another fiercely contested battleground in the culture wars. According to one side, permissive parenting and moral relativism is the problem and strict obedience, rigid rules, religious piety, and unquestioning acceptance of "traditional family values" is the answer. According to the other side, the family values camp is pining for a time that never really was. Besides, these parents say, such militaristic ideas of good parenting will create mindless robots unable to handle the moral complexities of modern life and citizenship.

Which side has the goods on how to raise decent kids? Ultimately, neither. Raising moral kids may not be easier than any other aspect of parenting, but it isn't the mystery the culture war makes it seem, either. Let's take a look at what's known about instilling values in kids.

What Psychologists Have Discovered

Morality is built upon other human capacities, the most fundamental of which is empathy. It is empathy, the ability to see life through another person's eyes, that makes people want to relieve the suffering of others, to sacrifice their labors or even their lives for a cause, to responsibly hold up their end in a group effort, and so on. This capacity develops in infancy as naturally and dependably as the ability to speak. When two-year-old Erica offers her upset brother some of her mashed peas so he'll feel better, she's demonstrating empathy. Because empathy is hardwired into children, parents can nurture it simply by praising it when they see it in action and not contradicting their child's impulses in this direction.

For Val and Stuart Schultz of Ithaca, New York, teaching and reinforcing empathy is an ongoing endeavor with their four children—Sammy, 7; Libby, 9; Jesse, 12; and Sara, 14. "[We say to them] 'Try and put yourself in the other person's shoes and think about how they'd be feeling before you say or act on something,'" says Val. "And it really seems to be working, I'm happy to say. The feedback I'm getting is just heartwarming. They are the ones who will help the underdog, or include the underdog, so in certain ways it's starting to show. It's very important to me to raise my children with these values because that's the small contribution I can make to the world and to peace."

Of course, just as it takes more than water to grow good roses, it takes more than empathy to "grow" morality. For kids to behave morally, they have to be self-disciplined, and they have to feel confident enough to do what's right even when it's difficult or others disagree. It also helps if they are relatively happy at home, because resentment and anger at parents can lead to vengeful, inappropriate behavior directed at others. Unfortunately, because most parents tend to rely on instincts, what their parents did with them, or they take other well-intentioned but poorly informed approaches, they often err in one or more of these areas.

People tend to fall into patterns when they parent, which can be broken down to three factors—acceptance vs. rejection, firmness vs. leniency, and autonomy vs. control. Parents vary in each of these areas—say, from extremely firm to extremely lenient—with most somewhere in the middle range. By looking at each of these factors in more detail, it's easy to see how parenting can be improved and how that can enhance children's moral development:

Acceptance vs. rejection. Accepting parents more freely praise their kids, are more affectionate with them, more attentive to their emotions, and take a more active interest in their lives. Children in these families feel comfortable going to their parents when they have problems, when they need help, or simply for companionship. Rejecting parents are colder, and not as responsive to their children's emotional needs. Sometimes this is by design, because the parents feel that too much nurturing spoils children. In other cases, the parents are just not very good at making their warm feelings known. Either way, the children grow up feeling lonely and unloved, and don't believe their parents will support them when times are tough.

Firmness vs. leniency. Firm parents clearly state rules that they expect their children to follow as well as the consequences for not doing so. When rules are broken, these parents consistently apply those consequences. As a result, their children grow up understanding what it means to be responsible for their actions. Lenient parents may be of several types. Some set very few rules—often, because they believe that rules kill the child's natural joyous spirit. Other lenient types do believe in rules and set them, but don't enforce them with any uniformity or energy. Children growing up in lenient homes often lack the ability to discipline themselves and are confused about what's okay to do and what isn't.

Autonomy vs. control. This factor concerns the extent to which parents will help their children develop their individuality. At the high end are parents who encourage their kids to express themselves and who ask their opinions, often. When their kids hit the teen years, these same parents applaud them for becoming independently thinking people with their own separate lives. Children raised this way feel that their thoughts and statements matter to their parents. They feel loved and respected unconditionally rather than pressured to agree with their parents for their approval. They aren't afraid to speak up for what they believe. In fact, they feel it's important to do so. In controlling homes, obedience—not individuality—is what counts. In fact, expressing independence in almost any way will be put down as disrespectful. Children in controlling homes feel they must bow to their parents' wishes in all matters, even if that means denying their own personalities.

It's not too hard to guess what works here for morality and good parenting in general, is it? Research consistently shows that the most emotionally healthy children come from homes in which parents are warm and accepting, firm when it comes to rules and discipline, and encouraging of their children's individuality. Temple University psychology professor Laurence Steinberg Ph.D., has written at length about parenting styles in his superb book *Beyond the Classroom*. He notes that of the hundreds of studies of parenting over the decades, no major study has ever argued that cold, laissez-faire, or controlling parenting is better.

Of course, that which is ideal is not always that which prevails. Psychologists like Steinberg have identified three common *parenting styles*— that is, combinations of the above factors that parents tend to fall into. Of these, "Permissive" parents rate high in acceptance, low in firmness, and high in autonomy. "Autocratic" parents rate low in acceptance, high in firmness, and low in autonomy. "Authoritative" parenting, the style that works best, rates high in acceptance, firmness, and autonomy. Authoritative parenting combines the strengths of the permissive and autocratic approaches and eliminates their weaknesses. It also produces the most morally able children.

However, since permissive and autocratic parents also make up a good portion of the population, we have a culture war in which both sides slam each other for a problem they each help create. Kids raised without much firmness can have trouble controlling their impulses and obeying rules. When they're young, they are more likely to fight, behave aggressively, and act out. As a group, they'll have more disciplinary and conduct problems later on. Kids growing up in less accepting homes may have lower self-esteem, which among other things can lead to prejudices, including racism. Kids raised without a sense of autonomy are more likely to experience depression and anxiety, both of which can affect decision making, moral and otherwise. Nor are they well-equipped or practiced in making their own moral judgments when the right thing to do isn't obvious.

Moral development requires considerable self-discipline and this is one of many ways in which the authoritatively raised kids shine. Thanks to the firmness of their parents' approach, these children internalize their parents' regulation of their behavior and regulate themselves as they mature. Their parents' acceptance of them leads children to develop a more positive sense of self, a more enthusiastic approach to life, better social skills, and ease in forming relationships. Finally, the respect their parents have shown for their individuality produces in these children a greater sense of responsibility, as well as greater industriousness, competence, self-reliance, and persistence when facing a challenging task. Not surprisingly, these kids also perform better in school than kids raised permissively or autocratically. Not all the qualities just mentioned directly affect moral development, but many of them obviously do.

In addition to preferring the Authoritative parenting style, child behavior experts stress that when teaching your kids morality, deeds matter much more than words. Kids instantly see through a parent's hypocrisy. By the same token, when they see their parents passionately committed to a cause, they are more likely to emulate that commitment in their own lives.

Other experiences that help kids develop an exceptional sense of moral commitment include volunteer service opportunities in the teen years, immersion in other cultures, relationships with diverse people, and a deeply affecting mentoring relationship. (Diversity is discussed elsewhere in this chapter, starting on page 96. Volunteerism and experiences with other cultures are discussed in Chapter 10.)

Teaching Morality in a Morally Complex World

For parents' moral lessons to "take," it's best that children see those lessons reflected in the world around them. But that's not going to happen with any consistency. We live in a time and place of deep moral ambiguity and confusion, in which leaders in our society—not to mention teachers, ministers, and police—disagree over many of the most basic moral issues.

What may be even more confusing to children are the discrepancies between what leaders—people children have been taught to respect—say and do. Children learn that lying, cheating, and breaking the law are wrong but see successful people doing all three of these things. In fact, kids will eventually learn that playing by the rules is considered ill-advised and naive in business, politics, professional sports, and many other parts of our society because you might give your opponent, or rival company, a competitive advantage.

Children also hear at home that people are more important than money. But they will often notice that priority reversed in both the public and private sectors. Nor will children observe much forceful challenge in public life to the morality of putting money first. However much ordinary Americans grumble about the super-rich, most hope they will someday be among them.

Again, children have a keen eye for hypocrisy so we're certainly not suggesting that you should hide the ways of the world from them—quite the opposite, in fact. If they don't hear a critique of mainstream values from you, they might get the idea that you agree with society's more questionable standards. You may then lose your moral credibility with them. This is in fact precisely what happened in the 1960s when the youth generation grew frustrated with with their parents' complacency about America's social problems and misplaced priorities.

We're also not saying you should make your kids jaded. But you should give them credit—they understand more than you may think and they can handle more moral complexity than you might imagine. Show them that most people are basically good even if they disagree about some basic values. But don't hide from them the fact that society is set up for some bad people to do well. What they'll then need to hear from you are ways people can succeed in the prevailing system without sacrificing their basic integrity.

This brings up one of the most important parts of morally guiding your kids: just being with them. Moral messages aren't simple and it takes time to get them across. Make the time to engage your children in lengthy conversations. Be involved in their lives, which will create more opportunities to talk. Moral questions will come up naturally because kids want to know what's right and wrong as part of their drive to figure out the world. They will ask troubling questions because the world is a troubling place, especially at their level of experience. Be ready for them with answers they can understand.

In your discussions, your kids will no doubt offer naive ideas about how to improve life—Alan and Hyiah's nine-year-old daughter Ariel, for example, would reorganize the entire economy to protect endangered animals. Acknowledge their good intentions and the ingenuity of their ideas and then explain how they may not work in current circumstances. But don't leave them without hope. If they feel the world doesn't support or reward good actions, they will wonder why they should even try. Certainly, you have your own list of stories you can tell about people who in your view have made a great contribution to society and were rewarded for doing so. Such stories will not only hearten your youngsters but also inspire them.

Teaching Morality Issue-by-Issue

You can't just address morality in a few broad brush strokes with your kids and then be done with it. The complexities of modern life won't allow it, nor will children's own developing complexity. Children face different issues at different ages. For instance, teens must deal with troubling issues relating to sexuality and drugs that weren't even relevant to them a few years earlier. As kids grow, so does the chance of them encountering morally complicated situations: Should they tell on a friend who has done something wrong? What action should they choose when doing the "right" thing puts one in danger? When teens begin to take their first jobs in private companies, they will see firsthand the foggy moral universe of business. As they begin to contemplate career paths, they may feel confused by conflicts between their own moral and material goals. See the Resources below for some excellent guides to raising moral children.

CHAPTER 3 RESOURCES

General

Magical Child: by Joseph Chilton Pearce (Plume, 1977).
  Pearce is a seminal Whole Parenting thinker. In this holistic classic on maximizing the developmental potential of children, he takes many controversial stands but ranks with Leboyer as a child advocate.
The Wonder of Boys: by Michael Gurian (Tarcher/Putnam, 1996).
  Addresses how to channel boys' potentially destructive aggressive energy so that it serves the positive purposes nature intended for it.

Reading to Your Child—Why It Matters

BOOKS ABOUT READING ALOUD
The Read-Aloud Handbook by Jim Trelease (Penguin, 1979).
  Trelease's classic guide makes a detailed case for reading aloud and includes one hundred pages of reviews of good read-aloud books.

Read to Me: Raising Kids Who Love to Read by Bernice E. Cullinan (Scholastic, Inc., 1992).

    This is a warm, wise, and informed argument for reading aloud, by a reading specialist and NYU professor. It includes reviews of good read-aloud books.

GUIDES TO GOOD CHILDREN'S LITERATURE

American Library Association Best of the Best for Children, edited by Denise Perry Donavin (Random House, 1992).

    This official guide reviews books, magazines, videos, audiotapes, software, toys, and even rich travel destinations such as the Smithsonian Museums.

The Best Toys, Books, & Videos for Kids by Joanne Oppenheim and Stephanie Oppenheim (Harper-Perennial, 1993).

    This book is based on *The Oppenheim Toy Portfolio,* an independent, nationally recognized consumer's review of children's media.

Books Kids Will Sit Still For by Judy Freeman (R.R. Bowker, 1990).

    The index of this general read-aloud guide to children's books, by an elementary school librarian, includes useful multicultural categories such as "Africa," "African Americans," "Mexico," "China," "Chinese Americans," and "Japan."

Eyeopeners! by Beverly Kobrin (Viking, 1988).

    An excellent, smart, exceedingly friendly guide to selecting good nonfiction for children.

The "Right" Toys—Playthings That Reflect Your Values and Help Your Children Realize Their Potential

BOOKS ABOUT TOYS AND PLAY

Playthings as Learning Tools: A Parents' Guide by Joan P. Isenberg and Judith E. Jacobs (John Wiley & Sons, 1982).

    Easy-to-understand explanations of child development and how play affects it. Excellent information on using ordinary household items as toys.

Who's Calling the Shots?: How to Respond Effectively to Children's Fascination with War Play and War Toys by Nancy Carlsson-Paige and Diane E. Levin (New Society Publishers, 1990).

    This revelatory book by two education professors show how the deregulation of children's television and the resulting takeover of programming by toymakers has changed the landscape of children's play.

Your Child's Growing Mind by Jane M. Healy, Ph.D. (Doubleday, 1987).

    Discusses how to maximize your child's developmental potential. Healy, a veteran teacher and mother as well as scholar, shows how the right toys and appropriate play meet kids' developmental needs.

GUIDES TO TOYS AND PLAYTHINGS

See *American Library Association Best of the Best for Children* and *The Best Toys, Books, & Videos for Kids,* reviewed above

TOY MANUFACTURERS AND MAIL-ORDER SOURCES

Culture Crafts (Lerner Publications), (800) 328–4929

website: www.lernerbooks.com

    A series of books that teach kids ages seven to ten how to make traditional crafts from a variety of cultures, including African and Mexican; $17 each. Call for a free catalog.

HearthSong, 6519 N. Galena Road, P.O. Box 1773 [both addresses needed], Peoria, IL 61656–1773, (800) 325–2502

website: www.hearthsong.com

This Waldorf-inspired company offers a lovely, inviting collection of hands-on toys, games, kites, musical instruments, and other fun stuff designed to help the "magical child" unfold.

The Natural Baby Catalog, 7835–3 Freedom Avenue NW, Suite 2, North Canton, OH 44720–6907, (800) 388–BABY
e-mail: nbaby@cannet.com

A good source of baby toys made of natural materials.

Bringing Diversity Home

Anti-Bias Curriculum: Tools for Empowering Young Children by Louise Derman-Sparks and the A.B.C. Task Force (National Association for the Education of Young Children, 1989); order the book by calling (800) 424–2460

A classic among progressive educators, this 150-page manual offers a wealth of strategies and readings for handling issues regarding disabilities, gender, race, and diversity with children between two and five years old.

40 Ways to Raise a Nonracist Child by Barbara Mathias and Mary Ann French (HarperPerennial, 1996).

Full of anecdotes and insights that resonate many layers deeper than most in this genre. It offers useful age-specific strategies, too.

Raising the Rainbow Generation: Teaching Your Child to Be Successful in a Multicultural Society by Darlene Powell Hopson and Derek S. Hopson (Fireside, 1993).

The Hopsons' approach to this sensitive subject is gentle, thorough, and compassionate. Particularly good is the section explaining how bias is usually a product of low self-esteem and poor self image. It has excellent examples.

Multicultural Books, Toys, and Other Resources

BOOKS AND OTHER PUBLICATIONS FOR PARENTS

Child's Play Around the World: 170 Crafts, Games, and Projects for Two-to-Six-Year-Olds by Leslie Hamilton (New York, NY: Perigee/Berkley, 1996).

Most of these activities rely on ordinary household materials. All foster a bond with, and teach about, children from other countries and cultures.

That's Me! That's You! That's Us! by Francenia L. Emery (Philadelphia, PA: The Multicultural Resource Center, 1998); order by calling (215) 438–2729.

Based on the premise that literature allows children to "walk in another's shoes," this immense, comprehensive annotated bibliography of multicultural books is organized by such categories as biracial experiences, intergenerational experiences, gay and lesbian issues, and gender equity.

RESOURCE GUIDES AND CATALOGS

Adoptive Families of America's *The Bookstore* catalog, 2309 Como Avenue, St. Paul, MN 55108, (612) 645–9955, (800) 372–3300 (orders)
website: www.adoptivefam.org

Adoption organizations such as this one probably provide the most comprehensive and useful sources of multicultural children's materials. In addition to addressing different cultural backgrounds, the catalog covers such topics as physical disabilities, learning disorders, attention disorders, building self-esteem, and teaching tolerance.

See also *Best of the Best for Children, Books Kids Will Sit Still For, Eyeopeners!,* and *Raising the Rainbow Generation* reviewed above and reviews of multicultural folktales, myths, and legends below.

Folk and Wisdom Tales

BOOKS ABOUT CHILDREN'S MAGICAL LITERATURE

The Ordinary and the Fabulous; by Elizabeth Cook (Cambridge University Press, 1976).

Cook beautifully describes the role magical literature plays in children's lives, compares different versions of the popular tales, and discusses the stories' significant symbols.

The Uses of Enchantment: The Meaning and Importance of Fairy Tales by Bruno Bettelheim (Vintage, 1975).

The best-known book on the subject. Although its reputation has been marred by controversy about Bettelheim, it remains a passionate and intriguing argument for the continued relevance of fairy tales to today's kids.

RESOURCE GUIDES AND CATALOGS

See *Best of the Best for Children* and *Books Kids Will Sit Still For,* reviewed on p. 127

TV or Not TV?

BOOKS AND OTHER PUBLICATIONS FOR PARENTS

Endangered Minds by Jane M. Healy, Ph.D. (Simon & Schuster, 1990).

Healy's book addresses the effect that several modern factors, including excessive TV, may have on developing minds. This is an important work that paints an alarming but not hopeless picture.

The Smart Parent's Guide to Kids' TV by Milton Chen, Ph.D., and Andy Bricky (San Francisco, CA: Bay Books, 1994). To order call (800) 358–3000).

The Center for Media Literacy (see below) calls this "the best book yet on why parents need to take control of their children's television watching." It includes an excellent resource list.

BOOKS AND OTHER PUBLICATIONS FOR KIDS

The Bionic Bunny Show by Marc Brown and Laurene Krasny Brown (Boston, MA: Atlantic Monthly Press/Little, Brown & Co., 1984).

This multiple-award-winner helps make kids wise to TV's tricks by showing them how TV shows are made. A video version narrated by LeVar Burton is also available (check your local library).

The TV Book: The Kids' Guide to Talking Back by Shelagh Wallace (Toronto and New York, NY: Annick Press Ltd., 1996).

Wallace covers TV production, program "hooks," advertising, TV violence, the future of television, and much more. She shows activist-minded young viewers how to fight back.

ORGANIZATIONS

Center for Media Literacy, 4727 Wilshire Boulevard, Suite 403, Los Angeles, CA 90010, (323) 931–4177 or (800) 226–9494
website: www.medialit.org

Excellent source of media literacy materials for home and classroom including materials that train parents and educators to teach critical thinking.

Should I Let My Child Watch Violent TV Programs?

BOOKS AND OTHER PUBLICATIONS

Big World, Small Screen: The Role of Television in American Society by Aletha C. Huston, et al. (University of Nebraska Press, 1992).

This is the official report by the American Psychological Association that reviewed exist-ing research on violent programming. It's surprisingly accessible.

Facets Non-Violent, Non-Sexist Children's Video Guide compiled by Virginia A. Boyle (Facets Multi-media, 1996).

The films are also selected for life-affirming, culturally diverse content.

Mind and Media: The Effects of Television, Video Games, and Computers by Patricia M. Greenfield (Cam-bridge, MA: Harvard University Press, 1984).

One of the earliest, and most comprehensive, analyses of the social and cognitive effects of video games and computers, and a cogent distillation of research related to television.

ORGANIZATIONS

Children's Television and Resource Center, 444 De Haro Street, Suite 117, San Francisco, CA 94107, (415) 864–8424

This group focuses on the effects of violence and advertising in TV and video games.

See also Center for Media Literacy listing on p. 129.

Should I Let My Child Play with War Toys or Violent Video Games?

BOOKS

See *Who's Calling the Shots?*, reviewed on p. 127

ORGANIZATIONS

The Lion & Lamb Project, 4300 Montgomery Avenue, Suite 104, Bethesda, MD 20814, phone (301) 654–3091

website: www.lionlamb.org

This organization helps parents find alternatives to violent toys and entertainment for children. Contact them for a parent action kit and information.

COMPUTER GAMES

SimCity and *SimEarth* from Electronic Arts, P.O. Box 7530, San Mateo, CA 94403, (800) 245–4525

website: www.ea.com

In *SimCity,* players actually plan out a city—either a real city such as San Francisco or Rio de Janeiro, or their own fantasy metropolis. Every planning or zoning decision affects the economy, environment, and quality of life, and players learn how the many elements of human society impact individuals and the community. A related game, *SimEarth,* does much the same thing from a global perspective. See the Electronic Arts catalog for new games in this series.

Raising a Moral Child

Beyond the Classroom by Laurence Steinberg, Ph.D. (Simon & Schuster, 1996).

Primarily about how parent modeling and child rearing styles affect children's school performance, the book also has much to say about how these factors affect children in other ways, including their moral behavior. It's research-based but presented in clear, easy-to-read language. Superb.

Bringing Up a Moral Child by Michael Schulman and Eva Mekler (Reading, MA: Addison-Wesley, 1985).

The authors, both psychologists, are modern, progressive, and flexible in their approach to difficult subjects such as sex and drugs. They don't preach which morals to adopt.

Rather, they show you how to best teach your own values. The book is comprehensive, nondogmatic, and developmentally oriented.

A Call to Character: A Family Treasury edited by Colin Greer and Herbert Kohl (New York, NY: HarperCollins, 1995).

This is a progressive alternative to the severe William Bennett book which he wrote from a social conservative's perspective. This collection includes stories, poems, and other writings that help develop values.

Teaching Tolerance by Sara Bullard (Doubleday, 1996).

Excellent at showing how authoritarian parenting can lead to racism and other forms of aggression and hatred. Bullard shows how important it is for children to feel secure and comfortable with themselves if they are to be comfortable and accepting of others.

family wellness

mericans have become so intrigued by alternative health approaches and so uncomfortable with conventional medicine that they are changing the face of healthcare. Adults spend billions of dollars every year seeing alternative practitioners. Herbs are becoming as common in home medicine chests as Tylenol. To win patients back, many medical doctors now profess openness to holistic methods where once they sneered at them as if they were an embarrassing relative. Some insurance companies are even writing policies that pay for care from licensed alternative practitioners such as naturopaths and acupuncturists. And yet, despite these accommodations by the healthcare establishment, more and more people are jumping ship, treating themselves at home with herbs and over-the-counter homeopathic remedies and seeing alternative practitioners even when they have to pay out-of-pocket.

Naturally, this revolution is affecting family healthcare, too, but in not quite such a headlong fashion. Parents who are holistically oriented are just as concerned, if not more so, about the side effects conventional drugs and procedures have on their kids as they are about their own bodies. However, they're far less willing to take the same chances with their children that they would with themselves. Many realize that little research has been done on the ability of alternative treatments to provide deep, lasting healing and relief, and that is immensely frustrating when they're already distrustful of conventional approaches.

What alternatives can be safely used with kids? Which are the most effective? When is conventional medicine the best option? In this chapter, we help you sort through what's known and what's not so you can make informed decisions regarding alternative professionals such as homeopaths, chiropractors, and naturopaths, and treat your kids effectively and safely with herbs. It is beyond the scope of this book to give you comprehensive guidance for all medical situations, but we do point you in the right direction to find more detailed information.

Holistic healthcare starts at home with preventive self-care, not in a healthcare professional's office. In this chapter, we cover family exercise, one of the pillars of holistic health, and its importance for children in their increasingly sedentary lives (we devote an entire chapter to another of those pillars, diet, because it's such a big subject). Even in most holistic households, chemicals and other toxins pervade the environs from paint to ceramic dishes. You have to be well-informed, as well as take a number of preventive steps, to protect your family—especially your youngest children, who are most vulnerable—from toxins around your house. We'll guide you to the best ways to secure the nursery and general home environment against the most common environmental health problems.

MICHAEL ALLEN JONES

Where teens are involved, the issue of drug abuse can't be ignored as a health concern. The politics surrounding drug use are so volatile that few public officials or drug educators feel free to tell the unfettered truth about these substances and how teens use them. We give you a perspective on the matter that you might not have heard or considered before. Teen sex, too, is a preventive health issue, considering the frequency of unwanted teen pregnancies and the dangers of sexually transmitted dis-

"holistic" or "natural"— what they mean for your family's health

Many people use the terms "holistic" or "natural" without really thinking about what they mean. Holistic or natural health for families is based on the following ideas:

- The body has a tremendous capacity to heal itself. By living close to nature's design for us and giving as much support as possible to the body's self-healing mechanisms, we maximize our chances for health and healing.

- Thoughts, emotions, and spiritual activities can have powerful effects on the body, both in preventing and healing illness. Conventional medicine acknowledges this principle but pays little heed to it in practice. Many alternative therapies also undervalue the nonphysical aspects of health and healing. Truly holistic therapies give equal consideration to mind, emotions, spirit, and body.

- Natural healthcare aims for a vibrant state of "wellness." Conventional medicine aims primarily for the absence of disease, a much lower state that is more susceptible to recurrent or new illnesses.

- We, not our healthcare providers, are responsible for our health. We act on this responsibility by becoming informed about health; by paying attention to the signals our minds and bodies send us; by eating sensible foods in sensible amounts; by exercising; and by otherwise making healthy choices. If we should fall ill, we learn what we can about our ailment and the treatment options available to us so we can be smart consumers of healthcare and active partners with the professional we select to help us.

- While technological innovations such as chemical drugs and surgery have saved countless lives and are the treatment of choice for many conditions, they inevitably have side effects and are overprescribed. Natural remedies and therapies, along with natural preventive self-care, should be emphasized whenever possible, particularly in noncrisis situations.

- Natural health is a state in which all the elements of life—pleasure, emotional fulfillment, spiritual fulfillment, learning, stress, work, self-expression, service to others, relaxation—exist in balance. A life that leaves out important elements is not balanced.

eases. We show you in this chapter how to establish open communication with your youngsters about sexuality and why it's so important to their sexual—and your emotional!—health.

HOLISTIC PHYSICIANS AND OTHER ALTERNATIVE PRACTITIONERS

The list of therapies under the umbrella of "natural" or "holistic" health is growing almost as quickly as the numbers of Americans attracted to them. In this section, we survey the primary systems families turn to when seeking an alternative to conventional medicine. Most of the therapies covered here are associated with some level of professional licensing. We do not review conventional medicine, still the therapy of choice for most emergency and other serious medical situations, as most readers have sufficient experience with orthodox physicians to draw their own conclusions about this field's successes and failings.

As knowledgeable health consumers well know, mainstream parents sometimes place too much faith in conventional medicine and thereby subject themselves or their children to dangerous or ineffective treatment. Holistically inclined parents often make the opposite mistake—they underrate the ability of conventional doctors to help their families and give alternative therapies undeserved bonus points just for being different. This uncritical attitude leaves these families vulnerable to dangerous and ineffective treatment as well.

We've tried to bridge this gap by noting valid criticisms of both conventional and alternative practices and referring readers to resources that will help them make informed choices. But in general, always take your child to an M.D. first if there is any chance she is seriously ill.

Traditional Chinese Medicine

History and description. Traditional Chinese medicine is based on ideas that could hardly be more different from those of conventional medicine. Yet on its own terms, it is a careful science with a long, glorious history. Practices such as acupuncture may go back thousands of years, but they are commonly used in China today alongside conventional treatments in modern hospitals. They have won grudging respect from Western physicians as well, who know that a considerable body of literature documents the success of certain Chinese medical techniques.

The health theories of Chinese medicine grew out of Taoism, an ancient philosophy that shows followers how to improve their lives—including their health—by bringing them in tune with nature and the universe. As such, Chinese medicine stresses preventive care. Traditional Chinese doctors show their patients that through a balanced lifestyle including moderate diet, exercise, and other habits, they can harmonize their bodies with the heavens and ward off disease.

When making prescriptions, Chinese doctors consider the properties of foods, herbs, organs, and lifestyle habits according to their doctrines of *yin/yang* and *five-element theory.* Yin and yang refer to the opposing but complementary qualities that exist, in various proportions, in everything in the universe. The five elements—wood, fire, air, earth, and water—represent the changing properties of things, which must be considered so a body can stay in balance in a constantly changing universe.

Chinese doctors also see anatomy differently than do Western physicians. Rather than focus on the physical organs, nerves, and blood vessels, Chinese doctors work with nonmaterial systems of bodily function (which they also call "organs") and the invisible pathways—or *meridians*—

that connect them. The invisible energy that travels in those pathways is called *chi*. Chinese medicine uses acupuncture, moxabustion (burning of herbs above acupuncture points), and acupressure (touching or massaging points instead of needling them) to influence *chi* flow for health and healing. Note that while acupuncture is the aspect of Chinese medicine that most fascinates Westerners, herbal medicine is actually used far more extensively, both for prevention and healing.

Uses. You might reasonably see a traditional Chinese doctor for any child's condition appropriate for alternative care (see "When Modern Medicine Makes the Most Sense" on page 150) and Chinese methods are particularly well suited to prevention, the soul of Chinese medicine.

Here in the West, people go to acupuncturists primarily for pain relief for such conditions as back pain, headaches, and arthritis. Western acupuncturists frequently treat smoking, alcoholism, and other substance abuse, as well. Interestingly, none of these are traditional uses of this ancient healing art. In classic Chinese medicine, acupuncture is a primary technique for everything from treatment of serious illness to anesthesia during surgery to prevention of ordinary colds and flu.

How to find a practitioner. Many states issue acupuncture licenses under such titles as Doctor of Oriental Medicine (DOM). Licensing typically requires graduation from a three-year course of study and clinical experience. In some states without licensing, anyone can call himself an acupuncturist, so check credentials before making an appointment. The fact that the practitioner may also hold a medical degree and license is not necessarily an advantage. Most states allow doctors to practice acupuncture with minimal training. On the other hand, a physician who had deeply studied Chinese medicine and acupuncture might be a valuable find indeed. See the Resources at the end of this chapter for organizations that can provide referrals or more information.

What else you should know. Chinese medicine views symptoms differently in children than adults. Pediatrics is a specialty of Chinese medicine, notes Ken Bendat, a licensed acupuncturist trained in China, so make sure your practitioner has been trained appropriately.

Choose your practitioner carefully. Classic Chinese medicine combines meticulously recorded knowledge—gleaned from centuries of practice—with intuitive and subtle skills that take long years to master.

Few acupuncturists schooled in America have learned Chinese medicine in all its complexity. Many practice primarily as pain specialists.

Strict vegetarians should know that Chinese "herbs" include animal products as well as botanicals and minerals. The typical prescription combines up to fifteen substances.

Ayurvedic Medicine

History and description. The recent fame of author and Ayurvedic physician Deepak Chopra and the support of the Maharishi Ma-hesh Yogi has pushed Ayurvedic medicine, the ancient health system of India, to the forefront of natural healthcare. Its practices go back at least 2,500 years, and are described in the Vedas, the earliest Hindu scriptures. In fact, it is considered the world's first healing system not based in magic and superstition. Thus, it may even predate Chinese medicine, which was first described in writing about 2,000 years ago.

Ayurveda shares more with Chinese medicine than its antiquity. Like the latter, it teaches that illness arises from disharmony and that, if properly supported, the body can heal itself. It also emphasizes preventive self-care such as proper diet, reducing stress, and adjusting one's lifestyle to the season. Ayurveda doesn't deny that infectious diseases can throw a body out of balance, too, but asserts that those who follow its preventive regimen are less likely to get those diseases in the first place.

---

healing stories 1: traditional chinese medicine

Leah Mazel-Gee, a licensed acupuncturist trained in traditional Chinese medicine, mainly sees adults in her Berkeley, California, practice. However with her own kids, Chinese medicine has made an important contribution, starting early in her son Aaron's life. Leah began giving Aaron Chinese herbs when he was about two. "He was really tiny [in the eighth or ninth percentile] when he was born and had really weak digestion," she recalls, "and the doctors gave me no answers." With the herbs and nutritional adjustments she made, Aaron started growing and now, at 11½, is in about the seventieth percentile, Leah says, with excellent health.

Leah generally prepares the herbs—a mixture can include ten or more substances—as a tea. Adults would normally drink a half a cup of such a concoction twice a day. But that's a lot to bolt down for a child, especially since the tea isn't likely to rate as a favorite beverage. So Leah boils the tea down until there's less than half a cup to consume per day. "It's not really the usual way to do it but I get results," she says.

She normally avoids using acupuncture needles with children, including her own son and daughter, because needles scare most kids. But she's found a mostly willing patient in Aaron, who took up the violin seriously at age 10 ½ and then began complaining of neck pain. "He's often a little squeamish about me doing it but he usually lets me," says Leah. She adds that Aaron's willingness is due in part to the treatments themselves, which have eliminated the pain and enabled him to keep up his heavy practice schedule.

Leah is getting more than just bodily responses to her treatments. "One of the issues I'm directing herbal treatment toward in Aaron is what I call prepubescent attitude." In Chinese medical theory, a child at this age is likely to have "liver-chi congestion." Certain herbs alleviate the condition and provide a literal attitude adjustment. "It really has helped," says Leah. "Even my husband admits it's made a difference and he doesn't always pay attention to the treatments I give the kids."

While the basic philosophy may seem clear, the details of Ayurveda are less familiar to Western thinking. Ayurveda sees the life force as being composed of three aspects—called dosha—symbolized by air, earth, and fire. Much as Chinese medicine categorizes everything in the universe according to its yin-yang and five-element properties, Ayurveda analyzes the dosha of everything, including the unique dosha makeup of each patient. Foods, seasons, and even times of day have their dosha character, too, and are considered when prescribing a diet, lifestyle, and daily routine that will keep health in balance.

For example, a teenager whose constitution is primarily *pitta,* the fire dosha, might be demanding, irritable, impatient, and quick to anger. An Ayurvedic practitioner would likely advise this person to reduce or limit consumption of stimulants such as spicy foods and increase exposure to sweet foods and cool, relaxing environments.

Ayurveda is one of the most truly holistic of all the major health systems, both alternative and conventional, because it notes that imbalance and illness will show up both in the physical body and in thoughts and emotions. In fact, "undesirable" thoughts are seen as one of the major causes of illness. And Ayurveda also uses mental/emotional as well as physical tools to treat. This is surprisingly rare in so-called holistic health, as you'll see.

Uses. Like Chinese medicine, Ayurveda has far more to say about preventive healthcare than does conventional medicine. As with any alternative therapy, it is always advisable to see an M.D. first for serious illness, unless the illness is one for which conventional medicine has no answers. But Ayurveda can be followed in conjunction with regular medicine. In fact, some health centers featuring Ayurveda have M.D.s on staff precisely for this reason.

How to find a practitioner. While Ayurveda itself isn't a licensable profession in the U.S., you may well find other licensed healthcare professionals, including M.D.s, who have studied and practice it. The advantage of going to licensed professionals is that they are more likely to make appropriate referrals when the patient's condition calls for it. Another desirable situation is a holistic health center where alternative practitioners work in cooperation with an on-staff M.D. See the Resources at the end of the chapter for an organization that may be useful in this regard.

What else you should know. The wealth and marketing reach of the Maharishi has made his organization a primary promoter of Ayurveda in the

U.S. The Maharishi's organization claims to have repaired the deterioration that Ayurveda suffered during centuries of foreign rule, consulting original Vedic texts to make sure the restored Ayurveda fit the classic mold. It renamed its version Maharishi Ayur-veda.

The Maharishi Ayur-veda literature promotes both the Maharishi's Transcendental Meditation and his herbal products. Meditation and herbs are both key tools in Ayurveda but only the true believers think the Maharishi brands represent an improvement over the "generics." Should you visit a Maharishi clinic, expect to encounter some of these true believer types among the staff.

Homeopathy

History and description. Homeopathy, the prescription of extremely dilute medicines to cure ills, may be the most mysterious of the alternative therapies. Modern science has no way of accounting for how it works and even practitioners struggle to explain it. Yet it boasts a clear record of success; in fact, in its early history, it proved far more effective than conventional medicine for some of the most serious diseases of the time.

German physician Samuel Hahnemann (1755–1843) created homeopathy at a time when medicine was dominated by so-called "heroic" practices with no scientific basis, including prescribing large doses of dangerous drugs that were little understood. Hahnemann seemed to be one of the few physicians who noticed the harm their profession was causing.

Hahnemann was also a trained chemist and a deeply spiritual man who believed that medicine's proper role was to safely support the patient's God-given healing powers. Driven to develop effective treatments that met this criteria, he began experimenting on himself with the drugs of the day. He soon noticed that many of the medicines that worked produced symptoms like the disease they were used to treat. For instance, chinchona—from which quinine, an anti-malaria drug, is made—gave him malaria-like symptoms. From these experiments came the first principle of his new therapy, the Law of Similars, or "like cures like." In other words, the best medicine for a patient was a substance that produced the same symptoms in a healthy person.

If Hahnemann had stopped here, modern medicine would have applauded him, for vaccinations and allergy desensitization are based on much the same idea. But he also noticed that even useful medicines caused disturbing side effects if given in large doses. To solve this problem, he developed a process of continually diluting the medicine until the side effects disappeared. He felt the process made the medicines even more effective, but it also made his new therapy perpetually controversial. Many of his preparations were so dilute that not a single molecule of the original substance remained. To Hahnemann, this may have confirmed the spiritual basis of healing, as if some sort of energy left behind by the substance was more powerful than the substance itself. But it drove—and still drives—orthodox physicians batty because their training makes it difficult to accept a healing method that can't be seen or measured, even if it works.

Despite the controversy, homeopathy caught on with the public in the nineteenth century, purely on the basis of documented successes with such horrific diseases as cholera, scarlet fever, typhoid, and yellow fever. Starting in the 1840s, the new but powerful American Medical Association (AMA) fought a determined and successful campaign against homeopathy, which it feared as economic competition. By the 1920s, professional homeopathy had all but disappeared in America. But the natural health revival of recent decades has fueled a comeback of this fascinating therapeutic approach. Today, many physicians—along with other licensed alternative practitioners such as naturopaths and many lay practitioners—prescribe homeopathic remedies.

Homeopathy doesn't make a distinction between physical, mental, and emotional problems. It teaches that disease affects the whole being, so remedies apply to nonphysical conditions as well.

Uses. Homeopaths recommend orthodox medicine for treating serious infections, infectious diseases, and other acute or emergency medical situations that may require antibiotics, setting of bones, surgery, and so on. In such instances, practitioners may recommend homeopathy alongside conventional treatment to support the healing process. More commonly, however, patients seek homeopathic treatment for:

- safe alternatives to chemical drugs for kids, pregnant women, and older people

- systemic upsets such as anemia or hormone imbalances

- chronic physical problems such as headaches, arthritis, high blood pressure, obesity, peptic ulcer, allergies, and colitis

- prevention of illness and maintenance of optimal health

- psychological and emotional upsets

How to fnd a practitioner. Most states in the U.S. recognize the right of licensed healthcare practitioners to practice homeopathy, and the remedies can be legally prescribed. Practicing true homeopathy requires considerable knowledge and skill because of the highly individualized patient interview and the thousands of available remedies. Look for practitioners—whether M.D.s, dentists, naturopaths, other alternative professionals, or lay homeopaths—who are intuitive, caring people as well as serious students of homeopathy.

There are a few of ways to identify shallow practitioners. Those who prescribe more than one remedy at a time are violating one of Hahnemann's basic principles, that a doctor should see what the first remedy does before prescribing another. And be wary if you feel you're getting a generic exam and treatment instead of something that is highly specific to your characteristics and condition. See the Resources at the end of this chapter for an organization that can help you find homeopaths in your area.

What else you should know. Orthodox doctors claim that those homeopathic remedies that work act as *placebos.* That is, the patient's belief in a practice's power to heal can sometimes be so strong that the body responds to her mind's suggestion. Although this probably explains the success of homeopathy in many cases, it also explains the success of orthodox medicine at times. However, homeopathic remedies also work on infants and animals. Presumably, these patients don't have any particular beliefs or expectations about the remedies.

Conventional doctors who scoff at the ability of such dilute substances to affect the body are also ignoring some similar remedies in their own black bag. For example, smallpox vaccine was developed from tiny amounts of material from cowpox lesions.

Homeopathic remedies are sold directly to customers in health food stores and pharmacies, a practice that homeopathic professionals don't support. They believe that patients should see a trained practitioner for all but minor complaints. Excellent guides to homeopathic self-care have been published, however. See the Resources at the end of this chapter for a review of one.

Finally, liquid homeopathic remedies have been diluted in alcohol, something parents may not want to give to their kids.

Osteopathy

History and description. Because they lack medical licensing, most alternative practitioners operate at a severe disadvantage. On the surface, osteopathy is the exception to the rule. Although classical osteopathy is based on ideas that are radically different from those of orthodox medicine, osteopaths are licensed to practice medicine in all fifty states. There is nothing that traditional doctors do that osteopaths aren't also licensed to do. They can perform surgery. They can prescribe drugs. And patients can bill most health insurance providers for their services.

However, note that you will have to look hard to find a true alternative practitioner among the current generation of D.O.s (doctors of osteopathy). The majority of osteopaths emphasize the orthodox medicine that they learn in osteopathic medical school. Only a few still practice the bone manipulation techniques that set them part from conventional doctors, even though they are trained in them as well. Modern osteopaths are, in effect, physicians under a different title, although osteopathy—which means "bone treatment"—in its original form represented a true holistic and natural approach to healing.

Much like Samuel Hahnemann before him, osteopathy founder Andrew Taylor Still (1828–1917) was a conventionally trained physician who became disillusioned with the methods of his own profession. His passion to create an alternative grew after he lost three children to spinal meningitis. Still shared Hahnemann's spiritual faith in the body's capacity to heal itself, and felt that the doctor's role should be to support that ability, which the toxic drugs of the day certainly did not. Personal experience and intuition led him to develop techniques of bone manipulation in which tension is applied to joints until they "pop." These techniques became the foundation of osteopathy.

The classic osteopathy that Still developed takes the holistic view that all of the body's organs and systems—including the brain—are part of an interrelated whole. Thus, a problem in any part of the body will affect other parts. Classic osteopaths see symptoms as signs of imbalance in the whole body. Unlike orthodox doctors, they are less concerned with treating symptoms than finding and correcting the cause of that imbalance. This paves the way, they feel, for the body's innate healing abilities to take over and eliminate the problem either on its own or with the help of further specific treatments.

Still achieved great success with his techniques, not only with musculoskeletal problems but even with serious infectious diseases such as pneumonia and typhoid. But determined to monopolize healthcare, medical organizations began a withering assault on osteopathy's credibility. After Still died, many osteopaths began modifying their practices to more closely resemble those of conventional physicians.

Uses. Very few studies have been done on the effectiveness of osteopathy with children's ailments. However, D.O.s have full medical training and make referrals to traditional doctors and hospitals as appropriate. So you or your family members might reasonably see them for any condition for which you would see a conventional physician.

Classic osteopathy, where you can find it, is said to be effective with musculoskeletal problems including work- and sports-related injuries such as back, neck, wrist, elbow, and leg pains; migraines and other headaches; respiratory problems such as bronchitis, emphysema, and asthma; cerebral palsy; infectious diseases (in combination with appropriate antibiotics); sinusitis; circulatory problems; and digestive disorders.

One of Still's students, W.G. Sutherland, developed an osteopathic specialty called cranial osteopathy (manipulation of the skull bones) that is practiced today with apparent great success by some D.O.s. Cranial osteopathy is reputed to be highly effective with children's ear infections.

Osteopathy can also be used preventively. For example, treatment of posture problems aligns the body with the pull of gravity and may prevent future musculoskeletal injuries and pain.

How to find a practitioner. Most modern D.O.s practice orthodox medicine, so you will have to request classic osteopathy if that is what you seek. See the Resources at the end of this chapter for professional organizations that can refer you to osteopaths, classic and otherwise, in your area.

What else you should know. Many modern D.O.s criticize classical osteopathy's fixation on musculoskeletal problems, which they say is overly focused on the physical manifestation of disease. They may have a point. Many so-called holistic therapies all but ignore the mental/emotional aspects of illness. For example, if emotional fears have led a patient to habitually hunch his shoulders, then manipulation only treats the effect, not the cause. Doctors trained in physical arts—whether osteopathy, chiropractic, or orthodox medicine—aren't always as sensitive as they should be to the emotional side of health, no matter how much they celebrate the mind/body connection in words. An osteopath who gives more consideration to mind/body factors than either classic D.O.s or M.D.s may indeed have something special to offer.

Chiropractic

History and description. Any health approach that challenges physicians' ideas and methods will draw orthodox medicine's ire. However, the controversy surrounding chiropractic is partly of this alternate therapy's own making, originating early in its history.

Daniel David Palmer developed chiropractic in the 1890s while searching for a single cause that explained all illness. His studies led him to focus on the art of spinal manipulation. Acting on his intuition, he claimed to have cured deafness in a local janitor and to have restored health to a man with a heart condition by pressing on key vertebrae. These two experiences convinced him that he had found the universal cause to disease that he had sought. However, true scientists would have gathered far more evidence than two case histories before drawing the conclusion Palmer did. And Palmer invited even more doubt because unlike the founders of homeopathy or osteopathy, he was a grocer by trade, not a trained physician.

According to Palmer's theory, which became the basis of modern chiropractic, the brain communicates with, and sends vital energy to, every organ through the spinal nerves. Vertebrae that press on these nerves interfere with the normal transmission through them, leading to disease. Palmer named these misaligned vertebrae "subluxations" and the manipulative techniques he devised to correct them "adjustments." By freeing up the blocked nerves, adjustments are said to restore normal transmissions, allowing the innate healing power of the body to take over and finish the job of recovery.

Palmer opened the first chiropractic school in 1897, its only admission requirement a $450 fee. He later sold the school and business to his son, Bartlett Joshua Palmer. B.J., as he was known, built his school into the foundation of a multimillion dollar empire, but it was essentially a diploma mill that marketed itself by loudly advertising its lack of entrance requirements and exams. B.J.'s father came to disavow his former school and the doctors it turned out. B.J.'s son David Daniel Palmer took over the school in 1961, upgrading its professional image without altering the basic healing philosophy and techniques it taught.

Chiropractic ultimately split into two main groups of practitioners. "Straights" practice strict, Palmer-style chiropractic; "Mixers" combine classical adjustments with other techniques such as physical therapy, other alternative forms of bodywork, and even nutrition counseling. Most chiropractors fall in the Mixer camp. A few rarely employ adjustments at all, using the chiropractic license as a legal cover to practice their own preferred blend of alternative therapies.

Uses. While research documents chiropractic's effectiveness in treating adults with back and neck pain, almost no such studies exist concerning children, who rarely suffer such ailments anyway. (When children have back pain, spinal infections and cancer should be ruled out by a physician.) To a lesser extent, patients also seek chiropractic treatment for migraines and other headaches, some of which are related to misaligned neck vertebrae; menstrual pain; stomach problems; allergies; asthma; and problems in the extremities such as hands and feet. It might be wise to determine if your chiropractor is a Straight or Mixer before going in for problems that do not involve the neck or spinal area. A Mixer is more likely to have the tools for treating the wide range of conditions just mentioned.

How to find a practitioner. In most towns of any size, you'll have your choice of D.C.s (doctors of chiropractic). As with any health professional, you are better off getting a professional or personal referral. All fifty states and provinces throughout Canada license chiropractors, and government insurance in both countries, as well as many private insurers, will cover treatment for certain conditions.

What else you should know. Despite the controversies that plague the profession, many chiropractic patients swear by their D.C. These satisfied customers include many who failed to get results from orthodox medicine.

Orthodox physicians criticize chiropractors for taking unnecessarily frequent and large X rays, exposing their patients to increased radiation. (The small X-ray films commonly used by allopaths require far less radiation.) Chiropractors respond to charges of reckless X-ray use by saying that modern X-ray equipment provides adequate protection for patients. You should ask your D.C. to verify that his machine is state-of-the-art and has been recently inspected as required by law. Be aware that overuse of X rays is particularly dangerous to children.

Keep in mind that chiropractic is philosophically disposed toward regarding almost every spine as needing adjustment, a fact that could make you unintentionally dependent on your doctor's services. Individual chiropractic treatments don't cost nearly as much as a visit to a conventional M.D. but the total treatment cost can add up over time.

Chiropractic is a "natural" therapy in that it doesn't rely on drugs or surgery and its basic thrust is to encourage the body's innate healing capacities. Yet it violates another core principle of natural medicine by teaching that health depends upon treatment by skilled practitioners rather than preventive self-care. And the notion that all disease is caused by subluxations is much narrower even than the disease theories of conventional medicine, not to mention the body-mind-emotions-spirit concepts of holistic health. Nevertheless, a dedicated search will turn up many true holistic practitioners operating under the chiropractic license, so be persistent and ask questions.

Naturopathy

History and description. In all its traditional methods, naturopathy sticks closely to natural health principles, particularly the concept of giving the body's innate healing capacity as much support as possible. Naturopaths teach their patients to take an active role in maintaining their own health by eating healthful foods, getting adequate exercise, eliminating toxins including alcohol and drugs, and making other lifestyle changes that allow the body to function at its peak. When the patient's condition requires professional intervention, naturopaths rely entirely on natural remedies, for they share other alternative practitioners' low opinion of the side effects of conventional drugs and surgery.

Beyond this, naturopaths are hard to pigeonhole because the profession has never developed the detailed philosophy that distinguishes other alternative approaches such as homeopathy or chiropractic. Naturopathy seems to have roots in the European health and healing spas that were in vogue in the previous two centuries. It gained the formal trappings of a health practice in 1900 when the first naturopathic college was founded by Benedict Lust, a German physician who had come to the U.S. eight years earlier. But Lust had no compelling health vision and naturopathy reflects his vague concepts. It is a field that attracts practitioners and patients who believe in common principles of health, but methods can vary widely from doctor to doctor.

Uses. Because naturopathy is an umbrella profession, the conditions for which your family would reasonably see a naturopath for will vary with each doctor's particular skills and specialties. Certainly, N.D.s (doctors of naturopathy) are a sensible choice when you think you or your child may be suffering from a lifestyle-related ailment, want to avoid drugs, and are willing to make some life changes to assist the healing. Many serious illnesses respond well to metabolic therapies (e.g., nutrition therapy) such as those that N.D.s practice.

The types of conditions for which people see homeopaths, Ayurvedic doctors, and doctors of Oriental medicine also apply, in general, to naturopathy. In fact, many N.D.s integrate aspects of other alternative therapies such as homeopathy, Ayurveda, acupuncture, acupressure, massage, and holistic bodywork into their practice. N.D.s are well-trained to make appropriate referrals to conventional physicians and specialists when necessary.

How to find a practitioner. Naturopathy is licensed in roughly one fourth of American states, most of those in the West. To become licensed, N.D.s take a four-year course of graduate study at one of the U.S.'s two accredited schools of naturopathy, the National College of Naturopathic Medicine and the John Bastyr College of Naturopathic Medicine. See Resources at the end of this chapter to locate a practitioner in your area.

What else you should know. Naturopathic education and training is considered quite strong. This wasn't always so—many middle-aged naturopaths became credentialed at a time when students could simply take a mail-order course and label themselves N.D.s. Be sure to check the education of any N.D. you plan to see.

Many naturopaths administer hair analysis tests, upon which they base recommendations for special diets or nutritional supplements. Hair analysis is a controversial procedure that has yet to be proven scientifically valid. If your N.D. relies too heavily on by-the-numbers approaches like this rather than closely observing the patient before him, he may not deserve your family's patronage.

A further caution: Whenever hair analysis—or even a medical blood test—is used as the basis to sell you a regimen of vitamin and mineral supplements, watch your wallet. Supplements are expensive and often constitute a lucrative side business for practitioners. You should be skeptical of any practitioner who profits by the sale of supplements rather than simply sending you to the nearest health food store for them. This isn't a particular sin of N.D.s. Many other health practitioners, including M.D.s, are caught in the same or similar conflicts of interest.

**healing stories II:
holistic medicine**

As we've noted, many so-called holistic physicians practice a narrow range of methods that, while alternative, may not truly qualify as "holistic." But such distinctions hardly matter when those methods produce spectacular results. Consider the report of Donna Garrett of Klamath Falls, Oregon.

Donna's son Timmy was born six weeks prematurely with a host of symptoms his doctors described as "premature lung disease," she says. The strong antibiotics they treated him with cleared up the symptoms, but over the next few years, a host of physical and developmental problems appeared including seizures, delayed coordination, and speech difficulties (Timmy wasn't fully verbal until he was five), and behavior problems. "He had trouble sitting still, completing tasks, and doing simple things like picking up toys unless I was right there to literally hold his hand," recalls Donna. "Discipline wasn't an issue because it really wasn't effective." Timmy also began to lose weight.

Timmy's doctors couldn't explain why these things were happening or what to do about them. When Timmy was six, he told his mother that his chest "felt funny" and he "needed medicine." So Donna took him in for more tests, which were again inconclusive. When the best the doctors could offer them was to repeat the test battery, Donna decided that it was time to pursue other options. Meanwhile, her employer, who had been diagnosed with cancer, had gone to see a holistic physician, Dr. Peters, in a nearby town. When her boss returned, he suggested Donna take Timmy for a consultation.

(continued on next page)

Holistic Medicine

History and description. "Holistic medicine" loosely refers to licensed M.D.s who combine various alternative therapies with orthodox medical practices. Despite the presence of an American Holistic Medical Associ-ation, holistic doctors have never fully organized to develop a detailed philosophy or standards that govern what and how they practice. As a result, practices in so-called holistic medicine range all over the alternative map. However, this may eventually change because holistic medicine is still a relatively young phenomenon.

"Holistic physician" has become a catchphrase that attracts patients who want something different from what conventional physicians offer but still want the experience, training, and the medical insurance eligibility that an M.D. license promises. "Holistic" *should* mean that the doctor considers mind, emotions, and spirit as well as the physical body when assessing and treating patients' health. But few doctors who call themselves holistic are that comprehensive. Take, for instance, the doctor whose alternative practices boil down to substituting nutritional therapy for drugs wherever possible. Admirable as this approach may be, it still only addresses the physical aspects of the whole person. To their credit, many physicians who call themselves holistic do honor the full meaning of the term.

Uses. Obviously, you can see a holistic physician for any condition a conventional physician might treat. You might also visit a holistic doctor for problems you wouldn't place in the hands of orthodox doctors, such as recommendations for a preventive health regimen, nutritional advice, or consideration of the emotional aspects of an ailment.

How to find a practitioner. A physician's ad in the phone book may indicate whether she is holistically inclined, although you're always better off to get a professional or personal referral before making an appointment. You might also ask to interview the doctor or her staff before making an appointment.

Many physicians who consider their approach holistic have joined the American Holistic Medical Association, which can refer you to member doctors in your area and tell you something about the practices/therapies they use. See the Resources at the end of this chapter for further information.

What else you should know. What many patients, and some doctors, seem to forget is that the faults of the orthodox don't automatically make the alternative better. Some holistically oriented physicians utilize alternative methods and remedies that have never been proven effective. Nor are holistic doctors automatically the best doctors in medical terms. As the saying goes, half of all doctors graduated in the bottom half of their class.

Of course, the best of the holistic approaches and techniques represent true advances over the severe limitations of conventional medicine. Your best strategy as a health consumer is to become well-versed in holistic principles yourself so you can recognize good practitioners when they cross your path. In the meantime, you can still get the best of what conventional medicine has to offer and avoid the worst by bringing your holistic perspectives and knowledge to your doctor's office, requesting what you want, and exerting control over your own treatment.

(continued from previous page)

Peters tested Timmy for food allergies and other systemic problems. He found a yeast infection in his intestines that accounted for Timmy's "camel's breath"—other doctors had told Donna Timmy should just brush his teeth better. Vitamin and mineral deficiencies explained his heart symptoms and seizures, Peters said. Tests revealed that Timmy was allergic to wheat, dairy, eggs, and food dyes, so Peters recommended major dietary changes.

"What I have now is a child who's gained about fifteen pounds and grown several inches," Donna says. "Discipline is no longer an issue. You can discipline him and he understands." Timmy, now eight, is even playing baseball—before seeing Dr. Peters, he didn't have the coordination to throw a ball properly. "All of it related back to how his system was functioning and what his system was lacking," says Donna. For proof, she points out that when Timmy stays with his dad for a few days (his parents are divorced) and doesn't follow his dietary regimen as closely, his symptoms begin to reappear until Donna gets him established back on his diet.

We spoke separately to Dr. Peters who confirmed that in his opinion many children diagnosed with attention deficit disorder or hyperactivity are suffering from systemic imbalance and/or allergies that can be corrected with diet. While he focuses on dietary and other physical recommendations with children, he strongly advises adults to confront their emotional issues, which he feels are a root cause of many physical symptoms.

SHOULD I CONSIDER ALTERNATIVE TREATMENTS FOR SERIOUS ILLNESS?

It's easy to get smug about natural healing when your kids stay flu-less because of the echinacea you drop into their juice or have fewer allergies because of the holistic diet they're fed. But suppose your child should become seriously ill? Now the choice of whether or not to rely on natural medicine has huge consequences, and the issue is rarely one-sided. Plus, your emotional state almost ensures that you won't be making these decisions when you're at your best.

We can't choose for you, but we can help you answer the following questions in the most informed way. Which conditions should you place in the hands of modern medicine and which should you turn over to an alternative practitioner? How do you know that a particular alternative method is the right one or even effective at all? Is there a middle ground that combines the best of what traditional and natural medicine have to offer? Where do your child's attitudes and beliefs fit? What about your child's quality of life?

When Modern Medicine Makes the Most Sense

Modern medicine is clearly your best choice when time is of the essence and medical techniques have a good record of success. Andrew Weil, M.D., perhaps the nation's most widely respected advocate of natural health, has written that modern medicine "is the most effective system I know" for acute trauma [for example, broken bones and other major bodily injuries]; acute bacterial and fungal infections and several other types of nonviral infections as well; hormonal deficiencies; and acute medical emergencies of almost any type. "If I had overwhelming pneumococcal pneumonia . . . I would want to be treated with penicillin," he says to illustrate his point.

Dr. Weil and many others in alternative healthcare express far less confidence in conventional medicine's ability to treat such conditions as viral infections, nutritional and metabolic diseases (adult-onset diabetes is a good example); most chronic degenerative diseases, allergies, asthma, arthritis, high blood pressure, autoimmune diseases, many forms of cancer, so-called psychosomatic disease, and mental illness. The average physician lacks both the training and philosophical orientation to deal with the emotional, spiritual, and preventive factors that can play a role in many of these ailments. And with several of these conditions (arthritis, high blood pressure, and noncritical allergic reactions, for example), natural health methods may simply be more effective. But Weil advises that any symptoms that are "unusually severe, persistent, or out of the range of your normal experience" be checked out by conventional physicians before you choose a treatment approach.

Natural medicine doesn't always cure what conventional medicine can't. In many cases, such as with most cancers, natural medicine may only offer the advantage of a better quality of life because its methods are less painful and assaultive to the body. While you may read of miraculous cures by this or that natural method, miracles are the exception, not the rule. Those who make miraculous recoveries are usually patients who have made dramatic lifestyle changes, followed their treatment regimen with a vengeance, and perhaps most importantly, believed that what they were doing would work.

Do not rely on the information in this section without doing your own research. Modern medical science is constantly advancing. A condition that was considered hopeless and terminal when these words were written may now be successfully treated by physicians. Patient responsibility—or in the case of an ill child, parent responsibility—is a watchword of natural medicine. Only when you have all the available facts from all sides of the issue can an appropriate choice be made.

For instance, when Phil and Michelle's then-seven-year-old son Gabriel first became ill with leukemia, they learned that the survival rate was quite high with conventional treatment by chemotherapy and radiation. Still, the side effects of those methods were so troubling that they wanted to weigh all their options. They consulted with several respected experts on holistic medicine, all of whom agreed that childhood leukemia was one of those cases where regular medical treatment was the most sensible and promising path.

Combining Natural Methods with Regular Medicine

Even when conventional medicine seems the best choice, natural medicine can usually make a contribution in a supportive role. If your child is ill with cancer, for example, it may well make sense to change her diet along the lines recommended in Chapter 5 for general health, because a body under assault from chemotherapy and radiation can certainly use the kind of reserve strength that good foods and vitamins supply. Exercise provides both physical and psychological benefits to seriously ill patients able to manage it. Exercise strengthens the immune system and muscles atrophied from inactivity and also helps to relieve stress. Norman Cousins, author of *Anatomy of an Illness,* has written convincingly about how laughter and play can help heal. And visualization and meditation techniques—for example, of tumors shrinking or radiation wiping out cancer cells—seem to improve the effectiveness of medical treatments.

But natural methods, too, should be applied sensitively, not shotgun-style, suggests Bernie Siegel, M.D., author of the bestselling *Love, Medicine and Miracles.* For instance, it wouldn't normally be smart for a young cancer patient to continue to eat hot dogs, which contain compounds known to be cancer-causing themselves. But if your child feels that life wouldn't be worth living without her favorite foods, you should pay attention—minds and emotions make at least as much difference in healing as good nutrition. And when you do suggest natural methods to your child, try to stick to only the one or two that make the most sense to you. If you recommend every holistic treatment under the sun, it may confuse her. It will also communicate an air of desperation that can't possibly be helpful to her state of mind.

Conventional medicine and natural methods don't always make good partners. For example, the professionals who preside over some clinics offering alternative cancer therapies may advise that you only pursue their program if you and your child are willing to forgo regular medicine entirely. This recommendation is not usually made because of professional competition but because many alternative treatments are designed to work in ways that aren't compatible with regular medicine. Like natural health methods in general, these treatments are intended to strengthen and detoxify the ill body; methods such as radiation and chemotherapy work by attacking the diseased body with extreme toxins. Obviously, you won't accomplish much by using treatments that work at cross-purposes to each other. Along the same lines, some alternative clinics will advise that you come to them as your first choice, not for a last desperate try after conventional methods have failed.

However, therapy combinations that were once unthinkable now make more sense. In cancer therapy, for example, chemotherapy/radiation is not the devastating regimen it once was. Thus, in many cases, alternative clinics welcome patients who want to use their methods in a supportive role.

Choosing the Appropriate Natural Method

Natural approaches work in dramatically different ways from regular medicine but you should still demand evidence that they are effective. Stories of spectacular cures and other successful natural treatments abound in magazines, tabloid television shows, and on the street. Even when the stories are accurate, they hardly prove that the methods will work for your child.

Ideally, you would only choose treatments that have been tested on children in randomized, double-blind, controlled experiments. But you won't always be able to find evidence of this order, even in conventional medicine, which is far less scientifically regulated than you might imagine. For instance, even over-the-counter drugs approved by the government may produce dangerous side effects, especially after long-term use. And, although it may be difficult to believe, the government doesn't require new surgical methods or diagnostic methods to be tested for either safety or effectiveness unless they involve new substances, which are regulated by the U.S. Food and Drug Administration.

Nevertheless, you still want to be as confident as possible that a method you choose—conventional or alternative—has worked, or at least shown promise, for some people. If scientific studies have been done on a method, you'll want to know about them. Thanks to computers, you can research these matters on your own from your home or at your local library. The Internet is a fertile source of this information, and most libraries have computers with easy-to-use software that includes thousands of articles from medical journals and health magazines, including natural health publications. For more researching treatment alternatives, see Michael Lerner's *Choices in Healing,* reviewed in the Resources at the end of this chapter.

The Role of Attitude and Belief

Some treatment methods clearly work much better than others, but it's just as clear that there's more to healing than choosing the right approach. Question people who have survived cancer and you will hear fervent claims that diet "did it." Or exercise. Or meditation. Or herbs. Or a master surgeon across the country. Or the Christian Science practitioner from their local church. Obviously, these methods wildly conflict in philosophy and practice, yet they have all produced their share of cures. So there must be some aspect of healing that is bigger than any particular technique and yet present in all of them. The only conceivable common denominator is attitude and belief. We suspect that in almost every case where a patient has beaten overwhelming odds against his recovery, you'll find that he had absolute faith that the method he chose would heal him.

Given this evidence, it's hard to imagine an argument for leaving your child out of the decision process, as long as she's old enough to understand the options. Ideally, you would research all the treatment possibilities, present them to her as objectively and positively as possible, and either leave the choice to her or choose together. (Many children won't want the burden or loneliness of choosing by themselves.) But choose does not mean "choose to avoid." As Dr. Siegel puts it, "When a patient says, 'I'm scared to death of surgery' and therefore chooses something else, I can't support that choice. Affirmation aids the body, fear is destructive. Treatment chosen out of fear is unlikely to be helpful."

Indeed, belief also plays a role in the very things that both children and adults fear about medicine. To illustrate the point, one fourth of all chemotherapy patients throw up *before* their next chemotherapy dose. This so-called anticipatory nausea is widely recognized in cancer treatment as purely the result of expecting bad things. Psychological techniques can dramatically reduce or even eliminate these side effects.

Belief can also be used to increase the power of medical treatments, as innovative doctors such as Siegel and Carl Simonton, a pioneer in the medical use of visualization, have shown. Rather than just letting your child be a passive receptor of pills or radiation, encourage him to imagine all the ways that the treatments are helping. Perhaps he can see the radiation as a precision laser zapping cancer cells or a ray gun knocking alien invaders from the sky. Perhaps the medicine is like a powerful stain remover that wipes clean everything in its path.

Quality of Life

When a child suffers from a long-running and life-threatening illness, quality-of-life factors should be considered every bit as seriously as the efficacy of the treatment. You want your child to emotionally support the treatment, not resent it. We've already discussed the questionable wisdom of forcing a "healing" diet on your child. The same goes for treatment routines that interfere with the things in life that your child considers most important. Obviously, your child's priorities may differ from yours, but remember who's the patient. Consider the example of

Sarah, a passionate soccer player but indifferent student who stays sick for several days after chemotherapy. It may be smarter to schedule the treatments so that she can take part in her sport as much as possible, even if that means more missed school days.

A FAMILY HERBAL

The current popularity of herbs shows that progress sometimes moves in circles. Until a renewed interest in natural healing began in the late 1960s, most doctors and consumers considered these remedies leftovers from a more superstitious time. Meanwhile, science's vaccines were defeating one horrific disease after another—smallpox, polio, diptheria. Their success seemed to prove that *these* were the medicines to be trusted.

Fascination with herbs spread quickly in the shaggy-haired counterculture of the 1960s and 1970s. But thanks to growing unhappiness with the side effects of synthetic drugs, the herbal customer base came to include neatly coiffed seniors and middle-class families, too. Today, mass-market versions of herbal products as well as booklets about them are peddled at the checkout stands of ordinary supermarkets all across America.

Nevertheless, the rediscovery of herbal medicine has caused its own set of problems. To find beneficial herbs and herb formulations, you'll have to wander through a maze of undependable products, unsubstantiated claims, pseudoscientific labeling practices, and misinformation from both herbal medicines' advocates and detractors. In addition, some herbs, despite being natural, can harm or cause discomfort, at least with certain uses.

To be a smart and careful consumer of herbal remedies for your family, you have to approach them much as you do natural health treatments in general. Be alert to special situations where conventional medicine really does make more sense. And keep an eye out for shams and hype.

What to Believe

Orthodox physicians and other traditional experts are constantly issuing dire warnings about herbal substances and the perils of treating yourself at home. These warnings are frequently overblown and conceal doctors' and drug companies' interest in preserving their share of the healthcare

**healing stories III:
homeopathy, naturopathy,
and herbs**

You don't hear many dramatic healing stories from parents who have long practiced holistic preventive health methods with their families, but not because the methods aren't effective. In fact, this health approach works *so* well that children in these families tend not to get sick very often, and when they do get ill they are rarely very sick.

Jennifer Battaglia of Rogue River, Oregon notes that her three kids rarely get whatever illness is going around school unless they're careless about washing their hands, a much-overlooked health factor in her opinion. When the kids are sick, she does most of the doctoring herself, with homeopathic remedies, herbs, supplements, and naturopathic water cures (fasting, soaking, and application of cold or hot water to the body). On rare occasions, she has also taken the kids to local naturopaths. "I use them mainly after I've used everything in my arsenal, which is quite large," she says. Only in emergencies does she take the kids to a conventional physician.

Jennifer can't remember natural methods ever not working—she's used them for ear infections, stomach problems, colds, and other common ailments. However, she points out that with homeopathic remedies, it's crucial that you find precisely the right remedy for the patient and condition, a process that requires some experience and knowledge. Jennifer has both—she grew up around homeopathic remedies because her mother

(continued on next page)

market. Nevertheless, you should still approach the herbal marketplace with some caution because of the following facts:

- *Some real dangers.* In a very few cases, consumers have become seriously ill after self-treating themselves with herbs. In a small number of those instances, the ill person has died. For example, the commonly used herb comfrey, contains substances called pyrrolizidine alkaloids which are known to be cancer-causing or harmful to the liver if ingested. Several children have died after drinking tea made from other plants—*not comfrey*—that contain these substances. By the same token, comfrey can be a powerful healing agent when applied topically as opposed to ingested (see p. 159).

- *Lax regulation.* The Food and Drug Administration (FDA) only lightly regulates herbal products, which it classifies as "dietary supplements," not drugs. It doesn't require makers to test products for effectiveness or even safety before marketing them. It only requires makers to assure the public that no ingredient "present(s) a significant or unreasonable risk of illness or injury."

- *Questionable claims.* Very few companies have scientifically documented the claims they make for their products. It's not hard to understand why. Testing according to the standards the FDA sets for chemical drugs could cost hundreds of millions of dollars per product. Because herbs can't be patented, companies would have a tough time recovering those costs.

- *Undependable quality.* As a result of loose regulation and a lack of research, the quality of herbal products, now over a $1.5 billion industry, varies widely. Plus, the form in which the product comes may be ineffective even if the herb in another form is helpful.

Of course, these problems have to be considered in the context of the overall quality and safety of the alternative to herbs, the chemical drugs prescribed by orthodox physicians. Many drugs that are closely regulated by the FDA are highly toxic and can produce dangerous side effects even when used as directed. In contrast, even naive herb users are in greater danger of wasting good money on ineffective, overly hyped products than on doing much damage to themselves. Nor are chemical drugs necessarily more effective than herbal remedies, although they do tend to be faster acting.

(continued from previous page)

used them, and Jennifer and husband Steve deal with natural remedies professionally in the natural foods store they own and operate.

Homeopathic medicines can be purchased in tiny sugar-coated pills, which few kids would reject. But it's trickier to give kids herbs and supplements. Jennifer mixes her concoctions with a small amount of juice that the kids can "shoot down" and then chase with a glass of plain juice if they wish. The beauty of this method is that they get the full dose, as opposed to mixing the remedies in a large glass of juice and having them refuse to drink more than a little bit. She also looks for herbs and supplements in chewable, flavored forms. The whole family takes chewable echinacea regularly to prevent colds and build up their immune systems.

Like Jennifer, Elaine Barker, who lives near Cave Junction, Oregon, does much home doctoring with her kids, drawing on over-the-counter homeopathic remedies, a small number of herbs, and vitamins and supplements. She also takes the kids to a well-known local holistic practitioner who is licensed both as a naturopath and a chiropractor. One of her favorite preventive regimens is a combination of zinc, vitamins A and C, and echinacea to prevent colds. "We've gotten through the whole winter without much ado, and I attribute that to preventive maintenance," Elaine says. When we spoke in the spring, poison oak was a constant problem in their woodsy environs. She was successfully treating the kids' itching with the homeopathics *apis mellifica 6x* and *rhus toxicodendoron* orally and tea tree oil (see page 164) topically.

In addition, herbs possess many outstanding properties, besides their relative safety, that pharmaceutical drugs do not. For instance, herbs such as garlic can correct blood pressure whether it's high or low. No pharmaceutical drug works in both directions like that.

Furthermore, herbal treatment often costs far less than treatment with drugs while producing as good or better results. For example, garlic pills sell for about one fourth the charge for the cholesterol-lowering drug Mevacor. The drug Proscar, prescribed for symptoms of an enlarged prostate, sells for almost two-and-one-half times the cost of saw palmetto, which may be as effective and is certainly safer.

Herbal Remedies That May Help Your Family

The following herbs have fairly well-documented histories of beneficial use. In many cases as noted, formal research has indicated potential medical value. But their listing here is not a recommendation that you use these products or that all uses are equally valuable or safe. Read carefully the notes below as well as the general cautionary advice above. And as a general rule, pregnant women should consult with their physician before using any herbal product.

Aloe Vera

JAMES WEEKS

Aloe Vera

Description and uses: A succulent native to eastern and southern Africa. Grown as an ornamental in warm regions of the U.S. and indoors by people who want this valuable home remedy at hand. The leaf gel and sap make an excellent treatment for burns, including sunburn, as well as for skin irritation and inflammation.

Precautions and comments: Commonly featured as an ingredient in skin creams and shampoos because of its moisturizing properties; however, such products usually contain too little aloe to produce much benefit. Those who take aloe internally for stomach disorders should be aware that it is a strong laxative. Reduce the dosage to avoid that effect. Overuse of aloe taken internally has been linked with bowel cancer. External use is considered safe, but some individuals are allergic. Apply a small amount behind the ear to test for an allergic reaction before using it. Refrain from use if stinging or rash results.

Chamomile

Description and uses: The tiny flowers of the common wild chamomile plant contain a beneficial oil. As a tea, it is used for muscle spasms, menstrual cramps, indigestion and other digestive problems, and as a mild sedative or relaxant for tired or frayed nerves. Applied topically, chamomile oil or ointment may reduce inflammation on skin or in mucous membranes or ease the pain of arthritis. Chamomile extract is sometimes used to heal wounds.

Precautions and comments: Make the tea from fresh herbs because the oil with the beneficial properties breaks down easily. Steep in a closed vessel for at least ten minutes to release the oils. Those who suffer allergies to ragweed or the daisy family may have problems with chamomile.

Comfrey

Description and uses: A perennial that grows wild in moist places through-out the U.S. and Europe. Extremely effective as a poultice for difficult-to-heal wounds.

Precautions and comments: Use only externally, particularly with children (see page 156), as it is safe when applied this way. Note that not all herb books mention that comfrey may be dangerous when taken internally.

Echinacea

Description and uses: Long known as a beneficial plant to the Native Americans of the central plains, where it grows wild. Also known as the purple cornflower. Boosts the immune system in times of low resistance. Also combats viruses and bacteria. Seems to help ease colds, flus, and sore throats. Re-search also indicates it may be useful in healing wounds and combating in-fection.

Echinacea

Precautions and comments: Continual use may reduce benefits; if using echinacea preventively, Dr. Andrew Weil recommends, alternate taking it for two weeks with not taking it for two weeks. People with allergies to the sunflower family may experience reactions. Test the potency of your echinacea by placing a small amount on your tongue and holding it in your mouth for a few minutes. It should cause numbness—if it doesn't, it won't provide benefits either, so save your receipts and return inef-fective products to the vendor.

Feverfew

Description and uses: A perennial plant that is cultivated and also occa-sionally found wild in California and parts of the Midwest and South. Can reduce the number and severity of migraine headaches, and help re-lieve any associated nausea and vomiting. A rigorous British study indi-cates that feverfew may reduce attacks in migraine sufferers by 25 percent.

Precautions and comments: Although some herbalists advise chewing the plant's leaves, this causes temporary mouth sores in some users. Can also be used as a tea or from a tincture. Some people suffer allergic reactions to feverfew. It must be taken daily for weeks or months to experience benefits, so it is more appropriate as a preventive than as an immediate remedy. Don't use during pregnancy.

Garlic

Description and uses: The same plant used to season food also produces strong medicinal effects, as has been known by many peoples for centuries. During the plague era in Europe, many people ate it, with apparent success, to gain immunity. Research indicates garlic can significantly lower cholesterol and reduce blood clotting. Helps control high blood pressure. Due to a compound it contains, called allicin, garlic works as a powerful antibiotic, fights fungal infections, and has antiviral and antibacterial properties. Eating several cloves of raw garlic when symptoms first appear can combat common colds. Warm garlic oil poured into a child's ear may heal ear infections in the early stages. Used preventively on a daily basis, garlic can help those who suffer from frequent yeast infections, chronic or recurrent infections of other types, or low resistance.

Precautions and comments: Although garlic has proven antifungal properties, it can cause allergic reactions, irritation, or even minor burns if used topically to treat diaper rash, as some recommend. Garlic is also too harsh and irritating to a child's tender skin to be used as a poultice for burns. Garlic pills coated with enteric dissolve in the intestine instead of the mouth, thereby cutting the odor and also improving the absorption of allicin, which seems to be one of garlic's most beneficial ingredients. Look for pills standardized for allicin content. Fresh garlic cloves cut into chunks and swallowed like pills may be more potent still. For children, embed garlic in something good-tasting such as cookie dough. People using anticoagulants should note that too much garlic may interfere with beneficial blood clotting. As a remedy, garlic must be used raw; cooking destroys the allicin.

Ginger

Description and uses: Like garlic, this common spice has a centuries-long history of medicinal use around the world. Controlled scientific studies have demonstrated ginger's value in preventing nausea such as motion sickness without the drowsiness produced by some commercial drugs. Clinical research also indicates that ginger can combat the nausea that occurs after surgery.

Precautions and comments: Could possibly interfere with blood clotting, although recommended therapeutic doses seem to be free of side effects. Large quantities can cause stomach distress.

Ginkgo Biloba

Description and uses: The ginkgo, native to the Far East, is the world's oldest species of tree. Increases blood circulation, including blood flow to the brain, which is why it is often recommended for the elderly to improve memory, concentration, and absentmindedness. Also used to treat headaches, tinnitus (ringing in the ears), leg circulation problems, and related cramps.

Precautions and comments: Ginkgo has also been known to *cause* headaches and nausea in some.

NATROL, INC.

Ginkgo Biloba

Goldenseal

Description and uses: The rootstock of this small, perennial plant, native to eastern North America, has long been treasured by Native Americans to treat a variety of conditions. Overharvested to near extinction, goldenseal is now cultivated for herbal remedies. Can be used as a disinfectant for wounds or to treat irritated or inflamed mucous membranes—for example, sore throat, canker sores, infected gums, tonsillitis, or sore tongue. Sold mainly in powdered form, either in bulk or in capsules. Unlike other herbs, it retains its potency as a powder.

Precautions and comments: Goldenseal has a strong, extremely bitter taste. If using it as a mouth rinse or gargle, consider yourself warned! Neither goldenseal nor any homegrown herbal remedy is recommended for children's eye problems. Do not use during pregnancy.

Milk Thistle

Description and uses: This annual or biennial plant grows in dry, rocky soils in western and southern Europe as well as parts of the U.S. Its seeds, fruits, and leaves have been used for many centuries in European folk medicine. Experiments show that extracts from the seeds and fruit help protect the liver against several chemical toxins as well as help regenerate the organ itself. Preliminary research indicates that milk thistle may also help repair liver damage from hepatitis and other chronic liver ailments. One compound in milk thistle, when taken intravenously, treats potentially fatal poisoning from the deathcap mushroom, which destroys liver cells.

Precautions and comments: Liver patients should be under the care of a physician and consult with them before using this herb. In folk medicine, milk thistle was once commonly given to breast-feeding women to stimulate milk production. Research has disproved this supposed benefit. Milk thistle has not yet been tested for safety with infants, so do not use it to treat newborn jaundice.

Mullein

Description and uses: A long-stemmed, biennial plant with a history of use in ancient Greece and throughout Europe. Also grows wild in the U.S. from the Atlantic coast to the Midwest. Tincture made from mullein leaves can be used to treat chest congestion, sore throats, hoarseness, and dry, bronchial coughs. Mullein oil can be used as ear drops to treat children's ear infections.

Precautions and comments: Considered nontoxic.

Passion Flower

Description and uses: A woody, climbing vine native to the southeastern U.S. The entire plant has medicinal properties. Primary benefit is that it relieves symptoms of stress or nervousness without sedating.

Precautions and comments: Much safer than chemical tranquilizers. Children with bedwetting problems should not be given passion flower because it promotes deep sleep and could keep them from waking to urinate. Do not use high doses of it during pregnancy.

Peppermint

Description and uses: The leaf and distilled oils of this common aromatic plant have been a staple in herbal medicine chests since ancient times. Taken as a tea, it improves digestion and treats nausea, heartburn, indigestion, discomfort from overeating, and other similar ailments. Peppermint tea added to bathwater helps relieve itching, as with chicken pox. Enteric-coated capsules of peppermint oil can be taken to treat distress of the lower gastrointestinal tract such as diverticulitus, irritable bowel syndrome, and other intestinal problems.

Precautions and comments: Not dangerous, but pregnant women should note that peppermint can interfere with iron absorption.

Saint John's Wort

Description and uses: Ancient peoples used this shrubby perennial with delicate yellow flowers, found throughout the world including the eastern region and Pacific coast of North America, to ward off evil spirits. Today, adults who suffer from depression are flocking to it as a natural Prozac. For children, it appears to be a potent remedy for many sleep disorders, including sleep loss from a recent tragedy such as death of a relative or pet.

Precautions and comments: Best to avoid using it as an antidote to bedwetting, another of its common applications, until more research is done. Saint John's Wort can increase photosensitivity, making a child more vulnerable to sunburn, so proper preventative care should be taken.

Saw Palmetto

Description and uses: Native to the southeastern coastal states, Georgia and Florida. The berries contain the medicinal substances. Popular treatment, especially in Europe, for ailments of the urinary tract, particularly prostate problems in men. Also used in Germany, where an herb's effectiveness must be validated by a government commission, to treat bladder obstructions. Useful for stimulating appetite.

Precautions and comments: Not known to produce any adverse side effects. But check with a physician before assuming that symptoms indicate a minor bladder or prostate problem.

Slippery Elm

Description and uses: The inner bark of the red elm tree contains a substance called mucilage which soothes irritated tissues and restores the mucous coating. Long a Native American remedy, slippery elm lozenges help treat sore throats and smoker's cough. Mix slippery elm powder with a sweetener and water and drink it to soothe and heal an irritated gastrointestinal tract. Add water only to make a poultice for treating burns, boils, and minor wounds.

Precautions and comments: Considered nontoxic for both internal and external uses.

Tea Tree Oil

Description and uses: Aromatic oil drawn from the leaves of a tree native to New South Wales. The leaves have long been used by Australian aborigines as a general remedy for various ills. Diluted to 10 percent strength in warm water, it is a potent disinfectant for wounds and other localized infections including vaginal yeast and Trichomonas vaginalis. Applied full-strength topically, it is particularly effective for fungal infections such as jock itch, ringworm, athlete's foot, and fungal growth on toe- and fingernails. Also recommended for boils. An Australian study has found it effective in treating acne.

Precautions and comments: Nontoxic and nonirritating for most people, but can spark allergic reactions in some. Not advisable for burns because of its potential to irritate.

Valerian

Description and uses: Long used by cultures from the ancient Greeks to Native Americans for a wide range of applications. Today, valerian is used mainly as a sedative. Experiments suggest that the active ingredient in the plant's root both depresses brain centers and relaxes smooth muscle tissue, easing the user to sleep. In smaller amounts, it can also be used during the day to calm nervous stomachs and other symptoms of stress. It may be taken as a tea, tincture, or encapsulated extract. Considered more powerful than most other herbal sedatives such as hops, with which it is often combined in herbal sedative products.

Precautions and comments: As with all herbs, pregnant women should clear use with their physician. Neither valerian nor any other sedative should be used to treat hyperactivity in children. Sedatives don't help and may lead to drowsiness, confusion, or erratic and impulsive behavior. Although valerian isn't likely to cause the heavy sleep "hangovers" that some commercial sleep aids do, some users do experience a mild hangover effect. They should reduce their dosage. Although the herb is considered safe, it may be best not to take it every night to avoid any chance of depressing mood or impairing mental functioning.

How to Shop for Herbs

The lack of industry-wide standards plus the difficulty of maintaining consistency in substances extracted from plants means that you must be a smart herbal shopper. Follow these guidelines for best results:

- *Buy tinctures or freeze-dried products when possible.* Tinctures are made by mixing the extracts of dried or fresh plants in grain alcohol to prevent spoilage and stabilize the herb's properties. Although the percentage of alcohol in a tincture is high, herbs in this form are highly concentrated, so the amount of alcohol in a single dose shouldn't affect you, writes Dr. Andrew Weil. To avoid alcohol altogether for you and your children, look for vinegar-based or freeze-dried products, which are also stable and concentrated.

- *Avoid bulk plants and powdered or encapsulated products in most cases.* Herbs in these forms have been exposed to air, moisture, and light, all of which can cause deterioration and loss of potency. For this reason, teas tend to be less reliable than tinctures or freeze-dried herbs, although several exceptions are mentioned below.

- *Look for reputable brands and manufacturers that strive for purity and standardization of their products.* If not grown organically or if handled improperly, herbs may be contaminated with pesticides or molds or even mixed with other plants. Although claims of standardization and purity on a product's packaging are no guarantee of effectiveness, they do show that the maker has measured the ingredients. For example, look for such words as "each tablet contains [#] milligrams of ____." Quantities of ingredients vary wildly in nonstandardized products. Tests have shown that some packages may contain little or even none of the most desired ingredients. Herbs grown organically or wildcrafted (harvested

taking herbs safely

All medicines, including natural ones, are toxic in large doses, and caution is always called for when giving anything to children, whose bodies can't tolerate near the levels of toxicity that adult bodies can. Take the following precautions for safest results:

- *Only take herbs if you feel you need them.* Despite what the FDA says, herbs are drugs, not dietary supplements. If you feel you might be able to accomplish the same healing with lifestyle changes such as more healthful habits, try that first.

- *Stop taking the herb if you experience troubling side effects.*

- *Pay attention to your experience.* All bodies are different. An herb with a stellar reputation may not help you or your child or may react negatively with your body's chemistry.

- *Read all warning notices on packaging and consult outside sources such as this chapter or the books recommended in the Resources at the end of this chapter before beginning self-treatment.*

- *Start slowly, with small doses.* Potency, concentration, and even ingredients can vary from package to package. Individual plants also vary widely in potency. If you feel you have found a standardized product, take only the recommended dosages at the intervals the manufacturer advises.

- *An herb's benefit for one condition doesn't guarantee its value or safety for other uses.* Tea tree oil is a good example. As noted, it is unquestionably a valuable disinfectant for wounds, but it can irritate burns.

- *Be wary of imported herbal remedies.* Some imported products are contaminated with lead or mercury, both of which are harmful to nervous systems, especially those of children.

- *Note the precautions for pregnancy, breast-feeding, and children.* Pregnant and breast-feeding women should always consult an M.D.—preferably one open to natural medicine—before taking herbal products. In general, herbs should not be used to treat infants—and certainly not without first checking with a pediatrician. Dosage levels will be less for children than adults—again, check with a pediatrician or other expert first if the herb is known to have side effects.

from wild plants) will likely also be purer and of higher quality.

- *Don't believe everything you read about herbs.* Many authors are too quick to praise botanical medicines and fail to note the cautions described by more responsible experts such as Andrew Weil, M.D., Kathi J. Kemper, M.D. (*The Holistic Pediatrician*), Varro Tyler of Purdue University, and James F. Balch, M.D. Nevertheless, you should own a reliable written guide to consult so you don't have to rely on makers' claims. See the Resources at the end of this chapter for reviews.

FAMILY EXERCISE

You probably already know that vigorous physical activity is crucial to your health. But even natural health buffs tend to think of exercise as something that's important mainly for adults because they're no longer kids taking gym classes in school, dancing to the Top 40, playing ball at the park, patrolling the sidewalks on bikes, and trekking with their scout troops.

However, many children and teenagers today are just as sedentary as their deskbound and couch potato folks. The average child or teenager today spends many of the same hours watching television that in past generations might have been spent playing outside with friends or in organized recreation. Video games and Net surfing eat up still more free hours where the only body part being worked is the hand on the joystick or mouse. In addition, children are often driven to school (or in the case of teenagers, they drive themselves) instead of walking or riding their bikes.

Kids get less exercise in school, too—Illinois is the only state that still requires all students in all public school grades to attend daily physical education classes. In many big cities, parents don't even feel it's safe for kids to play in front of the house, much less walk or bike to friends' houses or nearby playgrounds. Young peoples' diets have also grown less healthful, in part because of the high-fat junk foods pushed at kids in TV commercials, magazine ads, and even the public schools.

Girls in yoga–like stretch

Thus, it's no surprise that kids today are in much worse shape physically than children were thirty years ago. More than one in five children, both boys and girls, between the ages of six and seventeen are overweight. We tend to trivialize a few extra childhood pounds by joking that Joey is a little "chunky." However, the entire course of adult health can be set by bad health habits learned in childhood. For example, 40 percent of children ages five to eight already have at least one heart disease risk factor such as physical inactivity, obesity, elevated cholesterol, and high blood pressure, says the President's Council on Physical Fitness. That means that many of these kids are headed for an unhealthy and physically limited adulthood, and perhaps early death. Getting our kids moving isn't just about getting them in shape for the present, it's also about building habits that will help ensure them a long, vital life.

The Role of Parents

With school gym classes fading from sight, it's clearly up to us parents to motivate our children to get more exercise. But what can one do short of sheer physical force to get the kids off the couch? Plenty, say today's fitness professionals:

making exercise work for you and your family

Exercising as a family can be both a great togetherness activity and a mutual support system. But whether you and your children exercise together or separately, here are some tips that professionals offer for making exercise both beneficial and enjoyable:

- *Diversify.* One way to increase the fun-and-interest quotient of exercise is to combine a diverse group of activities. This will also result in better all-around fitness by working the body in a variety of ways. In addition, varied activities help prevent overuse injuries, such as tendonitis, that can occur when bodies are worked the same way all the time.

- *Ask the doctor.* If you're over forty, get a physical exam and ask your physician for exercise recommendations before joining your kids in any vigorous exercise program.

- *Watch TV or listen to music.* The link between television and sedentary living can be turned on its head if you use television or music to offset the monotony of riding a stationary bike or running on a treadmill. In the same vein, you and your kids can listen to your favorite tunes on a personal cassette player while running laps at the local school track. In fact, picking syncopated music to exercise to such as R&B or jazz can even enhance your workout by encouraging you to move more rhythmically, which increases flexibility and grace.

- *Work out with a friend.* If you can't work out with your kids, or if your teens aren't particularly thrilled with your offer of companionship, en-

(continued on next page)

- *Be an effective role model.* Begin by starting your own regular exercise program. Not that you should be doing this just for the kids. Our bodies are designed for vigorous work. If not used that way on a regular basis, they start falling apart faster than they should.

Set a positive example with your other health habits, as well. It's hard for your kids to get the point that health is important if the food you offer them and eat in front of them sends the opposite message. The same goes for smoking. Besides, our unhealthful habits don't just set a poor example, they also limit our ability to take part in physical activities with our children.

- *Teach your children the benefits of exercise.* Children should learn early on that regular, vigorous exercise helps prevent many of the health problems they see plaguing adults who are important to them. For example, proper exercise reduces blood pressure, helps women prevent osteoporosis by building bone density and offsetting bone loss, lowers cholesterol, builds lean muscle while reducing fat (a key to not only general health but also losing weight), strengthens the heart and helps keep it healthy, helps prevent adult-onset diabetes, helps offset the joint stiffening and bone loss associated with aging and inactivity, and may even prevent some forms of cancer.

Exercise also helps combat the symptoms of anxiety, depression, and tension, which affect young people every bit as much as older ones. For those already fighting weight problems, exercise improves the function of the appestat, which regulates the body's hunger signals so they more closely reflect the body's actual need for food. By the same token, the lethargy that slows down kids as well as their parents often results from too little physical activity.

- *Teach your child sports skills that you've acquired and learn others you can pass on.* Your peers may know you as "Rag Arm" or "Stonefingers," but you still have far more strength and athletic skill than your little ones can muster. Showing them the basic motor skills involved in sports, dance, and other vigorous youth activities, such as how to throw and catch a ball, gives them "a model to emulate and a goal to shoot for," writes Kenneth Cooper, M.D., the well-known fitness guru. It also makes it more likely they'll want to become involved in those activities later on, which will help them keep fit.

(continued from previous page)

courage them to start an exercise program with their friends or siblings. Buddying up is another great way to offset the boredom and hard work of some forms of exercise.

- *Choose family activities that provide good exercise.* Examples include walks, hikes, bicycle rides, swimming, and cross-country ski trips.

- *If exercise is too much of a chore, do the chores.* Remember, it doesn't take formal exercise to stay fit. Ordinary household chores such as raking leaves, mopping floors, and gardening can also do the trick, particularly if they're attacked with the same energy you or your kids would expend on a workout.

- *If your children take part in sports, match them with others at their same skill and developmental level.* Children who are more developmentally advanced or more skilled than their peers will dominate, and ultimately discourage, their opponents. Similarly, some children develop athletic ability at a slower rate than others their age. This disparity is one of the reasons less able and slower kids drop out of sports at an early age and become less fit. If your children haven't caught up to their peers yet, try to direct them into recreational programs that match kids according to their abilities.

- *Be alert to the possible negative effects of exercise.* Adults and kids alike can become addicted to exercise and/or its results, leading to injuries, obsession with body shaping, and a level of fatigue that interferes with the rest of life. Kids who are shy may use solitary activities like running to avoid social contacts.

- *Make your child's exercise about fun and health, not work.* The abstract notion of long-term health benefits isn't juicy enough to sell most people, mature or not, on sticking with something that isn't fun and comfortable. So the trick is to find activities that get us in shape without boring us silly or leaving us dreading the next painful workout. Val and Stuart Schultz and their four children (ages six to thirteen) ski almost every weekend in season (they live a half mile away from a mountain), in addition to biking and ice skating together. To Val, a nurse practitioner, it's important "to show the children that when your heart is beating a little faster, just how good that feels and that this is something we should strive for at least every couple of days."

It may be true that to be in top condition, people of all ages have to exercise until they "feel the burn." But feeling the burn isn't how many adults or kids want to spend the major chunk of free time that being fit requires. Nor need they. Studies in recent years have shown that more moderate forms of exercise—even common household chores—can produce solid health benefits if done often and vigorously enough. For example, an hour spent mowing a lawn with an old-fashioned push mower burns about as many calories as an hour spent swimming.

- *Make sports more about healthy enjoyment than work and winning.* If your children are involved in competitive sports, teach them how to play for fun while still giving a maximum effort. And be alert to coaches who put so much stress on winning and training that they drain the enjoyment from your child's experience. Studies show that youth fitness often declines at about age eleven or twelve, and one of the primary reasons is an unsatisfying encounter with competitive sports. For more on making athletics a positive and growthful experience, see Chapter 8.

In Chapter 8, we also show how experts view various youth sports and recreational activities for their fitness benefits. Many of these, such as bicycling, running, and tennis, are just as suitable for family exercise as organized youth sports.

PROTECTING YOUR CHILDREN FROM HEALTH HAZARDS AROUND THE HOUSE

When confronted with information about environmental health hazards, many parents feel the understandable urge to curl up like a pill bug and yell, "Go away!" You can't protect your family from everything, goes the argument, so why just scare yourself about things you can't control?

Well, that's just the point—you *can* prevent many of the problems outlined below. And some of them, such as lead poisoning, have serious consequences for children in particular. When it comes to household health issues, ignorance can get your family into serious trouble.

We have based our recommendations below on what is best for children, but pregnant moms should take similar precautions. And obviously, what is toxic to babies and small kids can affect teens and adults, too, although usually to a much lesser degree.

Lead

The problem for kids: Lead abounds in and around family homes, depending on their age. Most homes built before 1960 and many built before 1979 were coated in lead-based paint, indoors and out. Inside your cupboards, lead may lurk in the seams in food cans manufactured before 1991 or imported from outside the U.S. Kitchen- and dinnerware made from brass, bronze, or pewter or plated with silver may leach lead when used. So may handcrafted pottery, foreign-made ceramics (most domestic brands are foreign-made), fine crystal, and decorative dishes.

Inexpensive vinyl miniblinds sold in the U.S. from 1978 to 1996 were coated in a lead compound to make them more durable. Painted toys and furniture made before 1978, crayons made in China before 1994, chalkboard and pool-cue chalk, stained glass, and even many calcium supplements may contain lead. Many older homes also have lead in their plumbing systems (see drinking water section on page 172).

With so much lead around, it shouldn't surprise anyone that nearly one American child in ten has toxic levels of this heavy metal in their blood. The problem affects children in every social class and geographic area, not just poor kids in crumbling old houses and apartments. And the consequences can be critical. Lead can affect the nervous system, including the brain. The possible results of even low levels of lead ingestion include lowered IQs, attention deficit disorder, behavior problems, and learning problems.

What you can do: If you suspect your children have been exposed to lead, you should have their blood tested. Many pediatricians offer the test, a simple blood analysis.

You should also identify sources of lead contamination around your house and remove them without delay. Take the obvious steps first. Don't prepare or serve your infants or toddlers food in dishes, mugs, or utensils that you suspect may contain lead. (Adults should limit their own use of these items as well.) Get rid of suspicious toys, crayons, or chalk. Old furniture with deteriorating paint should go, too. Yes, you can buy commercial lead-testing kits but few reveal low-level lead contamination, which can still harm children.

The paint on your house may be a major lead source, so it should also be evaluated as soon as possible. Professionals can determine the lead content—do-it-yourself tests can't be trusted, say federal experts. If you do find lead-based paint on the walls, you don't have to remove it, but it should be covered up or sealed with paneling, lead-free paint, or wallpaper. But you may well want to replace or remove paint from moving or easily chewed surfaces such as doors, windows, sills, and wood trim, especially if the paint has deteriorated. Don't do the job yourself because you're likely to create even more of a problem with lead dust, debris, or fumes. Instead, hire lead abatement experts. Your local health department can supply a list. The job will cost several thousand dollars and children should be away from the house while the work is going on.

If your outside walls have lead-based paint, lead dust may contaminate the soil within a few feet of the house where kids sometimes play. Plant or otherwise cover the dirt to keep kids out, but by no means grow food there. In fact, you should also avoid growing vegetables closer than fifteen feet from a busy street or in areas exposed to pollution from a lead-based industry. Roads undergoing repairs or auto repair shops, if nearby, can also contaminate the soil around your home.

Mercury Paint

The problem for kids: Like lead, mercury can harm a child's nervous system. It can also affect children's muscular health. Until mid-1991, mercury-containing indoor paint was sold legally in the U.S. It remains legal in outdoor paint. Mercury vapors are heavier than indoor air and settle toward the floor, where young children play.

What you can do: Don't use outdoor paint indoors. Keep children away from the house when painting and ventilate well. Paint may emit fumes for months, so ventilate for a long time after painting. To prevent your kids from playing in soil contaminated by outdoor paint, take the same precautions you would with lead-based paint.

Drinking Water

The problem for kids: The very nature of water and the way it moves through the environment leads to pollution problems. Water seeps or percolates into places that aren't tightly sealed, including ground where chemicals have been spilled, picking up microbes and pollutants as it goes. These nasties then get carried back to groundwater and ultimately the basic water supply that is piped to our homes.

Businesses that don't comply with clean water laws and other companies dumping legal pollutants further compromise the water supply. So does "nonpoint" (that is, not concentrated in a single source) pollution such as the oils and heavy metals washed down storm drains from city streets. In rural areas, pesticide runoffs from agricultural areas and replanted forests contaminate private wells. In certain parts of the country, radon (see p. 174) may get into drinking water, especially in private wells or in community systems serving five hundred or fewer people.

Even if water gets to your home in good condition, it can pick up lead from your plumbing. If your house was built before 1930, it was probably lead-piped. Even houses built after that time may have plumbing joined with lead solder, which wasn't banned until 1986. The public water system pipes that bring water to your home may also leach lead. Roughly one in six Americans drink water with excessive lead levels, estimates the EPA.

If you have a private well and very young children around, you also need to be on guard for nitrates. These substances, from chemical fertilizer pollution, can cause brain damage and death in extreme cases with children under a year of age. Pollutants and microbes don't improve anyone's health but children are particularly vulnerable. Kids drink more than adults, especially in relation to their small bodies, and their undeveloped systems don't process toxins as readily.

What you can do: Get to know your local water supply—where it comes from, the most likely pollutants. Water that comes from a public water supplier is tested regularly by law and you can obtain a copy of the results. To test for lead in your own pipes, take a water sample to a professional lab—your state EPA or local health authority can probably refer you to several. Or use a national mail-order testing service, although reliability can vary. Comprehensive water tests can run about $200 but a simple lead test can be had for about $30. In some cases, local authorities will test for free. Private well users should test water periodically for problems in any circumstance, and immediately if the water changes color, taste, or smell.

The way you use your water can also minimize lead exposure. Never use water from the hot water tap for drinking or cooking because hot water is more likely to dissolve lead from the plumbing than cold. If a faucet has been unused for six hours or more, flush the system by running the water until it gets as cold as possible. However, this strategy won't work if you live in a high-rise building because of the plumbing system's design, so you may want to rely on bottled or filtered water instead.

Many families seek protection from contaminated water by installing purification systems. The problem here is that no single system can protect against all contaminants. Again, you should learn which contaminants are most prevalent in your water and select the system accordingly. Andrew Weil's *Natural Health, Natural Medicine* (see the Resources at the end of this chapter) includes an excellent discussion of the attributes of various water purification methods.

Finally, do your part to minimize public water contamination by using safe household products (see page 179), not pouring toxic chemicals and motor oil down your drains, and not spraying garden chemicals.

Radon

The problem for kids: When uranium in the earth's crust breaks down or is disturbed, it emits a radioactive gas known as radon. Invisible and odorless, radon rises from the ground into houses. In a house with a high radon level, a child may receive a radiation dose equal to thousands of chest X rays per year, possibly leading to lung cancer down the line. Radon is the second-leading cause of lung cancer, right behind smoking.

What you can do: Families that live in "hot spots" such as the uranium mining regions of Colorado, parts of Florida, and the so-called Reading Prong that stretches from eastern Pennsylvania to Connecticut, should test their homes for radon contamination. Test kits costing $25 or less can be obtained at a local hardware store in affected areas. If radon is present, you can reduce the level with ventilation or by sealing off places where it enters the house—crawl spaces, floor drains, cracks in basement floors and walls, and so on. Retest from time to time. As houses age and settle, new cracks appear that can let in the gas.

Asbestos

The problem for kids: If your home was built between 1920 and about 1978, you may find asbestos in vinyl floor tiles; linoleum flooring; flooring adhesives; ceilings (in paint, patching material, and soundproofing); wall, pipe, and furnace insulation; door gaskets and insulation in stoves and furnaces; and roofing and siding shingles. Materials containing asbestos release tiny, nearly invisible fibers when they are disturbed or deteriorate. When breathed into the lungs, the fibers can irritate tissues, causing irreversible scarring, lung cancer, and other cancers, although the problems may not appear for decades. Kids breathe more frequently than adults, making them especially vulnerable. They also do more breathing with their mouths, which provides a direct route to the lungs.

What you can do: If you suspect that asbestos has been used in your home, learn to identify the trouble spots or hire a specialist to do it for you. Intact, undisturbed asbestos won't shed fibers so don't rush to eliminate it. If you find asbestos dust that has collected for example, under a pipe, don't vacuum it. You will only scatter asbestos fibers into the air. Wet it down first, then wipe it up and discard it. If asbestos removal is warranted, hire a contractor certified for the job. Your state department of health will provide you with a list of asbestos specialists.

Lawn Chemicals

The problem for kids: In their bid to have picture-perfect lawns, shrubs, and trees, many families drench their yards in dangerous chemicals, inadvertently risking that their kids will someday develop catastrophic illnesses such as leukemia and multiple chemical sensitivity. As with agricultural chemicals in general, few of the garden chemicals commonly used by Americans have been cleared by the EPA for long-term safety. Most belong to a category called organochlorines, also suspected by many experts of causing reproductive system abnormalities and cancers. Children crawl around on the grass and climb trees, dramatically increasing their exposure. Their smaller bodies, faster breathing rates, and immature livers further heighten the risk.

What you can do: Start by accepting an occasional weed as a fair trade for your child's health. Learn healthy, natural forms of weed and pest control and take steps to improve the health of your garden, such as not overwatering your lawn; weeds and pests are attracted to unhealthy plants and soil. If you hire professionals to do your lawn and garden care, select those who minimize chemical use through methods such as integrated pest management. Certain plants—for instance, garlic, marigolds, peppermint, spearmint, onions, and leeks—repel insects with their fragrance. Interspersing them around your yard will reduce pest problems.

Indoor Air Pollution from Formaldehyde

The problem for kids: Pressed-wood products, including much children's furniture, are a notorious source of formaldehyde pollution, which "outgasses"—that is, passively releases vapors—over a period of months or even years after manufacture. Hardwood plywood, medium-density fiberboard, and, to a lesser extent, ordinary plywood also outgas this chemical. So does urea-formaldehyde insulation, which was installed in many homes between 1973 and the early 1980s. New carpets release formaldehyde, too, along with a host of other nasty chemicals. (Many natural-fiber carpets made from wool or cotton are no better in this regard—see below.) At low levels, formaldehyde vapors can cause respiratory irritation, watery eyes, and headaches. Higher concentrations trigger coughing, wheezing, dizziness, and even asthma attacks. High heat and humidity add to the problem, as does poor ventilation, common in today's heavily insulated homes. Again, children may be particularly vulnerable to these toxic vapors because they breathe more frequently and are less able to handle toxins in general.

What you can do: Pressed wood is tempting because of its low cost—even fine furniture manufacturers use it in hidden areas of their products. But you can eliminate or minimize outgassing by sealing pressed-wood furniture with polyurethane or lacquer. You can avoid carpet vapors by selecting alternative flooring such as natural-fiber area rugs without jute or latex backing. If you can't eliminate the source of outgassing, compensate with increased ventilation and air purifiers.

Indoor Air Pollution from Space Heaters, Gas Stoves, Wood Stoves, Fireplaces, and Central Heating Systems

The problem for kids: You probably aren't surprised that combustion appliances such as stoves, heaters, and fireplaces can pollute your indoor air. When natural gas, kerosene, or wood are burned, carbon monoxide, nitrogen oxide, sulfur dioxide, and particulates (tiny particles in smoke) may be produced. Many of these pollutants are heavier than air and settle toward the floor where kids play. They can spark asthma attacks, to which kids are more vulnerable than adults. In extreme cases, carbon monoxide vapors, which are odorless and invisible, can cause unconsciousness and death.

What you can do: Your combustion appliances came with safety instructions—read them! You should never use unvented combustion appliances such as kerosene space heaters for long unless you have cracked a window or placed the applicances in a fireplace. If you heat with a wood stove, avoid older models, which may not burn cleanly; stoves made after 1992 have been certified by the EPA for safe burning and also emit far fewer pollutants to the outdoors. Have your stove professionally installed, and have it inspected periodically to make sure vents are properly working.

Gas cooking stoves also contribute considerable pollution to indoor air unless certain precautions are taken. A range hood makes a big difference as does running an exhaust fan in a nearby window when using the stove. Check your pilot light to make sure it burns blue—yellow indicates that pollutants are forming—or better yet, get a pilotless stove.

If you have a central heating system, have it professionally inspected and maintained at regular intervals. Installing a carbon monoxide detector that sets off an alarm when levels are unsafe is always a good idea.

Sick Building Syndrome

The problem for kids: The chemical and gas problems mentioned above become even more of an issue in modern homes that have been tightly sealed and insulated to conserve energy. We're all for energy efficiency but many builders and families overdo it, leading to indoor air with dangerous concentrations of fumes from outgassed formaldehyde, carbon monoxide, and so on. If you or your kids experience sleepiness, nausea, eye irritation, irritability, or forgetfulness that goes away or diminishes when you step outside, you're probably suffering from what is called sick building syndrome. Again, kids' small size, immature anatomy, and fast breathing makes them even more susceptible than adults.

What you can do: Start by venting your appliances to the outside and installing exhaust fans to pull gases out. However, exhaust fans can reduce the home's indoor air pressure to the point that radon could be sucked in from the soil. Hazardous combustion gases from the chimney could enter the same way. To prevent this, open windows wherever exhaust fans are used or otherwise vent individual rooms.

Electromagnetic Fields

The problem for kids: For many years now, the media has alternately alarmed and reassured us with conflicting reports on the dangers of electromagnetic fields (EMFs), which are produced by the flow of electric current. Sources of particular concern include everything from utility substations and neighborhood power lines to small household appliances and home computers. Some experts suspect EMFs dramatically increase the risk of childhood leukemia, brain tumors, and lymphoma in people who are constantly exposed to them. Other widely reported studies have attempted to discredit this connection.

We think that erring on the side of caution is a wise approach in this case. Some rather influential parties—including utilities, appliance and computer makers, and builders—would rather that this issue just disappeared. We don't think there has been enough research on this matter to take any study as the final word.

What you can do: Relocate your children's beds if they are near where electric lines enter the house. Move fans, radios, clocks, lamps, and other small appliances at least thirty inches from the bed or where children frequently play. If your child uses an electric blanket or waterbed heater, only use it to preheat the bed. Unplug it—don't just turn it off—when they're under the covers. These same precautions should be followed by teens and adults as well.

In the rest of the house, family members should sit at least three feet from the TV screen, and thirty inches from computer monitors. Standing by an operating dishwasher is a bad idea, but appliances such as vacuum cleaners, electric shavers, and blenders that are only run for short periods shouldn't worry you. On the other hand, hair dryers should only be used sparingly.

You needn't pull up stakes just because you live near high transmission lines or a substation. On the scale of possible carcinogens, electromagnetic fields rank well behind poor diet or smoking. But you can certainly understand now why neighbors often protest when the local utility tries to build a new substation nearby.

Household Cleaning and Maintenance Products

The problem for kids: Few parents today have to be told to keep dangerous household chemicals out of reach of small children. But how many understand that locking them away is not enough? After opening the bottles and cans, many people store them that way. Behind locked cabinet doors, toxic vapors escape into indoor air that is being inhaled by rapidly breathing children. Also, freshly dry-cleaned clothes hanging in the closet may be adding tetrachlorethylene, suspected of being cancer-causing, to your home environment for days afterward. Poor ventilation and energy-efficient seals around doors and in walls compound the problem.

Among the problem products: paint thinner, glues, furniture polish, shoe polish, air fresheners, disinfectants, scouring powder, drain cleaners, toilet bowl cleaners, oven cleaners, window cleaners, bleach, spot removers, floor cleaners and waxes, wood preservatives, oils, wood varnishes, paint strippers, and adhesive removers. All of these chemicals poison the environment and water as well, especially when washed or poured down drains or discarded in unlined landfills.

What you can do: If you find the need to use chemical products, ventilate well. Store all packaging that isn't tightly sealed outdoors and away from areas where children play. And dispose of containers responsibly, as indicated on the packaging.

But you don't need to have all this poison in your family's midst. You can save considerable money along with packaging and other environmental stress by making your own cleaning solutions. For example, as Heloise has been teaching readers for decades, you can accomplish wonders with simple baking soda, water, and white vinegar. Or you can buy green products. Bon Ami makes a superior and widely available non-chemical scouring powder, and companies such as Harmony (formerly Seventh Generation—see the Resources at the end of this chapter) sell entire lines of household cleansers and other products that are safe for humans and the planet. Harmony products can be ordered by mail or found in many ordinary supermarkets as well as natural food stores. The latter institutions will stock many other chemical-free cleaning products on their shelves as well.

Indoor Pest Control

The problem for kids: The war you wage against ants, cockroaches, fleas, termites, and other tiny invaders may leave behind civilian casualties too, in particular your kids. At least one study associates a dramatic increase in childhood leukemia with homes in which pesticides are used at least once a week. Several of the most popular pesticides can attack the human nervous system or are cancer-causing. Many are also organochlorines, which, as indicated above, some scientists suspect lead to reproductive abnormalities and diseases. As with other toxins, young children and, of course, developing fetuses are especially vulnerable to these poisons.

What you can do: For every type of pest, including the dreaded termite, you can find a safer way of dealing with them. For instance, sealing cracks and holes outside your home and repairing poorly fitting outside doors and screens may solve your ant or roach problem. (See the Resources at the end of this chapter for books, including Schoemaker and Vitale's *Healthy Homes, Healthy Kids,* and other publications that describe pest-specific options.)

TALKING TO YOUR KIDS ABOUT DRUGS

What you are about to read will contradict nearly everything you hear from the most frequently quoted public and private spokespeople on teenage drug use. "Just Say No" or some variation is the only position considered socially acceptable for both public spokespeople and parents speaking to their kids at home. There is little evidence that this position has helped curb teen drug use—and considerable reason to believe, as we explain below, that it has actually helped encourage many young people to try drugs, or to graduate to harder drugs.

Our position is as follows: *We in no way condone drug use of any type,* but contrary to today's popular rhetoric, not all drug use is equally worrisome. The average teen who smokes marijuana with friends at weekend parties is not in the same league as a young person addicted to heroin. Although any reasonable parent would be concerned, the usual potsmoking youngster is not likely to suffer serious health consequences, become addicted, or try hard drugs. More to the point, if your child is determined to smoke marijuana, there's little you can do to stop him. Your bigger worry at that point should be that he not start hanging around with the wrong people (such as drug dealers or hard drug users), smoking when it endangers his safety or future (e.g. when driving, in school, or doing homework), or experimenting with truly dangerous drugs such as cocaine or heroin. Obviously, you must also be concerned that your child is breaking the law. Your best preventive strategy at this stage is to:

1. Learn the facts about drugs as documented in the independently funded (that is, not government-funded) scientific literature (see the Resources at the end of this chapter for books that will summarize that research for you);

2. Acknowledge these facts when you converse with your kids about drugs, even if the facts are at odds with popular rhetoric;

3. Only impose home policies for your child that are consistent with the facts, and otherwise maintain open communication and credibility with your teen so he feels comfortable discussing his concerns with you.

It is perfectly reasonable and appropriate parenting to make clear that you don't approve of drug use of any type. However, to forbid drug use is to tell your child that if he chooses to use drugs anyway, then he'll have to do it on the sly and rely completely on his friends for advice and information. That is a far more undesirable outcome, in our opinion, than reluctantly putting up with relatively inconsequential drug use to prevent more dangerous behaviors. Zero tolerance of drug use by young people is much akin to, and as ineffective as, "forbidding" teen sex. Most experts agree that preventing teen pregnancy begins with honest, open communication about sex and tolerance, if need be, of relatively safe sexual behavior. We have yet to see evidence that preventing abuse of dangerous drugs can be accomplished with any less openness, honesty, or, yes, tolerance, as uncomfortable as this is for parents to accept.

The Problem with Current Anti-Drug Strategies

Almost to a person, our political leaders try to prevent teen drug use by scaring kids with exaggerated or even entirely false pictures of what drugs do. They do this because it is considered politically suicidal to appear "soft on drugs." Partly because of pressure from these same politicians, school officials and government-funded drug researchers feel compelled to echo the same message, even when this message is clearly contradicted by research conducted by independently funded scientists.

We are not going to soft-pedal the dangers of some drugs. In particular, the manner in which heroin became the hip drug of choice in the Generation X rock, fashion, and party scenes of the 1990s should alarm parents. Never before has such a fiercely addicting and potentially fatal drug been so attractive to thrill-seeking youth.

But it is precisely because of such very real threats to our children that we need to rethink the message we give to them about drugs, both as parents and as citizens. *"Just Say No" and similar campaigns help create the very problem they are designed to prevent.* Our kids know that much of what society tells them, particularly about relatively mild drugs like marijuana, is laughably inaccurate. Many, frankly, know it from life experience. Others have learned the real facts just by looking them up at the library. Kids also know that most of the grown-ups wagging their fingers at them do their own drugs—legal or otherwise. As a result, most adults have lost credibility with teens on this subject. When the only real expertise is on the streets, teens will turn to their friends for facts and experiment with indisputably dangerous drugs, convinced that adults don't have their information straight on these substances either.

The information below is designed to give you a fresh perspective on this issue so you can establish a more constructive relationship with your children regarding drugs. Only when we adults begin using reality instead of fiction to discourage teens from taking drugs can we expect to be heard.

Who Uses Drugs

To put teen drug use in perspective, let's consider how common it is for adults to alter their consciousness. Alcohol is a drug. So is tobacco. Caffeine is a powerful stimulant that many adults feel they can't start their day without. Add in those who rely on tranquilizers or Prozac or smoke a little pot now and again and you soon realize that nearly every grown-up in "straight" American society takes some kind of drug some of the time. So do adults in other countries. In fact, drugs have been used in almost every culture in the world, throughout history. As young people approach adulthood, it is normal for them to want to do what adults do.

It is no less normal for teens to experiment with illicit drugs, especially relatively mild substances like marijuana. The desire to alter consciousness appears to be a basic human drive. This doesn't necessarily require illicit drugs—toddlers do it by spinning around until the room starts swirling. Young people and adults alike use everything from meditation to Hollywood special-effects movies to trippy dance music to get "out of their heads." But drugs are yet another way, and one that shouldn't surprise us in our push-button, instant gratification—seeking culture. According to a federally commissioned 1996 survey of 51,000 students, more than half of high-school seniors admitted to having used an illicit drug at least once. The numbers rise in the college years, when marijuana use peaks.

Teen drug use in no way means that kids are automatically on the fast track to bad grades, harder drugs, and general degeneracy. Just as many high-functioning adults smoke marijuana on occasion, so do many happy, well-adjusted kids who are good students and hang out with other good people. Most young marijuana users will steer clear of drugs they perceive as dangerous such as amphetamines and heroin. They pass through this phase of their lives with no obvious problems from drugs, probably cutting back or eliminating illicit drugs altogether by their mid-twenties. As Andrew Weil, M.D., and Winifred Rosen put it in their book *From Chocolate to Morphine,* use is not the same as abuse.

Unfortunately, some drug users will become abusers. Just as some adults will develop an addiction to alcohol or coffee, some youths will develop a dependence on pot. Some young pot smokers will also try harder drugs—marijuana use does not *usually* lead to harder drug use, but undeniably it *sometimes* does.

Because altering consciousness appears to be a common human impulse, it is unlikely that any antidrug program or policy will succeed if its goal is the total elimination of illicit drugs. Nor is the "Just Say No" approach likely to work in your household. We feel it is crucial for you to accept the fact that your teen may try drugs. You don't have to condone this behavior to be sensitive to the fact that not all drugs are the same and not all drug use is the same. Again, your best chance of preventing drug *abuse* by your teen is to maintain an open, communicative relationship in which you retain your credibility on the subject.

The Dangers of Drugs—Real and Imagined

When you discuss drugs with your children, it is crucial that you have your facts straight. And that means confronting information that runs counter to the propaganda coming from public officials. While there is much for parents to legitimately fear about teen drug use, most drugs don't quite live up to their bad reputations. Parents should understand this so they don't base their discussions with their kids on false, misleading information that teens can see through.

For example, the dark picture that "Just Say No" campaigners paint about **marijuana** so obviously conflicts with reality that many teens conclude that nothing adults say about drugs can be believed. Not that marijuana is without its dark side. It can cause fuzzy thinking, frayed concentration, and forgetfulness—an obvious problem for students—although the effects disappear when users stop smoking for a while. Irresponsible use can lead to accidents on the road or on the job. A small minority of users become dependent on marijuana and can have a hard time breaking the habit. Furthermore, studies show that marijuana contains more tars than tobacco, so it can damage lungs and bronchial passages in those who puff as often as a heavy cigarette smoker, although few do. Regular marijuana users do often develop a chronic, dry cough from respiratory irritation. But marijuana doesn't appear to cause any other physical damage, either to the brain or the rest of the body. No doubt, you have heard otherwise from certain "experts" and government representatives, but you won't find a single credible study that backs them up. For instance, as sociology professor and marijuana myth buster Lynn Zimmer points out, "Just Say No" types commonly cite a 1970s study by Tulane University's Edward Heath which showed that the brains of two monkeys exposed to marijuana smoke had been damaged. In the 1990s, a much better study using many more monkeys and more sophisticated methods and technology found that marijuana caused no structural changes to the brain. In 1995, editors of the British medical journal *Lancet* wrote that a review of thirty years of research reveals that "the smoking of cannabis, even long term, is not harmful to health."

The zero-tolerance crowd also promotes three other myths about marijuana that don't stand up to scrutiny: 1) that today's marijuana is much stronger than the pot of past years, 2) that new studies show the drug to be more unhealthful than previously thought, and 3) that marijuana use leads teens to try more dangerous drugs. These rationales are frequently offered to parents who wonder how to get their kids to say "no" today when they said "yes" in their youth. Again, no reliable studies validate any of these arguments. Although some highly refined "connoisseur" forms of marijuana may be more available than before, the "commercial grade" pot used by most hasn't changed much over the decades. No new health problems of any consequence have turned up; indeed, physicians are more interested than ever in marijuana's potential medical benefits. As for the "gateway drug" argument, the credible studies show just the opposite—that for the large majority of pot smokers, marijuana is the only illicit drug they will ever try, and many of them will simply use it a handful of times and then stop altogether. Certainly, many addicts use marijuana before hard drugs but that doesn't mean one causes the other. Many also drink alcohol first, yet no one is calling Budweiser a gateway drug. (For more on the questionable nature of drug research, see page 186.)

LSD creates a far more intense experience than marijuana, and its use by young people should concern parents far more than should marijuana use. Although no reliable research has ever shown it to cause brain damage, broken chromosomes, or any of the other physical problems usually mentioned by antidrug crusaders, there is evidence that it can help push people who are already psychologically imbalanced closer to the edge. Given that LSD is one of the most powerfully hallucinatory drugs around, you certainly wouldn't want your child driving or even crossing the street while using it. As a street drug, it may contain impurities or other illicit substances such as amphetamines. Most alarmingly, LSD use signals that your child is willing to try strong drugs, a major escalation from casual marijuana use.

The hip aura that now surrounds **heroin** use is terrifying. An accidental overdose—and the more inexperienced the user, the more likely the mistake—can kill. The primary danger of heroin is that it is powerfully addicting, driving users to take ill-advised risks. Interestingly, most of the other problems connected to heroin have less to do with its chemistry than the fact that it can only be obtained on the streets. In the typical scenario leading to overdose, the user unwittingly buys a packet that is much purer than she is used to and she injects too much. Heroin is actually not particularly toxic at usual dosage levels. The most common medical problem from long-term use is chronic constipation. [Many addicts look gaunt and suffer from a host of health problems because the street price of the drug is so high and addicts' craving so intense that they must spend all their waking hours raising money, often in illegal ways such as theft or prostitution. In the process, they tend to eat poorly and ignore other health needs.] But that only underscores heroin's dangers. A heroin user is quite likely to become a slave to the drug, taking extreme bodily and legal risks to obtain another dose. You should be very concerned if your child even spends time with people who use this drug.

Many of the other drugs young people try should also worry parents. **Cocaine** and **"crack"** users can easily become addicted and once they do, their drug habit can consume their lives. An overdose of **barbiturates** ("downers") can lead to death, as can mixing barbiturates and alcohol, not an uncommon combination. People who inject **amphetamines** may experience paranoia and hallucinations, and certainly aren't doing their hearts a favor. As with heroin, you should be concerned if your child associates with users of these drugs, even if they aren't now using such drugs themselves.

By far, the most dangerous drugs for teens are legal ones, **tobacco and alcohol,** because these are the toxic drugs young people are most likely to continue using as adults. Three quarters of teen smokers will still be smoking five to seven years later, and this habit may well compromise their health and shorten their lives. Few smokers have the self-control to use tobacco occasionally and nonaddictively. In fact, tobacco in the form of cigarettes may be even more addicting than heroin, although it less immediately threatens the user's survival. As for alcohol, teen drivers are hazardous enough to themselves and others without alcohol entering the picture. Many drinkers will become addicted, damaging their livers, brains, and peripheral nervous systems and risking a long list of other medical problems. Alcoholism resembles heroin and cocaine addiction in the way it takes over and destroys lives, and it may be even more difficult to treat. We should reserve some of the outrage we direct at drug pushers for the corporations that shamelessly advertise these legal drugs to our young people. The relatively small numbers of people who die from heroin or cocaine can't begin to compare to the vast numbers killed by cigarettes and alcohol.

How to Find Accurate Information About Drugs

More moderate drug experts stress the importance of basing your family decisions and discussions about drugs on accurate information. The problem is where to find it. Misleading statistics and reports abound, whether offered by government, law enforcement, and school officials; the media; or crusading organizations. Even well-intentioned authors writing about teen drug use often draw unknowingly from questionable sources.

That misinformation often begins in a seemingly unlikely place, scientific research. By doing a little digging in the library, any teen can discover that studies supposedly showing the dangers of drugs are notoriously unreliable. The reason has to do with the politics of drug control and how that affects research money. Most drug research is financed by government grants. But politicians only want to hear and promote bad news about drugs. They certainly don't want to hear, for example, about how to use marijuana or LSD safely, even though government does support research to determine safe amounts of alcohol.

Studies that confirm the message the federal government wants to send about drugs are publicized by politicians and officials such as the Secretary of Health and Human Services. Studies that don't are quietly ignored. In addition, scientists who reach the "wrong" conclusions know they are far less likely to get government funding in the future. Drug researchers understand this game and most of them play it by giving the system what it wants. But they pay a price in professional respect, because studies that politicians like tend to be riddled with faulty assumptions or other biases that are clear to the researcher's peers.

Much the same goes for the information offered by school officials or police officers in school programs. Undoubtedly many of those who teach in these programs know they are spreading falsehoods that many of their students see through immediately. But they also know that their jobs depend on not appearing "soft" on drugs. And soft these days means anything that varies even slightly from the official hard line.

Fortunately, you can find more objective information if you know where to look for it. We have listed two good books on the subject in the Resources at the end of this chapter. The authors include scientists who don't depend on government grants and other independent-minded experts who feel more obligation to young people and the facts than to anyone's party line.

Points to Remember When Talking to Your Kids

Preventing drug abuse begins with good relationships, not rules. No matter how firmly you lay down the law, your teen can still choose to ignore your wishes. And if you retaliate with even tougher sanctions, you risk isolating your child or further provoking him, both of which could lead to even deeper drug problems. Not that rules don't have a place, but they are most effective in the context of an open, supportive relationship that is based on trust, love, and two-way communication. Research out of Louisiana State University shows that kids who have positive, mutually respectful relationships with their parents are less likely to experiment with alcohol or illicit drugs. They're also less likely to select friends who might be considered bad influences.

Obviously, whether you decide to forbid drug use outright is up to you. However, if you do, you may simply be setting up your child to be disobedient. Parents' rules haven't done much to curb teen smoking or drinking. Nor, for that matter, have the laws against it. A more produc-

tive rule at home might be to forbid irresponsible or unsafe behavior—
for example, being high while at school or doing homework, driving a
car while intoxicated, or riding in a car with an intoxicated driver. If you
do make the rule, clearly communicate the consequences to your teens—
for example, losing their driving privileges or even their car—and make
sure you follow through if the rule is violated. At the same time, you don't
want your kids hiding dangerous behavior from you, so let them know they can call you any time of day or night and you will drive them home, no questions asked. Another alternative: Many towns and cities have free Safe Ride programs that will drive kids home without embarrassing them in front of their peers the way your presence would. Get your kids the phone number to put in their wallets.

We emphasize again that we don't mean to imply that you should approve of drug use.
We're simply suggesting that you take the tack most likely to be successful. School programs that give teens facts about drugs, help them develop decision-making and social skills, and show them how to cope with
anxiety and stress have proven far more effective in reducing teen drug
use than scare tactics. Apply the same thinking in your home: Train your
kids to make good judgments and then trust that they will make them.
Not because it's kinder and gentler, but because it works.

A few more tips:

Modeling. If you have your own troubled relationship with a substance,
legal or not, you must clean it up if you expect to have any credibility
with your kids on the subject. But we're not talking about the occasional
glass of wine with your pasta. Interestingly, parents who use substances
responsibly appear to be better models than do teetotalers. Professionals
have long known that problem drinkers are more likely to come either
from homes in which parents consume too much alcohol or homes in
which they don't drink at all. It appears that it's easier for kids to get the
concept of moderation when they can see it in action.

Reacting. If your child should come home drunk or high, hold back your anger and don't reveal how upset you are for a while, even if he's been driving. Let him know you're glad he's safe and allow him to sleep it off. If sanctions are appropriate, the next day is soon enough to enact them, after you've both had a chance to think about it awhile.

Remembering. Despite what the antidrug troops say, drug use hasn't changed all that much since you were in your teenager's shoes. Step out of your parent role for a moment and recall your own temptations when you were that young. Chances are that you're in a better position to be empathetic about your teen's experiences in this realm than your parents were with you. This is an immensely valuable tool—don't neglect it.

A Message That Young People Can Hear

There are many ways to urge kids not to use drugs that don't make you resort to false information and transparent horror stories. Start by reminding them that many of the drugs their generation is taking are illegal. "It may not seem fair to you that certain drugs are against the law when drugs like alcohol aren't," you might say. "But that's the law for now and not liking it won't keep you out of jail. The penalties for drug use today are really severe. That may not seem fair, either, but it means that if you get caught, it could hurt your future plans and perhaps haunt you your entire life. It could get you thrown out of school, cost you your job, or land you in prison. If you allow drug use to interfere with your schoolwork, that could hurt your future, too.

"And by the way, you aren't the only one affected by what you do. If you hurt yourself or someone else because of drug use or driving while high, the anguish you'll cause us is more than you can know. If you're arrested for drugs, you'll cause us a lot of trouble. It may also cost us lots of money to straighten out your legal problems, perhaps more than we can afford."

Because youngsters think they are virtually immortal, you want to state the dangers of driving while high or drunk in broader terms: "Almost any drug you take is going to hurt your driving. You're not only a danger to yourself when you are stoned, you're also a danger to others—passengers in your car, people on the road with you, and children playing by the street. In addition, if the police catch you driving while you're high, you could go to jail."

Kids aren't completely immune to messages about their health. That's why most teen drug users will confine their use to mild drugs like marijuana. But our overblown drug campaigns may lead them to make some unfortunate assumptions. So try stressing the following: "Some adults will tell you things about drugs that aren't true. But that doesn't mean that all drugs are safe. Most have their dangers, especially when you use them without having accurate information. And remember that you're getting these drugs on the street. You may be getting them from your friends but at some level, they're being put on the street by criminals who probably don't care much about what happens to the users. The drugs may be laced with things you don't want or aren't expecting. They also may be stronger than what you're expecting.

"I can't stop you from using drugs, much as I'd like to. But if you do choose to use them, make sure you know where the drugs come from, all the stuff mixed with them, all the things that might happen when you take them, and any precautions you should take. [*From Chocolate to Morphine* is a superior, teen-friendly resource on the latter.] You should be as careful about the things you ingest or smoke as you are about the things you eat."

Parents worry, for good reason, about the kind of company their kids keep if they do drugs. The majority of kids who do a little pot aren't bad kids, but you are right to be concerned that more unfortunate influences aren't that far away. Ask your teens to promise you that, if nothing else, they'll stay away from people who urge them to do reckless things or who are irresponsible in their own drug use. And point out to them that even if their drug sources are friends, the people at the end of that chain are large-scale dealers who are probably heavily armed, paranoid, and capable of just about anything. They should never deal with people they don't know, even if their friends say "he's okay."

This is barely an introduction to the difficult subject of teen drug use. For more information, turn to the books reviewed in the Resources at the end of this chapter.

TALKING TO YOUR KIDS ABOUT SEX

"My folks initiated exactly two conversations with me about sex," Alan recalls. "The first happened when I was in sixth grade. My whole class was taking 'Social Hygiene,' my school system's euphemism for sex education. The course didn't cover much more than basic plumbing, but as the time got closer, the playground buzz put it on the same level in my mind as the *Playboy* magazines my friends and I had nabbed from a neighbor's trash can. One afternoon, my mother was dropping me off at the library when she asked what I thought about sex, now that I'd learned what it was. I said that it seemed pretty bizarre. She avoided my eyes and said, 'Actually, it's very beautiful' in an endearing, stumbling kind of way. She never raised the 'beautiful' subject again.

"Dad made his first, and last, stab at 'The Talk' when I was sixteen. I'd been moping about the house for days after a girl I'd been dating broke the news she was going out with someone else. One evening, Dad, no doubt after heavy lobbying by Mom, came up to my room. He didn't ask me what was wrong. He just began relating his first sexual experience, although he was stiff, awkward, and vague about it. I felt compelled to explain that my depression had absolutely nothing to do with his story, which of course had fascinated me anyway. I didn't tell him that I hadn't even figured out yet how to move beyond a polite good-night kiss, which, come to think of it, is probably why my girlfriend was dumping me. I'm sure Dad was greatly relieved that I didn't have any embarrassing questions for him. We finished up the conversation talking about football. The original topic was abandoned forever."

As it turns out, most American kids get even less counsel and information from their folks than Alan did. Fewer than 20 percent of parents today have ever had a significant conversation with their children about sex, notes the National PTA. That may seem strange considering that so many of today's parents lived through the sexual revolution of the 1960s and 1970s. But the more telling factor here, sex educators point out, is that even those of us who came of age in more frank and bold times learned to be parents from *our* parents. And most of them were too inhibited to speak openly to us about sex. In other words, we still have no useful cultural tradition in America for handling the subject with our kids.

To complicate matters, only a small fraction of American schools offer comprehensive sexuality courses. In other districts, the courses are so restricted in scope that they have dubious value. For example, they often do not include discussion of contraception and other important topics such as homosexuality.

Why It Matters

Although well-intentioned, those who argue against early and frank sex education have either not read or chosen to ignore expert opinion on the subject. Statistics and research point clearly to the fact that American kids are being hurt by a lack of knowledge about sexuality:

- While many feel that teaching children about sexuality will increase their chances of having early sex, studies show the exact opposite. *That is, it is the teens with the least knowledge who are the most sexually active.* Considerable research demonstrates that teenage girls who receive honest, accurate information about sex are much less likely to get unintentionally pregnant. They're also more likely to delay starting sexual behavior.

- The U.S. leads all industrialized countries in teen pregnancy rates. This too suggests that early knowledge about sex is not the problem. Teens in Canada, England, the Netherlands, France, and Sweden have their first intercourse at roughly the same age as U.S. teens, yet teen pregnancy rates are less than half of those in America.

- Sexually transmitted diseases have always been statistically higher among the young. Today, AIDS has made this a life-threatening matter, and experts widely agree that lack of knowledge about proper protective behavior *besides abstinence* is a leading cause of the disease's spread.

- Lack of factual information about homosexuality causes anxiety in teenagers whose sexual identities are still forming and who are experiencing confusing thoughts and feelings. In some cases, these anxieties have led to suicide.

It's Up to Us

Children are going to learn about sex. Their natural curiosity ensures that. We can only control where they learn about it first, and whether they get accurate information. If we don't show them early on that it's safe to ask about sex and that we'll do our best to provide them with honest answers, they'll turn to far less reliable sources—their friends, the media, and their own florid imaginations.

But there's a lot more at stake here than misinformation. Research noted by the National PTA shows that children who have never discussed sex with their parents are more likely to satisfy their curiosity by experimenting. Still more studies emphasize parents' crucial role in helping their children make good decisions. Teens who discuss sexual topics with their parents are more likely to delay becoming sexually active and use contraception when they do start sexual activity.

Even in those rare cases where the school system offers a good sexuality course, that doesn't let parents off the hook. Most experts feel that if a child hasn't started asking questions by age five to six, parents should open the discussion on their own. Most schools that offer courses do so much later, closer to the time of puberty.

But educating your children about sex need not be seen only as a "should." It's also a terrific opportunity to build a more open, communicative, and intimate relationship with your children. While you may find the subject matter—especially the details of it—embarrassing at times, you would certainly want to convey to your children that making love is first and foremost about sharing love.

In addition to bringing you closer together as a family, talking to your children about sex can create a "safe space" for other sensitive discussions as well. A natural link exists between sexuality and other difficult subject matter that mystifies or troubles children—for example, drugs. If you want your children to feel they can come to you for guidance in making good choices about other crucial matters, this is where it starts. Questions about sex occur to most kids very early in life. How you respond to those questions lets your children know early on whether the door is open when issues get touchy.

Actually, says Alan, "openness was one of my parents' strong suits and it became one of the greatest lessons they taught me about parenting. Yes, my parents were awkward in the extreme when they talked about sex. But they never made me feel that this subject, or any other, was off-limits. As a result, I never felt I needed to do something crazy just to get their attention."

You should also consider the effects of the sexual messages that permeate our culture. Your kids will be bombarded with sexy imagery in advertising, television programs, popular songs, and even in the newspaper. Sex sells. All this lustiness makes adolescents feel pressured to become sexually active, as many have reported to counselors and researchers. Teens who feel safe to talk to their parents about sex are more likely just to talk about the pressures they feel rather than giving in to them. Talking openly with your kids about sex also communicates that sex is healthy and natural. Making it a secretive topic gives kids the idea that something is wrong with it. Final reason to talk to your kids about sex: If not you, who?

When to Start and What to Do

The first part of this question is easy: You should start answering your kids' questions whenever they start asking them. And those questions

homosexuality

In an inspired piece of Comedy Central election coverage, comedian Al Franken strolled amongst a large group of delegates relaxing during the 1996 Republican convention and asked them if they had ever had a homosexual dream. Without fail, everybody he asked would shake their heads and say nope, uh-uh, no way. To which he would always respond cheerily, "I have!"

Of course, all Franken was really admitting to was his own, well, frankness. Sex research shows that most heterosexuals have had homosexual dreams, fantasies, thoughts, or feelings. These are especially common during adolescence when hormones are surging and the psyche is changing from the self-centeredness of childhood to adult sexual identity. But they also persist in adulthood, because while most of us live exclusively heterosexual lives, our psyches play with all kinds of notions that we'll never act upon. Actual sex play between children of the same sex is also common among future heterosexuals and is just as natural.

Despite this, the topic of homosexuality is such a firestarter in America that few school sexuality programs dare address it in any meaningful way. Many of the mainstream educational materials neglect it as well. The persistence of antigay, "family values" rhetoric in the culture means that millions of parents under its sway aren't doing the best job of counseling their kids about sexual identity either.

So where does that leave adolescents who are struggling with the cataclysmic changes of puberty? In many cases, terrified. Their thoughts and feelings are shifting wildly, and they're very likely worried that the most momentary fantasy about people of their own sex will damn them to hell, or at least a living hell on earth.

The best way to handle this topic with your kids is the same way you should handle other sexual topics—with facts and loving, open communication. As with sexual topics in general, it is important that you base your statements on accurate information. It is also important that your children feel confident that they can come to you when they are troubled. Let's put this bluntly: Sidestepping or mishandling this subject can cause your preteens and teens tremendous emotional discomfort. In some extreme cases, teens have committed suicide over fears about being homosexual whether they were actually homosexual or not, so this is not something to be taken lightly.

(continued on next page)

could come as soon as your kids start asking about any other aspect of their world. We often forget that those charming, innocent little beings that we tuck in at night are also sexual beings. From birth, little boys get erections and little girls get vaginal lubrication. Both little boys and girls also get pleasure from fondling their genitals.

You'll notice that when your children start asking about sex, or mommy's and daddy's differing anatomy, the questions don't cause them the same embarrassment that they might you. Studies show that kids don't start feeling embarrassment about this subject until about age eight, long past the time you should have begun discussing sexuality with them. In fact, suggests Planned Parenthood, if you have forthright sex discussions with your kids from the beginning, they may never become shy about the subject and that should certainly be regarded as healthy.

Somewhere between the ages of nine and twelve, your children's questions will become less matter-of-fact, more personal, and more emotionally charged. Puberty is around the corner and they know it. They're worried about how they'll change, if they'll be attractive, and what sexuality means for them. If they don't raise these topics with you, you should with them, as early as when you see the first signs of facial hair in boys, breast development in girls, or pubic hair in either. And note that puberty may well come much earlier for your kids than it did for you, due to changes in diet and healthcare. For example, age twelve is a normal time for a girl's first period; just two generations ago, the normal age was sixteen.

Here are some tips to make your discussions with your kids more effective, comfortable, and satisfying for all of you:

- *Take the initiative.* Don't wait until they ask questions. Use everyday opportunities—for example, when you see your child noticing a sexy magazine cover— to raise the subject. This will give the message that sexuality is a normal and comfortable subject for conversation.

- *Teach responsibility and respect, and build self-esteem.* Preparing kids for sexual maturity takes more than just talking about sex. Teach your kids that every act has consequences. Also teach them to respect the rights and bodies of others and stress to them that they deserve the same. All of these things have obvious relevance to sexuality. In addition, building up children's self-esteem will help them resist pressures to have sex when they reach their teen years.

(continued from previous page)

The following information may be useful as well:

- *Homosexuality is not a disease.* In the view of both the psychiatry and psychology professions, homosexuality is not a mental illness. In other words, health professionals don't feel that homosexuals need therapy to be "normal" or that therapy could even make a difference. Homosexuality is simply a variety of human experience. Researchers don't know what makes some people gay and others straight, and may never know.
- *Homosexuality is not a choice.* No responsible researcher thinks that gays choose their homosexuality. The overwhelming majority of homosexuals report feeling an attraction to their own gender from an early age. Perhaps you've heard stories from "family values" advocates about homosexuals who have "converted" to heterosexuality, often after a religious experience. Whether or not these stories are true, they mean little. The fact that an occasional person "converts" to heterosexuality probably indicates he/she was bisexual, not exclusively homosexual. It in no way indicates that other gays could, or should, change their sexual identity.
- *Gays and lesbians have healthy relationships, too.* The homosexual population encompasses the same range of behavior as heterosexuals. Some homosexuals are decadent, as are some heterosexuals. Many other homosexuals live quietly in committed, monogamous, loving relationships.

While youthful homosexual thoughts and experiences do not determine mature sexuality, for some children the fantasies and desires will never stop. If this is so in your household, your child probably feels far more pain than you do and it's crucial that he/she feel safe to open up to you. Many parents in these circumstances blame themselves, as if a child's sexuality was a problem. Try to avoid this pitfall. Being gay is a trait that shows up in the population every so often, like red hair. It also may change at this age, so neither you nor your child should be drawing firm conclusions. But whatever the outcome, your child needs to know that he or she is still loved and supported. Your local chapter of Parents and Friends of Lesbian and Gays (PFLAG) is a terrific resource in these circumstances.

- *Don't segregate by gender.* Traditionally, parents have split the task of sexuality discussions along strict gender lines, mothers talking to their daughters, fathers their sons. But moms have a lot to share with their sons about sex—for example, helping them understand how girls feel about things—and dads can do the same for their daughters. These cross-gender talks can, and should, break down gender stereotypes about sex.

· *Don't let your inhibitions or what you don't know get in the way.* When your kids ask something that makes you squirm a little, it's fine to tell them that you're uncomfortable with the question before answering it. In fact, acknowledging your discomfort may well cause those disquieting feelings to subside. Of course, some parents subconsciously discourage their kids from asking questions about sex because they're afraid they won't have the answers. It's okay to tell your kids, "I don't know." Better yet, have appropriate reference material on hand and say, "Let's go look it up."

· *Examine your own sexual attitudes.* Confront your own sexual biases so you don't unconsciously pass them on to your kids.

· *Don't stop with "The Talk."* The whole notion of a single, comprehensive talk is a misnomer because sex education should be ongoing and "on demand," not a one-time session.

· *Don't punish your children for their natural curiosity.* If you find your kids exploring each other's genitals, it's fine to let play proceed if it's mutually consensual and between kids of similar ages. "Playing doctor" is a natural, healthy childhood activity, even if it is practicing medicine without a license! The real harm comes from parents showing revulsion, which may cause kids to conclude that something about their bodies or natural urges is bad. If you just can't tolerate it, "please react in a neutral rather than negative way," suggests physician/author Marianne Neifert, coauthor of *Dr. Mom.* "Practice responses such as, 'It seems a little cold in here. Wouldn't you like to put your clothes on?'"

· *Respect your children.* In one prominent survey, 65 percent of teens reported that they couldn't discuss sex with their parents. One of the most common complaints from teens: Every time they ask about sex, their parents accuse them of having sex or being in trouble. Unless your kids can trust you to trust them, they won't be coming to you for guidance, and that's where real problems begin.

· *Skip the scare tactics.* Attempts to frighten your kids with scary tales about pregnancy and sexually transmitted diseases don't work, say experts. Notes the National PTA, "studies consistently show that children are most likely to heed information that is given in an open, matter-of-fact manner that invites questions and discussion." Again, if you turn off your teens with a harsh or unforgiving attitude, they'll stop talking to you about sex, and that may lead to the very situations you're trying to prevent.

By and large, we have avoided advising you *what* to tell your kids about sex and only introduced the subject of how and when to talk to them. For more detailed information and useful support materials, see Resources.

CHAPTER 4 RESOURCES

General

The Holistic Pediatrician by Kathi J. Kemper, M.D. (HarperPerennial, 1996).
> Pediatrician Kemper gives recommendations for safely and effectively treating twenty-five of the most common childhood ailments. Draws on herbs, homeopathy, and other alternatives as well as conventional medicine.

Natural Health, Natural Medicine by Andrew Weil, M.D. (Houghton Mifflin, 1990).
> Weil's manual for wellness and self-care. Every holistic family should have a copy on their reference shelf, although little of the information is specifically about children.

Smart Medicines for a Healthier Child by Janet Zand, O.M.D., Rachel Walton, R.N., and Bob Rountree, M.D. (Garden City Park, NY: Avery, 1994).
> Well-organized, easy-to-use guide to treating common childhood disorders both holistically and conventionally. The holistic approaches covered include diet, nutritional supplements, acupressure, herbs, and homeopathy.

Holistic Physicians and Other Alternative Practitioners

BOOKS

Family Guide to Natural Medicine edited by Alma Guinness (Pleasantville, NY: Reader's Digest, 1993).
> Impressive, introductory guide to natural health including alternative therapies, herbology, diet, mental approaches, bodywork, movement therapy, and more.

Health and Healing by Andrew Weil, M.D. (Houghton Mifflin, 1983).
> Weil profiles alternative health approaches including their often fascinating histories. Also explores the role of belief in healing.

Homeopathic Medicine for Children and Infants by Dana Ullman (Tarcher/Perigee, 1992).
> Well-organized, easy-to-use guide by America's leading spokesperson for homeopathy. Ullman carefully notes symptoms for which parents should seek conventional medical advice.

ORGANIZATIONS—TRADITIONAL CHINESE MEDICINE

National Commission on the Certification of Acupuncture and Oriental Medicine, 11 Canal Center Plaza, Suite 300, Alexandria, VA 22314, (703) 548–9004
website: www.nccaom.org
> Contact for information on professional standards and licensing requirements.

American Association of Oriental Medicine, 433 Front Street, Catasauqua, PA 18032, (610) 266–1433

website: www.aaom.org

> Contact for referrals to practitioners.

American Academy of Medical Acupuncture, 5820 Wilshire Boulevard, Suite 500, Los Angeles, CA 90036, (213) 937–5514, (800) 521–2262

website: www.medicalacupuncture.org

> This professional organization represents M.D.s who practice acupuncture.

ORGANIZATION—AYURVEDIC MEDICINE

Maharishi Ayurveda School and Medical Center, 679 George Hill Road, Lancaster, MA 01523, (978) 365–4549

> Can both provide general information on Ayurveda and refer you to affiliated centers and practitioners. All centers have at least one M.D. on staff. The Center in Lancaster is an arm of the Maharishi Mahesh Yogi's Transcendental Meditation movement.

ORGANIZATION—HOMEOPATHY

National Center for Homeopathy, 801 North Fairfax Street, Suite 306, Alexandria, VA 223134, (703) 548–7790

website: www.homeopathic.org

> Can refer you to practitioners in your area.

ORGANIZATIONS—OSTEOPATHY

American Academy of Osteopathy, 3500 DePauw Boulevard, Suite 1080, Indianapolis, IN 46268, (317) 879–1881

website: www.aao.medguide.net

> For referrals to osteopaths, classic or otherwise.

Cranial Academy, 8202 Clear Vista Parkway, Suite 9D, Indianapolis, IN 46256, (317) 594–0411

> Contact to find a cranial osteopathic specialist.

ORGANIZATION—NATUROPATHY

American Association of Naturopathic Physicians, 601 Valley Street, Suite 105, Seattle, WA 98109, (206) 298–0126

website: www.naturopathic.org or www.aanp.net

> Contact for referral to practitioner in your area.

ORGANIZATION—HOLISTIC MEDICINE

American Holistic Medical Association, 6728 Old McLean Village Drive, McLean, VA 22101, (703) 556–9728

website: www.holisticmedicine.org

> Contact for referral to member doctors.

Should I Consider Alternative Treatments for Serious Illness?

BOOKS

Choices in Healing: Integrating the Best of Conventional and Complementary Approaches to Cancer by Michael Lerner (MIT Press, 1994).

> Outstanding resource for basic information on both conventional and alternative cancer therapies, including guidance on how to research treatment options.

Love, Medicine and Miracles by Bernie Siegel, M.D. (Harper & Row, 1986).

> Powerfully reorienting, inspiring, and wise on the subject of fighting, and living with, serious illness.

ORGANIZATION

The Plaintree Libraries' Institute for Health & Healing Library, 2040 Webster Street, San Francisco, CA 94115, (415) 923–3681; fax (415) 673–2629

> For a research fee, this consumer health resource can send a detailed report on the symptoms and alternative and conventional treatments (and national support groups) for just about any medical condition.

A Family Herbal

Natural Healing for Babies & Children by Aviva Jill Romm (Freedom, CA: The Crossing Press, 1996).

> Herbally oriented A–Z guide to children's symptoms and complaints. Tells when to call the doctor, offers nutritional suggestions, and shows how to create a basic herbal medicine chest and first-aid kit. Also covers some homeopathic remedies and includes discussions of pregnancy, labor, birth, and postpartum from a natural health perspective.

See also reviews under "General" on p. 197.

Family Exercise

See *Natural Health, Natural Medicine* reviewed on p. 197. While not geared specifically to children, Weil's book presents a moderate, enjoyable approach to exercise that is well-suited to family fitness.

Protecting Your Children from Health Hazards Around the House

BOOKS

Healthy Homes, Healthy Kids: Protecting Your Children from Everyday Environmental Hazards by Joyce M. Schoemaker and Charity Y. Vitale (Corelo, CA, and Washington, DC: Island Press, 1991).

> As befits its scientist-authors, the prose is sober, never alarmist. Long resource lists follow each chapter.

The Safe Shopper's Bible: A Consumer's Guide to Nontoxic Household Products, Cosmetics, and Foods by David Stenman and Samuel Epstein, M.D. (Macmillan, 1995).

> Clear, easy-to-read, and concise. Covers thousands of brand-name products, recommends the least contaminated forms of produce, gives advice for safe use of products, explores food irradiation and genetic engineering, and much more. Includes formulations for making your own household cleaning products.

ORGANIZATIONS

Environmental Defense Fund, 257 Park Avenue South, New York, NY 10010, (212) 505–2100 or (800) 684–3322
website: www.edf.org

> Source of several publications on home health hazards such as lead in kitchenware.

Seventh Generation/Harmony, 360 Interlocken Boulevard, Suite 300, Broomfield, CO 80021, (800) 869–3446

Source of environmentally friendly, nontoxic, and organic cleaning products, organic cotton bedding, as well as other products for healthy, green living. The company is soon to be called Harmony.

Talking to Your Kids About Drugs

From Chocolate to Morphine: Everything You Need to Know About Mind-Altering Drugs by Andrew Weil, M.D., and Winifred Rosen (Houghton Mifflin, 1993).

Best book we've seen for educating kids about real properties of substances. Must-have resource for parents of school-age children. Focused on preventing abuse of drugs, except those for which there is no safe use, such as heroin.

Marijuana Myths, Marijuana Facts: A Review of the Scientific Evidence by Lynn Zimmer and John Morgan (New York: The Lindesmith Center of the Open Society Institute, 1997).

Sociology professor Zimmer and medical professor/pharmacology researcher Morgan examine the correctness of statements about marijuana's harmfulness made by commonly quoted public and private authorities. Called by Andrew Weil, M.D., "the most accurate book on the effects of marijuana that has appeared to date." Also praised by conservative columnist William F. Buckley.

Talking to Your Kids About Sex

How to Talk with Your Child About Sexuality: A Parent's Guide by Planned Parenthood Federation of America with Michael Edelhart (Doubleday, 1986).

An excellent, progressive guide.

Call your local Planned Parenthood office for free educational brochures. Some also will supply reading lists compiled from local libraries' holdings.

a holistic family diet

alking about good nutrition makes most people nervous. Food provides some of life's most sublime pleasures. Why listen to some grumpy busybody who wants to take your fun away?

This is an entirely understandable feeling. Maintaining a healthy diet can mean a major change in a family's eating habits. After all, the typical American diet comes up far short of ideal, nutrition-wise, and helps create the high rates of coronary heart disease, colon cancer, diabetes, strokes, high blood pressure, and obesity (including childhood obesity) that are also typical in our society. If you want to help protect your children from a life threatened by these problems, it's best to establish good eating habits from the start.

Many people mistakenly think that improving their family's diet means sacrifice, but those who take the plunge often find that they are enjoying eating more than ever. After all, many healthful foods have richer, fuller tastes than their mainstream counterparts. Certainly organic fruits and vegetables tend to be tastier than those grown by huge agricultural corporations, who, in the process of breeding fruits and vegetables for better commercial properties (toughness to withstand mechanized handling, smoother appearance, and such), have often bred the taste right out. And the sweeteners and flours used in healthful foods are far less bland than the white sugar and flour that are staples of mainstream cooking.

Healthful eating leads to other new pleasures for your kids and you, as well—the pleasures of feeling and looking better, having more zip, not being sick as often, and not having so much trouble controlling weight. Says Kat Wild of San Diego, who has long pursued a healthy lifestyle with her husband Norbert and their two children, "When I see my friends who never wanted to bother with the details about food quality, I can see that it's taken a big toll on their skin, their hair, and their energy level." As for her kids' health, Kat notes that "they don't get the common colds and flus as easily, and when they get them, they get over them much faster."

In the following pages, you'll learn more about why you should feed your family more healthful foods and how to do it. We'll guide you to nutritious foods that resemble the "junk" that kids crave. You'll learn about aspects of vegetarianism and organic eating that you might not have considered and understand why vegetarian eating isn't for everyone. You'll also learn the basic rules for preparing foods so that you can preserve the maximum nutrients.

In addition, we'll cover special precautions for vegetarian families with developing infants and children. Healthful foods often cost more—you'll discover how many families have made it affordable. You'll learn that good nutrition is only one of numerous benefits of growing your own. We'll show you other ways of filling your kitchen with fresh organic produce if you don't have a backyard you can dig up. And of course, like so many others today, we offer our special secret for losing weight. Naturally, we think our way is better. We *know* it's healthier.

WHY HEALTHFUL EATING MATTERS FOR KIDS

It's not news that American adults lead most of the world in rates of heart disease and other diet-and lifestyle-related diseases. But research is starting to demonstrate that adult health problems don't appear suddenly in middle age. They result from a lifetime of poor choices, beginning in early childhood. As we saw in the previous chapter, close to half of American youngsters show at least one risk factor for heart disease by the age of five to eight. And the problem is getting worse, not better. The entire American population, kids included, is growing fatter.

No loving parent would intentionally endanger the health of her children by feeding them a diet that dooms them to life-threatening conditions later on. But the fact remains that most American kids and their folks don't eat wisely, so we have to ask why. The most obvious answer is that most parents simply don't know better. They tend to feed their kids the way their parents fed them. Unfortunately, the current generation of parents grew up in an era when far less was known about diet and when the myth-laden four basic food groups was the model of good nutrition.

Parents are swayed by bad nutritional advice from so-called experts, too. Medical schools don't spend much classroom time on nutrition, which is why most physicians have so little useful information to offer us on the subject. (In fact, parents who have studied family nutrition on their own may well know more about the subject than does their family doctor.) In addition, the guidelines issuing from professional nutritionists and dieticians and government bodies like the Agriculture Department are heavily influenced by the powerful food industries that supply the makings of the unhealthful American diet. After all, it was the meat and dietary industries along with government officials who developed the four basic food groups and promoted them to us. This dietary scheme—although originally well-intentioned—did wonders for those industries by emphasizing animal protein as the most important part of every meal. But we've since learned that it's also played a huge role in the profusion of diet- and lifestyle-related diseases that plague the Ameri-can population. Spokespeople for meat and dairy companies continue to promote the virtues of animal protein as if nothing has changed.

Another reason that American kids eat poorly is that their parents mistakenly believe that the extra fat and cholesterol kids consume doesn't matter because "they'll just burn it off." We now know that too much fat early in life predisposes children to illnesses and premature death in adulthood. Besides, kids aren't "burning off" calories the way past generations did, because of such factors as excessive television watching and cutbacks in physical education classes in schools.

We only have to look at our own experience to realize why it's important to start kids off with healthful eating habits. It's much easier to never start an unhealthful tradition like a big bowl of ice cream after dinner than it is to give it up. By the time children reach adolescence, they're probably eating much the way they will as adults and they'll have just as much trouble changing their habits as you do yours.

THE BASICS OF COMPOSING A HEALTHFUL FAMILY DIET

Consider Your Sources About Food

We've talked a bit about why mainstream nutritional advice is not always trustworthy. But leaving mainstream advice behind leaves you in a state of limbo. Once you start researching family nutrition on your own, you may find yourself awash in a stream of nutty ideas, fad diets, and unproved but fervent claims. Whom should you believe?

Start with this test—if the diet is extremely specific and the claims made for it just short of miraculous, steer clear. Differences in individual humans, seasons, climate zones, and many other factors affect how people respond to foods, making it impossible to recommend the exact same diet for everyone.

As for claims that a particular diet or food will absolutely prevent or cure certain illnesses, forget it. Yes, diet plays an important, even crucial, role in preventing certain conditions such as heart disease, but health also depends upon other important factors such as heredity, stress, and so on. People with the "right" genes may be able to live long, vital lives while violating every healthful living principle known to humanity, while those with the "wrong" ones or too much emotional stress may suffer problems even after a lifetime of broccoli and tofu. Diet has never been proven to cure major illnesses, although it certainly makes sense for sick people to eat as healthily as possible to support their body's internal healing abilities.

The nutritional information that follows is typical of advice issued by independent experts such as Andrew Weil, M.D., Charles Atwood, M.D., and the Center for Science in the Public Interest, and is backed by considerable research. It is also quite general, for good reason. What works for most people may not work for you or your children because of quirks in your biochemistry or physiology. Or what worked for you and your kids when you were younger may not work as you age. So nobody can tell you they know the perfect diet for you. Ultimately, you have to trust your own experience. That, and your commitment to be healthy no matter what adjustments you have to make, is what will lead you to a healthful diet.

The Real Basic Food Groups

In 1974, the weird and wonderful comedy group Firesign Theatre spoofed counterculture conceits with an album called "Everything You Know Is

Wrong." When it comes to nutrition, however, the Firesign title isn't far off. In the last couple of decades, research has turned much of what used to be thought of as good nutrition on its head. At the same time, researchers have validated many of the features of the diets promoted by holistic "crazies" in the 1970s.

A healthful family diet balances foods from three basic categories—carbohydrates, fat, and protein. It also pays attention to four additional categories—vitamins, minerals, fiber, and water.

Carbohydrates

Most of us grew up hearing that carbohydrates were fattening. However, besides being the *least* fattening, by far, of the three main categories of foods, carbohydrates are to the human body what gasoline is to a car. Our bodies fuel themselves by breaking down carbohydrates to glucose, the simple sugar that is carbohydrates' main component. This is well understood in poorer nations, which is why peasant diets are based around complex carbohydrate staples such as rice, corn, legumes, potatoes, and wheat. Experts here understand this as well—they commonly recommend that 55 percent of dietary calories come from carbohydrates, 80 percent of those from complex carbohydrates.

As the term "complex carbohydrates" implies, not all carbohydrates have the same nutritional importance. There are two main categories of carbohydrates: sugars, also known as simple carbohydrates, and starches, the shorthand term for complex carbohydrates. "Sugars" include such familiar foods as table sugar (sucrose), milk sugar (lactose), dextrose (corn sugar), and fruit sugar (fructose). The uncomplicated structure of these carbohydrates enables the body to burn them quickly, leading to a rapid rise in blood sugar and an energy spurt. You've probably observed unsophisticated athletes wolfing down candy bars for a quick energy burst. This mistaken strategy takes at least as much energy from the body as it gives. Because the body can't generally store the energy from simple carbohydrates, the energy spark from candy is soon followed by a rapid drop in blood sugar, and an energy slump.

Starches are absorbed by the blood far more slowly, leading to a much longer, steadier supply of energy than simple carbohydrates provide. People who eat diets centered around such foods as the staples mentioned above generally have a much easier time controlling their weight because they're not as hungry between meals, thanks to the slowness with which starches are digested.

That said, some starches are better for your family than others. Your family will be much healthier if you emphasize whole starches such as whole grain breads and brown rice over processed foods such as white flour and white rice. Food processing removes fiber, and destroys vitamins in the process.

You won't damage your family's health by using processed starches from time to time. In fact, processed starches supply just as much en-

ergy as whole grains. But if you rely on them too much, your family is being shorted on fiber and important nutrients. The standard American diet tends to be constipating because it emphasizes processed grains such as white flour over whole grains and is low in other important fiber sources such as raw fruits and vegetables. This almost certainly contributes to the country's high rates of colon cancer. (For more on dietary fiber, see page 216.) The claims made for whole, unprocessed complex carbohydrates can sound almost too good to be true, but in fact, these are the only foods not associated with America's leading diseases.

On the other hand, the bad news we've heard about sugars is largely true. Nearly everyone can tolerate a little sugar now and then. But in the large quantities that people typically consume (120 pounds yearly in Western nations!), sugars can lead to tooth decay, contribute to obesity and diabetes, and increase the risk of coronary disease by raising the levels of what are called triglycerides in the blood. Because of the infamous sugar "rush," high sugar intake can even cause depression, mood swings, and energy swings. Not all sugars are quite the same in this regard. For instance, white table sugar is known to be particularly destructive to teeth and may cause more of a "sugar rush" than does fructose or honey.

Sugars hide under the names of many aliases—molasses, brown sugar (white sugar plus molasses), honey, corn syrup, high-fructose corn syrup, maple syrup, raw sugar, and sorbitol and mannitol (the latter two are alcohol sugars used in supposedly sugar-free products). Many common processed foods contain substantial amounts of sugar, as well—for example, catsup, salad dressings, bread, soups, canned fruits and vegetables, crackers, and nearly every processed cereal in your local supermarket, including "plain" oatmeal, corn flakes, shredded wheat, and the like. Read food labels and see for yourself—remember that ingredients are listed in order of decreasing quantity and you'll note that sugar plays a major role in a staggering number of foods. (You should always read food labels so you can see beyond the hype on the packaging and know what you're really buying for your family.)

So-called health foods often utilize whole sugars such as honey, molasses, maple sugar, and raw sugar instead of granulated white sugar. These sugars do possess nutritional advantages (for example, the substantial amounts of potassium and calcium in molasses) over white sugar, which basically has no "nutritionally redeeming" value. But that doesn't make whole sugars important foods—their nutrients can be found in far more healthful foods as well.

Nobody's suggesting that you put your family on a sugarless diet. That might lead to armed revolt faster than it does better health! But you can reduce your family's intake to smarter levels by following a few simple guidelines:

- Serve naturally sweet whole foods such as fruits—raw, cooked, or dried—for desserts or snacks. Your children may love foods such as dried pineapple or papaya, which are candy-like in sweetness, color, and texture.

- Teach your children to satisfy their sweets craving with a small taste—a piece of nonsticky candy (better for teeth), a spoonful of ice cream, one or two small cookies.

- Reduce temptation by only keeping small quantities of sweets around. Half gallons of ice cream, cases of soft drinks, and bags of candy just beg to be consumed.

Fat

On average, Americans get 42 percent of their calories from fat, eight times what the body needs and way over the 20 to 30 percent "compromise" suggested by experts. Most of us know we should be eating much less from this food category. But we may not realize just what's at stake. The high-fat content of the American diet is linked to more fatal diseases—heart disease and various cancers among them—than any other food category. High-fat diets lay the groundwork for obesity, too. And since our vulnerability to these conditions begins early in life, parents should restrict the fat intake of their kids *once they reach the age of two* to the same low levels recommended for adults. But beware: Low-fat diets before age two can hinder a child's growth.

Many of us don't understand how fat hides out in the diet. Without that information, it's impossible to eat wisely. Here's just a partial list of common fat-laden foods: beef, pork, and lamb ("lean" cuts are still relatively high in fat); duck, goose, and unskinned chicken; whole milk and foods made from it (cheese, ice cream, butter, cream); seeds; nuts; olives; avocados; peanuts (a legume, not a nut); soybeans; oil fish (salmon, sardines, bluefish, mackerel, herring); fried foods of any type; chocolate; most fast- and snack foods; many restaurant foods; many prepared foods sold in supermarkets (including many foods labeled "no cholesterol" and "low fat"—see below); foods cooked in fats such as butter, shortening, or oil; mayonnaise; salad dressing; most sauces and gravies. In fact, the prepared foods you buy at your local health food store or natural foods restaurant may be just as fat-drenched as those in mainstream outlets.

Our body requires a certain amount of dietary fat for long-term energy storage and other purposes, but some sources are far better than others. Here are the important terms to know so you can improve your family's eating habits:

Fatty acids. These are the building blocks of fat.

Cholesterol. A waxy material manufactured by the liver, cholesterol is essential in small amounts for some bodily processes. However, the body makes all it needs, so dietary cholesterol adds nothing useful and large amounts increase the risk of coronary disease. Cholesterol is found only in animal products such as meat and dairy foods, not plant foods such as legumes or nuts.

Saturated fatty acids. These fats turn hard and opaque at room temperature. They're found mainly in meat and dairy products, along with hydrogenated (see below) vegetable products. The fats in tropical oils such as coconut and palm oils, widely used in fast food outlets and processed foods, are also overwhelmingly saturated. The body has no need for saturated fats; the fewer of them in the diet, the better.

Hydrogenation. This is the process of adding hydrogen to unsaturated oils to make them saturated or partially saturated. Hydrogeneration turns liquid fats to solid ones—examples include Crisco and other solid white vegetable shortenings as well as margarines. Hydrogenated oils are commonly used in commercial baked products such as cookies, including some "health food" cookies.

Polyunsaturated fatty acids. These fats are transparent and liquid both at room temperature and under refrigeration. They are found in vegetable oils such as sunflower, corn, soy, and cottonseed, which are common in salad dressings and "healthy" chips, crackers, and cookies sold in natural foods stores. The most unsaturated food oil—that is, the one with the highest percentage of polyunsaturated fatty acids—is safflower oil. Replacing saturated fats with polyunsaturated fats reduces cholesterol. However, diets high in polyunsaturated fats endanger health in other ways. When exposed to air, these fats can turn rancid, increasing the risk of cancer, speeding up the aging process, and causing other health risks.

Monounsaturated fatty acids. These are liquid at room temperature but thicken when cooled. Of the popular food oils, olive and canola oil contain the highest percentage of these fats. Peanut oil includes a significant percentage as well. Replacing saturated fats with these fats neither raises nor reduces blood cholesterol and heart disease risk.

Triglycerides. These fats are so-named because they combine glycerol with three fatty acids. Nearly all fats in foods come from these molecules, which increase the risk of heart disease when high levels exist in the blood. A diet high in saturated fats raises triglyceride levels, as does alcohol consumption, obesity, diabetes, estrogen supplementation, and high sugar intake.

To apply the above information:

1. Cut your use of all fats as much as possible. Radically reduce your family's intake of saturated fats, including hydrogenated oils.

2. Use monounsaturated fats when you cook (canola is the most versatile of these, especially for kids' palates, because it has no strong flavor).

3. Teach your family to appreciate simpler foods without adding fat—for example, bread without butter or margarine, main courses and side dishes without fatty sauces and gravies, air-popped popcorn without butter, and so on.

4. Learn to recognize the smell of rancidity and discard all oils and foods containing polyunsaturated oils that exude this odor.

5. Use recipes from low-fat cookbooks. Many delicious, rich-tasting foods can be prepared without excessive use of oil or other fats (see the Resources at the end of this chapter).

Unfortunately, some unscrupulous food companies have exploited the desire of many Americans to live healthily by deceptively labeling their products as containing "no cholesterol." These foods—for example, margarine, peanut butter, vegetable oils, and vegetable shortenings, plus foods containing them—are typically high in saturated fats, often from hydrogenation. Because they are derived from plants, they contain no cholesterol. However, your body will manufacture plenty of its own cholesterol when confronted with the high saturated fat content. And that cholesterol will stick to your family's arteries as surely as if they'd licked it off a spoon.

Protein

Experts used to teach that protein was the most crucial part of the diet and those who didn't eat prodigious quantities of it risked malnutrition. Now we know that it's far riskier to follow those obsolete recommendations than to eat a low-protein diet. Despite a wide disparity in eating styles and income levels, protein deficiency is virtually unheard of in this country. All whole foods contain at least some protein. So if you eat enough calories—and most Americans eat too many, not too few—you're almost certainly getting all the protein you need. That goes for kids and vegetarians, too. In poor countries, people often get by on diets of single whole starches without ever experiencing a protein shortage.

On the other hand, eating too much protein—typically, Americans eat two to four times the amount of protein they should—strains the liver and kidneys, which are forced to help process the excess. A protein overload also increases the body's excretion of minerals, including calcium. Excess protein taxes the digestive system, too, leading to energy loss and fatigue.

None of this is to deny the vital function of protein in the diet. The body relies on protein to grow and repair tissue. Because the body can't store protein, we need to take in a fresh supply of this nutrient every day and kids and people recovering from injury or illness need more than average adults.

The National Research Council, which compiles the familiar Recommended Daily Allowances (RDAs), advises that adults eat 0.36 gram protein per pound of *ideal* body weight every day. But note how little protein we're really talking about. For a 150-pound adult, the RDA amounts to only about two ounces daily, less protein than most Americans eat at every meal. The RDA for eleven-year-old kids is only slightly higher (0.45 gram per pound) than for adults. And the RDAs are intentionally set high, to cover most possibilities. The World Health Organization (WHO) recommends only 0.24 gram per pound of ideal weight for adults, 33 percent less than the RDA.

Nor do athletes or athletically active children need more protein than the rest of us. The body draws on carbohydrates, not protein, for its primary energy—knowledgeable athletes eat extra complex carbohydrates like cereals and pasta, not steaks and protein pills, before an event. Parents who stuff their sports-minded kids with protein in the belief that it builds extra muscle are also mistaken. Muscle is built through repeated exercise. Because the body can't store it, excess protein is conserved as fat, hardly an athletically desirable result. Young athletes such as football players who need to "bulk up" are the one exception to this rule. But even they should only be modestly increasing protein intake, and then only when exercising regularly.

To choose the best protein sources for your family, keep these guidelines in mind:

- *Beef, pork, and veal*—Medical researchers advise keeping beef eating to a minimum. Beef is loaded with saturated fat, much of which can't be trimmed off because it runs throughout the muscle tissue. A diet high in beef greatly increases cholesterol and the risk of coronary heart disease. And the normal forms in which beef is eaten—hamburgers, steaks, and roasts, etc.—supply far more protein in one meal than the body can use in a day. Despite the propaganda of the pork industry, all of the major drawbacks of beef apply to this meat, too. Veal, from beef calves, contains less fat than beef but is normally eaten in such quantities that the body still receives far too much protein and saturated fat.

Unless you buy from health-conscious sources, your family's red meats (beef) and white meats (pork and veal) will also contain residues of the growth hormones, drugs, and other questionable chemicals used to counteract diseases and create such commercial advantages as increasing the animals' weight. The effects of these chemicals are still unknown but potentially significant, particularly for children.

- *Poultry (chicken, turkey, duck, goose)*—Because most of the fat in chicken and turkey is attached to the skin, not in the muscle, these meats provide a relatively low-fat protein source if certain precautions are taken. First, remove the skin. Second, broil or bake *without added fat;* don't fry. Third, eat in modest quantities, keeping in mind the protein guidelines stated previously. Turkey provides a similar low-fat protein when eaten without the traditional gravy. As with other meats, most commercial poultry is fed hormones and drugs to overcome unhealthful conditions and increase weight. Look in health food stores and other alternative sources for free-range chickens and turkeys raised without these chemicals. Avoid duck and goose when possible—these meats are much higher in fat and cholesterol than chicken and turkey.

- *Fish*—In a perfect world, fish might be a near-perfect, low-fat protein source. But ocean and fresh water pollution has made this a problematic food, particularly for children. To complicate matters, the varieties most popular with kids, such as tuna and the freshwater species they might proudly bring home after fishing, are among the most worrisome.

  Most water pollution originates from inland sources such as industrial toxins, airborne pollutants from automobiles, pesticide run-offs, and sewage outfalls, so it is most highly concentrated in streams, rivers, lakes, and coastal waters. Pollutants tend to *bioaccumulate* in fish, meaning that larger fish (like tuna and swordfish) that eat polluted, smaller varieties end up with higher proportions of toxins in their flesh than the fish they feed on. These pollutants often include lead and mercury, known to accumulate in the human body and cause nervous system damage, with children at the greatest risk.

  When shopping for fish, consider that small fish are usually safer than bigger species, and deep ocean fish are usually safer than coastal and freshwater species. Tuna is a large, deep-water fish, and it's best to serve it only occasionally. Shellfish feed in coastal waters—eat only moderate amounts. Bluefish and swordfish are known to accumulate large amounts of mercury and should probably be avoided entirely by both kids and adults. Herring and sardines are considered among the healthiest species to eat because they don't feed on other fish and live in deep water. They also provide omega-3 fatty acids. Studies of Eskimos have shown these substances help offset heart disease risk from diets high in saturated fats. Other fish high in omega-3s include salmon and mackerel. Note that Norwegian salmon is farm-raised and may contain residues of chemicals used to fight disease.

· *Dairy products*—Chances are you grew up in a home in which Mom or Dad was always urging you to drink your milk to build strong bones. Many pediatricians and dietitians still give this advice today. But, in fact, considerable research indicates that the health benefits of dairy foods are overrated, especially when the negative aspects of these foods are considered.

Take their supposed benefit as a calcium source. Yes, milk products contain lots of this important mineral, but a diet high in dairy is more likely to cause calcium *loss* in most Americans because of the substantial protein content (although this is less of an issue with children because of their higher protein needs, especially before age seven—see page 218). Children do need calcium but they can get it in other ways.

Butterfat, the fat in dairy products, contains far more cholesterol than any other protein source and more saturated fat as well. The harmful effects are especially concentrated in cheese, which may contain up to 70 percent butterfat. For these reasons, low- and nonfat dairy products are much more healthful than regular milk, cheeses, and yogurt.

In addition, many people are allergic to cow's milk products and many more (especially people not of European heritage) lack lactase, the enzyme needed to digest milk sugar. When you do serve dairy products to your family, be alert to how they react to them. Symptoms of dairy allergies and lactose intolerance include bloating, drowsiness, flatulence, and digestive and intestinal problems. Allergic individuals usually do fine with goat's milk, and those with lactose intolerance can handle fermented cow's or goat's milk products such as yogurt, kefir (a yogurt-like drink), cheese, and buttermilk. Taking an enzyme supplement with milk can eliminate lactose intolerance problems as well.

One final caution on dairy products: These foods increase mucus in the system. Withholding them helps ease congestion when you or your kids are ill.

Most of us would terribly miss dairy foods if we were eliminate them entirely. However, adults and kids would be better off eating them only as occasional treats and in the lowest-fat versions available (1 percent fat or nonfat milk and yogurt, for example).

· *Eggs*—Eggs are another problematic protein source. Egg white provides high-quality, low-fat protein but the yolks are high in cholesterol, so it's best to serve whole eggs only occasionally.

· *Legumes (kidney, black, garbanzo, Anasazi, soy, and mung beans; peas; peanuts, lentils)*— As a group, legumes may have more going for them, health-wise, than any other protein source. Except for peanuts and soybeans, they contain little fat. The protein in legumes is mixed with high complex carbohydrate content, so you can consume fairly large portions of these foods without suffering the consequences of excess protein. Most are also among the most inexpensive protein sources. And such legumes as soy products, lentils, and black beans have a special appeal for those trying to give up the meat habit—rich in flavor, they can taste quite meat-like, depending upon how they're prepared. You can buy some soy-based products that are nearly indistinguishable from meat in look, texture, and even taste.

Other than soybeans, legumes don't supply whole proteins by themselves. But that shouldn't really concern you—contrary to old thinking, we now know the body builds complete proteins from incomplete ones by mining microorganisms and cellular material from the intestinal tract.

The main drawback of legumes has more to do with comfort and social acceptability than health. Because they contain some carbohydrates that are hard to digest, legumes can cause bloatedness and flatulence. Try black beans and Anasazi beans, which have fewer of the problem carbohydrates, if other legumes cause your family trouble. Also try cooking your bean dishes slowly in water over low heat until they begin to break down into the liquid, which improves both flavor and digestibility.

One more minor caution—some legumes contain natural toxins. Cooking destroys the toxins in most cases, but you should avoid raw garbanzos, which in large quantities can cause a dangerous immune system disease called lathyrism, and serve foods such as raw peanuts, raw peanut butter, raw peas, and raw lentil or mung bean sprouts in moderation.

- *Nuts and seeds*—It's better to use these foods as occasional treats. While they are high in protein, they are also high in fat.

- *Grains*—Grains supply only modest amounts of protein although, again, you need not worry much about protein once your kids reach age eleven or so. If you have younger kids, note that combining grains with legumes provides the full complement of amino acids, the basic building blocks of protein. In many poor countries, legume-grain combinations such as beans and tortillas form the basis of the main population's diet. Protein considerations aside, grains are crucial to the diet for their complex carbohydrate content.

Vitamins and Minerals

The body doesn't make its own vitamins, but it can't do without them so it depends on foods to provide them. We need the right vitamins in our system to remain healthy. Minerals play a crucial role in bodily processes, too—for example, calcium is vital for bone formation.

Many experts maintain that as long as you eat a balanced diet with a variety of fresh fruits and vegetables, whole grains, and legumes, you won't need to use vitamin and mineral supplements. That makes perfect sense to those of us who believe that natural living automatically produces good health. However, many nutritionally oriented physicians, naturopaths, and other natural health practitioners do advocate vitamin supplementation, particularly for those who eat deficient diets. In addition, some argue that environmental pollution, the emotional stresses of today's fast-paced living, and other contemporary factors make optimal health impossible without the outside help of these substances.

The supplementation issue remains controversial for several reasons. First, many practitioners sell the supplements they recommend, an obvious conflict of interest. As we mentioned earlier, be skeptical of practitioners who prescribe their own supplements instead of having you obtain supplements independently. Second, the value of many supplements remains unproved. However, supplementation does make good sense in many cases and even the most orthodox of physicians use it therapeutically for certain conditions.

If you do decide to supplement your family's diet with vitamins and minerals, be aware of the associated risks. Supplementation can endanger your family's health in some cases, and waste considerable money and effort in others. Several vitamins (A, D, E, and K) and most minerals can build up to toxic levels in the body, particularly with the "megadosing" popular today. Actual cases of vitamin toxicity are rare but taking too much iron, sodium, selenium, or zinc can cause mineral toxicity. Other supplements make little sense in their popular usage—for example, as mentioned above, taking calcium supplements is undermined by a high-protein diet. In addition, vitamins and minerals often interact with the body's chemistry in complex ways that must be taken into consideration. For example, too much vitamin C can inhibit the body's absorption of copper, an important mineral. Before undertaking a course of supplements, it's always best to consult an expert source—preferably not the same one selling you the pills.

Fiber

Fiber proves that nature finds a use for everything. Fiber is the part of edible plants that the body can't digest, but that's precisely what makes it so valuable. Because the body can't break it down, it passes through us pretty much intact. And on its way through the intestines, it pushes the food along with it. If your family takes in enough dietary fiber, along with adequate amounts of water, your bowels are far more likely to move regularly and completely.

On average, Americans eat about twelve grams of fiber daily. Physicians and nutrition experts recommend two to four times that amount, and not just for comfort in the bathroom. As a population, Americans suffer extremely high rates of colon cancer, especially compared to populations in countries with high-fiber diets, so researchers feel quite strongly that dietary fiber makes the crucial difference in preventing this deadly disease. If you base your family's diet on whole plant foods, which is also the healthiest approach in every other way, they'll get plenty of fiber as a natural byproduct.

Fiber also makes weight control easier. Whole grains and cereals (for example, oatmeal, millet, and the breakfast cereals listed in "Healthful Foods with Kid Appeal" on page 222) are low in calories yet digest slowly because of their high-fiber content. (Not true of most fruits, which despite high-fiber content, digest quickly due to their enzyme structure.) These foods absorb water as they run through the body. As a result, they make you feel "full" much longer and reduce your desire to snack.

If you eat the high-fiber foods advised in this chapter, you shouldn't have to turn to fiber supplements such as bran-enriched foods and commercial products like Metamucil, which exist mainly to compensate for the inadequate fiber in the American diet. However, if your family does use bran products, be sure to drink plenty of water with them. Otherwise, they may backfire and constipate you by absorbing water already in your system. Also note that high-fiber foods and supplements can increase gas—if that becomes a problem, moderate your intake.

Water

Bodies don't run any better without adequate water than do, say, dishwashers. In fact, water serves a similar function in both—carrying away wastes. For example, our kidneys help purify our blood by flushing out the toxic wastes that build up in our bodies both as byproducts from normal metabolism and otherwise. If we don't run enough water through the system, some of the wastes stay put and do damage.

Water performs other vital tasks in our bodies as well. It helps digestion, transports nutrients in the blood, maintains proper body temperature through perspiration, lubricates joints, helps transport solid waste out of the body, and facilitates the growth and repair of body tissues. Although the body signals us when it needs more water by making us thirsty, some people ignore those signals or simply forget to drink—kids are especially prone to this. Other people attempt to satisfy their thirst with liquids that end up hurting more than helping. For instance, alcoholic beverages and coffee are diuretics that promote fluid loss, not retention. The high protein content in milk can stress the kidneys if the body has already taken in adequate protein.

As a result of neglect or mistaken ideas about what the body needs, many kids and adults walk around in a state of partial dehydration. You don't need a complicated test to identify this. Just look in the toilet after you or your kids urinate. Dark yellow, smelly urine means the body isn't getting enough water. Constipation may also indicate water deficiency.

In addition to monitoring your kids in the bathroom, do them a favor now and for their future health by teaching them to slake their thirst with water. The body wants water when it's thirsty, so water or drinks that are mainly water, like tea and flavored mineral waters, are what it should get. A thirsty body isn't asking for calories, so feeding it high-caloric drinks like sodas, milk, and so forth instead of water, which has no calories, contributes to weight gain. Infants need 11–43 ounces of water or fluids every 24 hours (increasing as they grow). School-age kids need 48–60 ounces per day, and adolescents need 73–90 ounces.

That said, the purity of the water your family drinks really matters, especially as you drink more of it. Very few public water sources, including sources of bottled water, are completely trustworthy and kids are more vulnerable than adults to the chemicals, heavy metals, and other contaminants commonly found in water. For more on this issue and what to do about it, see the discussion on page 172.

JAMES WEEKS

Putting It All Together: Dietary Considerations for Kids

In their years of greatest growing, kids will need a somewhat different diet than the rest of your family. The major considerations concern protein and fat. Infants should take in about one gram of protein per pound of ideal body weight through their first year, says the Nutrition Research Council. Protein requirements taper down to about half a gram per pound by age seven. By age fifteen, requirements for both boys and girls drop to nearly the same levels recommended for adults. Regarding fat, you should keep your children's fat intake to the amount suggested above for your own diet—20 to 30 percent of total calories—after age two. Before then, don't restrict your baby's fats.

With the above exceptions, the ideal family diet looks like this:

LOW in protein (especially animal protein), simple sugars, fats, processed foods of all kinds.

HIGH in complex carbohydrates (with an emphasis on whole grains, cereals, legumes, fruits, and vegetables), water, and variety (which helps ensure sufficient intake of vitamins, minerals, and other nutrients).

Vegetarians may need to take a few special precautions. Those are covered later in this chapter.

GETTING YOUR KIDS TO EAT WELL
IN A JUNK FOOD WORLD

No matter how hard you try to keep your kids' innards "pure," they step into nutritional no-man's land when they go to other kids' homes or when they join their friends at the mall. Meanwhile, ads on TV, in kids' magazines, and public school walls tempt them with foods that are the nutritional equivalent of Astroturf. What's a conscientious parent to do? More to the point, your children will ask, what's a hungry kid away from home supposed to eat?

Kat Wild took her cues from a health-conscious friend who had already been through the food wars with her children. "She realized that the gap between what she fed her family and what the rest of the world ate was beyond what she could deal with. So she decided that, 'In this home, we eat [healthful foods].' Then when her kids were out, which was not the majority of the time, they could do the burgers and the pizza, because being part of the greater group was every bit as important as being nutritionally perfect. So that's what we do with our kids, and let them use good sense. That's always the last thing said as they hit the door, 'Use good sense.'"

Dorise Treiger of Ashland, Oregon completely agrees with this approach. "I think it's best not to be dogmatic, to allow some treats sometimes or to allow them to have meat, even if you're a vegetarian. I think you get a lot less rebellion that way." She and her husband Jay only offer healthful foods at home but out in the world, their teenage sons Ben and Noah are free to buy what they want. They also allow their boys to order what they want when the family eats in restaurants. Both Noah and Ben have developed a taste for candy and Noah in particular enjoys meat although it's rarely served at home. But neither boy feels the need to rebel because their parents haven't given them anything to push against. The Treigers also teach their kids that there are times when good manners trump good nutrition. "We always felt that when you're [at someone else's home] and you're given food, you take it," says Dorise. "You might not hop up and down about it, but you say 'Thank you very much.'"

Some parents may fear that once their kids get a taste for how their friends eat, they'll be hooked for life. But most of the parents we spoke to reported just the opposite. Kat Wild maintains that her kids have never developed a fancy for junk food: "They love the thrill of having it but they don't really eat it much. They'll eat a little of their Halloween candy, but they're not that interested. That goes for junk snack foods, too. They'll want to buy it, and on occasion I'll let them, knowing that after everyone's had their fill in one sitting, it will sit there until it turns to dust." Lori Cangilose's vegetarian children have tried chicken and fish in restaurants but "none of it sticks with them," says Lori. "They never say, 'Oh, can we go out and get chicken?'"

The Cangiloses regulate their children's, and their own, sugar intake by occasionally indulging their sweet teeth when eating out. "If we do want to get something, we all share it. We'll get a few forks and one dessert and pass it around. We talk about how fabulous it would be if every meal was like this, because it's a taste nirvana, but it ends there." The Willefords also deliberately break their diets on occasion as a way of maintaining discipline. They live on an island near Seattle without a single fast food outlet to tempt them, so every few months when Lynn and son Brook go to the mainland together, they stop at Burger King for lunch. "It's so exotic," laughs Lynn.

There's no need to lower your health standards when your children's friends are visiting. The Treigers always serve their boys' guests healthful foods such as fresh fruit. "If they really are hungry, they'll eat it," says Jay. The same goes for drinks. "They might say, 'Don't you have anything except water?' and we say, 'No, that's it.' Well, if you're really thirsty, water tastes great."

The older Cangilose boys have taught Lori to take a different tack. "Even though they like eating alternatively and they're proud of how they've eaten, there's another side to it," observes Lori. "It's like, 'Why can't it just look normal?' So we make a deal. If I know their friends are coming, I'll pick the most normal food that we eat and fix that. When we go to a school potluck, my ten-year-old will say, 'Okay Mom, what are you bringing? To bring something really strange would be worse than bringing nothing at all.' So I'll fix something that looks 'normal' and is still healthy, like pasta."

The Treiger's experience to the contrary, children may well wish to veer from the family diet as they become more independent, particularly as they pass through the rebellion phase. When Brook Willeford's tastes changed, his parents found it worked best to reorder their priorities about food. "Brook had a period in his early teens when in reaction to his upbringing he became totally interested in sweets, and would indulge himself with his own money," Lynn recalls. "That seems to be over now, and he's become moderate about them. It's always been tough to balance my desire for him to eat the most nutritious diet and his own tastes and desires. Generally we chose not to battle about food, because I believe dinnertime is so important to the life of a family that I didn't want to spoil it."

Introducing New, More Healthful Foods

Few experiences will test your parenting ingenuity like trying to get your kids to accept new foods. We consulted a couple of parenting veterans for their tips.

Always give them the option of spitting the food out, advises Laura Davis, veteran mom and coauthor of *Becoming the Parent You Want to Be.* In her book, she and coauthor Janis Keyser cite a study by Leann Birch and D. W. Marlin that showed that kids are more likely ultimately to accept a new food if they have several chances to try it and the option of rejecting it.

Lori Cangilose has experienced great success with what might be called the Farm Plan, letting kids grow the vegetables she wants them to eat. "If you've got room in your yard or even if you just have a box on the patio if you're in an apartment, they'll eat things they normally wouldn't just because they planted the seed and watered it. I don't think we've ever brought peas inside. Vincenzo, the baby, just stands out there eating them. There's something special about watching them grow and then eating them."

Lori has made another clever trick work for her—stealth ingredients. "When I want my family to try something new, I just keep adding it in small amounts to what they're already eating. I gradually increase the amount until before they know it, they've gotten used to it."

Of course, adults can resist just as fiercely as kids when it comes to changing long-held and cherished eating habits. Modeling counts big-time when guiding your kids to more healthful foods. So here's the two-word secret to adopting a more body-friendly diet of your own: Tastes change!

That's right, you can learn to like new foods and let go of old, un-healthful favorites just by giving yourself two or three days to make the transition. Vegetarians who were once burger-and-steak-loving carni-vores have experienced this with food after food. Get your confidence up with a relatively simple shift—say, to a cheeseless pizza (natural food com-pany Amy's makes a great frozen one). Then move on to seemingly tougher changes—butterless toast and potatoes and so on. You'll find that there are plenty of swell-tasting treats out there that you once may have rejected as "rabbit food." Soon, you'll start feeling better because you're feeding your body what *it* likes and dietary changes will come easier still. And then when you urge your children to try new things, your voice will ring with experience: "Yes, kids, this can be done."

healthful foods with kid appeal

The trick to getting kids to eat more healthful foods is to find or make things that are similar to what they would eat if health didn't matter. Many of the following foods may not be "perfect," but they are relatively healthful and certainly far better than their mainstream equivalents. We've kid-tested all of them with great success. The majority of the brand-name products can be found or ordered at most natural foods stores; some will be carried in mainstream stores, too, in a "health foods" section.

BREAKFAST CEREAL
Barbara's Breakfast O's
Barbara's Shredded Spoonfuls
Barbara's Puffins Crunch Corn Cereal
Breadshop Puffs 'n Honey

CONDIMENTS
Annie's Naturals barbecue sauces
Knudsen & Sons conserves (use in place of jams or spread on
    toast instead of butter)
Millina's Finest catsups
Nasoya Creamy Dill and Herb salad dressings (use in place of
    mayonnaise. Nasoya also makes a mayonnaise substitute)

PASTA
Annie's Homegrown Macaroni & Cheese
Deboles Artichoke Elbows & Cheese, Artichoke Shells &
    Cheddar (essentially macaroni and cheese)
Deboles pastas (Varieties with artichoke, semolina, and durum
    wheat flours taste like "regular" white flour pasta. Whole wheat
    pastas do not.)
Millina's Organic, Fat-Free pasta sauces

PIZZA
Amy's varieties
Pizsoy varieties

SANDWICHES
Ken & Robert's Veggie Pockets
Wholesome & Hearty Foods GardenBurgers

(continued on next page)

WHY VEGETARIANISM, AND FOR SOME PEOPLE, WHY NOT

Our culture has come a long way in how it views vegetarianism. The public once regarded diets without meat as kooky and potentially dangerous. Experts more or less concurred. They cautioned that unless vegetarians were extremely careful in how they planned their meals, they could undermine their health by not getting enough protein and other essential nutrients that meat supplies.

Today, federal health officials consider vegetarianism a healthy alternative approach that accomplishes the dietary goals they consider most important. As explained above, the old worries about the dangers of meatless diets, such as too little protein, have largely disappeared in the face of new information. Meanwhile, it's now common knowledge that meat and dairy products are a primary source of dietary fat and cholesterol.

Mainstream experts have yet to take the next step, which is to declare vegetarianism the *preferred* healthful diet. But you don't have to read very far between the lines to see the superiority of meatless eating, because all cholesterol and most saturated fats come from animal products. Meats are also compromised by human-made substances—for example, the hormones and drugs fed to beef cattle and poultry and the polluted waters in which most fish live.

Health is just one of several reasons that people turn to vegetarianism. Others include:

Ethical issues. Some people feel that to eat meat when the body doesn't need it is cruel, particularly considering the inhumane conditions in which meat animals are often raised and slaughtered. Says Dorise Treiger, who maintains a mainly meatless home with her husband and sons, "The more I've read about other ways of living, the more I've asked myself, 'Do we really need to enslave these critters so we can eat them?'"

Environmental issues. Livestock production is a leading cause of environmental devastation. Meat raising requires far more gasoline and water use than plant-based agriculture to feed an equivalent number of people, because meat is so much higher on the food chain. (It takes about seven kilos of grain to produce one kilo of pork, and about five kilos to produce a kilo of beef.) Manure tends to pile up in far greater amounts in livestock operations than the land can absorb, and the excess

(continued from previous page)

SANDWICHES
Yves Tofu and Veggie Fat-Free Wieners
Whole wheat pita pockets filled with cooked vegetables and
    topped with low-fat dressing

MAIN COURSES
Amy's Vegetable Pot Pies
Lumen Foods Heartline Meatless Meats (Soy products—cook
    them with water for an amazingly meat-like addition to cas-
    seroles, burritos, and soups or serve them dry for jerky-like
    snack.)
Build-your-own burritos with cooked Heartline Meatless Meats,
    cooked beans, and salsa
Chicken or turkey breasts and drumsticks, unskinned and cooked
    with no or minimal fat
Alta Dena, Continental, and Stonyfield Farm low-fat and nonfat
    yogurts

SNACKS
Barbara's Cheese Puffs Bakes (Lights)
Garden of Eatin' corn chips
Health Valley fat-free cookies
Sweet fruits and vegetables: watermelon, cantaloupe, grapes,
    oranges, tangerines, apples, strawberries, carrot sticks, celery
    sticks, etc.
Air-popped popcorn

SODAS*
Crystal Geyser Juice Squeeze
Knudsen & Sons Spritzers

*"Healthful" soft drinks are far preferable to sugar- and caffeine-laden mainstream products. However, the phosphorus in carbonated beverages can cause bone loss and so they should be served only occasionally.

polluted rivers and groundwater. The huge proliferation of beef cattle in recent years has led to overgrazing and compacting of the land, which ruins once-productive agricultural lands. The rain forest is disappearing in tropical countries largely because ranchers are clearing the land to raise beef cattle for export to rich countries like ours. And believe it or not, the methane from cow belches, flatulence, and manure piles makes a significant contribution to the greenhouse gases behind global warming.

World hunger. The world may be facing an eventual food shortage because of the combined effects of an expanding population, destruction of prime agricultural lands, and the increased consumption of meat by people in rapidly growing economies such as China's. The world's grain supplies would go much further and feed far more people if meat-eating in all nations dropped.

Healthcare inflation. Although policymakers don't often mention it, meat eating plays almost as big a role as tobacco in driving up healthcare costs. If Americans ate less meat, the rates of heart disease, strokes, colon cancer, breast cancer, obesity, osteoporosis, Type II (non-insulin dependent) diabetes, kidney stones, gallstones, and diverticulosis would all fall, in many cases dramatically.

Types of Vegetarianism

"Vegetarian" means different things to different people. Technically, the term covers four different types of diets:

- *Vegans, or "strict vegetarians,"* don't eat foods, including eggs and dairy products, derived from animals in any way.

- *Lacto-ovo vegetarians* don't eat meat, seafood, or poultry, but do eat eggs and dairy.

- *Lacto-vegetarians* don't eat eggs or meat but do eat dairy foods.

- *Semi-vegetarians* eat modest amounts of meat, particularly poultry and fish, on occasion.

Are Vegetarian Diets Dangerous for Children or Pregnant Women?

Many dietitians and physicians—perhaps including your family doctor—retain old prejudices about vegetarianism, particularly as a diet for children. But as Kathi J. Kemper, M.D. (*The Holistic Pediatrician*) writes, "children can grow perfectly well on vegetarian diets." By and large, vegetarian parents need only follow the general rules of good nutrition outlined above, with a few minor exceptions:

- *Fat for infants.* Vegetarian diets tend to be much lower in fat. As mentioned above, children under the age of two need more fat because of the tremendous weight gain they're undergoing. In baby's first year, you might offer her such foods as thinned nut butters (except peanut butter), avocado, whole goat's milk and yogurt, egg yolks, and so on. Some experts feel it is best to delay potentially allergenic foods such as egg whites, peanut butter, and cow's milk products until about one year of age, although if neither parent has a family history of allergy, you might try these foods, too. At one year, baby will probably be ready to eat mashed versions of what the rest of the family eats, but keep the fat content high with the foods just mentioned, ice cream, cookies, and so on. Just remember that by age two, children can and should follow adult guidelines regarding fat.

- *Protein for infants and pregnant and lactating moms.* Many people, including conventional dietitians, don't realize that vegetarians generally take in a lot of protein. Still, vegetarians do tend to eat less protein than meat eaters so parents should be aware that infants need three times the protein, per pound of ideal body weight, as adults, and from age two to seven still need about twice as much as adults do. Pregnant women should eat almost twice as much protein as other adults, and lactating moms about 50 percent more than normal.

- *Vitamin B12.* Vegan diets, those with no animal products whatsoever, don't supply any B12 so vegan parents should supplement. Non-vegan vegetarians will get enough of this vitamin just by eating small amounts of dairy products.

- *Calcium.* Calcium is found in many foods besides milk—for instance, cooked greens such as collard greens, broccoli, sesame seeds, molasses, and tofu—although some of these are foods that few kids like. Parents who keep their kids on milk-free diets need to ensure that they get this important mineral in supplements if not in food. If you use calcium supplements, avoid those with dolomite or bone meal, both of which may be contaminated with lead and other toxic heavy metals. Calcium supplements can cause some health problems over the long term unless magnesium is taken as well.

- *Vitamin D*—In most cases, even minimal exposure to the sun gives the body what it needs to produce this vitamin. During winter months, most people get their vitamin D from dietary sources such as butter, egg yolks, fortified milk, and fish livers. Children who aren't fed these foods may need vitamin D supplements, especially when spending nearly all their time indoors.

- *Iron.* Although red meat supplies iron in way that is uniquely easy for the body to absorb, vegetarians can get the iron they need from foods such as cooked greens, whole grains, dried beans, raisins, prunes, and apricots, as well as from occasionally cooking in iron pots and pans. But don't overdo it—recent research indicates that iron excess may cause more serious health problems than does iron deficiency. Iron accumulates in the body and can reach toxic levels. Supplementing with iron pills or iron-containing multivitamins is not a good idea except for menstruating women and those following a physician's advice.

Why Not Vegetarianism? While the arguments for vegetarianism may seem powerfully persuasive, natural health is ultimately about *health,* not meatless diets. And from a strict health perspective, it is possible—and some people find, even preferable—to include a little meat in the diet now and again. Nature designed the human body to be amazingly resilient. Animal products may not help health much, but small amounts don't hurt much, either.

Besides, what works for most people doesn't necessarily work for everyone. For example, some people feel they do better with some animal protein. The Willeford family knows the principles of holistic nutrition and adheres fairly closely to them but they do eat small amounts of meat. "Our lean and active bodies seem to need it," says Lynn. Many other former vegetarians have reached similar conclusions.

Nor does eating meat constitute the same ethical dilemma for everyone. Kat Wild's family integrates meat eating with their spirituality by drawing on a Native American tradition of gratitude to nature. "When we eat meat, we thank the animal that gave its life and we promise to help build a better world with all the energy it's giving us," says Kat, whose mother is Native American.

Health-conscious people who venture to places where few vegetarians have gone before—the homes of certain friends and relatives, for instance!—can have trouble getting enough to eat without breaking their diets or making awkward requests (such as, "This is a lovely meal you've served, but I don't eat anything on the table—would you make me something else?"). Although the world is changing, it's still tricky to keep to a rigidly vegetarian diet when many of your social contacts don't. If you do choose to include some meat in your family's diet, note the guidelines detailed elsewhere in this chapter for doing so healthily.

WHY ORGANIC?

Organic food buffs would probably answer the above question with one of their own: Why feed your kids potentially dangerous chemicals whose sole purpose is to kill other living things? The term "organic food" refers to crops grown in a way that replenishes soil and is oth-

> ### what about macrobiotic diets?
>
> Macrobiotics grew out of the same principles of yin and yang that you encountered in Chapter 4 in the discussion of traditional Chinese medicine. Macrobiotic theory classifies foods according to their yin-yang properties. For instance, yin foods are acidic in pH and sweeter and yang foods are alkaline and saltier, among several criteria. A balanced diet is built around foods such as brown rice that are considered fairly balanced between yin and yang. Followers of this philosophy eat other foods, of course, but always with an eye toward offsetting foods that are more strongly yin with those that are more yang and vice versa. In addition, they avoid foods toward the extremes such as meats and eggs (extremely yang) and sugar or honey (very yin). The result is a vegan diet that is low in fat, cholesterol, and calories and high in fiber and fresh vegetables.
>
> Advocates of macrobiotics may not be able to substantiate all of their claims—for instance, some insist without proof that macrobiotic diets cure cancer—but research has confirmed that those who eat this way tend to have lower cholesterol and blood pressure than most Americans. Whether these diets are healthy for children and pregnant women is another question. Certainly, the more extreme forms of a macrobiotic diet in which followers eat little but brown rice are inappropriate and dangerous. But even more varied macrobiotic diets may be too rigid and limited to supply all the nutrients kids and moms-to-be need, or the fat that infants require. As with all vegan diets, followers should make sure they get enough calcium and vitamins B12 and D.

erwise environmentally sustainable. It also refers to meat animals raised without feed additives and hormones, but we'll concern ourselves mainly with plant foods here.

In organic farming, crops are grown largely without agricultural chemicals such as pesticides, herbicides, chemical fertilizers, and fungicides. The media often calls all such chemicals "pesticides" for short. Pesticide defenders—including mainstream food companies, nonorganic food growers, and the chemical industry—claim that no one has ever proved that today's farm chemicals harm humans. They're technically correct in most cases but cynically deceptive. Few agricultural chemicals have ever been tested or even monitored for adverse health effects because the EPA takes the position that they are innocent until proven guilty. In other words, the EPA allows growers to use them until tests can be completed, a ludicrous stance considering that, as health guru Andrew Weil, M.D., writes, "[Pesticides] can't possibly be good for us. The only question is just how bad they are."

The few tests the EPA does conduct leave much to be desired. First, they are usually geared toward measuring health effects on adults. Yet, as the National Academy of Sciences points out, kids are likely to be far more sensitive to the chemicals than are adults, and they eat six times the amount of fruit adults do, which dramatically increases the chemical doses they receive. Second, tests are mainly conducted for effects on men, yet women have more body fat and many of these chemicals accumulate in fat. Third, the government only tests the chemicals at hand, such as the residues on foods in a normal adult diet. It doesn't consider the additional exposure from nonfood sources such as drinking water and lawn chemicals.

MICHAEL ALLEN JONES

Finally, until now, the EPA has tested primarily for cancer-causing properties. Yet disturbing evidence has emerged in recent years that pesticides, along with many other human-made chemicals, may be leading to stunted reproductive organs in infants, increased rates of testicular and breast cancer, lower fertility in men and women, and other reproductive abnormalities. The above-mentioned health effects have been observed in wildlife exposed to high doses of pesticides and related chemicals, and also in laboratory animals. The tie to pesticides has yet to be proven in humans with similar problems, but many experts feel the connection is too plausible to neglect.

As for those few chemicals, such as DDT, that have been tested, found dangerous, and banned, many, including DDT, are still used in foreign countries with lax regulations and make their way back here in imported foods, which is permitted by our global trade agreements. Despite what you may have heard, agricultural chemicals cannot be completely washed off your produce, so residues are commonly found in food. That goes for wheat products, too, such as flour, bread, and pasta, because wheat is one of the most heavily sprayed crops.

Of course, it's also possible that we receive such small amounts of chemicals from food that we really don't have to worry. But don't you think that caution in this case is wiser, especially where kids are concerned? And that means that parents, including nursing moms, should consider minimizing the intentional exposure received by their children and children-to-be by emphasizing organic foods. Jay and Dorise Treiger began buying exclusively organic food even before their first pregnancy. "Once we started looking into the prevalence of poisons in the regular food and saw that there was a choice by eating organic, we decided there wouldn't be any question," recalls Jay.

As with vegetarianism, there are social as well as health reasons for buying organic foods when you can. For example, tens of thousands of farmworkers worldwide die each year from agricultural chemical poisoning, and many farmworkers' children suffer serious birth disorders, especially in Third World nations such as Mexico and other Latin American countries where worker protections are weak. Kat Wild always strives to buy the most healthful foods possible for her family, "but our big motivation [for buying organic foods] was realizing that people are working in all those toxic chemicals and they are Native Americans like us, only they live across the border."

Agricultural chemicals also contribute to many of our most devastating environmental problems. They pollute rivers, lakes, and coastal waters. They contribute to air pollution and global warming, and have hastened the decline of many species of birds, fish, and animals by poisoning what they eat. Chemical agriculture has also helped create an international topsoil crisis, endangering the planet's ability to feed a burgeoning population. When you buy organic foods, you send a message to food, chemical, and agricultural corporations that you refuse to contribute to this devastating cycle.

Buying organic does present its own challenges, though. First, organic produce costs significantly more. Second, it isn't always guaranteed to be free of potentially dangerous pesticides. The premium prices that farmers can charge for organics has motivated some to falsely label their produce. This is made easier by the fact that only a few states—California, Oregon, and Maine among them—have laws governing how the term "organic" may be used. New federal standards proposed in 1997 may end this problem but only if the government can resist intense pressure by mainstream food industries to undermine the standards. In addition, even food grown in true organic fashion can be contaminated by pesticides that blow in from nearby, nonorganic fields. The better natural food stores are aware of these problems and will do their best to control for them. Thus, you should only buy your organic produce from dealers you trust to have their customers' best interests at heart.

healthful food preparation

You make quite an investment of time and money to select the most nutritious foods for your family. Obviously, you don't want to destroy all that nutritional worth in the food preparation stage. Follow these guidelines to maximize the health value of the meals you serve:

- *Raw foods.* Uncooked fruits and vegetables contribute vital nutrients and fiber to a healthful diet. Increasing the proportion of these foods in your family's meals and snacks also helps control your family's intake of dietary fat, food additives, sugar, and salt, so long as you aren't adding these things back in with dressings, flavorings, and condiments. Do be aware that certain raw foods—for example, celery, alfalfa sprouts, white mushrooms, peanuts and many other legumes—contain trace amounts of naturally occurring toxins. You needn't strike them from your family's diet, but you shouldn't serve them every day. In most cases, cooking destroys the toxicity.

- *Steaming and pressure cooking.* From the standpoint of both preserving nutrients and conserving energy, these cooking methods top the list. Plus, you don't need to add fat to steamed and pressure-cooked foods.

- *Boiling.* This is another good, no-fat cooking technique but it is not as desirable as steaming and pressure cooking because some of the vitamins and other nutrients leach into the boiling water. Save the nutrient-rich cooking water for soups.

- *Stir frying.* Stir frying preserves most nutrients and produces relatively low-fat results if you minimize your use of oil and cook only until veg-

(continued on next page)

You can never fully eliminate pesticides from your family's bodies no matter how carefully you shop for food. Even organic farms use controlled amounts of some chemicals considered safe by the organics industry and the EPA. Farm chemicals permeate the soil, water, and air—even humans in the remotest regions of the earth show traces in their systems. But you can dramatically reduce your family's exposure by choosing organic foods whenever available.

LOSING WEIGHT

The "secret" to losing weight and keeping it off, for kids as well as adults, couldn't be simpler: Eat less, exercise more. To lose weight, you have to burn more calories than you take in. Eating less handles the intake side of the equation, and exercise increases calories burned. Exercise also maintains or builds lean muscle mass, which keeps the metabolism at a high level, making your body a quicker-burning machine.

By itself, the low-fat, low-protein, high-fiber, high complex carbohydrate diet recommended in these pages leads to better weight control, without counting calories. As mentioned above, it keeps to low or moderate levels the most concentrated sources of calories—meats, other fatty foods, and simple sugars—and it emphasizes lower-calorie foods such as whole grains, cereals, and pasta. In addition, the latter foods, because of their high-fiber content, are more filling, resulting in less snacking and bingeing. Of course, overeating of even the "right" foods adds pounds. However, in many cases, overweight people don't really eat that much, they just make poor choices about foods.

In addition to guiding your children to healthful food choices, be sure to explain the dynamics and deceptions of dieting to them. Although it counters all the hype you hear in the media, the worst way to lose weight is by dieting. The purveyors of fad, quick-result diets have put a big one over on the American public and some of them are starting to pay for it. If you've followed the news in the last few years, you've noticed that many of the brand-name diet programs have gotten themselves in legal trouble for making dishonest claims to the public. These diets tend to work by starving the body for carbohydrates. Weight in the form of water and lean muscle mass falls away in the beginning because the body is burning protein to make up for the carbohydrates it prefers as fuel. But

(continued from previous page)

etables are tender, but still crunchy. Avoid deep-frying—deep-fried foods are drenched in fat. Also, rancidity and overheating of the oils makes them carcinogenic, and the smoke from overheated oils is carcinogenic to breathe.

- *Broiling and baking.* Both of these cooking methods are safe so long as fat is not added and foods are not overly darkened, which can turn the outer layers carcinogenic.

- Cookware. Stainless steel is best. Iron cookware used in moderation may help vegetarians by adding iron to their diets. Aluminum (not including aluminum-bottomed stainless steel) should be avoided if possible: Acidic foods react with aluminum cookware, absorbing traces of the metal, which then ends up in your body; aluminum cookware can also damage vitamins in the food.

- Microwave ovens. Many holistic types ban microwave ovens from their kitchens, fearing everything from radiation poisoning to nutritional meltdown. In fact, microwave radiation bears no relation to the kind of cancer-causing radioactivity that we associate with nuclear bombs and power plants. Nor does it damage food in ways different from other ovens—in fact, it preserves nutrients better than most cooking methods. But radiation leaking from damaged or defective microwave ovens can damage human tissue exposed to it and may cause subtler health problems as well. So follow the manufacturer's instructions for care and maintenance of your oven and get it checked if you suspect a leak, and don't let your kids stand near the oven while it's on.

the weight never stays off. The water weight comes back when the water is replaced and the loss of lean muscle lowers the body's metabolism, making it harder to keep pounds off when the dieter resumes normal eating.

Dieting also causes other internal body changes that increase the probability of weight gain later on. This is why for dieters, no special program ever makes a permanent change and they're always looking for the next book or miracle program to make the difference. As any expert who doesn't have a book, video, or program to sell you will confirm, the only way to control weight permanently and healthily is to adopt lifestyle changes such as those suggested in this and earlier chapters.

Of course, many children, teenagers, and adults bypass the diet fads and severely cut their calories on their own, getting by on tiny meals or small amounts of junk foods. This strategy is both dangerous, because it can deprive the body of essential nutrients, and, like other diets, is counterproductive. The body doesn't understand "diet." When calories drop too far, it thinks "Red alert! Starvation!" and lowers its metabolism to conserve energy. The more frequently a person diets, the more efficient the metabolism becomes, meaning it needs less and less food to maintain weight. This leads to the dreaded yo-yo syndrome of diet, weight gain, diet, weight gain, which is not only frustrating but more unhealthy than just staying fat.

As a parent, you should help your children feel good about themselves no matter how much weight they're carrying. And be sure to model only healthy weight loss behavior, for their sake as well as yours. There are no shortcuts to long-lasting weight control and fitness.

BUDGETING FOR HEALTHFUL FOOD

Once you and your family start eating more healthily, you'll notice two things immediately: how much better you all feel, and how much more you're paying for the privilege.

No doubt about it, it costs more to eat better. White flour, sugar, coconut oil, pesticide-sprayed food, and the foods that contain these ingredients may have little else to recommend them, but they are far cheaper than their more nutritious alternatives. If you're a coupon clipper, you'll also soon notice that none of the coupons stuffed into your mailbox and newspaper apply to truly healthful foods, although some may be labeled "natural."

What's going on here? In part, quality costs more. Natural food companies tend to use higher quality ingredients and take fewer shortcuts in preparing their foods for market—they know that their customers care as much about health as they do price. Other reasons include complex economic factors such as economies of scale. For example, most of the natural food companies are simply not big enough to get the best price breaks on packaging (which often costs more than the food itself), buy the most efficient machinery, or ship on the biggest trucks. Nor are most big enough to supply the major food retail chains, which buy in vast quantities to keep prices low and beat the competition.

Still, by knowing a few tricks, you can cut the price of your healthful food purchases considerably. Try the following:

- *If your city has a nonprofit natural foods store or co-op, patronize it.* Many cities and towns still feature community-oriented natural foods stores or co-ops, a leftover from the late 1960s and early 1970s, that get healthful food and related items "to the people" at the lowest possible prices.

- *Buy in quantity.* Many local food co-ops and natural food stores allow you to order packaged foods by the caseload and produce by the carton at deep discounts or even wholesale. If yours doesn't, form a buying club with like-eating friends and purchase directly from the same distributors that service the stores. Even when buying through a store, splitting costs with friends often makes sense, says Lori Cangilose, "because it's hard to go through a whole box of organic apples before they go bad."

- *Cook more and buy packaged foods less.* A large pot of vegetarian legume chili or soup can supply a week's worth of meals cheaply, deliciously, and nutritiously. Whole, nutritious foods such as brown rice can be purchased in bulk or in ten-plus-pound sacks and used as the basis of inexpensive meals, with vegetables and soy products added for flavor and protein.

- *Check prices at large retail outlets.* The buying power of large chains enables them to beat smaller outlets in the price wars. If price is your main concern, you will often do better in the health food department of a chain store than at the local co-op, particularly on sale prices. Many large grocery chains carry organic produce in their produce bins, too, particularly in large cities.

- *Join a subscription farm.* Although you assume some of the farmer's risk, this strategy normally delivers fresh, organic produce to you at considerable savings over market prices. (See page 234.)

- *Buy produce locally and in season.* Crops grown locally don't carry high transportation costs; buying them also supports local farms and economies. When crops are in season, their prices are lowest and flavor fullest.

- *Fill your family's bellies with cheaper staples before you give them expensive treats.* Lori Cangilose makes sure her boys have finished their lunch before they start in on the family's expensive organic fruit supply: "I have to point out that for us to have healthy food that hasn't been gassed or sprayed, we have to consume it in a way that makes it affordable."

- *Grow your own.* To reduce their food purchases, Kat Wild's family has planted nine fruit trees and a garden in their urban backyard. In most years, the Willefords have grown enough fruits and vegetables for the summer, with some left over to freeze for the winter.

Of course, the greatest savings from healthy eating come from the intangibles. How do you put a pricetag on the health of your family? Remind yourself, too, that your improved health should also result in lower medical and dental bills, higher productivity at work, and improved school performance from your kids, who should have more energy and miss less time due to illness.

BUYING PRODUCE THROUGH SUBSCRIPTION FARMS AND COMMUNITY-SUPPORTED AGRICULTURE

So maybe you're not someone who feels at home digging around in the soil. This doesn't mean you have to forget all dreams of getting closer to your food source. By hooking up with local community-supported agriculture (CSAs) or subscription farms, families all across the country are getting steady supplies of fresh, pesticide-free produce, feeling more connected to nature's seasons and bounty, supporting earth-friendly farming, and taking regular, educational field trips to boot.

Here's how subscription farming and CSAs work: Both require a financial commitment—typically up front—from subscribers or "shareholders" to help pay for a local farmer's operating costs. In return, these investors take home a portion of the farm's harvest, usually on a weekly basis. Both types of farms typically grow their crops free of the synthetic fertilizers and pesticides found on conventional farms. And many of them go a step further, adhering to organic farming methods designed to sustain and replenish the earth's fertile soil. Many farmers use the terms "CSA" and "subscription farming" interchangeably. But for those who make a distinction, subscription farming represents the more conventional veggies-for-dollars swap, in which the produce is sometimes delivered to convenient drop-off points or even to your door. CSAs invite their supporters to participate actively in some of the administrative and agricultural activities of the farm, including occasional harvesting.

At the Brookfield CSA farm in South Amherst, Massachusetts, shareholders and their families drive right up to the farm once or twice a week (depending upon the season and whether they've bought a whole or a half share). While the kids run around or join the local "quack pack" to check up on new ducklings and piglets, their parents fill bagfuls of freshly harvested fruits and vegetables. And, if they've signed up for meat items, they'll stock up on poultry or freshly cut slabs of pork or beef as well. Then Mom and Dad might peruse the messages on the "Pick Your Own" chalkboard to see if beans, peas, berries, or herbs are ripe for plucking—in which case, the kids will probably be only too happy to oblige. "Of course, if raspberries are in season, they never make it home," says Cynthia Barstow of Amherst, Massachusetts, mother of Willy, age four, and Emily, age five.

Logistics demand a somewhat different set-up at the Live Power Community Farm in Covelo, California. Because many of this CSA farm's subscribers live in San Francisco, some three-and-a-half hours away, the farmers haul their collective share of the bounty each week to a wholesale organic vegetable warehouse in the city. There, neighborhood representatives meet and divvy up the produce to be dropped off for individual families. Three or four times a year, farmers Steve and Gloria Decater host work weekends and pot-lucks for the shareholders and their families. During these excursions, parents and children alike help harvest the vegetables, gather the eggs, or watch apprentices milk the cows.

MICHAEL ALLEN JONES

A myriad of important and inspiring forms of social and communal interactions can orbit around a community-supported farm. CSA farms in and near Hadley, Massachusetts; Washington, DC; and Pittsburgh contribute produce to local food banks for the hungry. In Santa Cruz, Calfornia, the Homeless Garden Project CSA provides jobs for the local homeless. And in a number of regions, CSAs reapportion their shares so that low-income families can afford to join the fold. Simply put, this system of farming can go far beyond buying a bushel of veggies for a week's worth of suppers.

CHAPTER 5 RESOURCES

General

Natural Health, Natural Medicine by Andrew Weil, M.D. (Houghton Mifflin, 1990).
> This book provides as much detail on diet as you'll need and is moderate where it needs to be. It has few particulars on children.

Cookbooks

Cooking Without Fat (Health Valley Foods, 1992) and *Baking Without Fat* (Health Valley Foods, 1994), both by George Mateljan.
> High fat content can ruin the health value of meals made from natural foods. Mateljan's cooking and baking principles help you make all your meals more healthful ones. *Cooking* isn't a vegetarian cookbook but contains recipes for many vegetarian entrees.

Why Healthful Eating Matters for Kids

Dr. Atwood's Low-Fat Prescription for Kids by Charles Atwood, M.D. (Penguin, 1995).
> A detailed exploration of why low-fat diets are best after age two. The book gives advice for eating in hotels, restaurants, on airplanes, and so on, and includes recipes, some of which include sugar.

What Are We Feeding Our Kids? by Michael Jacobson, Ph.D., and Bruce Maxwell (New York, NY: Workman, 1994).
> Practical advice on feeding kids healthily, with hard-hitting criticism of food makers, government, advertising agencies, and schools for failing to protect young people from destructive eating habits. A good first step for those who eat a conventional American diet now.

Why Vegetarianism and for Some People, Why Not

Better Than Peanut Butter and Jelly by Wendy Muldawer and Marty Mattare (Ithaca, NY: McBooks Press, 1998; to order, call 888–266–5711).
> Two vegetarian moms penned this book of recipes for quick vegan and vegetarian meals with kid appeal. It lists vegetarian resources and online services and Web sites.

The Vegetarian Child by Lucy Moll (New York, NY: Perigee, 1997).
> Filled with useful tips about surviving as a vegetarian family in a meat-filled world, the book covers dietary needs for developmental stages, vegetarianism during pregnancy, recipes, and healthful foods that kids will enjoy. Moll provides a sensible approach that allows for occasional "sinning."

Buying Produce Through Subscription Farms and Community-Supported Agriculture

ORGANIZATIONS

The Biodynamics Farming and Gardening Association, P.O. Box 29135, San Francisco, CA 94129–0135, (800) 516–7797, (415) 561–7797
website: www.biodynamics.com
> This is a nonprofit group that promotes community supported farming by underwriting training for biodynamic growers and maintaining a database of over 550 community supported agriculture (CSA) farms and gardens across the country. Contact them for an introductory brochure or list of CSA farms in your state.

Center for Sustainable Living, CAP Project, Wilson College, Chambersburg, PA 17201, (717) 264–4141, ext 3247

>Covers both urban and rural farms in their network. Will send information packets upon request.

"The Community Farm" Newsletter, 3480 Potter Road, Bear Lake, MI 49614, (616) 889–3216

e-mail: fsfarm@mufn.org

>Eight-page quarterly for $20/year with news about community farming from as far as Canada and Japan.

Community Supported Agriculture West, P.O. Box 363, Davis, CA 95617, (530) 756–8518.

email: csawest@caff.org

website: www.caff.org

>Maintains information on CSAs west of the Rockies. You can find CSAs near you on their website.

Michael Fields Agricultural Institute, W2493 County Road ES, East Troy, WI 53120, (414) 642–3303

>This organization will mail a directory of, and information about, CSAs in the upper Midwest—from Ohio to the Dakotas and Nebraska.

Northeast Sustainable Agriculture Working Group, P.O. Box 608, Belchertown, MA 01007, (413) 323–4531.

e-mail: nesfi@igc.org

>This organization will mail list or offer referrals to CSAs in the northeastern and mid-Atlantic states.

6

the learning family

 hat if learning were something children loved doing because they loved how it felt when their world expanded? What would education be like if the whole child were encouraged to develop more than just the verbal, logical, and mathematical abilities most schools concentrate on? How enthusiastic would kids be about school if it focused more on who they might become and less on what employers need them to know?

As we pondered these questions, Phil recalled an account one mother gave him a few years ago of her first visit to a Waldorf school, based on the ideas of holistic philosopher Rudolf Steiner (see page 259). Entering the kindergarten classroom, which had no one in it at the time, she burst into tears. "What I saw," she said, "was a very light, airy classroom that had a softness about it—no harsh teaching materials, with soft colors, silk, and toys made from wool. It touched a deep part of me, spiritually. I thought, 'Why didn't *I* get to go to a school like this?' It understood a child from a deep level."

Waldorf schools may not be to every family's tastes, but the glowing terms in which so many discuss them and their stark contrast with conventional schools' methods dramatize the state of childhood education today. The country where free public education was born still struggles with the concept of what education is, what it should accomplish, and how it should approach the child. In the absence of a cultural consensus, parents have to determine for themselves what priority education has in their family and what should be emphasized in that education for their children. For families that make education a top priority, that may mean becoming deeply involved in the local public school system, enrolling their kids in an alternative school, or even homeschooling their children.

We believe the sometimes confusing array of educational choices is actually a plus for families. As a society, we have erred in assuming that education should be something done *to* our kids by some external agent called "school" and that it should conclude when a person finishes formal schooling and begins a career. The shallowness of this concept has motivated many parents to make learning their own family value, to encourage their kids in their education, and even to join them in that great adventure.

Family learning is a cornerstone of Whole Parenting. In the following pages, we'll help you actualize your own learning vision for your children. We'll give you ideas for learning projects you can do with them at various stages in their growth. We'll cover the primary choices you face when your children reach school age, both in the public school system and in alternative education. We'll

MIRIAM JACOBS

show you how to turn your home into a holistic learning center that nurtures all aspects of the child's self. We'll guide you in teaching your children to be skilled *critical* thinkers. And our Resources list at the end of this chapter will provide further options and explorations for your family.

TEACHING YOUR CHILD TO THINK CRITICALLY

Teaching children to think critically is not a parental responsibility much talked about in America today, for reasons we'll soon make clear. It's also a responsibility about which many parents would rather not be reminded. Show your kids how to think and there's no telling what they'll start questioning—their religion, family rules, the need to graduate.

By critical thinking, we mean the ability to analyze and evaluate information, to not confuse assumptions and opinions with facts, and to draw the most likely conclusion from several diverse sources of information. Educators call this "high-level" thinking, in contrast to the simple recall of facts, known as "low-level" thinking.

Unfortunately, low-level also means average, because society hasn't prepared most of us to do otherwise. Low-level thinkers simply absorb information and react to it. Many of us are aware intuitively when people are trying to fool, manipulate, or mislead us. Far fewer of us have learned the specific skills needed to identify just how we're being tricked, much less stop the flow of our own erroneous thinking.

Your children live in a world where everybody from politicians to advertisers to special interest groups will be battling for their hearts and minds. Critical thinking is the "secret decoder ring" that will equip your kids to see through the persuasive techniques of salespeople, candidates, issue groups, and corporate public relations campaigns. It will also make them less likely to believe dubious information they hear on television or talk radio, or read in newspapers and magazines. Finally, critical thinking will enable your children to test ideas for their merits rather than accept them merely because "that's what everyone" thinks or does.

The Vital Skill That No One Teaches

Why is teaching critical thinking your job? Well, if you don't do it, who will? Few public school systems give critical thinking the emphasis it should have. Rarely is it applied to every subject and by every teacher, as it should be. And in many areas of the country, critical thinking is side-stepped altogether when it comes to politically sensitive subject matter such as alternative interpretations of U.S. history.

Nor are children likely to get help with this crucial skill from other adults in their lives. Few religions encourage dissent or even the questioning that might lead to it. Although many companies now encourage employees to suggest improvements in company methods and products, few want employees challenging the business' goals or philosophy. Essentially, we live in a society that talks much more about freedom of thought than practices it.

Why Critical Thinking Counts

Here are just some of the areas in society where your child will need critical thinking to participate at a high level:

Citizenship. To make good decisions as citizens and voters, your children will need high-level thinking skills. Every time a political office or issue is at stake, competing candidates or groups will fight bitterly for your children's loyalties and few will do it by simply telling the truth. It takes sophisticated thinking to separate facts from rhetoric and make sound democratic decisions.

The workplace. Critical thinkers go further in the work world. The average business may not be a bastion of democracy, but employers do value people who can critically manage information. For example, when companies want to develop new products or create marketing campaigns to sell existing products, they need people who can make sense out of masses of data, understand important social trends, and think clearly beyond wishful or fearful ideas.

The media. To get to the bottom of stories that matter, your children will have to know how to search out information from independent sources and evaluate it on their own. No critical thinker can rely as completely as before on the media outlets that Americans have traditionally trusted. Today, most of America's leading media outlets are owned by massive corporations that also own many non-media businesses. This creates any number of possible conflicts of interest, because no corporation wants its media companies covering stories that could hurt its other businesses.

In addition, the television networks now expect their news departments to contribute to corporate profits in a way that wasn't so true in previous eras. That means more emphasis on entertaining viewers and satisfying advertisers and less on straight news reporting and analysis. Fluff and sound bites are ever on the increase, and context is disappearing from the airwaves.

Nor can citizens turn to public media any longer for information that is free of commercial considerations. To survive, public TV has to keep all its sponsors, corporate and government, happy. In the process, important stories are ignored or rejected.

In short, only critical thinkers know how to identify reliable information in this media environment, or even where to look.

Commerce. To make wise purchasing decisions, your children will have to sort through misleading advertising and product labeling, corporate public relations pieces carried by news programs as news stories, and other misinformation that will confront them from every corner of their world.

Beginning a Home Curriculum in Critical Thinking

The following list covers some of the most important critical thinking skills. The most basic of these skills can be learned by children as early as age seven. None are so complex they can't be comprehended by the average teenager. Start this training as soon as your kids are ready for it. And, yes, we're fully aware that you may need to brush up your own critical thinking before teaching your kids about it! See the Resources at the end of this chapter for help.

Categorization. Play a categorization game with your younger children (ages seven and up) by having them devise categories for items they've collected—shells, leaves, dolls, animal models—and decide in which categories the items belong (for example, with animal models, such categories as "mammals," "reptiles," and so on). Categorization teaches them to observe each item closely, compare it to others, and evaluate how it should be classified.

Questioning standard explanations. Point out to your kids that many of the ideas that they take for granted today were probably considered radical when they were first introduced. For example, the idea that the earth revolves around the sun rather than vice versa was considered completely outlandish when astronomer Aristarchos of Samos suggested it in the third century B.C.E. It wasn't until almost 1,800 years later, when Copernicus proved it to be true, that scholars accepted that their planet wasn't the center of everything.

Kids should also learn that the commonly accepted explanation may not be the only possible one. You can teach this principle with a fun learning game. Have your kids suggest an alternative for a commonly accepted "fact" or theory. For instance, have them concoct another rationalization—besides genes—for why children resemble their parents. Let their imaginations run wild—the point isn't to get the right answer but to break the habit of lazily accepting everything on faith. (And beware of your own lazy thinking—your kids may point out to you that some people also resemble their dogs!)

Understanding science. Your children will probably learn in high school science classes what is meant by "controlled" studies, "double-blind" studies, and other important concepts about scientific methods. But they may not learn much about how science or pseudo-science is used to manipulate public opinion, including theirs. Nearly everyone with an argument to make cites studies to prove their point. Will your child understand how assumptions built into those studies can limit or distort their outcomes?

For example, many medicines for adults are tested mainly on young, adult men to see if they should be labeled safe. The researchers assume that what's true for those test subjects will be true for everyone. But we've learned otherwise—drugs may behave quite differently in the bodies of women or the elderly.

Your kids should also understand that scientists only consider a study valid if its results are replicable—that is, if other scientists using the same data and methods will produce similar results. Studies used to sway the public to an extreme point of view often can't pass this or other important tests.

Your kids should know the difference between causation and association, too. For example, as we saw in Chapter 3, kids who watch lots of TV tend to have poorer physical fitness. But TV doesn't *cause* poor fitness. If more people exercised instead of consuming potato chips while viewing, TV would be correlated with excellent fitness!

Finally, your kids should understand that it's important to know who funds a study. If the money comes from people or organizations with a strong interest in a particular outcome, and the study just happens to produce that outcome, the study should be regarded with considerable skepticism until independent scientists can evaluate it.

Assessing information sources. Clearly, your children should learn that something isn't necessarily true just because they read it in a book or see it on TV. They should know how to recognize both good and inadequate documentation, and take questionable sources such as sensationalistic programs and literature for what they are—entertainment or propaganda, not carefully presented fact. They should also realize that even widely re-spected experts can make mistakes or have questionable ideas.

Being willing to reach unpopular conclusions. If your children are good criti-cal thinkers, they won't reject any idea out of hand. They will evaluate it on its own merits, rather than whether it is the accepted idea of their peer group, others they identify with, or mainstream experts.

Understanding the thinking of those who disagree. Critical thinkers constantly re-examine their own ideas, often by reconsidering the arguments of their opponents.

Recognizing stereotypes. Point out to your children the stereotypes—of mi-norities, of women, of businesspeople, and so on—that frequently ap-pear in popular movies and television shows. Teach them that stereotypes can be favorable as well as unfavorable.

Learning to recognize ethnocentrism and religiocentrism. One of the subtler skills of critical thinking is noticing when a writer or speaker's opinions about another race, religion, culture, or group are colored by the crite-ria of his or her own. The Opposing Viewpoints book series, which comes in junior and adult versions (see the Resources at the end of this chap-ter), helps develop this ability and many others discussed above.

Of course, you have to be willing to have your children reject some of your most cherished ideas if you want to raise critical thinkers. But should this happen to you, listen to your kids carefully—no matter how young or naive, they may have a point!

CREATING A POSITIVE EDUCATIONAL ENVIRONMENT AT HOME

A brilliant orchestra of wildflowers and native plants greets you as you approach the front door of Beverly and Jim Fety's home in Rogue River, Oregon. However, nearly every other space on the property has been dedicated to the growing of the Fety's three children, thirteen-year-old Lauren and ten-year-old twins Allegra and Stuart.

Inside the cozy cedar house, the Fetys have provided each child a table for learning and art, Allegra's in a corner of the living room, Lauren's and Stuart's in the kitchen. The tables are stocked with paper, writing instruments, colored pencils, paints, and other art materials. A microscope sits in the kitchen for whoever wants to use it. Against a living room wall rest stacks of cardboard blocks for creative construction projects. In a utility room, an organizer unit spills over with crafts materials that the children can select whenever inspiration hits. The unit's disorderly state reveals that it hits often.

The upstairs, modest in size and furniture, also overflows with learning tools. In the kids' bedrooms and the hall lives what Beverly and Jim describe as "the core of everything we do with our kids," their extensive book collection. Dozens more books, from the library, lean against a bedroom wall. What the house doesn't have is a television and sound system, although a small boom box upstairs gets a workout playing talking books, a current favorite of the kids, and music.

The learning and growth opportunities continue outdoors. The lawn is wide enough for small-scale sports and spontaneous dramas. The sandbox is big enough for all three kids and a couple friends—the ultimate for imaginative and social play, says Jim. A stand of pine trees borders the lot on three sides, giving the children daily lessons on nature's ways in Oregon.

As any educator can tell you, the kids who do best in school often come from homes like this one that are virtual extensions of the classroom. The Fety's approach is just a variation on a theme—for example, the absence of TV also precludes certain learning opportunities, as we point out in Chapter 3. But the Fety house still demonstrates several aspects of how a home environment can support the learning children do in school. The Fety kids are partially homeschooled—Jim, a teacher in the local elementary, and Beverly, a former teacher, move them back and forth between homeschooling and public education as it suits the children's individual learning styles. Homeschooling parents have a special obligation to provide their kids with educational materials. But even children who attend public school learn best when education doesn't start and stop with the school bell.

A Holistic Approach to Home Learning Environments— The "Multiple Intelligences" Model

When making your home a better environment for learning, you may want to think more holistically—that is, cover a broader range of subjects and learning methods—than traditional educators do. In that vein, consider the ideas of psychologist Howard Gardner. In his 1983 book *Frames of Mind,* Gardner suggested that there is much more to intelligence than the verbal, logical, and mathematical abilities that standardized tests measure. Although public education, and Western culture, tend to prize these abilities above all others, Gardner feels that the human family displays many other forms of intelligence that are just as crucial to a functioning society. To encompass all of them, he developed what he called his theory of "multiple intelligences."

JAMES WEEKS

You can probably recognize your own strengths and the strengths of your children in the following description of the eight intelligences that Gardner has identified. Following each intelligence, we have listed several types of educational tools and/or activities that help develop it. Although our lists are intended for the home environment, they are adapted from the work of Thomas Armstrong, a holistically oriented psychologist and Gardner disciple who developed similar lists for the ideal classroom:

1. *Linguistic intelligence*—The verbal ability measured by IQ tests and the SAT (Stanford Achievement Test). Gardner says poets display this ability in its purest form. *Tools/activities:* An *up-to-date* encyclopedia, atlas, and dictionary are fundamental to any home with school-age children; regarding the former, the Colliers and World Book sets are especially kid friendly while still being useful to adults. Storytelling, reading aloud, discussions, and talking books (books on tape) all foster language development. Magazine subscriptions help children deepen knowledge in a wide variety of areas related to their favorite subject. Most educators feel a child should have access to a computer by midway through the grade-school years, although some holistic educators and Waldorf schools feel that computers before junior high age limit a child's imaginative play. You can't have too many books, but remember that quality counts as much as quantity. Build your book

collection cheaply through yard sales, library sales, publishers' clearinghouse catalogs, and remaindered books at bookstores.

2. *Logical-mathematical intelligence*—The ability required to excel in science and mathematics, as well as logical pursuits such as law. This is the other intelligence, besides verbal, measured by IQ tests and SATs. *Tools/activities:* A microscope is one of the most important home learning tools but one of acceptable quality, such as the Bausch and Lomb models, costs several hundred dollars; many school systems make microscopes available for students, icluding homeschoolers, to borrow. Other valuable tools in this category include science kits, science books and magazines, strategy games such as chess or checkers, computer software, and detective games. Don't neglect financial education in this category—a children's savings account is a good way to start. Finally, keep in mind that many holistic educators feel that children shouldn't be exposed to logical pursuits before about age seven.

3. *Spatial intelligence*—In Gardner's words, "the ability to form a mental model of a spatial world and to be able to maneuver and operate using that model." This type of intelligence is possessed in abundance by engineers, sailors, painters, sculptors, and surgeons. *Tools/activities:* Blocks and other such undetailed construction toys are the indispensable items here, say developmental experts. Other helpful items include charts, maps, diagrams, a telescope, graphics software, cameras, carpentry tools, optical illusions, drafting materials, visualization exercises, and art supplies.

4. *Musical intelligence*—The ability to effectively use melody, rhythm, harmony, and other musical elements for self-expression, composition, and so on. *Tools/activities:* Music, along with the other arts, helps children integrate all the intellectual disciplines and also develops creative problem-solving skills. Research shows that music education may improve math abilities and language skills. Melodic musical instruments (piano, guitar, electronic keyboards, woodwinds), percussion instruments (tambourine, drums, maracas), a metronome, recorded music (see Chapter 7 for more on recordings for children), family singing, toy instruments, homemade instruments, and natural sounds such as birds chirping and wind rustling leaves all nurture musical intelligence.

5. *Body-kinesthetic intelligence*—The ability to solve problems or make things using all or part of one's body. This type of intelligence is best demonstrated by athletes, dancers, surgeons, and crafts people. *Tools/activities:* You can help your child develop in this area with the aid of large open outdoor spaces such as lawns, exercise and play spaces indoors, gym equipment, model-building kits, trampolines, swimming pools, carpentry equipment, modeling clay, sports equipment, video games, costumes for drama, and even animals (Alan's daughter Ariel has greatly expanded her body-kinesthetic abilities by chasing and catching her chickens.) Education of the body has long been denigrated in Western education but in a non-Western culture such as China's, neglecting the body would be unthinkable. See Chapter 8 for information on popular youth sports that promote body/mind integration.

6. *Interpersonal intelligence*—The ability to understand others, including what motivates them, and also the ability to work cooperatively with others. Successful psychotherapists, salespeople, religious leaders, managers, teachers, and politicians possess this gift. *Tools/activities:* Group games, team sports, social play, clubs, committees, social events, group projects, discussions, peer counseling, and peer tutoring help develop interpersonal intelligence. Note that many otherwise gifted individuals are rendered ineffective by their inability to relate well to people. "People skills" lead to both personal satisfaction and worldly success.

7. *Intrapersonal intelligence*—The ability to see and know oneself with a minimum of self-delusion and to use that knowledge to function effectively in the world. This type of intelligence is not particular to any profession but is obviously possessed by extraordinary people in a variety of endeavors. *Tools/activities:* This intelligence, although native to some, also develops with the help of such activities and "atmospheres" as mediation, awareness exercises, self-esteem training, individual sports and games, individual projects, self-paced learning, and personal spaces in which a child can spend time alone such as a fort, tree house, or playhouse.

8. *Naturalist intelligence*—The ability to understand, analyze, and utilize the natural environment. This type of intelligence is demonstrated by many environmental scientists, environmental

activists, and nature-lovers. *Tools/activities:* A flower or vegetable garden, nature exploration kits, backyard exploration, items from a nature museum gift store, nature videotapes, microscopes, magnifying glasses, pets, aquariums, and terrariums all develop a child's sensitivity and capacities in the natural world. See also Chapter 9.

You'll notice that the Fetys' home encourages learning in every one of Gardner's categories. In addition, the Fetys have supported their kids in undertaking a full "curriculum" of special classes and youth programs—soccer, ballet, piano, tap, dancing, and art. However, the home environment plays a fundamental role that no outside course can. It demonstrates to children that learning isn't a "have-to," or something external to day-to-day living. It's a big part of what life is all about, it's fun, and it feels good.

A Space of Their Own

Children are far more likely to take full advantage of the educational tools and activities you provide for them if they have their own work space to use them in. (They should be ready for one by age two.) Work spaces give kids a sense of control and power over their world, especially if they also have writing, art, and craft supplies at hand that they can choose from for self-initiated projects. Having their own desk or table also leads to good study habits later on, say veteran teachers. Here are some things to keep in mind when setting up your child's "home office":

Furniture. For toddlers, almost any surface that they can sit or kneel at can be made to work, but kid-scale furniture is best because it will feel to them more a part of their own little world. Ideally, the furniture will be big enough and have an extra chair so a friend or parent can join the party, too.

As kids grow, the furniture has to grow with them. Discourage studying on the floor or bed. If they write or read in unnatural positions, your young students will tire sooner.

Location. Younger kids do much better near the action center of the house, usually the kitchen or family room. They feel reassured by having Mom or Dad nearby and inspired to do their own work beside parents who are preparing meals, balancing the checkbook, and so on. Whichever place you pick, make sure it's one where you can have a forgiving attitude about the messes kids make as they feed their growing brains. But parents should also be prepared to redirect their childrens' activities, says Bev Fety: "If the child's behavior is way out of hand, the environment is usually out of synch. Instead of ranting that Johnny's drawing on the wall with the crayons, put the crayons away for now and take the blocks out."

The kitchen or an adjacent room may be just the right spot for older children, too, so you can easily answer their homework questions. But if your kids are easily distracted by noise and activity, it's better to find them a quieter place.

Organization. Clear-plastic, stackable boxes can be found in almost any home center store or hardware department; these help manage the ever-expanding collection of arts-and-crafts materials and don't need labeling because the contents are visible. Make sure your child can reach what he needs. And make sure to provide plenty of display space for your child's artistic output or prize school papers—a special place that shows how proud you are of what he's done.

Beyond the "Stuff" of Learning: Parents' Role

While children will gravitate to appealing learning tools and projects on their own, there is much you can do to actively encourage your kids' desire to learn. Start by showing an interest in and reinforcing what they're learning in school, as Lynn and Blake Willeford do with their son, Brook, age seventeen. "If he's taking astronomy, we borrow our friend's telescope for a month and set it up on the deck," says Lynn, who with her husband has made their Washington home a well-rounded learning environment for Brook, much as the Fetys have for their kids.

Perhaps the most encouraging action you can take is to have your children observe you happily learning in your spare moments, too. "We read all the time," notes Lynn, "so Blake claims Brook became [an avid] reader in sheer self-defense. It's not unusual to see all three of us reading in the living room at night. We also always looked things up immediately if we didn't have the answer, rather than saying 'I don't know,' so by the end of the dinner hour there was likely to be an atlas or a volume of the encyclopedia on the table. We've also used our travel experiences as educational opportunities. There's no doubt in my mind that our own curiosity about the world fostered Brook's."

PARENT-CHILD LEARNING PROJECTS

You don't have to stock up on textbooks, toys, tools, or technical know-how to make sure that your child's imagination stays active or his intellect is stimulated. Play in itself helps kids develop their sensory motor perception, their large and small muscle coordination, their hand-eye coordination, and their vocabulary. It's easy to incorporate learning and fun into everyday acts and chores such as cooking, sorting clothes, picking up around the house, or walking around the neighborhood. Ideally, you might want to try activities that cover a range of experiences from verbal games to tactile crafts to imaginary play settings. Here are some ideas grouped by category and offered in ascending order of age-appropriateness:

Tactile Activities

- *True Grit.* In an area that you don't mind getting dirty, try pouring dry backyard dirt or sand (or too-old cornmeal, grits, or cream of wheat from the pantry) in a dishpan or broiler pan; then give your toddler a plastic bottle filled with water, a mini muffin tin, spoon, and spatula and watch what she pats, slaps, molds, and stirs up. This type of play fosters experimentation with physical properties—for example, making sand soupier or more crumbly.

- *Edible Experiments.* Cooking teaches such basic skills as planning, measuring, and timing—not to mention basic chemistry. For instance, a pancake or cookie recipe can be the forum for your child learning what happens when a rising agent like baking soda is combined with something acidic, like a tablespoon of yogurt, lemon juice, molasses, or vinegar. Have your child practice making batches with and without each acidic ingredient; and discover which of the four creates the best texture and taste. This activity is best for ages five to ten.

Figuring and Sorting

- *Food Facts.* After you return from grocery shopping, ask your pre-kindergartener to separate the foods that need to stay cold from the stuff that doesn't need refrigeration. Older kids might be asked to separate the fruits from the grains, the vegetables from the dairy products, and the oils from the meats or beans.

- *Map It Out.* As your eight- to ten-year-old begins to understand such concepts as left and right, north, east, south, and west, try coaxing her to draw a large map of your neighborhood.

- *Country Crops.* To instill an even broader geographic understanding in your child, help him cut out the faces of friends and relatives from some of your spare photos. Next, using a map of the United States or the world on the wall, ask your child to help you attach these photos of folks you know to the appropriate cities, states, or countries.

- *Budget Help.* The next time you need to order from a catalog, give your seven- to ten-year-old the book and a limited budget. Tell him what you'd like to purchase and let him figure out the best buys for the dollar, as well as how much you'll spend and how much you'll have left.

- *A Make-Believe Menu.* Ask your kids to conjure up their ideal three- or four-course menu. At first, make this a game. But eventually, you can introduce the concept of food groups and ask your kids to pick balanced meals as an exercise in higher-level sorting.

Word Play

- *What's the Riddle?* With your child, take turns coming up with a description that could be a good answer to an unasked question, for instance, "A smiling daddy." Then both of you could brainstorm about the most appropriate question, perhaps "What do you get when you tell Dad you love him five times a day?" or "What happens when you make a face like this _____ at Dad?" Exercises that approach a challenge from a different angle encourage vocabulary building, the recognition of causal relationships, and other kinds of creative thinking.

- *The Missing Link.* Ask your child to say a word, any word, then follow it up with a completely unrelated word of your own. Your child, for instance, might blurt out "dog," and you might say "cloud." Your child now has to discuss some connection between dogs and clouds; perhaps he might note that some clouds are shaped like dogs or that in the winter, some dogs breathe clouds of air. This helps kids develop the language needed to form "connective tissue" between ideas.

- *Fifteen Ways to . . .* This list-making endeavor also fosters creative thinking. While you take notes and keep count, challenge your child to come up with fifteen uses for an empty aluminum foil roll or an eggshell or a jar.

- *Finish the Story.* At the dinner table, offer up the opening scene of a story—a favorite in Stephanie's household is entitled "The Grape Who Got Away"—and take turns trying to make this tale as tall and outlandish as possible. This is a fun exercise to enhance language development and inventive thinking.

Fantasy Play

- *Winter Pool.* "In the winter months, we yearn for summer activities so we recreate them in our home," says Karen O'Dougherty. She and her five- and three-year-old daughters spread a down comforter out on the floor. The girls then get in their bathing suits, suit up their dolls as best they can, and "teach" the dolls swimming lessons, with the comforter as the pool. "We talk about getting splashed and how cool the breeze is on our wet bodies," says Karen. "The key is to recreate the pool scene as much as possible. The more images and sensations I portray for them, the more they participate in the fantasy. My three-year-old daughter was so absorbed in the fantasy one day she pretended to cry when she got water up her nose!"

GETTING THE MOST FROM YOUR PUBLIC SCHOOL

Although many of us dream of educational Shangri-las for our children, the public schools most of us have inherited offer a starkly different reality—ongoing budget woes; overcrowded classrooms; art, music, and physical education cutbacks; and physical deterioration. No mother or father can single-handedly fix what ails America's schools, but they can make steady advancements one step at a time.

To get the most out of your child's public education, you'll need to invest time, both at school and at home. Rest assured, your efforts will be rewarded: In a comprehensive survey of more than 85 studies conducted between 1980 and 1995, researchers found that when parents were involved in their children's education, students had better grades and test scores, more completed assignments, more positive attitudes, and higher expectations from their teachers.

The following suggestions show how families can maximize their children's public school experience—by helping their children *and* their schools succeed.

Helping Your Child at School

Here are some significant ways you can make a difference in your child's school experience:

PHIL CATALFO

Get to know her teacher. The first and most important task you should undertake on your child's behalf—getting to know your child's teacher—sounds obvious. Yet it's worth discussing because so many parents go about this process the wrong way and in doing so, set the tone for a less-than-productive school year.

Your first interaction with the teacher should not revolve around a problem. Instead, make that first encounter casual, friendly, and supportive. Set aside time to meet the teacher during the first week of school. Find something positive to say about the class or the homework right away—for example, "What a creative idea that was to assign an oral history of our family— we'll have fun putting it together." This lets the teacher know that you're engaged but not overly critical and it will open the door for her to share her goals and observations about your child. During these initial talks, you might want to let her know what your child's special interests are and how he learns best. Let your tone convey that you'd like to be partners with the teacher, and that you assume that she, too, only wants what's best for your child.

"When my son was in second grade, I became something of a cheerleader for his teacher," says Titilayo Bediako of Minneapolis. "I'd send her notes at the beginning of every week about his progress at home and about any positive things I could find to say about her assignments." Perhaps the fact that Titilayo is also a schoolteacher (at a different site) engendered more empathy than most parents might feel, but her tactics are still instructive.

Keep in mind as you observe your child's teacher in action that you can't expect public school instructors to be immersed in all the principles and philosophies of holistic learning. However, most public schools are at least making progress in that direction by adopting an integrated curriculum—that is, instruction in which a variety of academic disciplines converge. A lesson plan about the Mexican festival, Cinco de Mayo, for instance, might include a history of the celebration, some Spanish vocabulary, a hands-on papier-mâché art project (with the students using applied math to duplicate the recipe for 30 kids), a social studies poll, and a class newsletter.

Observe the class periodically. This should be step two on your school-involvement agenda, as time permits. At some schools, teachers adopt a sort of open-door, any time policy. In others, instructors—or their principals—will ask you to make an appointment to observe. While you're there, don't be surprised if the teacher puts you to work collating, filing, or even grading student papers. Go ahead and cooperate as best you can while still tuning in to the classroom dynamics. Are children being encouraged to take chances? Is the teacher playing to each child's strengths? Does she acknowledge or praise students' achievements? Is she making every effort to connect her lessons to her pupils' life circumstances, interests, or needs?

Among other things, you'll want to pay attention to how reading or cooperative learning groups are set up. Are all the groups mixed racially, and ability- or gender-wise? Are all the "slow" readers seated together? What about "troublemakers"—are some students constantly labeled in negative terms?

When a fifth grader we know in public school reported that her teacher had chastised her for forgetting her homework one day, her mother was far more concerned about the nature of this scolding than the fact of it. If this student ever forgot her homework again, the teacher allegedly said, she'd be assigned to a learning group of four boys whom the teacher had identified as troublemakers less than a month into the school year. "You must have felt humiliated," the girl's mother said to her. "Yes," said the student, "but, Mom, think of how those boys must have felt."

This comment helped the mother to realize that "these kids were probably far more traumatized than my daughter was." So the mother wrote up her concerns about the classroom grouping in a letter to the teacher. Although the teacher didn't respond favorably, eventually the mother and her daughter attended a meeting with the other parents and their children. "It was like a debriefing dinner where we parents listened to how the kids felt about the class," the mother recalled. "After listening, the adults spoke to them about how they shouldn't let bad experiences keep them from learning. This session let them know that we weren't blind to their rights."

If you have concerns about how students are grouped in your child's class, ask questions. If the teacher's answers suggest students are clustered according to their abilities, that may be cause for concern. Studies show that ability grouping or "tracking" can have a detrimental effect on learning because it pigeonholes the supposedly slow learners and can limit what they learn. What's more, tracking within, say, reading or math groups, tends to perpetuate academic divisions by offering the "fast" track student stimulating work that everyone ought to have, while offering the "slow" track student the more rote and repetitive work.

Once you've gotten to know your child's teacher, her curriculum, goals, and general teaching style, consider making a more tangible contribution to the class. You might try writing up a list of activities that you'd be willing to do—offering to read at story time, cleaning up, demonstrating a scientific principle, and so on.

Become familiar with homework. How the teacher handles outside assignments merits a great deal of attention. Make sure the take-home lesson plans are stimulating and relevant to what's going on in the classroom. Homework sessions, after all, shouldn't feel like drudgery or punishment to your child. They should offer him a chance to show his academic strengths outside the classroom. Ideally, some of the homework given should require your child to interact with you. Look for instruction sheets that suggest the degree of help a parent should give on an assignment or ask the teacher how much help is appropriate.

Review your child's progress. Teachers should allow you to do this over several weeks—before report card time. If no such mechanism is in place, you might ask the teacher to let you review the work at school, or you might suggest that she send your child's portfolio home for you to look over.

Get to know the staff in the front office. Having a good rapport with the school secretary, for instance, will certainly help when you want to meet with the principal quickly. And it may make you privy to new policies being developed, not to mention the daily traumas and dramas of student life. Such a relationship can also help you gauge where the most help is needed.

Keep an eye on the next grade level. Network with other parents to find out who are the better teachers and what you can expect. For a sneak preview of a next-grade class, you might approach that teacher with an offer to help out in the classroom.

Helping Your Child's School

Becoming an active, involved parent instills another value worth cultivating in your family: a sense of community. By rolling up your sleeves
and pitching in, you reinforce the notion that your family has a role in
the school—and that school is important enough to play a big role in
your lives. "Seeing me so active in their schools helps my girls feel more
connected," says Viviane Arzoumanian, mother of two who served for
years on the steering committee and in the parent-teacher organization
at her daughter's school in Brooklyn. "Besides, the fact that I know everyone seems to give *them* some status too," she adds with a laugh.

Here are more suggestions on creating a strong presence at school:

- *Become active in the parent's association or PTA.* As you might expect, most
  PTAs are involved in a variety of school activities including fund-
  raising, curriculum enrichment, parent education, building safety,
  and ground improvement.

- *Join or start a Welcoming Committee for new parents at the school.* This helps create
  a new pool of involved parents to call when veteran PTA parents are
  about to burn out.

- *Participate in a carpool.* If none exists, post a flyer on the school bulletin
  board to start one. Be willing to extend your carpooling beyond your
  own child's classmates. This not only encourages friendly interaction
  between students of different ages, but invites upper- and lower-
  grade parents to exchange important information about the school.

- *Reach out to help other parents get involved by acknowledging the many facets of their
  lives.* You might, for instance, offer to swap baby-sitting stints so that
  you and your fellow parents can take turns going to key PTA or school
  policy meetings. The mom or dad who attends the meeting can report
  back to the baby-sitting parent. This kind of networking is especially
  helpful for single parents who want to stay involved.

- *If you find meetings too frustrating, volunteer for some grunt work.* For instance, you
  could try cooking, typing up announcements, or calling up local
  businesses for donations. These tasks have a beginning, middle, and
  end, which is a lot more than you can say for *some* committee work.

- *Join committees that you feel passionate about.* Your passion will keep you interested and engaged, help get things done, and inspire your kids.
  When the Berkeley, California, school board decided to restructure

and rebuild its elementary and middle schools five years ago, Robin Baker joined a team of parents, teachers, administrators, and community members to review plans for renovating the Washington School her five- and eight-year-old attended. Over the next two to three years, the group met regularly with other school movers and shakers to make decisions ranging from the square footage of new classrooms to the reservation of room space for a preschool site on campus. "I knew when I joined the committee that my own kids might not be the ultimate beneficiaries of our efforts," she says. "But I think it's important for people to not buy out of the public school system and let it go to hell in a handbasket."

- *Be aware of some of the safety and environmental issues on the school grounds.* For months, says Carol Silverman Saunders, she and fellow parents at her first grader's school in Westchester complained about the smell of smoke. As it turned out, the smell came from the school's ancient electrical wiring system, which eventually caused a fire that severely damaged the building. Unsatisfied with the district's response to the crisis, Carol soon moved her family to another city and started a school safety committee at her kids' new school "where we looked at fire safety and roof safety." Her experiences with school building safety also inspired her to cowrite a book on the topic (see the Resources at the end of this chapter).

- *Approach local businesses to see if they'd be interested in cooperative ventures with your school* (see the partnerships program listed in Resources).

- *Help revive the arts.* Art and music curricula are often among the first to go when cutbacks in school spending are made. Yet research shows that when kids are exposed to the visual arts and music, their learning in other areas—math and spatial reasoning, in particular—is enhanced. You may need to persuade your PTA to earmark funds to hire an art, music, or drama teacher who is skilled at working with kids.

- *Support increased funding for public schools.* This is how Parents for Public Schools (see the Resources at the end of this chapter) got started. You can participate in such a campaign by registering voters on school campuses, or joining a phone tree, or passing out leaflets.

Waldorf, Montessori, Charter, and Other Alternative Schools

In recent years, critics from nearly every corner of society have blasted public schools for not doing a good job. We think that's unfair—we get the public schools we pay for, and many states and municipalities don't pay much, particularly in low-income neighborhoods. Education has also been hurt by a nasty convergence of social trends, including a rise in latchkey kids, too much television, and too little reading. And for that matter, many schools are meeting or exceeding the standards set for them, without getting much credit from the public for it.

But for some parents, the issue is less the job the schools *are* doing than the concept of what they *should* be doing. To these parents, it's the very methods and the goals of public education that are the problem. Oft-expressed comments by these parents include the views that public schools are too dogmatic, too nationalistic, too competitive, too materialistic, too authoritarian, or too insensitive to minorities. Many feel that the public schools fail to educate the whole person because they're trying too hard to train workers for business and government. Some parents worry that the schools are too inflexible to suit the individual learning styles of their children.

For all of the above reasons and more, many holistic and progressive families choose to educate their children outside common public schools, whether through homeschooling, private schools such as Waldorf or Montessori education, or publicly funded options such as charter schools. However, once they start with these programs, they often find mixed results there, too. Alternative education may provide you and your children with an immensely satisfying experience, but only if you let go of the notion that it will be perfect.

Waldorf Schools

You don't have to understand the unique approach of Waldorf schools to grasp that there's something very different going on here. Waldorf classrooms may have tables and chairs but students rarely sit at them. At the Waldorf School of the Rogue Valley near Alan's home in southern Oregon, the first grade class spends much of its time outside on the school's forty-acre rural property, studying the living systems of the land's wetland and creek and observing the habits of the deer, elk, coyote, ducks, geese, herons, and sheep that share the space. The fourth grade class studies fractions by baking muffins and pizza. Fifth graders are completing a display on the Oregon Trail for the local library, combining studies in history, art, and geography. Bodies are almost always in motion here. And judging by the absence of bored faces, minds clearly follow.

Holistically oriented families who prefer alternative education for their children often consider Waldorf schools first. No school serving a large number of students can meet every parent's hopes and ideals. However, for almost eighty years, Waldorf curriculums have pursued a careful, intelligent, and heartfelt plan of whole child education while producing results that would make any public school principal beam.

Waldorf schools follow the ideas of Austrian-born and educated Rudolf Steiner (1861–1925), whose wide-ranging thinking led to profound innovations in everything from education to spiritual philosophy to agriculture (Steiner invented biodynamic gardening). Steiner felt the surest way for schools to contribute to a better world was to turn out more fully realized people. "We shouldn't ask: what does a person need to do in order to fit into the existing social order?" he wrote. "Instead we should ask: what lives in each human being and what can be developed in him or her? Only then will it be possible to direct the new qualities of each emerging generation into society."

Steiner, who founded the first Waldorf school in 1919, believed that education could be vastly improved by bringing its rhythms and content more in line with the developmental needs of the child. He felt that the public schools of his day pressured children to grow up too quickly to meet the needs of a fast-paced society. Play is the serious work of childhood, he believed. If you divert children from this task, he claimed, they will pay an inevitable price, including the curtailing of their creative and imaginative powers. Along those lines, he also felt that a school that blended arts and academic education would produce students who were more creative in their thinking and who took a more lively interest in learning.

If you went to traditional schools, little of what Waldorf schools do will look familiar to you. For example, Waldorf students keep the same teacher for the first eight grades after kindergarten, the idea being that an instructor who really gets to know the students and their parents can do a better job of teaching. Students learn two foreign languages, beginning in the first grade, to open them to other cultures. Reading isn't encouraged until children are 6½ or 7 beacause Steiner believed that reading isn't developmentally appropriate until then—interestingly, research shows that children do learn to read more quickly at this age. The arts—music, drama, painting, drawing, sculpture, and so on—permeate every aspect of the curriculum, even mathematics and the sciences. Wholeness is the watchword of Waldorf—all teaching engages multiple disciplines and multiple senses.

Waldorf education places a high priority on learning by doing. All boys and girls from kindergarten to high school learn "handwork" skills such as knitting and crocheting and receive musical instruction, starting with wooden flutes in the first grade. Students also take part in large-scale projects such as carpentry and gardening. These practical arts are used to develop coordination, perseverance, patience, and a sense of accomplishment; they're thought to aid intellectual development as well. Sciences are taught via experiments that turn students into little Galileos, enabling them to discover basic principles for themselves. "We learned about conduction, convection, and radiation, and unexpectedly found gold's melting point when we [accidentally] melted Miss Crawley's wedding ring," wrote students Megan Adler and Eberley Wedlake about the physics experiments in their sixth grade class at the Rogue Valley school.

THE WALDORF SCHOOL OF ROGUE VALLEY

The beauty, mystery, and interdependence of the natural world also plays an important role in Waldorf teaching. Ideally, a Waldorf campus sits in a natural setting such as the Rogue Valley school does. Inside, nature abounds as well—playthings, furniture, and as many teaching materials as possible are made from natural materials such as wood, wool, and cotton.

How does all this impressive theory work out in real world terms? Quite well, by nearly all accounts. Waldorf students perform strongly on standardized tests compared to their public school peers. Every year, graduates are accepted to many of America's finest colleges. Parents are probably Waldorf education's harshest critics, but that may be a result of the "Mercedes effect," suggests Waldorf parent and substitute teacher Alan Wright, whose wife Denise is the Rogue Valley school's kindergarten teacher: "Public school is free and here I'm paying four, five, six, seven thousand dollars a year. So, parents expect to get what they pay for." And even most parents who object to this or that aspect of their local Waldorf school seem to feel the benefits far outweigh the problems.

Still, some facets of Waldorf education will initially frustrate or confuse parents who otherwise share the school's goals. One of the most frequently voiced issues concerns rigidity. As with any ideology, some Waldorf schools have been accused of sticking too closely to Steiner's original philosophy when compromise for individual situations may be called for. Jay and Dorise Treiger sent their two sons to the Rogue Valley Waldorf school for much of their elementary period. "In general, we were pleased with the Waldorf approach," says Jay. But the Treigers felt that Waldorf's policy of treating all children the same, regardless of ability (which they do to discourage competition), was too unbending. They agree that in the earliest grades, kids profit by not feeling rushed into achieving. But, Dorise adds, "In fifth or sixth grade, when kids awaken to their differences from each other, I would have liked to have seen a little more flexibility in encouraging our kids' strengths and addressing their weaknesses." Waldorf schools are independent of each other, sharing only a curriculum, not organizational ties. Thus, some programs will be more flexible than others. Then again, too much compromise can dilute Waldorf's special qualities, some would say.

Some mothers and fathers also feel confronted by what is expected of them as Waldorf parents. Waldorf schools want parents to be involved with the school and their child's education. "It doesn't work well when parents just drop them off and pick them up," notes Alan Wright. (Of course, this is true with public education, too.) Waldorf schools also encourage parents to modify their home lifestyle if need be to support the Waldorf process. In some households, the suggested changes may seem extreme: little or no TV, few or no video games or visits to the video arcade, and less media in general for children in younger grades. Also few or no detailed mass-market toys, more nonspecific toys made of natural materials, and regular bedtime and waking rituals—to strengthen the child's will, the theory goes.

But even the Wrights, deeply committed as they are to Waldorf philosophy, cut the occasional corner at home. "I tend not to make compromises in the classroom because I feel like this may be the only time where the children get what we're trying to give them," says Denise. But at home, "there are times when Crystal or Eli want something like Barbie dolls or guns or some plastic toy. We don't really agree with it and we really want to give them a more natural material, but I don't want to be an oddball when other parents are allowing them to have these things. So we'll say, 'Okay, we'll get this' but then it may be a long time before we get something else that's not a Waldorf-type toy."

Many prospective Waldorf families wonder if the schools are sufficiently connected to the "real" world. They worry that ideas conceived in early-twentieth century Europe don't necessarily apply to near-twenty-first century America, but the fact is, corporate employers today are hungry to hire exactly the type of fluid-thinking, creative students that Waldorf turns out. Businesspeople love to see children involved with computers early on, because computer whizzes are useful in today's high-tech workplace. Waldorf programs do introduce computers, but much later than in "wired" public schools—after puberty, when it is felt to be more age appropriate.

The Christian symbolism employed in the schools will upset some non-Christian families. Waldorf schools don't favor or teach Christianity over other religions, but they have adopted the Madonna-and-child as a nurturing, maternal symbol; the image is present in all classrooms.

Finally, circumstances make the transition from Waldorf to public school an issue for many families. Of the one hundred-plus American communities served by Waldorf schools, few are able to support a full K–12 program. Some offer only a kindergarten, some only an elementary program. So ultimately, many Waldorf students end up transferring to public schools, where the greater emphasis on skills and competition can be disorienting until the students settle in. On the other hand, some Waldorf alums feel the biggest transition problem is that public schools simply don't compare to their Waldorf experience.

Montessori Schools

Maria Montessori (1870–1952), the first woman physician in Italy, became a schooling innovator by accident while working with so-called "mentally defective" children, whom she tried to educate along with doctoring them. They progressed so far under her guidance that they passed the standard school examinations in Rome. Where do we go wrong with "normal" kids, she asked herself, if my disadvantaged students could do nearly as well as them? She found some answers a few years later while successfully trying her ideas with children from the slums in Rome. Although she insisted that her work was broader than an educational method, the day care center she began directing in 1907 became the first Montessori school. Today, America is just one of many countries dotted with them.

Montessori schools aren't as closely identified with holistic values as Waldorf education is. However, their philosophy and learning methods still make an easy fit for most holistically oriented families. In particular, their nonauthoritarianism and respect for the developmental wisdom of nature appeal to parents who find these qualities lacking in public schools. Unfortunately, only a few American Montessori programs include elementary grades; most offer only preschools.

You'll see the Montessori philosophy in action as soon as you step in the classroom. Instead of group learning, individual children will be engaged at various learning stations around the room or even moving between indoors and the play and garden areas outside, entirely on their own initiative. In Montessori schools, children are left free to be naturally attracted to learning, play, and social activities as their developmental drives inspire them. Left to their own devices, the theory goes, children reflect upon what works for them and what doesn't and learn the limits and promise of their own abilities. Teachers provide only minimal guidance—for example, giving individual children introductory lessons on new learning materials to which they're drawn. Teachers also strive to draw out new children and step in when a child does something to annoy others. What they don't do is plan and deliver lessons, because every child is learning at her own self-directed pace. Not that the teachers aren't highly trained, but the training directs them to stay out of the child's way as much as possible. They're also taught to be alert to the child's ever-changing needs and growth.

Everything about the Montessori classroom and the way it is maintained is designed to reinforce the philosophy. Learning materials are organized so children always know where to find them and the kids themselves share the responsibility for returning everything to its proper place when they're done with it. Children practice real life skills such as cooking and cleaning on real stoves, refrigerators, and sinks. They learn that reality sometimes hurts by using real knives to cut fruit and hot irons to press clothes. They learn waiting, patience, and respect for other's activities because a classroom only includes one of each learning material or piece of equipment. They study nature, compassion, and social responsibility by taking care of plants and animals, exploring outside, and peering at the natural world through a magnifying glass or microscope. They absorb aesthetic concepts in a pleasing atmosphere of bright and harmonious colors, good music, well-designed furniture, and high-quality learning objects. They also practice art and music with materials and instruments specific to their culture and other specially designed Montessori objects that transcend culture.

Although Montessori education emphasizes individual pacing, it also encourages social development. For instance, children aren't segregated by age, so older children naturally help younger ones learn. And, of course, they're always free to relate with their classmates so long as they don't step on their rights.

Some experts and parents criticize Montessori schools for being too rigid, for suppressing initiative, and for pushing children too far in the areas of neatness, order, and self-control. Some also say the schools place too much emphasis on intellectual pursuits at an early age. Others feel the method discourages imagination and creativity, particularly in the supposed narrow way children are encouraged to use the special Montessori materials. As in any school environment, parents trying Montessori need to stay alert to how their children are doing. However, they also need to be patient to let the educational philosophy do its work.

When searching out a Montessori school for your child, be aware that the parent organization that certified the school will affect how your child is taught. In America, disagreement over Montessori's methods has led to a philosophical split in the movement and the confusing spectacle of two primary certifying organizations—the Association Montessori Internationale (AMI) and the American Montessori Society (AMS). Schools affiliated with the more traditional AMI adhere tightly to Maria Montessori's original ideas. The AMS is no less admiring of Montessori but stresses that the methods must be adapted to American culture and the needs of American kids as those change over time. Its affiliated schools are more likely to blend some non-Montessori techniques with the basic method.

Charter Schools

Where it exists, the charter school option allows groups of citizens from parents to teachers to activists to entrepreneurs to start their own alternative schools, paid for by diverting money from public education funds. If you like the idea of Waldorf or Montessori education for your kids but can't afford the tuition, there is a chance that a charter school in your area offers a publicly funded version. And if not, the charter school option enables you to start such a program on your own and get public money to pay for it, so long as you can find enough like-minded parents or teachers to share in the effort.

when a child constantly complains about school

Let's face it: Not all schools create a warm and safe environment for all of their pupils and not all instructors have your child's best interests at heart. Overcrowding and minimal staffing can result in a lack of supervision on school grounds. Sometimes a student's distaste for school stems from bad chemistry among her classmates or between the child and her teacher. And sometimes the problems originate outside the classroom.

Short of abandoning the school or the school system, what's a progressive, humane mom or dad to do?

First, investigate. If your child is complaining about bullies in the bathroom or cookie theft in the cafeteria, try checking it out for yourself by volunteering as a hall or lunchroom monitor. It takes less than an hour of your time and what better way to get to know the social climate of the school? If school policy changes need to be made to correct the situation, you'll have the firsthand information you need to make recommendations.

If your child is upset because of his teacher, first listen carefully to his complaint. It's important to hear and validate your child's feelings, but also keep your objectivity. It's too soon to take sides, and you'll need to hear the teacher's perspective on what's going on. If you lead your child to think that you're going to charge right into the classroom and demand changes, he may manipulate the situation to no good end.

Next, depending on your child's age and level of maturity, you might

(continued on next page)

The legislation that creates charter schools usually frees them from most public school regulations, although they may be required to satisfy certain performance standards. As of this writing, some twenty-five states and the District of Columbia have authorized charter schools and many more will likely follow because of a burgeoning "school choice" movement.

Although conservatives comprise the majority of those demanding school choice, charter schools have made friends all over the philosophical map. Civil rights leaders who doubt that public schools will ever treat minorities fairly have created Afro- and Latino-centric charter schools. Environmentalists have set up nature-oriented charter curriculums. Holistically oriented parents and teachers have started charter schools that follow the Waldorf or Montessori model. Still other charter schools serve more traditional academic goals. For example, in Colorado, where charter school legislation was passed in 1993, charter start-ups have included a science-and-technology academy, a preschool for "at risk" kids, and a school for the gifted.

According to progressive educator and *The Power of Their Ideas* author Deborah Meier, charter schools share one big advantage, no matter what educational philosophy they follow: They're on a human scale. Like Waldorf schools founder Rudolf Steiner, Meier feels that good education depends on strong human relationships, which are only possible in small schools of no more than a few hundred students. In small schools, all students, teachers, and administrators can get to know each other and decisions can be made that everyone can live with. That rarely happens with large, "one size fits all" public schools and fractured communities.

Instead, valuable time and energy gets wasted as bitterly opposed factions battle over content or teaching methods. And education suffers as deep compro-mises are made to keep all sides "happy." Presumably, such ideological clashes are less likely to happen in charter schools, which are often formed by people of like mind.

Nevertheless, charter schools are public, so they retain the democratic goal of equal opportunity for everyone. State laws require "open enrollment policies," guaranteeing that the schools are nonsectarian (including maintaining the separation of church and state), tuition-free, and nondiscriminatory with respect to ethnicity, gender, national origin, and disability.

If you have charter schools in your area, you may also be able to use them as a lever to get existing public schools to make changes

(continued from previous page)

arrange for him to come with you to talk to the teacher. Be careful not to sound accusatory, but also try not to make statements that are so vague as to be misunderstood. The following example is both diplomatic and direct: "Sam says he likes the story hour lessons—especially the one about Anansi the Spider—but he also gets upset and embarrassed when he hears you yelling at him."

In most cases, the teacher will respond in conciliatory tones while insisting on orderly conduct in the classroom. Since good behavior is a goal most parents can agree with, it's important for your child to see that you support the teacher's need for it while supporting his need to be treated respectfully. If you suspect that the teacher is overreacting to your child's behavior, you might offer some insights about your child, for example: "When Sammy would get up from the dinner table while I was talking to him, I used to think it was a sign of disrespect, but now I think that that's just where he was, developmentally. He's the kind of kid who has to move around sometimes."

If your efforts to resolve differences fail, approach the senior administrator—in public schools, the principal—and ask whether your youngster can be transferred to another class. Be sure to frame your request in terms of your child's needs, rather than any shortcoming on the teacher's part—even if you feel strongly that the latter is the real impetus for switching. But be prepared to take your grievance higher up—all the way to the school board, if necessary—if your request is not granted.

you want. In a Twin Cities, Minnesota, school district in the early 1990s, parents tried to get administrators to offer a elementary-level Montessori program. The administrators cited a heap of obstacles and said it couldn't be done. Frustrated, the parents requested a charter to run their own Montessori school. Like magic, the district's obstacles disappeared and their public Montessori elementary opened a few months later.

Of course, despite their exciting potential, charter schools are also prone to the problems of all small, innovative programs: inadequate funding, poor execution of the philosophy, too few students for the program to be vital, and so on. Note too that conservative enemies of public education are promoting charter schools as part of a grand strategy to undercut common public schools. None of this is to say that a local charter school won't meet your family's needs but these are factors you may want to keep in mind.

Other Alternative Schools

The broad social changes that swept America in the 1960s and 1970s produced a tidal wave of experimental alternative schools, both private and public, some of which survive today. You'll have to do your own investigating to see what options exist in your area. If your region includes a sizable counterculture community, there's a fair chance you might find a bare-bones alternative private school, with parents and other volunteers keeping the tuition to a minimum. If you live in a city with a progressive activist community such as New York, your public school system may still include some "schools-within-schools"—optional programs that exist alongside mainstream schools in the same buildings—or free-standing alternatives. These schools may feature such methods as self-paced learning, apprenticeships, age-mixing, less emphasis on grades and testing, more emphasis on electives and special projects, and so on.

Other Points to Consider About Alternative Education

Whatever alternative program you're evaluating for your child, keep in mind that "alternative" doesn't necessarily mean "better." Like everything else, alternative school programs of any type will have their strengths and weaknesses. In addition, holistic/progressive alternative schools as a group tend to have certain limitations you should evaluate before sending your child down that path:

Teacher considerations. Holistic education works best when the teachers are well-trained in the philosophy and methods practiced and dedicated to the students' growth. Teachers in a self-paced program also need to be exceptionally sensitive to their students' needs and educational impulses at any particular moment. In other words, these programs require exceptional people to run them successfully.

Student considerations. Even the best alternative programs work better for some children than others. Educational environments that emphasize freedom of choice are best suited to children who are highly motivated, independent, self-disciplined, and assertive. If these qualities don't describe your child at this time, will the school you're considering be able to draw your child out or keep him on track? If your child might have a learning disability or unusual learning style, will the school be able to identify it and work with it?

Parent considerations. Would you describe yourself as dedicated to your child's education? Does your home environment support learning? Does your work permit you or your spouse to be involved in your child's schooling or is your involvement limited to dropping off and picking up your kids at either end of the day? What goes on at home makes a big difference to the success of any school program, but the structure of a more traditional program may work better for kids whose parents aren't as able to contribute to the educational process.

Evaluation of students' progress. It's important to ask how the alternative school you're considering measures the progress of its students. Studies document the success of established programs like Waldorf education. For some other alternatives, comparable data may not exist, in which case the school should have some way of proving to parents and schools at the next level that its students are progressing as expected. Although many progressive/holistic alternative schools de-emphasize standardized tests, it's not too much to ask an alternative school to be accountable for its results. A school that rejects even subjective tests and progress reports may be too lax for all but the most inner-motivated and bold children.

HOMESCHOOLING

When you hear the word "homeschooling," perhaps you think of children writing in workbooks under their parent's watchful eye. Or perhaps you think of little Margie learning to add and subtract by watching Mom or Dad balance the checkbook. Or a curious child following her parents around, asking questions as they come up to constitute the lesson of the day. Or religious families teaching their kids Bible lessons along with ordinary history and biology.

In fact, every one of these images accurately depicts how some families approach homeschooling. As you'll see below, homeschooling is a very big net containing a wide variety of philosophies, approaches, and motivations.

Who Homeschools, and Why They Do It

As many as several hundred thousand American families educate their children at home. (Exact numbers are impossible to determine, because some families homeschool on the sly, without registering with local school authorities.) But beyond a do-it-yourself attitude toward education, homeschoolers cover a wide spectrum in everything from purpose to method. Many parents, including Alan and Hyiah, homeschool for secular reasons, ranging from a belief that they can do a better job at home to just wanting to spend more time with their kids. This group includes a surprisingly large number of public school teachers, many of whom feel they can replicate what schools do well and improve on what they don't. A small number of families homeschool because the flexibility meets their special needs, including having children in the entertainment industry or pursuing junior sports careers, frequent traveling, and so on. Finally, a large proportion of homeschooling families are fundamentalist Christians who want to inject religious teaching and conservative family values into their children's education.

Among the broad group of secular homeschoolers just described are a large number of parents won over by educational reformer John Caldwell Holt's 1981 book *Teach Your Own*. Holt preached a form of home education called "unschooling," based on the idea that children are biologically programmed to acquire knowledge. Left to their own devices, wrote Holt, kids will tell you what they want to learn when they're developmentally ready to learn it. For families who approach it this way, homeschooling isn't just about teaching at home—it's truly an alternative theory of education. Children aren't taught to read until they ask to be taught, don't learn math until they show the desire, and otherwise are encouraged to follow their own interests.

You might worry that a child educated this way could fall hopelessly behind her publicly schooled friends. Indeed, parents who practice this form of homeschooling do tend to go quietly crazy if, for instance, their kids aren't wanting to read "on time." But "unschooled" children demonstrate an extraordinary capacity to catch up. Val and Stuart Schultz' first three children began their schooling at home. Two learned to read between ages five and six but the middle one was close to nine. "That was so late for me that I would have anxiety in the middle of the night," recalls Val. "But I just thought, 'well, she's a bright kid' and she was the one who loved to listen the most to my reading. As long as she was going forward, that was my yardstick, not her siblings. That was hard for me, but I'm just so glad now that I didn't interfere because she's reading way above grade level and just devouring the books."

To Val, homeschooling in general and unschooling in particular made intuitive sense: "Just to allow these kids to read as late as they wanted to into the night without having to say 'Gotta go to bed now because you've got school in the morning' was heaven for me. If they found water striders on the pond that intrigued them, we could do a unit study on that, just take it to the next step. 'Oh, what happens to these guys when ice forms on the pond?' It's just amazing how it can evolve given the time at home to do that and an interested adult who can get a net to catch those striders and a magnifying glass to look at them and books about them."

Not that homeschooling need be a radical switch from formal education. Some families do better with structure, preferring organized lesson plans and starting and ending homeschooling activities at the same time each day. Others simply "go with the flow," integrating learning with the family's daily life without a fixed agenda. Some use classic textbooks and workbooks, or ready-made curriculums marketed to homeschooling families. Others prefer to rely on libraries, museums, creative projects, and life experiences. In many areas, the public schools offer support to homeschoolers, allowing them to use computer labs, check out microscopes and textbooks, or even attend single classes or play team sports without being fully enrolled. Some also provide tutoring.

One of homeschooling's greatest advantages is its flexibility—you can adapt or blend approaches to suit your family's ways and child's learning style. For instance, you might use textbooks for math, enroll your child in a public school science class, and teach other subjects when you sense they're ready to learn them. And of course, you can always reshuffle the deck as your and your child's needs change.

Homeschooling and the Law

All fifty states allow you to educate your children at home. Some states require families to file an affidavit declaring their intention to homeschool; others do not. In certain states, homeschooled children must document their progress by periodically passing standardized tests. In some regions, politically ambitious district attorneys or revenge-seeking school administrators have been known to harass homeschooling parents on occasion, even where the law fully protects them. However, such harassment is the exception and homeschoolers have usually prevailed in these cases.

Your local librarian or homeschooling support group should be able to provide you with a copy of your state's laws on homeschooling. Homeschooling Internet sites can also lead you to this information. If legal harassment is a concern, you can protect yourself in some states by registering your home as a private school. National correspondence schools such as Clonlara in Ann Arbor, Michigan (see the Resources at the end of this chapter) also provide legal cover as well as a contact teacher and a prepared curriculum, an attractive option for families who prefer structured learning. In many areas, persons providing tutoring services to homeschoolers register their business as a private school without walls, which protects their clients as students in their institution.

In most states, organizations have formed to offer support to homeschooling families. While some serve purely social or academic functions, others fight legislative and administrative battles on behalf of their members. That's not always for the best—some of these organizations pursue political or religious agendas that don't necessarily represent the interests of their diverse membership. For instance, some state organizations have lobbied for strict homeschooling laws that favor curriculum-based learning and discriminate against "unschoolers," or parents who wait until their kids are developmentally ready to learn certain subjects. Before you join a support group, make sure its values match your own. Better yet, ask yourself if joining is a step you need to take—in most cases, you'll do fine, legally and otherwise, without anyone holding your hand.

Social Skills

"When will [your child] get to be with other kids?" Your friends and relatives will ask you this within seconds if you announce your intention to homeschool. In truth, homeschooling often proves to be far superior to public school for social development. Homeschoolers aren't segregated with kids their own age, as they would be in public or private school, and spend more time in the everyday adult world. They will still get plenty of contact with their same-age peers if they take part in soccer, ballet classes, scouts, or whatever. But unlike their publicly schooled friends, they're more likely to be comfortable relating to adults and older children. A county school superintendent in San Diego told Alan that the homeschooled kids who occasionally took part in public school activities there tended to be "a little more outgoing, a little more vocal, a little less reluctant to answer." Overall, they were more willing to learn, and more eager to take part in voluntary activities than the public school students.

But homeschooling can isolate your child if you don't make sure he gets the social contact he needs or if you live in a rural area, as many homeschooling families do. Kids can get lonely when their home is on a mountaintop and public school is one way to remedy the situation.

Are All Parents Qualified to Teach?

The rule-of-thumb in homeschooling is that if you completed high school, you're qualified to teach your kids. As the poet William Butler Yeats wrote, "Education is not the filling of a bucket but the lighting of a fire." However, as Yeats implies, you'll do a much better job at homeschooling if you also love learning. And even "unschooling" requires dedication. Jim and Bev Fety alternate their three children between homeschooling and public school as it suits their learning styles and development. "Teaching involves a lot of thought, preparation, and follow-through," says Jim, himself an elementary grade teacher. "I think a lot of [homeschool parents] talk a good show but don't always do it." Adds Bev, "Homeschooling is not being home with a pile of workbooks and absorbing by osmosis. You need to sit down with the children and work with them."

If you feel insecure about your ability to teach, keep in mind that homeschooling has certain built-in educational advantages that help offset the gaps in your "training." In a typical public school classroom, a student may only get a few minutes per day of one-on-one instruction from the teacher, and in overcrowded classes, not even that. Homeschoolers maintain that the one-to-one (or -two or -three) teacher/student ratio enables them to accomplish the equivalent of one day of public school teaching in just one or two hours at home. Plus, as *Magical Child* author Joseph Chilton Pearce once noted to Alan, children are biologically programmed to learn from their parents. In his view, a classroom teacher is at best an imperfect substitute.

Still, for homeschooling to be successful, you and your kids should enjoy each other's company almost endlessly. In some families, parents and kids find they need long breaks from each other for the health of their relationship. In those cases, outside schooling—public or private— may be a better choice.

Hard Proof: How Homeschoolers Do on Standardized Tests and Getting into College

A number of studies have validated the effectiveness of homeschooling as an educational alternative. One often-cited study conducted by a combination of homeschool advocates and public school professionals researched the performance of Washington homeschoolers on the Stanford Achievement Test over a five-year period. As a group, homeschoolers scored well above national norms. Even children of parents not educated beyond twelfth grade somewhat exceeded the national averages, which underscores the point that parents need not be college educated or professionally trained to give their kids a quality education. Sarah, who was homeschooled up until middle-school age, is the only one of the Schultz children who has undergone standardized testing and she's in the ninetieth percentile, says Val, her mother.

As for college, homeschooling's most famous success story may be that of John Quincy Adams, who jumped from homeschooling directly into Harvard. Today, Harvard is just one of hundreds of American colleges that regularly accept homeschoolers. Indeed, many institutions actively seek out the creative, motivated, and unconventionally educated students that homeschooling typically produces. Of course, homeschoolers will have a much tougher time hurdling the admissions barriers at tradition-bound colleges that still rely mainly on transcripts and teacher recommendations. Do your homework about a college's admissions criteria before applying. Homeschooling literature abounds with good advice on how to ease the transition from home education to college.

How Much Does Homeschooling Cost?

Ready-made curriculums, tutors, and correspondence school arrangements can add up quickly for families that choose those homeschooling routes. But educational materials need not cost much if you take full advantage of libraries, public school programs, and free and low-cost children's educational programs in your community. You can collect many other useful items by combing through garage sales, library sales, and thrift stores.

By far, however, the largest cost you'll bear is the potential earnings sacrificed because you or your partner is staying home to do the teaching. Here, too, creative solutions can help fill the hole. For example, Mark and Helen Hegener of Tonasket, Washington literally supported their family with homeschooling, having built a home-based business around it. They started Home Education Press, publishers of *Home Education Magazine* (see Resources), in the early 1980s and apprenticed their children in it, which gave the kids some real world training and helped Mark and Helen to get more work done.

CHAPTER 6 RESOURCES

Teaching Your Child to Think Critically

Thinking for Yourself by Marlys Mayfield (Belmont, CA: Wadsworth, 1991).
> Covers both basic and advanced critical thinking skills for writing effectively. Essentially, it's a college text but it is suitable for bright high school students, too. It is also useful for parents who want to sharpen their own thinking before working with their kids.

The Opposing Viewpoints book series (San Diego, CA: Greenhaven Press).
> Each OV Junior book focuses on one critical thinking skill, for example, *Prisons* focuses on detecting bias while *The Palestinian Conflict* focuses on identifying propaganda techniques. Other titles include *AIDS, Alcohol, Animal Rights, Death Penalty, Drugs and Sports, The Environment, Gun Control, The Homeless, Immigration, Nuclear Power, Patriotism, Poverty, Prisons, Smoking, Television, Toxic Wastes, The U.S. Constitution, Working Mothers,* and *Zoos.*

Creating a Positive Educational Environment at Home

Multiple Intelligence by Howard Gardner (New York, NY: BasicBooks, 1993).
> Gardner explores applications of his theory in this scholarly, not commercial, book.

See also homeschooling resources below, your best sources of information on this topic.

Parent-Child Learning Projects

The Mudpies Activity Book by Nancy Blakey (Berkeley, CA: Ten Speed Press, 1989).
> This small paperback is full of line drawings and fun ideas for art projects, edible science experiments, and gardening (for kids ages two to twelve).

Playwise: 365 Fun-Filled Activities for Building Character, Conscience, and Emotional Intelligence in Children by Denise Chapman Weston and Mark S. Weston (New York, NY: Tarcher/Putnam, 1996).
> An impressively organized collection of well-considered play activities designed to teach children about people skills, self-awareness, independent thinking, stress management, self-esteem, and unconditional love.

Your Child at Play: One to Two Years by Marilyn Segal, Ph.D. and Don Adcock, Ph.D. (Mailman Family Press, 1985).
> Reading this book, you'll feel like you're in the hands of master teachers who have gained their wisdom about toddlers both by experience and intuition. The authors tell parents how to push the limits of the moment in order to reap the most benefit from play. The book is illustrated with numerous black-and-white photos.

Getting the Most from Your Public School

BOOKS

The Elementary School Handbook by Joanne Oppenheim (New York, NY: Bank Street College of Education, 1989).
> Oppenheim provides a thoughtful discussion about how a meaningful partnership between parents, school, and child can work. She lays heavy emphasis on issues pertaining to kindergarten through third grade.

Getting Ready: The Education of a White Family in Inner City Schools by Lois Mark Stalvey (Morrow, 1974).
> The author chronicles her gradual disillusionment with fellow white parents who talked like liberals, but lived like conservatives and her dawning horror at the tremendous discrepancies in the treatment of black students and white students. A generation-old classic.

Learn & Live (Nicasio, CA: The George Lucas Educational Foundation, 1997).

This resource kit includes a one-hour videotape narrated by actor Robin Williams and a 285-page book about new innovations in public schools nationwide. For a website preview of the book, key in www.glef.org

To order the kit, call (888) 475–4371.

Safe at School by Carol Silverman Saunders (Minneapolis, MN: Free Spirit Publishing, 1994).

This book covers the gamut of safety issues in schools.

ORGANIZATIONS

National Association of Partners in Education, 901 North Pitt Street, Suite 320, Alexandria, VA 22314–1536; (703) 836–4880; fax (703) 836–6941.
e-mail: NAPEhq@NAPEhq.org

This organization helps schools create partnerships with local businesses for donations, supplies, and career instruction.

Parents for Public Schools, 1520 N. State Street, Jackson, MS 39202; (800) 880–1222
e-mail: PPSChapter@parents4publicschools.com
website: www.parents4publicschools.com

Founded in 1989 in Jackson, Mississippi to recruit middle class families back into public schools, this group tries to build bridges and strengthen schools across the economic and racial divide. It has more than fifty chapters in some twenty-four states. Contact them to start up a chapter in your district.

Waldorf, Montessori, Charter, and Other Alternative Schools

BOOKS

The Parents' Guide to Alternatives in Education by Ronald Koetzsch, Ph.D. (Boston, MA: Shambhala, 1997).

This is an accessible, amazingly comprehensive guide to alternative education—Jewish Day Schools, Mennonite and Amish schools, multiple intelligences education, and so on, plus Waldorf, homeschooling, and the other familiar approaches.

Time to Choose: America at the Crossroads of School Choice Policy by Amy Stuart Wells (Hill and Wang, 1993).

Wells offers a revealing look at the school choice movement. She reviews the various options now being considered by parents and voters nationwide under the banner of "school choice." This is a superb history of the alternative school movement of the 1960s and 1970s.

ORGANIZATIONS

American Montessori Society, 281 Park Avenue South, Sixth Floor, New York, NY 10010, (212) 358–1250
website: www.amshq.org

This group accredits Montessori schools and teacher training programs according to its innovative updating of Montessori's original methods.

Association Montessori Internationale—USA (AMI-USA), 410 Alexander Street, Rochester, NY 14607–1028, (716) 461–5920 or (800) 872–2643
website: www.montessori-ami.org

This group accredits traditional Montessori schools and teacher training programs. It also sells by mail order Montessori-related books and materials.

Association of Waldorf Schools of North America, 3911 Bannister Road, Fair Oaks, CA 95628
website: www.awsna.org

A clearinghouse of information about Waldorf programs in the U.S., Canada, and Mexico. They can assist initiatives to start Waldorf schools in your local area. They also consult with public schools that want to incorporate Waldorf principles in their classrooms.

Homeschooling

BOOKS AND PUBLICATIONS

Home Education Magazine, P.O. Box 1083, Tonasket, WA 98855, (509) 486–1351, (800) 236–3278
website: www.home-ed-press.com

> Every issue is packed with contributions from readers on homeschooling tips for teaching various subjects, worthwhile projects and field trips, and so on. It offers excellent coverage of homeschooling political issues as well. The ads and indexes are good sources of homeschooling resources.

Homeschooling for Excellence by David and Micki Colfax (Warner, 1988).

> This is a general guide to homeschooling by parents whose homeschooled sons went on to Harvard. It tells the Colfax's fascinating story and advises readers on basic homeschooling tools and subject matter.

Schooling at Home, edited by Anne Pederson and Peggy O'Mara for *Mothering* magazine (Santa Fe, NM: John Muir, 1990).

> This anthology covers most of the subject areas such as teaching reading, writing, art, and science. It offers a strongly holistic perspective.

ORGANIZATIONS

Clonlara School, 1289 Jewett, Ann Arbor, MI 48104, (313) 769–4515
website: www.clonlara.org

> Clonlara School is a fully accredited private school-without-walls that provides curriculum, contact teachers, transcripts, a private school diploma, and legal cover for homeschooling families nationwide.

John Holt's Bookstore, 2269 Massachusetts Avenue, Cambridge, MA 02140, (617) 864–3100
website: www.holtgws.com

> This is a source for books, videos, and homeschooling materials. Holt's organization also publishes *Growing Without Schools,* a bi-monthly journal primarily containing parent contributions à la *Home Education* magazine only briefer.

7

the artful family

Time was when parents and educators believed that learning the arts and exercising their creativity made children "well-rounded." Public schools embraced this vision. Children could choose between playing the classics in the school orchestra or pop tunes and marches in the marching band. Schools at all levels put on plays and middle- and high schools offered full-time drama departments.

Suddenly, those days seem very far away, at least in some parts of the country. School districts across the nation have axed arts programs in the wake of budget crunches, and many schools in poorer districts now offer no arts courses at all. So if the arts and creativity matter to you in your parenting, it's falling to you now more than ever to bring them into your children's lives.

In the following pages, we'll show you many possibilities for doing just that. We suggest several ways to participate *with* your children, from telling them stories to helping their dance or theater classes put on productions and perhaps even playing one of the adult roles. We'll discuss how musical expression enhances young people's lives, from babyhood onward, and offer ideas about how to involve your kids in music training without being overbearing about it. Finally, if your child is still an infant and keeping you up one exhausting night after another, we'll point you toward a musical method for relaxing her to sleep. This method defies everything you've ever read on the subject, but perhaps unlike what you've read before, it works!

MICHAEL ALLEN JONES

THE ART OF STORYTELLING

In simpler times, family and community life featured a communal activity all but lost today—the art of storytelling. Young and old would assemble together around bonfires, in the village square, in living rooms, and other family and social gathering places to share tales passed down for generations or simply invented on the spot. Today, storytelling is enjoying something of a revival at libraries, festivals, prisons, theaters, churches, and on radio and television. But in the family home itself, what may be the world's oldest art is mostly a lost art.

Fortunately, even if a substantial yarn hasn't been spun in your family in a couple generations, you can revive this ancient tradition in the time it takes you and your kids to make your way to the couch. For storytelling is one of the most accessible art forms—all it requires is an imagination and a mouth. And much like reading aloud, it is also one of the most intimate activities you and your kids can engage in.

In fact, a storytelling session can be an even more dynamic way to relate to children than reading aloud. Without the word-prompts from a book, you're forced to turn off the automatic pilot, dwell in the moment, and build a tale. Meanwhile, your child imagines pictures to go with your words, thereby completing an interactive circle of communication. And chief among the messages conveyed is that she is special enough to inspire a tale created for her alone.

Storytelling enhances young lives in other ways as well. Listening to stories lets children try out new ways of acting and being, all within the safe bounds of their own imagination. Listening to stories also helps children develop an ear for language, an important prerequisite for reading later on. This art form serves a more social function as well: "Stories keep kids hip to what's expected in the community—and to the values that their community holds dear," says Gay Ducey, mother of two grown children and a librarian and storyteller by profession.

But where do you start? How do you come up with stories that will both delight and inspire your kids? "Don't think of it as a performance," advises mother and storyteller Diane Ferlatte. "Just think of it as a conversation, a shared experience." Try drawing on your own past to spark your first story: "When I was in school . . ." and go from there. Family stories are actually an ideal place to begin because they give children a sense of continuity and comfort, knowing that their parents and grandparents, aunts and uncles were once children who played, loved, struggled, and grew, too.

Take, for instance, Thandiwe [last name withheld]'s account of how her mother's family reconciled with Thandiwe's mom after she left home to live with Thandiwe's dad. This gem sparkles with tidbits about forgiveness, family ties, and Jewish culture. "When my mother ran off with my dad, her family was outraged," Thandiwe says, noting that Mom was only nineteen and Dad was non-Jewish. "So they wanted to disown her. But once you have a kid in this faith, you're back in because Judaism is passed down through the mother. One day when I was about a week old, my father looked out the window and saw my great-grandmother stepping briskly up the walkway. 'Uh-oh,' he warned my mom, 'Here comes your grandma and she's carrying a load of bags with her.' 'Are they shopping bags?' my mom wanted to know. 'Yeah,' said Dad. Mom rushed to the window and shrieked, 'Oh, my God, that means she's moving in!' And sure enough, she unpacked and stayed about a week," Thandiwe laughs. "Dad didn't get it. You see, shopping bags are a Jewish grandmother's suitcases." Not surprisingly, Thandiwe's daughter Shona loves to hear the tale over and over.

Tell your kids stories about themselves, as well—moments when they made their parents especially proud, stories about their birth, and so on. Kids love being reminded that they, too, can contribute to the family lore.

Other Stories Kids Need to Hear

Over time, family stories won't completely satisfy our children's yearnings for a good yarn. Sooner or later they will also want to hear stories of other people and creatures—crafty animals, brave and resourceful heroes and heroines from other places and times. We need to hear these traditional stories or myths, according to the late mythologist Joseph Campbell, because they tell—or rather, remind—us who we are, as individuals, a culture, and a people.

"When you tell children some of the more archetypal kinds of stories, they are able to see themselves inside the tales," says Diane David, a Waldorf schoolteacher in San Francisco and mother of six children between the ages of ten and twenty-two. "One week, I remember telling my kindergartners the story of Snow White and Red Rose, the Grimm fairy tale about siblings. Snow White was the quiet one and Red Rose was rambunctious. After the third or fourth reading, this little boy wanted to know 'is Red Rose a boy?' He was able to live so deeply inside the story that he clearly identified with this character."

So let the stories you tell cover everything from family memories to animal allegories to epic poems and timeless archetypal legends. Look for stories that are nourishing, comforting, exciting, miraculous, explanatory, or encouraging. In our resource list at the end of this chapter, we provide a few such story collections from a range of cultures, plus some how-to books that combine tips with suggested stories to tell.

In the meantime, parents interested in inventing stories with a holistic spin to them might want to incorporate some of the following suggestions:

- *Try telling stories in which animals and things in nature—rocks and trees and the wind, sun, or moon—speak.* Such characters bring us closer to those cultures in which people lived more intimately with nature. It also suggests to kids that perhaps we do inhabit a world that speaks back to us, and paves the way for the humane and earth-friendly precepts we'll be teaching later.

- *Be mindful of what your child needs to hear.* Perhaps he's anxious about a new school he's about to attend or an upcoming visit to the doctor. Create a story that addresses his concerns and comforts him. Are two siblings using rude language with one another? "Try a story about a group of gnomes who experienced frogs jumping out of their mouths every time they said a bad word," suggests Diane David.

- *Tell stories with messages that go beyond your youngster's immediate needs, including larger lessons worth teaching.* Some theme ideas: giving back what you take from nature; appreciating differences between people; being your brother's keeper; respecting the wisdom of elders; standing up to peer pressure; taking care of the Earth; savoring friendship; resolving conflicts peacefully; finding one's courage.

- *If it feels natural, try giving your heroes or your likable characters an unusual accent for a change of pace (just be consistent with it).* This helps your child make friendly connections with people who sound different from them and it certainly counters the xenophobic messages that kids encounter from Hollywood.

- *Emphasize dialogue.* Don't *tell* how a character acts or feels, suggests Diane Ferlatte, "bring the character alive with your voice." A big bear who's full of himself, for example, probably speaks in deep, booming, authoritative tones.

- *For more vivid imagery, incorporate most of the five senses in your telling.* For example, describe sounds and smells of the setting. Describe the appearance of characters as well as the sound of their voices and texture of their skin.

- *Use similes or colorful comparisons in key descriptions.* For example, "he rushed into the room like a gust of wind." This will help your child develop an ear for metaphor, and encourage her to master this art herself.

- *Coax young listeners to participate.* Ask what they think will happen next, or what they might do in the same circumstances. Or you might ask your child to fill in the dialogue—especially during a story that's been repeated several times: "And the little red hen said. . . ." onsider throwing in some singing, too. Younger children love to join in when stories have a repeated lyric or tune in them.

- *Allow kids to interrupt and ask questions.* Your story can wait, their curiosity can't. Besides, their queries will let you know what interests them, and may offer guidance about where the story needs to go.

a dozen ideas for family tales parents can tell

What my parents once did to amuse us

When you were born

When your brother/sister was born

My first day of school

The day I got into big trouble

My worst vacation ever

The first time I got lost

My most embarrassing moment ever

Grandpas say the funniest things

How Auntie stood up for herself in public one day

The day I broke something that belonged to someone else

My favorite childhood hiding place

- *Permit your children to listen in their own way.* "Younger children might listen while they rip open and reattach their Velcro binders," says Gay Ducey. "Teenagers might look like they're totally immobilized by cool, but don't worry about it. All kids have different listening styles."

In the end, make storytelling easy on yourselves. Start slowly and be casual about it. "Our culture gives us this message that unless you are extraordinarily talented, you shouldn't be practicing storytelling," says Ducey. "But perfection isn't important. Storytelling is a folk art and it belongs to folks."

TEACHING CHILDREN TO APPRECIATE AND PLAY MUSIC

Children need our help in learning many things, but learning to love music isn't one of them. Children are born musical. They sing as they skip down the sidewalk or mix their green beans and applesauce. They're dancin' fools in the living room and master percussionists in the kitchen. We parents can do much to enhance their appreciation of music's finer points. We can encourage any musical talents they make apparent. But our desire to have our children "do something with music" can also backfire because it only takes a few bad experiences for children to conclude that getting serious about music just isn't worth the pain.

Looking to your own past may show you just how that happens. Perhaps you have your own grim memories of Mom or Dad making you stay inside and practice your piano when your friends had just come to the door to request your company. Or maybe it was the school band leader who spent the term teaching the class the marches of John Philip Sousa when your biorhythms were crying for rhythm and blues. Fortunately, as a parent drawn to holistic ideas, you may be better oriented than most to guide your children to successful and satisfying experiences with music. For one thing, your preference for child-centered parenting makes it less likely that you'll push a musical agenda on your children that reflects your interests more than theirs. For another, holistic approaches to education apply to music, too, and may increase the chances of a child's success.

Why Music Education Makes a Difference

If all children are musical, why does specific training in music matter? For one thing, children who learn to play music have the ability to create it for themselves without depending on the performance or recordings of others, and they have that ability for the rest of their lives.

Music also provides a lifelong social tool—what could be a better and more fulfilling way to get together with others than to make music? In addition, music shares with other arts the ability to teach life skills that

go far beyond learning to read music and plunk the piano keys. Waldorf schools recognize this— singing and learning to play instruments is an integral part of the curriculum for all students. In Waldorf philosophy, music is valued both for its own artistic sake and because it "brings a strong harmonizing and humanizing force into the student's life, strengthening the will and capacities for the future" (from "An Introduction to Waldorf Education" by Rudolf Steiner College in Fair Oaks, California).

Laying the Foundation: Guiding Your Children's Musical Experiences in Their Early Years

Preparing the ground for your child's musical education can actually begin in utero. The womb may not be the perfect listening room but the sounds will get through. Research and the reports of countless parents confirm that infants exposed to music before birth are significantly more responsive to it in the early stages of development, as long as the sounds are at moderate volumes.

Few parents can resist the urge to impose their tastes on their kids, but the trick to opening the ears of babies and children is to make their musical environment as rich and varied as possible, beginning with the recordings you play at home. If you don't feel experienced enough to find good new music on your own, consult reviews in reliable publications such as the *All Music Guide, The Rough Guide to World Music,* and *The NPR Guide to Building a Classical CD Collection.* Or ask for recommendations from the staff of an independent record store. Unlike their chain-store peers, they are generally passionate and knowledgeable music fans who will be only too glad to point you in some promising directions.

As your children grow old enough to appreciate and enjoy live music, taking them to a performance may provide just the inspiration they need to request music or dance lessons. And don't be dismayed if they're drawn more to the spectacle than the art at first. Louie Perez of the rock band Los Lobos remembers that it wasn't just the music that grabbed him at the Mexican variety shows he attended with his mother in downtown Los Angeles: "There'd be this big extravaganza of dancers and singers. And it always led up to the main attraction, which was always a star Mexican singer. There would be a twenty-piece mariachi up there with the outfits, the silver, the embroidery, the lights bouncing and flickering off this stuff, and suddenly the main guy would come out. He'd be on horseback, the horse would be covered in silver, he'd come out with a microphone and just start singing. As a little kid, I'm thinking, 'Man, this is incredible!' "

Obviously, if you play an instrument or sing, performing for your children may have an even more powerful effect on them than the strangers up on a stage. Don't worry about impressing your kids when you perform. It's seeing you enjoy yourself and entertain others that will stick with them.

The quality of the musical toys you buy for your little ones also makes a difference in the way they relate to music. The better toys are available in specialty stores and through catalogs such as HearthSong. When your children have toys that make real musical sounds and have the look and feel of real instruments such as the Music Maker, it's just a short step for them to want to play a trumpet or the piano. And in the meantime, they experience the thrill of creating beautiful sounds with their own hands or mouths. (See the Resources at the end of this chapter for information on Hearth-Song and the Music Maker.)

As another option, you might try enrolling your children in structured musical education programs keyed to early childhood. Some of these, such as the Kindermusik system, are essentially early child development programs that use music as the medium. For example, the Orff Schulwerk program takes children as early as infancy. Most such programs involve movement as well as pure musical activities. Some programs—notably again, the Orff system—use special, simplified instruments so children can create music without having to first master the technical difficulties of "real" instruments. Other childhood music courses, such as the Suzuki program, are aimed at eventual study of serious music, although they begin working with children as young as two. (For contact information on several of the better-known programs, see

Sound Choices by Wilma Machover and Marianne Uszler, reviewed in the Resources at the end of this chapter.)

Music Lessons—Who, When, What, Where

Music may be for everyone, but learning to play a serious instrument clearly is not. In his terrific music education book and public television series, *Marsalis on Music,* renowned trumpeter Wynton Marsalis doesn't sugarcoat anything about the process. "Almost no one likes to practice," he tells his young audience. "We all want to be heroes, but we just don't want to fight the dragon." He goes on to describe what makes practice so disagreeable: "You have to spend time working on things that you can't do, which makes you feel bad about yourself. Often, it's just terribly boring, the same thing repeated over and over and over again until you get it. And you have to be inspired to want to practice. There must be some reason besides 'I don't want to make a bad grade,' or 'My parents will kill me,' or 'I don't have anything else to do.'"

We agree. So while we highly recommend laying a good musical foundation for your children, the final impetus has to come from them if music lessons are going to take. They also need to understand that learning music requires real commitment. If they ask you for an instrument and lessons, they should agree to keep up their end by practicing. Says Val Schultz of Ithaca, New York, who herself plays piano, "Sammy [her youngest] wanted to play the violin at four. I just said 'That's too early.' I wanted to see if he asked for a while. He asked for a year and a half. I got that this kid really wants it, and that's when I started lessons for him."

Fortunately, kids are wired to make lessons work. They are impelled by their developmental drives to learn. They are "in their bodies," which is crucial to understanding rhythm. They tend to be more focused in the here-and-now than their harried parents so when they listen to music, they really hear. And they aren't as likely to be hung up about performing for an audience at recitals.

Here are the major issues you'll face with formal music instruction:

The right instrument. When your children announce that they want to take lessons, they may or may not have a specific instrument in mind. For kids, finding the right instrument is kind of like finding the right puppy. Instruments are buddies, sometimes for life, so choosing one is a highly personal matter. Don't be surprised if your child's choice confounds

your expectations and contradicts your advice. But don't let the decision
be a hasty one, either. Your child should have the chance to sample several instruments or perhaps view a variety in action at a youth concert in
your community before settling on one. Some schools and community
centers offer special summer programs in which children
can experiment with several instruments and generally test
the whole idea of lessons.

The right teacher or program. A good music teacher will be
attuned to each child's individual learning style and adapt
to it, will emphasize praising the positive rather than crit-
icizing the negative, will figure out strategies that take advantage of your child's strengths, and will assign music that
your child enjoys. The last point is crucial. If your child
seems unusually resistant to practicing, ask what's going
on. The problem may well be with the assignments. If the
music your child practices doesn't particularly excite her
even when she gets it right, where's the satisfaction?

LEAH MAZEL-GEE

For very young children, you'll want to look for a couple of additional qualities in a music teacher. Programs
and instructors for young children, especially in the preschool years, should involve movement and emphasize
rhythm. There is no such thing as "head" music at this age.
An appropriate teacher will also be gifted at recognizing when individual children are bursting with energy and find constructive ways of chan-
neling it, perhaps into the very movement and rhythm activities we just
mentioned.

Along with these holistic criteria, you should evaluate a teacher by
more traditional standards. Does the teacher have a formal musical education? Some musicians, including many very good ones, are self-taught
and have never learned to read music or studied music theory. Keep in
mind that they can't teach what they don't know. Is the teacher a disciplined person, starting and ending the class on time, keeping appoint-
ments, and so on? It takes a self-disciplined person to teach your kids
the discipline of practice and preparation for performance. Finally, you
need to assess the progress your child is making. Often, even the best
teachers have their limitations and there comes a time for moving on to
someone who can take your child to the next level.

All of these criteria apply to school programs and teachers, too.
Arrange to visit your children's music classroom and observe for a while,

and question your kids at home. If they're not enjoying the music they're playing or the person at the front of the room, this may be the last music class they'll ever want to take. You should seriously consider switching classes or finding a private alternative if their musical motivation is at risk.

The right age. According to the "child-centered" approach, your children should start music study whenever they let you know they're motivated to do it.

The Radio Years

Once kids reach the age where they're listening to the radio on their own and buying their own CDs and tapes, horrifying things start to happen. We hear repulsive sounds only vaguely resembling music blasting from their rooms. We glimpse their musical idols on television and know that the end of civilization is near. We're convinced that the emotional and financial investment we've made in their musical education has turned to toxic waste. Worst of all, we recognize that we're reacting just like our parents did when we entered the "radio years" a few decades ago and we suddenly feel very, very old.

But realizing that we're acting like our parents is the key to understanding our problem and reconnecting culturally with our children. Young people's music is designed to get our goat. This takes its most extreme form with rock, where the rebellious spirit of the music virtually demands that it alienate all of those who have come before—not just parents but even previous generations of rockers.

We may forget that such certified pop music geniuses of earlier generations as Bob Dylan, Jimi Hendrix, and Elvis Costello were considered weird and only marginally talented not only by parents but also by many of the young people who first heard them. Although all the music your teens listen to may sound the same to you, it most assuredly is not. The current generation of popular musicians includes its share of unique and valuable artists just as yours did, even if you don't immediately understand what's so special about them.

So, if your teen comes to you with her favorite CD in hand and says, "You gotta hear this song," do her the courtesy of listening with her. Try as best you can to transcend your musical biases and really hear. You still may not "get it" and it's okay to say that, but she'll appreciate your effort to cross the great generational divide. And she'll love the opportunity to prove to herself once again that she's light years ahead of you in coolness, which helps meet her need to see herself as a separate person with her own tastes and ideas.

The Future of Music and How It May Affect Your Kids

Actually, the future has arrived. Technology has made it possible for people who don't know a single guitar chord or note on the piano to make sophisticated music, so long as they have musical talent. The pop world is already exploding with young stars who don't play instruments in the conventional sense. Instead, they manipulate taped segments and electronic sounds to beats supplied not by a rhythmically gifted human being but rather a computerized machine.

What does the advent of musical technology mean for your children? Among other things, it means that they won't necessarily have to spend years practicing scales and chords just to approximate the music in their heads. While "real" instruments haven't become obsolete, it's clear that fewer and fewer people—children included—will be investing the time and effort needed to master them. This isn't a prediction—it's a trend with a several-years-old heritage already in popular music.

So all is not lost if your child resists your wishes and turns down piano or violin lessons every time you raise the issue. More than ever before, age and stage of life present no barrier to those who wish to express themselves musically. Indeed, the trend toward electronics means that both new forms of artistic expression and new musical career opportunities are opening up for young people who master the emerging music technology. And getting kids to spend more time at the computer has never been as tough as getting them to practice their piano lesson, has it?

MUSIC TO SOOTHE YOUR BABY WITH

In virtually every culture of the world, parents have turned to music to help ease their baby to sleep. The first lullabies probably came to their creators spontaneously—velvet-soft little songs punched up on the spot from that infinite jukebox otherwise known as parental intuition. Today, parents who are weary or self-conscious of their own voices can choose from a marvelous selection of recorded lullabies, from culturally diverse international collections to lullaby albums by adult music stars. Many parents also play quiet, soothing instrumental recordings while rocking their little ones. Others take the biotech approach, turning to recordings that evoke the sounds of the womb.

There's only one problem with all these sonic techniques—what if they don't work right away? What if it's *you* that starts to go under while baby's cooing, "Let's party!" You know the scene—it's 3:00 A.M., your eyelids feel like rocks, your body is shutting down cell by cell, and your little one seems to have transcended the biological need for sleep. What's worse, you've got a crazy day starting early in the morning, you may be facing another night like this in twenty-four hours, and the lack of rest is piling up like dirty dishes. If this sounds too, too familiar, you also know that it's just the beginning of a most vicious cycle—you get tenser and tenser and that tension vibrates through you right into the little body in your arms. There's no way baby will go to sleep with that going on.

We call this the Theory of Contagious Agitation. Fortunately, this theory implies its own solution, The Theory of Contagious Relaxation. It goes like this: Don't worry about baby's taste. Find the music that relaxes you, music you wouldn't mind listening to all night, in case it comes to that. As you groove to whatever cool sounds work for you, you'll start to let go and just enjoy hanging out with your little one. Dance around the room with baby as your partner. Get funky with the beat. Forget about slumber—you and Junior wouldn't want to miss the next smokin' cut, would you? Sure enough, as your muscles loosen up with the rhythm, so will the muscles of the one you're holding. Sleep— baby's, then yours—should soon follow.

Yes, we know this violently clashes with the advice given in shelves full of parenting books. Walk your baby round and round to low lights and soothing sounds, traditional parenting experts say in knowing tones. So go ahead, try it their way. But we're willing to bet that unless your baby is one of the "easy" ones, you'll come crawling back to this page, muttering about wimpy lullabies and back-to-the-womb tapes under your breath.

Does the type of music you choose for your baby-dance matter? Absolutely—it should be music you like but there's no escaping the fact that certain types of music are more likely to drain tension from tight muscles than others. Don't forget that babies have a hair-trigger startle reflex, so sudden assaults of sound as in hard rock or Beethoven's Fifth won't be well received. We suggest mellow "body music": sweet '60s soul music like Smokey Robinson or Marvin Gaye. Ambient electronica. Reggae. The easygoing blues of Taj Mahal or Keb' Mo'. The comfy gait of the Grateful Dead. The atmospheric jazz of Roy Hargrove or Bill Frisell. The western swing of Bob Wills or Asleep at the Wheel. If you're dozing on your feet and fear for baby's safety, pick it up a little. Aretha. Otis. Ani DiFranco. Sonny Rollins.

Alan's son Ajene also confirmed another tenet of the Contagious Relaxation Theory: Volume doesn't matter. Don't shatter your baby's eardrums but you needn't keep the control knob at lullaby level, either. Remember the key: It has to work for you, too.

Many terrific lullaby albums have appeared in recent years, some so sweet you may want to end your own evening with them after baby has floated off to dreamland. Go ahead and try them—what's to lose but a little more shut-eye? But if they don't work for their original purpose and you decide to test our theory, remember that the first dance is parent's choice.

THEATER AND DANCE FOR CHILDREN AND FAMILIES

It's an hour before curtain time at Stillpoint Dance Studio's annual holiday production of *The Nutcracker,* and the room buzzes like a high-tension wire. A steady stream of families with dancers in tow pours through the double doors of the combined auditorium/gym at Lincoln Savage Elementary. Mothers of the grade-school age performers hustle them into the restroom to make last-minute adjustments to their makeup and hair. Other young dancers chat with their friends; some are chasing each other around the room. Backstage, intensely focused teenaged performers warm up muscles chilled by the cold rain outside and practice their most challenging moves. Several costumed adults stroll the area as well, trying to look more relaxed than they feel.

Although essentially a dance recital for all of the school's students, from age four to adults, *The Nutcracker* is also a handsomely mounted entertainment for a rural community in southern Oregon that gets scant exposure to such things. But the production isn't just about the performers prancing about for adoring kin. This event involves whole families for months beforehand, with many parents helping out behind the scenes and a few even playing adult roles in the production, right up on stage with their kids. By the weekend of the two performances, many parents have already put in long hours assembling props, setting up lighting, and sewing costumes. Those who will be dancing or acting have fit numerous rehearsals into their already overbooked lives. Other moms and dads handle logistics during the performances themselves, selling home-baked refreshments, taking tickets at the door, setting up chairs and risers hours before, and taking down and cleaning up the room afterward.

These whole-family aspects are the "bonus surprise" of children's theater and dance. Not all parents take part—some are only able to drop their children off at class and pick them up at the end. But the opportunity remains to make these classes a parent-child "thing" and many of those who take advantage of the opportunity say the hours spent doing so are among the most poignant of their lives.

Children's Dance Classes—Creative Expression, Centering, and Therapy

What your children get out of dance classes will depend to a large extent on what they want from them, but the potential benefits—artistic, social, developmental, and more—are so comprehensive that the classes can meet a variety of needs:

Artistic expression. In many regions, arts aren't funded at all in the public schools. When the arts aren't validated in the school experience, they can cease to be part of "kid culture" with the result that artistically inclined children find themselves ostracized by their peers for being different. As Nancy Gordon, who operates and teaches at Heartland School of Dance in Grants Pass, Oregon, points out, dance classes are one way of providing a place for "the artistic soul to go and express itself."

Centering. When dance teachers stress centering techniques in class—and not all do—dance can lead students to be more balanced in both mind and body. Centering techniques show students how to move gracefully by beginning all movements from the center of their bodies, just below the navel. The process also creates a beneficial side effect, because centering the body also tends to center thoughts and feelings.

Technical instruction. Obviously, students also learn specific dance moves, although Lori Cangilose, who teaches at Stillpoint, feels this can be overdone, especially at the younger ages. "You see their faces fall, and their minds go right out the window [when classes stress too much technique]," she notes. She advises parents to avoid technique-heavy classes until their children reach age seven. Prior to that time, Lori prefers to introduce movements that relate to her students' everyday life, "anything that gives them an experience to move from," such as the butterflies fluttering outside the dance studio window on a spring day.

Flexibility and other holistic exercise benefits. Students learn the value of staying flexible from early dance training. Dancing also strengthens the body in subtle ways that go deep into the connective tissue, which has applications to most sports as well as dance. Dancers learn body awareness in a way that few others do, too. They feel comfortable in their bodies in a way that many people don't, which often carries over into adulthood. They also know precisely where their bodies are as they move, which not only enables them to move more gracefully but helps them avoid the stiffening that most people experience as they age.

Discipline. Students learn discipline both because they have to follow instructions and because they must observe moves their teacher demonstrates and then emulate them.

Therapy. Psychotherapists trained in dance therapy, which developed from modern dance, use dance exercises to help patients express blocked emotions, recover blocked memories, improve communication, and regain a sense of self. But these effects can also occur spontaneously in dance classes. Lori mentions a student who had been abused at home; in her free times in class, she "was dancing out her dreams."

CITICENTRE DANCE THEATRE

"Okay," you may be thinking, "but what if I want all these swell things to happen for my *son?* He thinks dance is for sissies." Most boys need a pathfinder before they'll try dance classes. They're more likely to chance it if a friend or brother goes first, but such brave souls aren't easy to find. Male teachers help make classes "safe" for boys, too, as do dances involving masculine themes—swords, battles, and so on.

Children's Theater—A Garden That Grows People

From the standpoint of personal development, children's theater may be even more transformative than dance. In theater classes, children are pushed—in the best classes, gently—to exceed themselves; common are exercises in which everyone is required to perform silly or outrageous stunts in front of the group. Because everyone is doing it, it is both safe and socially approved to make an absolute fool of oneself. In such an environment, self-consciousness won't survive for long.

Being in a play also requires children to take responsibility—to memorize their lines, to work hard in rehearsals, to work cooperatively with others, and to cover for production errors on stage. This helps explain why theater is such a terrific crucible for children's social growth. "The kids form really tight friendships," notes Nancy Gordon, who also teaches children's theater classes, "because those are friendships where they took chances together and where they counted on each other. 'If I forget my line, you whisper it to me or say my line instead.' " Of course, children must be ready to accept that level of responsibility. Nancy, for one, requires that her students be at least nine years old.

Playacting contributes to children's personal development in many other ways as well. In the course of rehearsing different characters, students try on different social and emotional roles including those of authority figures such as parents, doctors, kings, and queens—a welcome break from their usual position in life. They also get to practice expressing strong feelings in a controlled setting. Drama develops focus, too. Children must simultaneously remember their lines, stay in character, and react to the other characters. In addition, they learn to solve problems in an emergency, of which any complicated production will have its share. And certainly the pride of achievement from having participated in a great endeavor that entertains others helps build children's self-esteem.

On the intellectual plane, theater can bring children into contact with great literature. Spiritually, acting can contribute to moral development because most plays in which children act have heroic figures with whom they identify and good triumphs over evil. And in ways different from dance, theater also helps children develop physically. The long rehearsals build stamina and even muscular strength. Theater also promotes mind-body integration because actors must learn to move in a relaxed, controlled, well-coordinated manner.

Dance and Theater Family-Style

If you can make the time to participate in some way, your child's theater or dance productions can be a nearly unbeatable family togetherness activity. Productions would be impossible without adult volunteers, but duty aside, helping out allows parents to share a memorable experience and sense of accomplishment with their children.

When parents take part in the classes themselves or volunteer to fill adult roles in productions, yet a different kind of magic happens. In Nancy Gordon's theater classes, for example, adults often experience the same kinds of personal expansion that their children do. Even more intriguing are the relationship dynamics unleashed when parent and child attend classes together. "At first, it's very hard for the parent to stop being a parent," says Nancy. "They'll watch their kid and get upset if their kid isn't [doing what she's supposed to]." So Nancy makes it clear that during class time, she is the one in charge and parents have to let go. "Which they do," she says.

"What happens then is you see your kid in a completely different light," Nancy notes. "And the child sees her parent in a completely different light, scared to say her lines, too. You practice your lines together. You have something to talk about and interact with when you're going home and to rehearsal. You sing the songs. It's just a completely different interaction than the usual parent–child relationship, and I think it's wonderful!"

CHAPTER 7 RESOURCES

The Art of Storytelling

BOOKS AND PUBLICATIONS

Bury My Bones but Keep My Words: African Tales for Retelling retold by Tony Fairman (Henry Holt, 1991).

> Wonderfully evocative and colorful African tales handed down orally and presented by the author for you to retell creatively in traditional village style.

Homespun: Tales from America's Favorite Storytellers by Jimmy Neil Smith (Crown, 1988).

> Maybe it's the poignant and personal biographies of the twenty storytellers featured here, or maybe it's the varied selection of stories they've told that makes this collection so magical. A how-to section in the back details such topics as "Discovering Your Story," "Using Your Voice," and "Changing and Adapting Your Story."

Storytelling magazine (quarterly), P.O. Box 309, Jonesborough, TN 37659, (423) 753–2171.

> The periodical of choice for America's growing storytelling movement.

Teaching Children to Appreciate and Play Music

BOOKS

Marsalis on Music by Wynton Marsalis (Norton, 1995).

> Gorgeously designed and illustrated companion to the PBS series comes with a CD of examples. Lucid and simple explanations of music fundamentals—rhythm, melody, how to read music, practice tips, terminology, and more. Speaks engagingly to young music students. This one works for adults, too.

Rubber-Band Banjos and a Java Jive Bass: Projects & Activities on the Science of Music & Sound by Alex Sabbeth (John Wiley & Sons, 1997).

Fun and stimulating activity book that teaches both music basics and music science—for example, how the various instruments make their sounds and how music is recorded. Simple, well-designed projects using household items and materials.

Sound Choices: Guiding Your Child's Musical Experiences by Wilma Machover and Marianne Uszler (Oxford University Press, 1996).

Sensible, holistic, and friendly advice keyed to needs of each individual child. Covers musical experiences and education from infancy through adolescence and includes a chapter for children with special needs. Extensive, annotated resource lists of books, recordings, CD-ROMs. Good discussion of early childhood music programs such as Orff Schulwerk, Kodaly, and Suzuki.

INSTRUCTIONAL TAPES

Homespun Tapes, Box 340, Woodstock, NY 12498, (800) 33-TAPES.

website: www.homespuntapes.com

Founded by 1960s folk music icon Happy Traum. Over two hundred video- and audio-tapes of music instruction, primarily on instruments for playing folk or roots music. Tapes feature renowned instrumentalists such as Richard Thompson, Chet Atkins, Doc Watson, Rory Block, Dr. John, and of course Happy himself. Some book/CD combos and instruments, too.

QUALITY TOY INSTRUMENTS

The Music Maker, distributed by Peeleman/McLaughlin Enterprises Inc., 4153 South 300 West, Murray, UT 84107, (800) 779-2205

website: www.europeanexpressions.com

The Music Maker is an all-ages stringed instrument that has the look and feel of a fine stringed instrument but can be played by a four or five year old. Caution: quite difficult to tune, especially by a nonmusician. An Oppenheim Toy Portfolio Best Toy award-winner.

See also HearthSong listing on page 127.

8

fields of play

Not so long ago, Americans generally agreed that children's participation in sports made them better people. Sports build character and train leaders, it was thought. Presidents and senators had often been varsity sports stars in their high school and college days. High school graduates had a much better chance of getting into certain elite universities if sports were mentioned on their application along with good grades and other extracurricular activities.

But many families now wonder if youth sports still fit in the scheme of wholesome childhood endeavors. To many parents, pro sports stars are spoiled, immature, self-centered, and greedy, and they're less than thrilled that their kids idolize and imitate these athletes. Sports are also too aggressive, too competitive, or—in the case of, say, football—too dangerous, some contend. Nor are many moms and dads happy about the values modeled by overheated and insensitive coaches, not to mention hotheaded parents of some of their children's teammates.

We share these concerns, but we also believe that sports can teach children important life lessons that will better equip them for success later in life. Sports don't do this automatically—much depends on the personal qualities of the adults involved in youth sports programs. But with the right leadership, sports provide children learning opportunities that few if any other endeavors in their young lives can match. We'll show you in this chapter how to identify and maximize those for your child.

From a holistic point of view, athletics offer other benefits, too. Some sports will not only raise your kids' physical condition but sharpen their emotional and mental functioning, too. As we show you later in this chapter, certain sports help achieve what holistic teachers celebrate as "mind/body integration." In surprising ways, as we'll illustrate, sports can even generate teachable moments about mystic spirituality.

Yet youth sports programs can also be fraught with problems. In the sections that follow, we'll give you some guidance on dealing with those. We'll give a detailed rundown on both the fitness benefits and dangers associated with popular youth sports. And because competition and aggression doesn't have to be present for a physical activity to be fun and good exercise, we'll introduce you to cooperative and noncompetitive games that your kids may enjoy even more than the old standbys.

A HOLISTIC VIEW OF COMPETITIVE YOUTH SPORTS

When kids enter the world of competitive youth sports, they link up with cultural traditions that go back thousands of years. Popular sports such as handball evolved from games played by indigenous peoples. Soccer began as a European peasant game in Roman times. The combination of physical esthetics, which the ancient Greeks celebrated in their sports, and the physical and mental challenges the various games present, help make sports one of the most enduring and universally popular pastimes we have, and most kids take to them enthusiastically, often at an early age.

Parents have good reason to encourage their children to take up sports. Athletics offer much to growing bodies and developing minds. However, moms and dads should also bear in mind a number of important pitfalls and cautions.

Why Competitive Sports—A Holistic Perspective

Young bodies want to run, jump, throw, hit, chase, and be chased. Young minds also want to play games. They want to learn, by working out in imaginary or contrived circumstances, how to solve certain problems or succeed in certain social situations. Competitive athletics provide an excellent opportunity to do just that, through choosing teams, risking failure, abiding by the concept of fair play, accepting "the rules," and abiding by the decisions of an impartial universe (that is, umpires and referees). These are all essentially social experiences and values, and they're learned nowhere more acutely than in sports.

On the physical side, sports teach hand-eye coordination (from hitting, kicking, throwing, or catching a ball, for example), balance, timing, and certain aspects of body/mind integration (see page 300). Sports also provide a superb forum for learning to set and achieve goals. Kids learn the psychological skill of committing oneself to the long-term pursuit of individual or team objectives, such as enduring the drudgery and boredom of practice and conditioning in order to achieve better performance or win a championship.

Plus, compared to more lethal alternatives, allowing ourselves the chance to participate in the charged atmosphere of competitive sports is probably one of the healthiest ways we can let off steam. "We all have aggressive instincts," says child psychiatrist David Ritvo, the father of two young athletes and a longtime youth-soccer coach. "Being able to channel them into this setting and not act them out elsewhere is a sign of strength of character." And even when things do get rough during a game, he says, "Better they should act out aggression on a playing field than on the streets in a gang." When tensions build up in day-to-day life—as they do even for kids—sports can provide a much-needed pressure-relief valve.

With today's frantic lifestyles, the informal sandlot games and unstructured play of the past are being replaced by an overly-structured daily and weekly calendar, including demanding sports schedules, for today's youngsters. This is unfortunate—the individual and group processes that occur when kids are left on their own are an essential part of their development, and adults shouldn't interfere with that. Besides, kids have a way of structuring their play to be about fun, whereas adults tend to structure sports to be about winning.

Still, Ritvo notes that "sports can provide a model of how to negotiate life in a civilized society. One of the values of playing in a team sport is learning the lessons and rules of social conduct." Done properly, he says, an organized program "can offer kids a more supervised sandlot experience."

Are Competitive Sports for *My* Child?

To help determine whether your child is ready for organized sports, or for taking the leap from organized recreational to competitive play, parents should follow their kids' lead. Do your children love the game? Do they want to play three or four times a week? Do they have the ability to play at a higher level? It's also important to look for signs that the child is ready to risk failure, in the form of striking out, dropping a ball, missing a crucial jump shot, or allowing a goal.

If all those conditions are met, and if you're not trying to cajole your child into competitive sports to meet your own need to compete and win, then the odds are good it will be a valuable experience. On the other hand, if your son or daughter is more interested in the social aspects of sports, doesn't seem to have an intense drive to compete, shies away from pressure situations, or prefers quieter, more solitary pursuits, then better to keep his or her athletic endeavors more recreational—and then, only so long as it's clear they remain enjoyable.

For more on your child's physical readiness for sports, see "The Health Benefits and Risks of Your Child's Favorite Sports" later in this chapter.

What Are Sports For? Or, the Valuable Life Lessons of Competitive Sports

In the adult world, both professional and international sports organizations are dominated by two imperatives: winning at all costs, and making big pots of money. But in the world of the young, sports are first and foremost a high form of play. Any adult hoping to encourage her kid in sports, or become involved in the child's sporting life, owes it to her child to always remember that athletics are supposed to be *fun*. Youth sports, even at a competitive level, should always place fun at a premium.

But besides fun, and the obvious benefit of physical fitness, competitive sports can enhance kids' physical and emotional well-being in other important ways:

Teamwork. Competitive sports require players to work together to achieve a common goal. Of course, much the same can be said about the cooperative games described later in the chapter, but in competitive games, the stakes are higher, and the players' attachment to the outcome is greater. No matter how skilled an individual player may be, he or she can seldom carry a team to victory all alone. Even if that's possible in a given game, it's almost never possible over an extended period like a season. At higher competitive levels, the opposition is just too great. Besides, going solo is almost always at odds with the nature of the game. If this lesson is learned well in youth, it will prepare the child for the myriad ways in which she will need to collaborate with others in her personal and professional life later on.

Camaraderie and community. Playing together, struggling together, and winning and losing together gives kids and adults alike an almost ineffable sense of closeness. For boys and men, in particular, sports can provide an opportunity to experience—and express—an intensity of loving friendship rare among males in our society. This experience can help kids learn that other people matter, that it's valuable to care for others, and that you are supported by those around you.

PHIL CATALFO

Coordination. The demands of a competitive game require players to juggle many physical and mental skills to accomplish a specific strategic task or game objective, often within seconds. This experience promotes a responsiveness of body and mind that is indispensable to modern life.

Self-esteem. Overcoming physical challenges, and acquiring new physical skills, can do wonders for a child's self-esteem. An otherwise unathletic kid who smacks a baseball sharply between the outfielders will feel on top of the world—and be motivated to try it again, even if the next few efforts don't work out quite as well. Over time, a child who may never aspire to higher levels of sport will still feel more roundly competent than before. As Ritvo says, athletic accomplishments "can add to a child's sense of who they are. . . . They become a person who is capable in this way."

Identity as a growing person. Once children get past the earliest developmental stages, such as learning to walk and talk, sports involves some of the most notable and easy-to-recognize physical milestones kids will experience in their young lives. They can measure their progress quite clearly—"I can throw the ball a *whole lot* farther than I could last year, Mom!"—and can feel their increasing abilities practically bursting from their bodies.

Self-control. The rules of a given sport make plain what is allowed and what isn't, and in order to play, kids are forced to accept those parameters, or risk being ejected from the game or team. In sports, whining, complaining, fighting, or generally acting like a pest not only won't get you what you want, but might cost you the chance to play altogether.

Setting and pursuing goals. Kids don't start out with much in the way of long-range plans. They generally follow their impulses and when they find something pleasurable, they do it over and over again. But in sports, it is often necessary to *strive* to do something. With proper guidance and encouragement from coaches and parents, kids can learn to set tangible goals for themselves, and will pursue them with amazing dedication.

Overcoming adversity. For many kids, sports is the first context in which they will experience failure, loss, or disappointment at a deep level. Yet the spirit of sports is to take every game as a new opportunity and embrace every new challenge without dwelling on past failures (or for that matter, successes). Ironically, there are benefits to losing, in that there are some things we can *only* learn by transcending loss. For instance, a young baseball hitter can improve by having to figure out what led to an unexpected strikeout. Besides, losing can make players not just better competitors, but better people by learning how to be gracious in defeat as well as magnanimous in victory. And learn they will because no one wins all the time.

Sisterhood. Not so long ago, even youth sports were almost completely dominated by males. Happily, as a result of newer laws such as Title IX, a federal rule requiring colleges to spend comparable amounts on women's and men's athletic programs, as well as shifts in prevailing social attitudes, women and girls today have abundant opportunities to pursue recreational and competitive sports. Girls' basketball, softball, and soccer programs, in particular, have proliferated greatly in the last two decades, to the point where the U.S. national women's soccer team became the best in the world, and two women's professional basketball leagues are attracting fans and media attention. Among other things, this makes available to girls strong role models in the person of admirable female athletes and coaches.

Integrity. When we talk of "good sportsmanship" (called the more gender-fair "sporting behavior" in soccer), what we're really describing is integrity—that quality of character which will not take unfair advantage, which will play by the rules, which strives to win but never to injure or demean, and which seeks a fair contest in which the opponent is respected. The "good sport" understands that this kind of integrity not only produces the most enjoyable kind of game, it also produces the most enjoyable experience of self. In other words, if you win by cheating, insulting, or deliberately injuring an opponent, you wind up with a hollow victory and a diminished self. Whereas if you and your opponent respect each other, you will both be aiming for the best you can be; indeed, you respect your opponent *because* he or she challenges you to be your best.

Despite unfortunate modeling by some pros they watch on television, even kids as young as seven or eight can be taught to conduct themselves proudly and civilly on the field and sidelines—and if they can learn to do that in sports, they can learn to apply that elsewhere.

The Shadow Side of Competitive Sports

Any parent whose kids are involved in (or even considering) sports should be mindful of—and try to mitigate or reverse—the uglier aspects of these pastimes. Most of what we're referring to here stems from the obsession with winning. Of course, the objective of any game is to win, and we don't mean to suggest that players, coaches, or spectators shouldn't strive to do it. But in youth sports, when winning becomes the sole focus to the exclusion of players' physical and emotional development, and when it results in unacceptable behavior, we have lost sight of the real purpose of the program.

It's usually pretty easy to tell if the adults in charge of a competitive youth sports program have things in the proper perspective. If the coach stresses effort, teamwork, learning, and encouragement, the players will most likely have a positive experience. On the other hand, if the coach stresses winning over progress, provides little technical instruction to help players improve, or is a "screamer," the participants will probably become disheartened and may even decide to quit the program.

Even when the adults involved have the proper frame of mind, a young athlete can bring with him a host of unhelpful attitudes about himself, teammates, or the nature of competition. We've all seen kids get down on themselves for failing to make a big play, and there's nothing wrong with that kind of disappointment. But when a young athlete is so frustrated with a single failure that she forgets recent successes, someone needs to step in and restore composure and perspective, and remind the player and team that *learning* from mistakes and failures is the only way to redeem them. When star athletes berate their own teammates for mistakes, they need to be shown that there's a difference between demanding the best from yourself and your teammates, and becoming obnoxious and overbearing with your colleagues.

Because of the atmosphere in adult sports, many parents new to youth sports assume that a certain amount of verbal abuse is not only acceptable, but almost *necessary* to make the sporting experience complete. This can include everything from booing the umpire, to taunting the opposing team, to foul language, to personal attacks on specific players or coaches. Otherwise mild-mannered and decent folks can become downright psychopathic when their kids' (or in their minds, their own) athletic honor is at stake. When this happens, it's essential that others on the scene make it clear that such language or behavior will not be tolerated—for the sake of the kids *and* the adults.

A Parent's Short Survival Guide to Competitive Youth Sports

To make sure your child will have the best possible experience in a given sports program:

- *Be Involved.* Become a coach, referee, team manager, or other volunteer of significance. Sports are not just baby-sitting programs. In fact, most youth-sports organizations rely heavily on volunteer parents. By becoming involved, you're setting a great parenting example for your kids, as well as helping to make the program available in the first place.

  Even if you can't give much time, attend as many games as possible. Your kids want you to see them play! Kids really thrive on their parents' witnessing and acknowledging their athletic prowess. Parent spectators often imagine that their kids need to hear them shouting instructions throughout a match. In reality, players hear few specific comments amid the din of sideline or bleacher chatter. But they do hear cheering.

- *Make your comments positive ones.* If your child asks for feedback on her performance, don't shy away from pointing out things that could be improved, but be sure to make those observations in the context of ample encouragement and acknowledgment. Parents and coaches alike would do well to use the "sandwich" recommended by sports psychologists Aubrey Fine and Michael Sachs, authors of *The Total Sports Experience for Kids:* "a positive comment about effort, followed by a technical instructional effort, followed by another positive comment." A good example, from Fine and Sachs: "Nice try on that grounder. Next time make sure your glove is positioned in front of you and you're blocking the ball's path with your body. You'll get the next one. Keep up the good effort!"

· *Introduce the notion of organized sports slowly and gently.* Start your child off in a strictly-recreational program—one in which no scores are kept and the focus is on instruction, participation, and high-spirited fun. Some kids are best suited to recreational, as opposed to competitive, sports, anyway. If this is the case with your child, by all means encourage it. Even athletically-gifted kids sometimes prefer to maintain a somewhat casual involvement in sports, rather than pursue them wholeheartedly.

If your young athlete does have the talent and desire to play at a competitive level, you will need to summon the dedication to be transportation engineer, support crew, equipment manager, venture capitalist, and peanut gallery all at once. You may soon wonder where your former life disappeared to. Unscheduled weekends may become a dim memory, and all sense of balance in family activities may be lost. But all those problems can be solved, and are more than outweighed by the sheer joy of watching your son or daughter run, leap, slide, throw, or kick their way into a starring role in their own fantasy.

POPULAR SPORTS THROUGH THE BODY/MIND LOOKING GLASS

If you think Whole Parenting means things like teaching your kids to meditate and buying them nonviolent toys, you may well wonder why we're talking about ice hockey and football. The fact is, youth athletics can contribute to the development of not only young bodies but also the minds, emotions, and spirits that inhabit them. This is particularly true when you consider that childhood sets the course for the rest of life. Sports can release human potentials in your kids that might otherwise never be tapped.

how to deal with obsessive, sports-crazed adults

One of the biggest problems parents encounter when their kids become involved in organized sports programs is coming to grips with a bizarre species known to frequent playing fields. We're talking, of course, about the abrasive adult whose obsession with winning is such that he—and it usually is a he—makes everyone around him miserable unless his team obliterates the opposition. Many kids quit teams or drop out of a sport entirely because of unpleasant experiences with these types.

While this person—let's call him Mr. Mouth—can be a coach or a spectator, the potential to do harm is greater for coaches, so we'll concentrate our remarks on them. Keep in mind, though, that some of the following recommendations also pertain to an unwelcome presence in the bleachers:

- *Don't overreact.* When you first notice shouting, unpleasant, foul, or abusive language, control your impulse to get into a confrontation with Mr. Mouth. First, simply observe. Is this an isolated incident or part of a consistent pattern? If the behavior is consistently inappropriate, then you should take the next step.

- *Take notes, preferably written.* It's very important to cite specifics—frequency and verbatim comments—if you're going to pursue a complaint with the organization or even just have a conversation with the coach.

- *Talk with other parents.* Do others share your concern? Other parents may be able to paint a fuller picture of who the coach is and how he handles his coaching responsibility. Or your concerns may be confirmed, in which case you and your fellow parents may provide each other with enough mutual support to voice your concerns in a way that will get positive results.

- *Talk with Mr. Mouth.* Do this away from the kids, preferably, and not at a practice or game. Start with a positive before addressing the negative. For instance, say you appreciate his devoting so much time to the kids on the team. Then, state your concerns clearly, calmly, and courteously. Ask him to explain how what you're referring to fits into his coaching philosophy and his overall aims for the team. Then, listen. You may be surprised by what you hear. He may turn out to be a lot more reasonable than you expected, or may have a very good explanation for what you saw or heard. Or he may confirm your worst fears, in which case you should say, as cooly as possible, exactly what your expectations are: "I really don't want my kid or anyone else's kid belittled or yelled at. I'd much rather see them taught the skills or tactics they need to learn, and be encouraged to believe in themselves. Winning is not nearly as important for them as learning skills and teamwork." If he disagrees, hear him out and conclude the conversation before it escalates into an unresolvable argument. You'll still have served your purpose, which is to put the coach on notice about your needs and standards, and the fact that you feel he's not meeting them.

Sports can also upset the balance in young lives and bodies. It all depends how the activity is approached, and to some extent, which sport is chosen. We cover the physical and mental/emotional health attributes of youth sports elsewhere in this chapter. Here are some other factors you might not have considered:

Sports and Spirit

Sports won't turn your children into enlightened sages, but in sometimes surprising ways, they can lay a foundation, especially in the teen

- *Wait a little while to see if anything changes.* If you notice improvements, contact the coach again to acknowledge them: "I wanted you to know I'm really grateful that you've used a different tone of voice with the kids lately. They seem to be having a lot more fun together—I know Heather is enjoying practices and games much more." During this time, also compare notes with other parents. If several weeks pass without appreciable improvement, you're ready to take the step described immediately below.

- *Contact the organization sponsoring the program.* A letter is best, but a phone call will do in a pinch. Seek out the highest appropriate official. In large programs, the official may not know every player and their family, so begin by giving as much background about your family's involvement as you can. Then detail the behavior that troubles you, including your attempted resolutions with the coach and the results of those efforts. Conclude by stating what you would like to see the official do, but realize that she or he will have to investigate first, and doing so will take time. The most you can expect at this point is an acknowledgment that your concern is legitimate and that the organization takes it seriously.

- *Become more involved in the program.* When it comes to upholding a "community standard" of behavior, nothing will give your opinion more clout like paying the dues of volunteer involvement. Maybe next year, Mr. Mouth will *have* to satisfy you or risk losing his status as coach.

If you suspect your child or any other kids on the team have had their feelings hurt by the coach, make sure they get plenty of encouragement and comfort from you and the other parents. Tell them exactly how you think what the coach did or said was wrong. Also remember to tell them that *some* of what the coach said may have been okay, even if it was hard to accept. If, for instance, your kid made a mistake or could have tried harder, she needs to learn from the situation. Explain, too, why people talk and act as her coach did—about how sometimes people get so focused on winning that they lose sight of what it *really* takes to win (teamwork, skills, mutual support), not to mention the fact that sports are supposed to be fun. Also, give your kid a chance to vent her concerns and frustrations. For example, writing a letter to the coach, even if it's never sent, might help her feel better.

Whatever else happens, don't let your kid become so disheartened that she decides to drop out. That is the worst thing that can happen in these situations. Instead, encourage your child to try again, to come back for another season with another coach, to think of all the fun, pleasurable aspects of playing the sport, and so on.

years, for a child's eventual interest in spiritual matters. At the very least, observations your children make in athletics may open the door for you to have a conversation with them about life's mysteries, because in the course of even a young sports career, dedicated athletes sometimes have spontaneous, mystifying experiences that are best explained by the language of spirit.

As Esalen Institute founder Michael Murphy has pointed out, sports are a kind of Western yoga. The laser-like focus required to perform well can build skills of concentration and mental clarity like those produced by meditation. The mental rehearsal (visualization) techniques practiced by many athletes are essentially spiritual exercises adapted to sports. The long-term commitments and regular practice regimens of sports resemble the dedication required in many spiritual disciplines.

Athletes, including child athletes, also learn to cultivate other mental states like those celebrated in spiritual life. For instance, athletes quickly learn that they must be "in the moment" to perform at their best. They also know that the quality of the performance at hand depends largely on detaching themselves, Buddha-like, from thoughts about the previous performance, good or bad. Basketball and football players make their best moves when they let go of trying to think or will their way through the maze of the opposing team. The clearing of the mind that precedes such athletic creativity is essentially a state of moving meditation like that taught in Zen Buddhism or spiritually based martial arts such as aikido.

PHIL CATALFO

Young athletes, like athletes at any age, will find themselves in the midst of extraordinary, spiritual-like experiences in the normal course of an athletic career. Players in fast-moving sports like football and basketball will experience time appearing to slow to a crawl, putting them in a state of hyperawareness where they can make complex decisions in just a few chronological seconds. Almost all young athletes will know the exhilaration of being in "the zone" where human imperfection disappears for a time and they can do no wrong.

We don't want to make too much of the spiritual implication of youth sports, because few child or teen athletes are reflective enough at their young age to see these extraordinary occurrences in mystical terms. But if yours is a spiritually oriented family, you may be able to talk to your children about life's great mysteries by drawing on examples from their athletic pursuits.

Sports and Body/Mind Integration

Body/mind integration refers to such things as "groundedness" and moving with grace and balance. It also refers to a balanced life, in which the life of the body plays an equal part with the life of the mind, heart, and spirit. A lack of body/mind integration writes itself into the body's structure, starting early in life. Hunched shoulders, heads slung forward on necks, rigidity, tension, awkwardness—all of these conditions indicate a poorly integrated life. For example, awkwardness often stems from a lack of full awareness of the body as it moves.

Body/mind integration from an early age helps prevent problems such as back trouble later on. A body that is hunched, rigid, or awkward is also poorly aligned with gravity, which means that gravity's pull will worsen the condition over the years. In other words, misalignments that originate in childhood will almost certainly lead to aches and pains and perhaps more serious conditions such as disabling back problems when a person loses the suppleness of youth. Body/mind integration affects children in their current lives, too, because it can enhance their musculoskeletal development and give them the joy and confidence that comes with natural grace and vibrant health.

Many physical activities in which children commonly participate can provide your kids a more integral athletic experience. Dance and martial arts such as aikido pursue this goal directly by teaching students to move from their "center," a point at the center of the abdomen that the Japanese call *hara*. Moving from the center is the basic skill required to move in a balanced manner. In addition, dance and martial arts teach grace and moving with full attention out to the ends of the limbs—it is virtually impossible to perform these activities properly without this level of awareness.

Among conventional sports, soccer and basketball rank high as body/mind integrators. Soccer, with its emphasis on foot and leg skills, gets awkward, nervous, and spacey children "out of their heads." Kids, and adults, who think too much move in an unbalanced fashion and are easily knocked off their feet because all that energy in their heads pulls the center of gravity upward. In soccer, the attention paid to the lowest part of the body draws the center of gravity back down to its natural spot just below the navel. An emphasis on dribbling skills and elusive moves in basketball has the same effect. Players can't dribble or move well unless they are centered and grounded.

Some sports inherently unbalance the body. Sports that place most of their emphasis on the child's strong side—for example, pitching in baseball, the serve and one-handed ground strokes in tennis—can lead to bodies in which one side becomes much more developed than the other. Sports that emphasize being good with both hands and both feet—another strength of both soccer and basketball—have the opposite effect.

They develop bodies that are far more balanced than average. Most people favor their strong side—to play soccer and basketball well, young players must bring their weaker side up to speed.

Too much of a good thing also upsets balance. Young athletes who spend so much time practicing their sport that little time is left for schoolwork, other interests, and family and social relationships can hardly be called balanced no matter how well they move. The same goes for kids who take games too seriously. Val Schultz is happy about the success her oldest daughter, Sarah, enjoys in soccer and basketball but she is not at all happy about the emotional costs. "When my daughter goes into tears over losing, I think that's a little bit much," she sighs. True, the intense preparation to be a top athlete or dancer or martial artist makes possible the moments of transcendence that we refer to above. But somewhere in that regimen is also a point of balance. And perhaps only you, since you know your children best, can help them find it.

THE HEALTH BENEFITS AND RISKS OF YOUR CHILD'S FAVORITE SPORTS

Like most things that are truly rewarding, youth sports carry their risks. To participate in organized or recreational athletics, your kids will have to put their bodies on the line. No sport is truly injury-free.

Still, there is much we parents can do to reduce the numbers and severity of athletic injuries. To make sure your young athletes have maximum protection, start with the following preventive steps:

- *The right, well-fitting equipment.* Ask coaches and other parents for advice on what to buy and learn all you can about how the equipment prevents injury. Make sure your kids know how to put on and secure their equipment and regularly inspect it for wear so you can replace pieces as needed. Don't leave it to coaches to teach your kids safety consciousness. Talk to your young athletes about why they have to use their mouthpieces, keep their helmets buckled, and so on.

- *Properly maintained facilities.* Soccer, baseball, field hockey, or other outdoor fields must be clear of grooves, ruts, holes, and rocks and obstructions too close to the action such as benches and stakes. Indoor courts for basketball, volleyball, and so on must be kept dry and clean. Proper landing pads must be in place for gymnastics and track and field. Know whose responsibility it is to maintain facilities—in school sports, probably the athletic director's—and take any concerns to them immediately.

- *Proper conditioning.* This doesn't count as much with younger kids because of their rubbery bodies and almost bottomless energy. But by high-school age, kids who aren't ready—physically or mentally—to play get hurt much more often, making conditioning the most important means of injury prevention. Conditioning means more than just general physical fitness. It also refers to fitness for the *specific* activities required in the sport, development of skills specific to the sport, good nutrition, sufficient sleep, and motivation to play. For example, not being in the game mentally can drastically affect timing and judgment. Nor can your children cram conditioning the way many kids cram studying. Getting in shape has to start well before the season to be effective in preventing injuries.

- *Adequate stretching, warm-ups, and cool-down exercises.* A proper conditioning program will include stretching at least several times weekly to build some residual body flexibility. In addition, teenage athletes should fully stretch out before practice or a game, followed by properly warming up beforehand and gradually cooling down afterward. Coaches should be supervising these aspects of your youngster's sports preparation.

- *Well-prepared, sensitive coaches.* The quality of your child's coaching will affect her safety in several ways. A qualified coach will insist on proper conditioning, knowledge of and obedience to the game's rules, disciplined play, good technique, good sportsmanship, and precautions during extreme weather, all of which help prevent injuries. Good coaches will also make sure that facilities and fields are as safe as possible and that all possible preventive steps have been taken in the event of injuries. In addition, good coaches are good people who realize that while winning counts, safety counts more.

- *Adequate rest and emotional well-being.* Fatigue and emotional stress can affect concentration and lead to injury. Kids are easily knocked off center by emotional incidents such as turmoil with a parent or a friend. Do what you can to send your child to her game feeling centered, both mentally and emotionally.

- *Grouping players by size instead of age.* This matters most with boys fourteen and over in contact/collision sports such as football, rugby, ice hockey, and wrestling, writes John F. Duff, M.D., author of *Youth Sports Injuries.* In general, the adults in charge of youth and school sports will make sure competition is balanced by size, with a pre-participation physical exam a crucial part of the decision making. But if you're still concerned that your child doesn't have the size or development to protect himself, you may want to get a second opinion from a physician or youth sports expert.

- *Well-prepared, sensitive officials.* Once the game starts, it's up to the officials to enforce the rules governing safe play. That means knowing the rules inside out and blowing the whistle as often as it takes to make sure the rules are followed. As a parent, you too should know the rules so you can tell if officials are doing their jobs. But don't berate the refs from the stands—take up the issue with the responsible parties after the game. Better yet, get trained as a referee or umpire yourself. Then you can make sure at least one official is doing a good job!

- *Sitting out when hurt.* Pros, and many athletes at lower levels, take strong medication or simply "suck it up" to play with pain. Your child isn't being paid millions of dollars to risk a crippling injury. You need to be alert to coaches who will push kids to risk further injury just to get a win. You also should make sure that your children report their pains to you and their coaches. They may try to hide an injury so they won't miss a game or lose their position on the team.

Health, Fitness, and Injury Issues with Specific Sports

The health and fitness information below is largely based on the activity itself. Of course, there's nothing to prevent a young baseball player, for example, from building superior fitness on his own even if the sport itself doesn't provide much of a workout. A couple of general comments:

- The overuse injuries referred to below come from repeated stress of a single part of the body. Most often, they occur because a specific motion is practiced intensively, as is the case with the classic example, "Little League elbow." These injuries aren't serious enough to disable your child permanently or even require much treatment. However, they can take months to heal and will knock your child out of sports participation during that time. Teaching your kids to back off when they first feel pain will help prevent injuries from developing.

- As a rule, sports with high injury rates for teens—football and ice hockey, for instance—are relatively safe for younger children. Sports injury rates go up dramatically at the high-school level.

The following guide will alert you to the injury risks associated with the most popular youth sports as well as their health and fitness benefits:

Ballet and Other Dancing

Health and fitness. Young dancers may *look* like they're in great shape but to get much aerobic benefit, they need to keep moving at a vigorous level for twenty to thirty minutes several times a week.

injuries. Young children rarely hurt themselves in dance. Teens, however, may suffer a variety of minor injuries including stress fractures, strains to various muscles and the back, and tendonitis and sprains in various joints. Most of these are overuse injuries and of no long-term concern. Falls, of course, can cause fractures.

Baseball/Softball

Health and fitness. Very little benefit for cardiovascular fitness, overall strength, or muscle endurance. Nor does playing these sports burn many calories. Pitchers and catchers get more of a workout than players at other positions, who spend most of their time standing or sitting.

Injuries. The injury rate compared to other major sports is quite low, and most injuries are minor. However, the worst baseball injuries—from being hit in the head by a pitched or batted ball—are in rare instances fatal. The fatality rate for young players is second only to football's. Players are also at some risk of ankle and finger fractures. Batting helmets and face masks reduce the risk of serious head injuries. Breakaway bases help prevent sliding injuries.

Basketball

Health and fitness. At the recreational level, basketball doesn't produce much cardiovascular fitness because of the stop-and-go action. However, conditioning for organized ball often includes both cardiovascular and strength training. And basketball at any level burns a heap of calories.

Injuries. The overall injury rate is high but the overwhelming majority of those hurts aren't serious. Very few basketball injuries require surgery. Interestingly, teen girls suffer higher rates of surgical knee injuries than boys of the same ages. Other common injuries are to the ankle (sprains, most not serious), foot (stress fractures), back problems (some serious), fingers, and eyes. Frequent overuse injuries include "jumper's knee."

Bicycling

Health and fitness. When young riders pedal fast, tackle plenty of hills, and use gears that force them to work hard, they can build strong cardiovascular fitness without the bone and joint shaking caused by running. Cycling builds muscle strength in the back and legs, too. The potential downside includes tight hamstring muscles (back of the upper leg) and a loss of leg flexibility overall because legs are never fully extended when pedaling.

Injuries. Traffic is an obvious hazard. Tired kids shouldn't ride on the street. Nor should any child take off without a proper helmet—head injuries from a fall can be catastrophic.

Cross-Country Skiing

Health and fitness. A superior fitness builder from almost every standpoint: cardiovascular, muscle strength and endurance, and flexibility.

Injuries. Young skiers suffer very few injuries.

Downhill Skiing

Health and fitness. Runs of ten minutes and longer can build good cardiovascular fitness but shorter runs punctuated by stopping and riding the lift back to the top don't provide the sustained activity needed for significant health benefits.

Injuries. The risks from falls and collisions are well-known—major knee injuries, fractures, thumb injuries from getting caught up in the ski pole straps, shoulder injuries, and to a lesser extent, head injuries. Make sure your kids only attempt slopes appropriate to their skill level. Good conditioning and equipment is essential to help prevent injuries.

Equestrian Sports

Health and fitness. Active sports like polo build a moderate degree of fitness in all major categories. Obviously, when the rider's level of activity drops, so do fitness benefits. However, sophisticated riding of any type not only gives the rider a thorough workout but requires a moderate level of fitness just to do it well.

Injuries. One of the most dangerous of all sports, both at the recreational and competitive levels. Major risks include serious head, spinal, and upper extremity injuries. Jumping adds other risks—in a spill, the rider may injure major joints or even be trampled or crushed by her horse. Risks do go down as riding experience increases. Proper helmets are a must to help prevent head injuries.

Field Hockey

Health and fitness. Excellent for cardiovascular fitness and can build high muscle strength and endurance as well.

Injuries. Knee injuries in field hockey, exclusively a girls'/women's sport in America, are not uncommon and frequently require major surgery. Players also risk serious back injuries and stick injuries to the face. Mouth guards help prevent dental damage.

Figure Skating

Health and fitness. If your youngsters have sufficient skill and skate hard enough for a long enough time, they can get a good cardiovascular workout. The vigor with which they move their bodies will determine whether or not skating improves their muscular fitness. Leisurely recreational skating provides only low-level benefits.

Injuries. Most injuries on the ice are of the overuse variety, from constantly repeating jumps, moves, and routines.

Football

Health and fitness. In general, football training provides good cardiovascular conditioning and is an excellent strength builder. However, specialization by position means that not all players may be subjected to the same training regimen. Extreme weight gain for the lineman positions is not healthy and can lead to obesity in the off-season when training ends. Pay attention to the diet your son follows to gain weight for football—see Chapter 5 for more on this subject.

Injuries. Few injuries other than the usual bumps, bruises, and sprains occur in Pop Warner football, because young players are smaller, more elastic, and less aggressive, says Dr. Duff. But for kids age fourteen and over, football is the most dangerous youth sport. The nature of the activity leaves every player banged up and one out of three players will suffer an injury requiring at least moderate treatment. Frequent injuries include head injuries (most are mild concussions but some are serious), stretch injuries to the neck, shoulder injuries (often serious), knee injuries (in one out of four high-school players), and ankle injuries. Any of the above injuries may be serious enough to cause permanent damage, including brain damage, and about twenty high school players die or are paralyzed every year from injuries to the head or neck. Ruptured spleens are infrequent but possible. Football practice begins in summer, when insensitive coaching can force players to do too much on hot days, risking heatstroke and other medical problems.

Gymnastics

Health and fitness. Fitness benefits depend on the event although most gymnasts practice a variety of them. Gymnastics builds good muscle strength and flexibility. Other benefits are modest, with the cardiovascular value low.

Injuries. It doesn't look safe, and it's not—gymnastics has one of the highest injury rates in athletics. Falls and dismounts can cause dislocations, back problems, and serious fractures. The endless repetitions in training often lead to overuse injuries, particularly to gymnasts' elbows, knees, and spine. Occasionally, gymnasts suffer catastrophic head and neck injuries. The need to be thin for competitive reasons can lead to improper and severe dieting and ultimately malnutrition or eating disorders such as bulimia. Query your kids to make sure they feel good about the state of the equipment they're using and the skill of their spotters.

Handball/Squash/Racquetball

Health and fitness. As a rule, handball offers a slightly better workout than squash, which in turn works players harder than racquetball. But all three can build pretty good cardiovascular fitness if: your youngsters are playing others of similar ability; both players have the skills to sustain rallies; and points are played without long breaks for players to catch their breath. These sports exercise all the major muscle groups.

Injuries. The most serious risk in these sports is to the eyes, so make sure your kids understand the importance of wearing goggles.

Ice Hockey

Health and fitness. Excellent for cardiovascular fitness and muscle strength.

Injuries. Youth league hockey has a low rate of serious injuries, but this is not so in high school, where players slam into the boards and opponents with force, in part because they put too much trust in their protective equipment. Common injuries include separated shoulders, traumatic bursitis of the elbow, and head injuries, most not serious, thanks to headgear. Frequent knee and ankle injuries and some dislocated shoulders occur, although most aren't serious, as do wrist fractures, some of which are quite serious. Goalies can suffer serious injury if the puck strikes their throat. Neck injuries, including broken necks, are a risk with younger players, whose necks aren't as strong as mature players'. Players are also vulnerable to groin and thigh injuries.

Lacrosse (Boys')

Health and fitness. Lacrosse produces excellent cardiovascular fitness and moderate-to-excellent benefits in other categories as well.

Injuries. About one out of two players will require medical attention for an injury at some point. The injury patterns resemble those in football and ice hockey (see above), although 70 percent of injuries are minor.

Lacrosse (Girls')

Health and fitness. See boys' lacrosse above.

Injuries. The noncontact rule in girl's lacrosse makes it a much less risky activity than boy's lacrosse. The major injuries—facial fractures and knee ligament and cartilage tears—don't occur very frequently.

Martial Arts

Health and fitness. Martial arts vary but in general provide a superior all-around workout from the standpoints of cardiovascular, flexibility, and muscle strength and endurance.

Injuries. The injury rate for children is below I percent. For adults, rates are significantly higher. Injuries to shoulders, elbows, wrists, and toes are the most common.

Roller-Skating and Roller-Blading

Health and fitness. See figure skating.

Injuries. Falls can lead to fractures or head injuries so make sure your kids put on their elbow pads, knee pads, and helmets before they lace up their skates. Also try to convince them that trying stunts they're not ready for could be a painful experience.

Rugby

Health and fitness. Rugby produces a high degree of cardiovascular fitness and also builds strong legs and arms.

Injuries. Injuries to head, shoulder, knee, and other large joints occur frequently although the rates are lower than in football.

Running

Health and fitness. Strictly in terms of cardiovascular fitness, running is the leading exercise option for all ages. It also is a great leg strengthener, although it does little for upper body strength. Running can reduce leg flexibility, which increases pain and injury risk, although younger runners will be less affected than older ones. Running near heavy traffic is a bad idea because the runner's accelerated breathing causes her to take in lots of exhaust fumes.

Injuries. The jostling of running, particularly on hard surfaces like concrete and to a lesser extent asphalt, can lead to overuse injuries of the knee, lower leg, and foot. These injuries may sideline your teen runners for a while but they aren't serious. The strain on the legs increases for heavy runners and runners who are in poor condition or haven't stretched out first. With preteens especially, watch out for heat exhaustion and dehydration. Teach your children to replace lost fluids and encourage them to run on softer surfaces such as school tracks and dirt paths.

Soccer

Health and fitness. Excellent for cardiovascular fitness. It builds good leg strength and moderate strength in the abdomen and back.

Injuries. Soccer is one of the safer sports, particularly at the youth league level. Frequent injuries include sprained ankles and an overuse injury called "soccer foot" or "soccer toe," none of which cause permanent trouble. Serious knee-ligament tears do occur, but rarely below high school level because youth league players have more elastic bodies and joints. Less frequent injuries include fractured wrists and mild concussions. Shin guards provide some added protection.

Swimming

Health and fitness. Swimming provides a superior cardiovascular and over-all fitness activity so long as your child swims at a workout, not leisurely, pace. For young athletes recovering from leg injuries, swimming will keep them in shape without stressing their lower bodies because the water bears their weight. For similar reasons, swimming is an excellent exercise for overweight kids.

Injuries. Competitive swimmers suffer a fairly high rate of overuse injuries because of the intense training regimen. Common overuse injuries include tendonitis of the shoulder, and for swimmers who do the breast stroke, a form of knee strain. Chlorinated water can take its toll on skin, eyes, hair, and mucous membranes.

Tennis

Health and fitness. Highly skilled players who sustain long, hard-fought rallies without long breaks in between will get a modest cardiovascular workout. Otherwise, the average tennis game—whacking the ball a couple times then walking to retrieve it—offers little in the aerobic fitness department although it does aid flexibility and balance.

Injuries. At lower levels of play and competition, young players suffer few injuries. But as competition and training schedules become more intense, feet, hand, knee, and shoulder injuries occur with some frequency.

JAMES WEEKS

Track and Field

Health and fitness. The benefits depend upon the event. Middle- and long-distance running, along with the sprints, produce the best all-around fitness.

Injuries. Most events are relatively safe with respect to major injuries beyond the usual muscle pulls and tears, overuse injuries, and sprains. Events such as the high jump, pole vault, long jump, and triple jump may cause injuries either on takeoff or landing—again, primarily tears, pulls, and sprains along with the odd fracture.

Volleyball

Health and fitness. When played at a high level with long rallies, volleyball builds good cardiovascular fitness, muscle strength and endurance, and flexibility.

Injuries. Player collisions cause many injuries so make sure your children's coach does a good job of coordinating the team on the court. Floor burns and hard-hit balls do damage too, with ankles, knees, shoulders, and fingers most vulnerable. Heavy training and play can lead to such overuse injuries as jumper's knee and shin splints.

Waterskiing

Health and fitness. The more fit young skiers are, the more cardiovascular benefit they're likely to get—the real value comes from longer continuous skiing and longer total time. Waterskiing at most levels builds good muscle strength and endurance.

Injuries. The most common serious injuries are to knee ligaments. Other risks include major muscle tears to the groin and thigh. Recreational skiers suffer higher rates of injuries than do competitive athletes.

Wrestling

Health and fitness. Excellent for cardiovascular fitness and muscle strength.

Injuries. The nature of the sport—force applied to a twisted body—leads to a high injury rate at the high-school level of competition. Injuries to the knees (some serious), hands, and fingers are common. Other frequent injuries include bloody noses, neck sprains (rarely serious), and shoulder injuries including strains and dislocations. Wrestling without headgear can lead to "cauliflower ear," a deformity resulting from scar tissue buildup. Some wrestlers damage health—and a few have died—from rapid, last-minute weight loss to qualify for their weight class.

For more on the injury risks of youth sports, see Dr. John Duff's *Youth Sports Injuries,* reviewed in the Resources at the end of this chapter.

Steroid Abuse in Youth Sports

In their search for any conceivable competitive edge, both male and female athletes as young as high-school age have long taken male sex hormones, also called anabolic steroids, to enhance strength and stamina. Steroids help increase muscle and bone mass. They enable athletes to train more rigorously, too. Users can take fewer days off because the steroids speed recovery from hard workouts.

Anabolic steroids, available under such names as Dianabol, Anavar, Anadrol, Winstrol, and Depo-Testosterone, are obtained illegally because they are listed by the government as controlled substances. They can have adverse health consequences, both physically and mentally. Steroids weaken resistance to disease and can make the user weaker, not stronger, in later life. They often increase aggression including extreme episodes called "'roid rage" and can cause confusion, impulsiveness, and poor judgment among other behavioral consequences. Female users may develop male secondary sex characteristics such as deeper voices and facial hair in addition to bulky muscles. Abuse can be hard to stop, especially if young athletes believe their opponents or competitors for their position on their own team are using these drugs. It is beyond the scope of this book to discuss the therapy for steroid abuse. If your child is an abuser and you seek professional help for him or her, we recommend that the professional have specific expertise in sports-related drug abuse.

COOPERATIVE AND NONCOMPETITIVE GAMES

If you were always the last one picked for your schoolyard teams, if your young teammates tormented you for muffing an easy play, if your teams always lost and you "knew" you were the reason, or even if you just recall shuddering as these things happened to kids around you, you know in your gut the argument for cooperative and noncompetitive children's games. The very structure of traditional sports ensures that some kids will suffer deep and sometimes lasting emotional pain because not everyone can win and because not all players were created equal.

Some parents appreciate alternative games from another perspective, too. Many believe that the ugly side of our competitive, winner-take-all society is also reflected in its sports, even at the youth level. In particular, many parents believe their young athletes are being taught the "killer

instinct"—that is, beating their opponents by shattering their confidence—
at a much too impressionable age. Not all parents appreciate having *their*
children's confidence shattered, either.

In the mid-1970s, an alternative games movement arose to address
such concerns. Inspired by such leading-edge thinkers as *Whole Earth Catalog* founder Stewart Brand and author/aikido teacher George Leonard,
so-called "New Games" grew from roots in the counterculture, antiwar,
and human potential movements of that era. As Leonard noted in *The
Ultimate Athlete,* the games of many cultures don't even involve competition.
New Games emphasized play, fun, and the well-being of the players over
competition, although not all New Games were noncompetitive.

New Games were aimed first at adults, not kids, but authors such as
sports psychologist Terry Orlick extended the alternative game idea to
children. Orlick noted that children were far more vulnerable than adults
to emotional wounds from losing or being snubbed by teammates or
coaches. He promoted games in which there were no losers, all children
participated equally, it took cooperation to achieve success, and the main
point was just to have a blast.

The Case for Cooperative Games

As a former collegiate gymnastics champion, Orlick speaks from experience. In *The Cooperative Sports and Game Book,* he offers a withering critique
of traditional youth sports that is not easy to dismiss. As he points out,
many youth games and programs are structured so that only a very few—
and in some cases, only one—can win, with everyone else coming up
short. The constant pressure to measure up and the stress from losing or
being berated by others drives the fun right out of the game for some
kids. In fact, the emotional pain scars many young people so deeply, he
says, that they begin avoiding competition altogether. Some even conclude that they are seriously flawed people because of their failures at
sport. We have become so enthralled with the emotional benefits of winning, Orlick concludes, that we have completely lost sight of what it costs
the kids on the losing side.

As a remedy, Orlick offers games such as the following:

- *Togeth-air Ball (Collective-Score Volleyball).* Players on both sides of a volleyball net—or string or line in the dirt—work cooperatively to keep the
  ball in the air as long as possible. Based on a Caribou Eskimo game.

- *Shake the Snake,* a game for young children. Children group themselves as either Shakers or Stompers. The Shakers each hold one end of an eight-foot rope between their thumb and first finger and wriggle the other end of the rope on the floor as they run about the room. The Stompers, as their name implies, try to wrest the ropes from the Shakers by stomping on them. A Stomper who succeeds picks up the fallen rope and joins the Shakers. The ropeless Shaker joins the Stompers. With an uneven number of children, make more of them Stompers than Shakers.

- *Deacove Rounders.* Named for creator Jim Deacove, this game is a non-competitive form of baseball played on a baseball field. As with traditional baseball, two teams play, one at bat and one in the field. But the batting team keeps hitting until it scores the same number of runs as players on the team—e.g. a six-person team bats until it scores six runs—which it can't do without the help of the team in the field. Here's how it works: a groundball of any type counts one base; an infield fly, two bases; an outfield fly, three. Runners on base advance accordingly when their teammate hits the ball. Cooperation occurs because no hit counts until the ball is stopped. Grounders must be fielded before they roll to a stop and flys must be caught. Therefore, the fielding team works hard to help the other team score its quota of runs so it can take its turn at bat. To keep the game moving, batters who don't get a hit after three pitches let the rest of the batting order hit before trying again. However, pitchers are clearly motivated to serve up easy-to-hit balls. There are no assigned positions in the field—players rotate, playing each position in the course of the game.

Not all cooperative games are as active as these. Some, especially those designed for younger children, are more like party games than traditional sports. You will find other ideas for cooperative games in *The New Games Book* and *More New Games,* now out of print but available in many libraries. New Games tend to be energetic and are readily adaptable to kids. Their creators have made as few rules as possible to allow for maximum creativity. New Games follow only three general dictums: Play Hard. Play Fair. Nobody Hurt.

A Possible Middle Ground—Traditional Sports Played with a Cooperative Heart

While the benefits of cooperative games may seem obvious, that's no reason to discard traditional sports like so much junk mail. Games like baseball, basketball, tennis, football, and soccer haven't survived all this time for nothing. They are highly evolved activities that provide many millions of people worldwide with some of their greatest pleasures in life. Indeed, few if any cooperative games can match the degree of challenge in traditional sports, which is so refined in baseball, for example, that the difference between a successful stolen base and throwing the base stealer out is usually a matter of inches. For many teens and adults, only such games will be stimulating enough to attract them. Besides, traditional youth sports need not be played as a competitive brawl. Games that have winners and losers can also be fun, teach cooperation, involve everyone, and do all the wonderful things ascribed to so-called cooperative and New Games.

Tim Gallwey, author of the classic *The Inner Game of Tennis,* points out that competitive sports can be an immensely valuable tool for personal development when winning is viewed as "overcoming obstacles to reach a goal." In other words, only when your children's opponents make their best effort can they push your kids to make theirs. Thus, both sides must cooperate if either is to achieve new heights of accomplished play. Seen this way, winning a game becomes less important in its own right than as hard evidence of a supreme effort. If you can communicate this spirit to your children, they will get much more from their sports, no matter how well they do. And you, too, will notice the difference as they grow from the experience.

Try the following ideas for investing the sports your children play with some of the benefits of alternative games:

- *Play a mixed-ages, mixed-gender, mixed-skills game.* Set up a touch football, basketball, softball, or soccer game with teams that mix kids and adults, boys and girls, men and women, and the skilled and lesser-skilled. With teams this diverse, we can almost guarantee that the game will be about fun and mutual support first and foremost.

- *Practice teamwork.* Most traditional sports have cooperative elements that require tight coordination between two or more players for a play to work. Practice these with your kids or work with them to do the same with their friends.

- *Play catch.* A good game of catch with a football, baseball, softball, or whatever requires a decent throw and some effort by the receiver to complete the exchange. What could be more cooperative than that?

- *Encourage your children to play sports with friends of comparable ability.* Sports played between good friends have a special quality, so long as the players' abilities are similar enough to make the acitivity a true game. Friends play to win but generally not to the point of grinding their buddies' self-confidence into the dirt. When the game is over, so is the combat.

- *Acknowledge cooperative play when watching sports with your kids.* This may require first learning how to watch team sports yourself. That is, don't just concentrate on the player with the ball, widen your focus to see what his or her teammates are doing to help make the play successful. Acknowledge the good blocks in football, the good screens and passes in basketball, hitting behind the runner in baseball, and so on. The winning team almost always plays more cooperatively than the losers—note that to your children as it makes itself evident in a game.

CHAPTER 8 RESOURCES

A Holistic View of Competitive Youth Sports

BOOKS AND PUBLICATIONS
Good Sports: The Concerned Parent's Guide to Competitive Youth Sports by Rick Wolff (Champaign, IL: Sagamore Publishing, 1997).
>   A smart, accessible rundown of what's wrong with youth sports, and how parents can remedy it. Written by a frequent contributor to *Sports Illustrated.*
Positive Coaching by Jim Thompson (Portola Valley, CA: Warde Publishers, 1995).
>   Subtitled "Building Character and Self-Esteem Through Sports," the book focuses on a philosophy of "relentless positivity" and offers a perspective that is both sensible and inspiring.
The Total Sports Experience for Kids: A Parents' Guide to Success in Youth Sports, by Aubrey H. Fine, Ed.D., and Michael L. Sachs, Ph.D. (South Bend, IN: Diamond Communications, 1997).
>   Two sports psychologists look at competitive youth sports from the perspective that winning isn't "the only thing," but trying to win is.

Popular Sports Through the Body/Mind Looking Glass

An Athletes' Guide to Mental Training by Robert Nideffer, Ph.D. (Human Kinetics, 1985).
>   Sports psychology pioneer Nideffer teaches mental techniques for performance enhancement and overcoming performance anxiety. Many exercises are drawn from holistic body/mind methods such as meditation, visualization, and biofeedback.
The Ultimate Athlete by George Leonard (Viking, 1974).
>   A groundbreaking book on the spiritual aspects of sport.

The Health Benefits and Risks of Your Child's Favorite Sports

Rating the Exercises by Charles T. Kuntzleman and the editors of *Consumer Guide* (Morrow, 1978).
Details the physical fitness benefits of a wide variety of sports.

Youth Sports Injuries: A Medical Handbook for Parents and Coaches by John F. Duff, M.D. (Collier, 1992).
Comprehensive, clearly written, and well-laid-out guide to injuries in youth sports. Covers prevention as well as how to identify and treat injuries. Includes a short section on how to involve children with disabilities in sports.

Cooperative and Noncompetitive Games

The Cooperative Sports & Game Book by Terry Orlick (New York, NY: Pantheon, 1978).
Orlick claims all his games are kid-tested. Chapters on games for kids ages three to seven, eight to twelve, and adults including remakes of traditional sports, games from other cultures, tips on games for preschoolers, and suggestions for creating your own games.

The Second Cooperative Sports & Game Book by Terry Orlick (Random House, 1982).
Two hundred more cooperative games for kids and adults.

9

greening your family

omewhere in the grade-school years, today's children begin
to understand that things they have taken for granted up to
now—enough clean water to drink, forests, pandas, elephants,
tigers, and other magnificent species featured in their favorite books—are all big question marks in their future. They can't necessarily recite the specifics of the loss of natural resources and wildlife
but they get the big picture: They are being handed a planet in a precarious and rapidly declining condition.

Children can go two ways with this information. They can feel that
the situation is so overwhelming that there's nothing they can do about
it. Or they will look to be environmental heroes, convinced that doing
their part really will make a critical difference.

Which of these alternatives our kids choose is largely up to us as parents. When we show them ways they can help preserve and restore the
earth, they feel more confident about the future and empowered to do
something on the planet's behalf.

Making environmentalism a family value isn't just about helping our

kids feel better about things. Raising environmentally conscious kids is also one of the most profound contributions parents can make to the planet itself. Daunting environmental problems such as global warming, deforestation, and pollution of the ozone layer can't wait much longer for us to react to them. Only if the lifestyle of the current generation of children includes recycling, conservation of water and energy, low-emission transportation, and other resource- and pollution-saving steps will the earth remain a comfortable place to live.

This chapter begins on a spiritual note, as we discuss teaching your children the wisdom of nature and a sense of place. By having a greater appreciation for the wonders of the natural world and their place in it, your kids will be more motivated to be considerate of nature. They'll also have a better understanding of just what the planet needs from them. Next we cover the simple, greener lifestyle changes you can teach your children, and other lifestyle changes you can model for them. Finally, we touch on a simple restoration project—planting trees—that the whole family can do together. Collectively, these actions send an important message to your children: The planet's going to make it, but only if we all get behind it and push.

TEACHING YOUR CHILDREN TO APPRECIATE THE WISDOM OF NATURE

Teaching kids to appreciate nature's wonders doesn't need to be justified. It's simply part of their being more fully alive in the world. But you can hardly blame us sneaky Whole Parenting types if we have other agendas in mind, too. If our children learn to care deeply for animals and plants and the natural systems of which they're a part, they're likely to care enough when they grow up to help protect them.

Actually, it doesn't take much teaching to turn children on to natural wonder. There's nothing more instructive about the natural world than just hanging out in it, so most of the activities described below are just variations on this simple theme. By the way, you can find bundles of additional ideas along these lines in the books reviewed in the Resources at the end of this chapter.

Sensory wake-up. Pick a quiet, natural spot to sit with your kids—near a lake, in the woods, in a park, or even in your backyard if appropriate. Have everyone close their eyes and just take in the sounds for a few minutes. Then open your eyes and add sights to what you've noticed with your ears. Now without talking, begin to walk around, touching and sniffing what's around you—the earth and grass beneath your feet, the rocks and plants around you, the fallen leaves and twigs, and so on. Respect for the earth begins with intimate familiarity with it.

Natural medicine chest. Learn what herbs grow in your area, where they grow, what they do in the body, and how to identify them. (See "A Family Herbal" on page 155 for some of the most effective and useful medicinal plants.) Take your children on an excursion to find some—or to a local herb garden—so they can see how nature provides medicines for so many of our ills. You can grow and use herbs at home, too.

Natural recycling depot. On a stroll in the woods, find a rotting, fallen log and show your kids all the life forms it harbors—your stump may provide a home to insects, lizards, squirrels, mice, fungi, plant life, and so on. Near the log will be fallen leaves, pine needles, and other "refuse" from the surrounding trees that will rot and contribute their energy and minerals back to the forest's health. Demonstrate to your kids how the forest is a complete system that depends upon the recycling of its dead matter as much as the survival of its living things.

Meet your neighbors, the birds. Buy or make several bird feeders and place them around your yard within easy sight through windows. Soon several of your feathered neighbors will be dropping by for a snack. Be sure to have field guides on hand so you can learn your neighbors' names. To make simple bird feeders from pinecones, tie long strings to the end of each cone and then spread a little peanut butter in the spaces between the cones' bracts. Hang the cones from branches in your yard.

Snowflake "collection." Put a few sheets of black paper in your freezer to keep them cold. When it begins to snow, give the frozen paper to your kids and send them out to catch some snowflakes. The black background will show off the facets of each flake with maximum clarity and the cold surface will allow your kids to observe the flakes for a while before they melt. Ask your children how each flake is alike (each has six arms, unless some have broken off) and how each is different (each has a unique pattern).

Animal detective. After a snowfall or not-too-heavy rain, go outside with your kids to search for animal tracks. Have them note where the tracks go and see if you can figure out together what kind of animals made the tracks and what they're up to.

Garden world. We've already given you several good reasons to plant an organic vegetable garden—for example, growing healthful food and getting your kids to eat more veggies. Here's another one: It's a perfect experiment for Ecology 101. Backyard agriculture with your children gives you the opportunity to discuss the ecology of the soil, observe the critters (wanted and unwanted) that visit or inhabit the place, and watch the growth process from seed to edible plant.

Seashore detective. The next time you take your children to the beach, suggest they sift through the sand and sort through the piles of seaweed and other natural debris for evidence of different marine plant and animal species. Have your kids count all the different plant pieces, shells, feathers, and fish bones to paint a picture of the variety of life in this ecosystem.

Eco-tube. Nature documentaries on TV can provide a superb education about wildlife and the environment. Such shows as PBS's *Nature* and *Wild America* and the many nature programs on The Discovery Channel do an outstanding job of teaching viewers about animal behavior and the ways that environmental degradation threatens various species' survival. Even shows not written for kids will connect with them because of kids' fascination with animals. Nature shows also make worthwhile viewing for families to share.

As with any child game or learning experience, never forget your purpose—to entertain, delight, and educate your kids. That won't happen if you stick so closely to the activity's "rules" that you turn your children off. Go with the flow—*their* flow. If they want to improvise or go do something else, so be it. That's nature's way, too, and your sensitivity to it helps teach the lesson you wanted them to get in the first place.

HELPING YOUR CHILDREN DEVELOP A SENSE OF PLACE

From early in their lives, we talk to our children about what it means to be a citizen of a place—about being considerate to the family's neighbors, about the public parks and other facilities that belong to everybody, about what it means to vote. But there's another form of citizenship that often gets neglected in these conversations, what poet Gary Snyder calls citizenship of the "deep old biological communities of the land." This isn't just about being better environmental citizens. It's about, as Snyder puts it, observing the etiquette of the place we live, being grateful for what its original residents—plants, animals, rivers, mountains—contribute to make our lives better, understanding how to use the tools of the place, and learning "the songs that it takes to live there."

Essentially, we're talking about getting to know the neighborhood and all of its inhabitants and all of their interlocking relationships in a profound way. This understanding of local ecology, including our human role in it, is also a big part of what's called building a "sense of place." Children love this sort of learning. They naturally want to know more about the animals and plants they see every day, and where the rivers come from, and how the mountains got there, and why people cut trees and clear land. For parents, too, this can be a wonderfully satisfying exercise, for how many of us wouldn't want to expand our sense of place if only we had a reason to make time for it? Our children, and their curiosity about the place they're inheriting, provide that reason.

Your community abounds with resources for teaching a sense of place. Try some of the following family activities for starters:

- Purchase or borrow from the library books that explain the local and regional ecology and how the local economy depends upon it so you can answer questions your children ask. Also obtain nature field guides so you can help them identify any species they observe.

- Your local natural history museum almost certainly offers low-cost or free classes for young people on the flora, fauna, and geology of your region. Nature and outdoor stores may offer such classes as well.

- In state and national parks near your home, rangers will offer guided hikes and talks about the land and life forms it supports.

- Take your own excursions and hikes with your children, armed with field guides and binoculars so you can identify species. But put the books down at times, and just observe the relationships of your fellow ecological citizens there.

· Discuss the local water and weather cycle with your children and how it affects ordinary life in your area, including how the local economy is affected by the weather.

· Show your children how certain industries in your area depend upon the resources of the land. Perhaps some local resource—dependent industrial plants offer tours that you and your children can attend.

· Discuss local and regional environmental issues with your children. Explain varying points of view about them as best you can and possible solutions that might benefit all contending parties.

· Talk to your children about conflicts between natural and human borders—for example, how the things people spray on their grounds or into the air above their property can affect the water other people, animals, and plants drink and the air they breathe.

· Talk to your children about the endangered species in your area and how their numbers came to dwindle.

There is, of course, a larger lesson here to teach your kids—that the land, its climate, and its plant and animal, including human animal, inhabitants are all connected. But this perhaps is a lecture best left undelivered. Simply getting to know your place in the ways already suggested will make this teaching abundantly clear.

TEACHING YOUR CHILDREN TO CONSERVE

Young children don't understand the concept of "waste." Where does water come from? In their minds, the tap. Just turn it on and there's always more. And who needs a Supreme Being? Just flip the switch and Let There Be Light! Unfortunately, the evidence suggests that few children, in affluent countries anyway, ever grow out of this particular form of magical thinking. Most of us put more stuff in our garbage cans each week than families in some countries *own*. Then there are the thousands of tons of fossil fuel energy we consume lighting and heating our dwellings or driving our vehicles.

A quick scan of the numbers confirms the role of our "little" household in planetary decline. Industrialized nations make up only 22 percent of the world's population, but they generate 91 percent of its industrial waste, 93 percent of its industrial pollutants, 95 percent of its hazardous waste, and 74 percent of its carbon dioxide emissions. And we Americans are by far the worst of the lot, yet our extravagant ways are precisely the model that billions of consumers in the developing world can't wait to emulate.

If we make clear to our kids what's at stake, they will be anxious to help reverse these trends. Children feel closer to nature and identify with it more than most adults do. And kids have a simpler set of morals than we do. They're far less likely to split ethical hairs when it comes to saving birds and trees. Thus, it's often we who have to change, consuming less and conserving more. It then becomes a simple matter to teach our kids how to do the same.

Below we focus on the "conserve" side of the equation. But please note that our lists sample only the most *kid-friendly* activities you can undertake. When it comes to curbing your family's use of materials and energy, there's much more you can do as an adult. Modeling that behavior (see the Resources at the end of this chapter for ideas) and explaining to your children why you are taking these steps is just as powerful a lesson as the activities you do with them.

Shopping

· Before buying anything—books, toys, bikes, cars, furniture, appliances—research whether you can get what you need used. Show your kids that there's an entire economy of used items out there—stores, garage sales, columns of secondhand goods in the newspaper's classified ads, and private publications like *The Car Trader*.

· When you shop with your kids for toys and clothes, show them how things that are poorly made lead to more use of resources. Encourage them to select things that are durable, which is also a good lesson in design and quality, and teach them the environmental value of taking care of their things.

- Show your children how much material goes to waste as discarded packaging and encourage them to save trees and other resources by rejecting items, such as individually wrapped snack foods, that are over-packaged.

- When you go shopping with your kids (as well as alone), bring bags with you and refuse unneeded bags at the checkout counter.

- Buy large, economy-sized items to save packaging and involve your kids in redistributing the item into smaller containers at home. For example, buy large bottles of shampoo and have them help you pour the shampoo into smaller bottles to distribute to each bathroom.

- Buy items made from recycled materials such as recycled-content office paper. Explain to your kids how such purchases help conserve the earth's natural resources.

Saving Water

- Teach your kids that leaving the water running while they brush their teeth sends several wasted gallons down the drain every day, which can add up to thousands of gallons a year. And running the water while they wash dishes will waste several times that. Show them how to do the dishes by filling a sink with soapy water, rinsing in a modest stream from the faucet, and always turning off the water when it's not being used.

- Involve your kids in buying and installing low-flow shower heads and faucet aerators (flow controllers). Together, you can also fill a plastic jug with rocks and water to take up space in the toilet's tank. Encourage them to take short showers instead of baths, too. Teach them that all of these actions together will save the planet many thousands of gallons of clean water every year and that low-flow faucets also save power when hot water is run.

- If you run your tap for a minute or two (as you should) to clear out unhealthful impurities before drinking, fill several bottles or pitchers afterward and get your drinking water from them. Have your kids help and explain how doing it this way saves water.

- Take your kids with you to the nursery to buy outdoor plants, selecting attractive food plants instead of ornamentals when you can and low-water varieties when you can't. Once you explain your strategy, they'll probably be fiercer about saving water than you are.

Saving Electricity, Gas, and Gasoline

- With kids in tow, purchase and install compact fluorescent bulbs for the commonly used light fixtures in your home. Explain that each bulb uses only one fourth the energy of a regular bulb and that this helps prevent air pollution, acid rain, and global warming, thereby saving the lives of animals, fish, and plants.

- Remind your kids that TVs and radios use polluting power too and should only be on when someone is viewing a specific program, not when they're just channel-flipping.

- Teach your kids to do their reading whenever possible in a room that is lit by daylight or already occupied.

- Encourage your kids to walk or ride their bikes whenever possible instead of asking to be driven. Explain how cars contribute to air pollution, acid rain, and global warming and model your concern by forming carpools for school and their outside activities.

- Explain to your children that it wastes power to stare into an open refrigerator rather than opening it only when they know what they want.

- Tell your kids that they should turn their computer monitors off if they're going to be away from them for more than a few minutes. Sure, the screen saver looks cool, you can say, but you get plenty of chances to see it in the normal course of using the computer.

- Teach your kids how to save power by opening and closing curtains, shades, and windows at the appropriate times to heat or cool the house. Explain to them that air conditioners are wasteful, power-hungry appliances that should only be used as a last resort. Demonstrate how you can control your house's temperature on hot days by keeping windows open at night to let in cool air and closing them early in the morning to shut cool air in and warm air out.

Saving Raw Materials

- In the kitchen, demonstrate to your kids that it's much less wasteful to dry their hands on a dish towel and clean up messes with a sponge or

GORDON PIPER

rag rather than use paper towels. Show them that plastic bags can be washed, dried, and reused as can aluminum foil in many cases. Have them store their uneaten food in washable containers instead of plastic or aluminum wrap.

- Pack your kids' school lunches in reusable plastic containers and use lunch pails instead of bags.

- Make sure your kids observe that you always attempt to repair or reuse something you already have before purchasing something new.

Another Way to Make a Difference

Assist your children in writing letters to company CEOs to complain about environmentally destructive products and express gratitude for planet-friendly ones. Explain to your kids that while individual consumer behavior is important, letters are even more powerful because most companies see them as representing many more people like the writers themselves.

INVOLVING YOUR CHILDREN IN RECYCLING AND COMPOSTING

Recycling has long been the most user-friendly form of environmental citizenship. With curbside pickups, community recycling centers, and recycling bins at local retailers, this green behavior requires little more effort than carrying out the trash and, cumulatively, it makes a real difference.

What recycling does for adults' spirits it can also do for kids. Children love doing things that Mom and Dad approve of and that help other living things. But just as meaningful to them is that fact that most recycling activities fall well within their developing capabilities. Even toddlers can lug aluminum cans or newspapers to their proper bin. Once kids reach school-age, they can help with almost every aspect of recycling—separating colored glass bottles, composting, even helping out at the local recycling center. Motivated teens have often started and managed recycling programs at schools that didn't previously have one.

For parents, recycling provides no end of "teachable moments" for environmental lessons—about how waste strains the planet's resources, about responsible consuming, about nature's own processes for recycling raw materials, about green economics. We imagine that you are well aware of all the different aspects of recycling. But you may not have thought about all the ways your kids can participate or the potential learning opportunities involved. Try some of the following:

Do the stomp, the stomp, the aluminum can stomp. Many recycling centers request that you flatten your aluminum pop cans before dropping them off. This may be a chore for you but your school-age youngsters will see this as glorious fun and a permissible way to be destructive and constructive all at once. Toddlers may not have the weight to do their own can smashing but they'll enjoy being the "set-up" person who places the cans on the floor for their siblings to stomp.

The hand-me-down sweep. Help your kids go through their closets and toy shelves and box up things they don't need. They will be especially proud to pass on their belongings to other children if you take them with you to the place where you drop the items off—the Goodwill, Salvation Army, or hospital.

Garbage stew. Build or buy a compost bin or simply designate an area for a compost pile in your yard. Even your toddlers will proudly collect the hair off hair brushes, apple cores, and other easily handled organic wastes to add to the compost. They'll also love assisting you in adding the leaves, grass clippings, coffee grinds, and other kitchen wastes. They won't be much help when it comes to giving the pile the occasional turn with a shovel it needs, but if they have their mini-shovel on hand, they'll be pleased to try. To give your kids a special thrill, and speed up the composting, buy some red worms at the local nursery or bait shop and turn them loose on the pile—while your kids are watching, of course. Explain how nature takes all this garbage and turns it into rich food for plants. For example, the worms eat garbage and turn it into soil.

Green computing. Put a box by the family computer so that you and your school-age kids can drop used computer paper in for recycling. But place a separate box next to it for paper that has only been printed on one side so it be placed back into the printer for draft copies. Teach your kids that while printing on both sides of the paper is a good thing, it's even better when they can avoid printing altogether and simply store data electronically on the hard disk or floppies.

Activism 101. Schools generate many tons of waste per year, from paper to beverage cans to cardboard packaging. The cafeteria alone will produce huge quantities of such recyclables as cans, glass bottles and jars, and of course uneaten and spoiled food. If your teen has the green bug, suggest that she investigate the state of her school's recycling and take the initiative to fill any gaps she finds.

A recycled world. Your kids will feel far more motivated to do these jobs if they see the results of it in the world. When they accompany you on shopping trips or are just tooling about the house with you, point out the various items that contain recycled materials—the boxes that many of their favorite cookies, crackers, and cereals come in (recycled cardboard packaging will be gray on the inside); possibly a large portion of the family's daily newspaper; special "green" products such as recycled-content office paper, and more. Some companies these days are even making fabrics such as T-shirt material from discarded plastic pop bottles. If your kids still doubt that anybody really uses all this "junk," show them the listings of companies in the yellow pages that buy or sell recycled commodities.

There is just one downside to involving your kids in the family's recycling—they may try to "out-green" you. They will be absolutely uncompromising, wanting to reuse or recycle the tiniest scraps of things. At times, you'll feel that you need to give them a lesson about proportion. At other times, they'll teach you just as much about not cutting corners!

TEACHING YOUR CHILDREN ABOUT SIMPLE LIVING

We just looked at the impact our extravagant lifestyles make on the limited resources of the planet. Here we look at the negative messages our lifestyles send to our children, and what we can do to turn that around.

Many American consumption patterns have little to do with *need.* We don't *need* an 1,800-square-foot home or a closet full of the latest fashions just to protect us from the elements. We may need a car to get us to work or our kids to school but we don't necessarily need a new, trendy, or big one. We don't need a faddish soft drink to slake our thirst—simple water will do the job, far more effectively and cheaper.

We overconsume because we let advertisers convince us that things we want are things we need. This confusion of wants and needs leads to a virtual addiction to consuming. It also makes it very difficult for us to talk our kids out of the $150 sneakers or $50 doll they think they need to make them feel secure.

Limiting consumption isn't a matter of sacrificing, or shouldn't be anyway. As Vicki Robin, coauthor of *Your Money or Your Life* (see the Resources at the end of this chapter) writes, it's a matter of knowing when enough is enough. Sacrifice ultimately backfires by building up resentment and a desire to splurge to make up for past deprivation.

Most of the recommendations below are also tenets of the "simplicity" movement, which is made up of a broad group of Americans who for various reasons—including a desire to escape the workaday rat race, an overdose of consumer debt, inadequate income, a wish for greener living, and an opposition to commercial culture—are reducing their debt, increasing their savings, and most importantly, cutting way back significantly on their purchases. Because the behavior we model for our children is even more important to them than the words we speak, the following recommendations address parents' actions as well as kids':

- Whenever you experience the urge to buy something, ask yourself the following questions: Is this something I really need? How much am I likely to use it? Is it worth the amount of my life I spent to earn the money to pay for it? Do I already own something that could meet my needs or wants just as well? When your kids plead with you to buy them things, go through the same questions with them. This sort of reflection helps defeat advertising, which is based on the hope that we won't examine its questionable and often silly assumptions.

- Instead of shopping to fill your time, spend that time serving others—assisting at your child's school, coaching your child's sports team, visiting an elderly person—and see how the experience compares to the pleasures of "recreational" shopping.

- Limit the amount of time your children watch television. Television feeds the consumption habit in several ways. It exposes your kids to a flood of commercial messages, which research shows children are more vulnerable to than are adults. Television also takes the place of activities such as social play with other kids. Such activities are intrinsically satisfying and reduce the desire to fill emotional needs with purchases.

- The next time your kids ask you to buy them the latest hot clothing item that "all the kids are wearing," take the opportunity to educate them about how corporations create fads and trends, and also how they plan for fads and trends to expire so they can replace them with new ones. Ask your kids how they feel about allowing their emotions to be manipulated like that.

- When you do spend money on yourself and your family, try spending it less on frivolous material objects and more on things that help you grow intellectually, spiritually, and emotionally—educational courses, self-development workshops, spiritual retreats, sports training, and nature excursions. Such activities can dramatically improve quality of life, a claim most advertisers make for their goods but can't deliver. This form of consumption can easily be sustained even by our threatened environment. It also addresses the root cause of much overconsumption—the futile attempt to satisfy inner, nonmaterial desires such as the desire for higher self-esteem with outer, material objects.

FAMILY TREE-PLANTING

When people see an old, majestic tree, they often imagine, "If it could speak, what stories it might tell!" Some trees have watched generations, even whole civilizations, come and go. Some have survived hurricanes, tornadoes, and wars. The biggest ones lord over their surroundings, tall, wizened, and strong. But if trees *could* talk, they'd probably yell, "HELP!"

Forests once covered about 40 percent of the earth's land surface. Today, almost a third of that forest cover has been cleared away and much of the rest is being felled at a horrific rate. When trees go, we lose benefits to almost all life on earth. Homes for birds, animals, and insects disappear. So do nuts, fruits, and raw materials that would have become paper and lumber. Shade for creatures and plants on the ground is gone. Lost too are the fallen leaves, twigs, branches, and bark that would otherwise decompose and replenish the soil so it can nourish other growing things.

Trees and the plants they help support also prevent erosion because their roots bind the earth together. They help clean our air and make it breathable by absorbing carbon dioxide and releasing oxygen. This same attribute helps offset global warming. Planted on the sunny side of buildings, trees provide natural air conditioning and reduce energy dependency, which also affects global warming. Trees nourish our souls, too, and they are friends to our children. They greet them with outstretched "arms" and invite them to climb up in their branches for a different view of the world.

No wonder then that tree planting is considered one of the most important forms of environmental restoration. It's also one of the most accessible, so it makes a perfect low-tech, high-yield project for the family. If you and your kids want to make an ecological contribution together, what makes a more lasting impact on the landscape?

Tips for a Successful Tree-Planting Project

It isn't particularly complicated to put a tree in the ground and have it grow. But if you're aiming your project for property other than your own, a little planning is clearly required. And even planting in your own yard requires a little more know-how than wielding a shovel and turning on the water. Here are some tips:

- If planning a public project, check with your local civic center or city- or town hall to be sure you have the proper permits or authorization from the parks department or other committees governing the area you want to work in. If you want to contribute work to privately owned property, approach the owners with your offer and be sure to let them know what to expect—when you'll be on the property and how long the project will take.

- Ask your area garden clubs, parks department, or your state division of forestry for advice on community projects. You might even end up with contributed saplings or native plants and wildflowers to plant around your tree. Some organizations might also supply you with tools and a person who can answer any further questions you might have. Ask for what you need—you might just get it.

- Select a planting date that works in the tree's favor. Early spring or in the fall are the best times to plant trees and shrubs.

- Seek the advice of an expert before you dig in. A little library research and a chat with a local nursery expert will tell you what kind of tree to plant in the local soil and how to prepare the soil with peat moss and fertilizer.

- Remember that trees need space above and below ground, so don't plan locations that are too close to buildings or under phone and electric wires. And allow for proper space between saplings if you're planting more than one.

- Make sure your planned location has easy access to water.

Once you've found a good planting site and done the other basic research and planning suggested above, you're ready to get your hands dirty. The following advice is general. Certain variations may apply depending on the type of tree you're planting and the conditions of your soil. If you have instructions from the source that supplied the tree, follow those instead:

1. Dig a starter hole a foot or more deep to check for drainage. Poor drainage could result in root rot. Fill the hole with water and check it to see if it drains out within twelve hours. If it does, the drainage system doesn't need your help. If it doesn't, you'll need to dig the hole a little deeper to make room for a few inches of rocks or gravel at the bottom.

2. Widen the hole so it fits the natural configuration of the roots plus some room to grow. The hole should be a foot deeper than the height of the roots and twice as wide as the span of the roots.

3. Loosen the soil on the sides and bottom of the hole to give root tips room to grow and assist with drainage.

4. Put the sapling or other young plant in the hole and begin to shovel soil around the roots, pressing it firmly to support the plant in an upright position. Pack the soil firmly to remove large air pockets.

5. When the hole is 3/4 filled with soil, saturate the soil with water. If the plant settles into the hole, pump it up and down in the soil until you have raised it to the proper level. Fill the remaining 1/4 of the hole with soil and water some more.

6. Water faithfully to keep the soil damp, especially if rainfall is scarce. Don't let the soil dry out but don't overwater, which could lead to root rot. Keep in mind that a sapling will be especially thirsty in its first growing season. Adding a three-inch layer of mulch, wood chips, peat moss, or leaf mold around the trunk will help keep the soil moist and save water.

7. A young sapling generally needs support from stakes and wires to keep it upright. But it should still be able to sway in the wind a bit; swaying strengthens the trunk. Once the tree is strong enough to fully support itself, remove the supports.

You and your family needn't try to out-Johnny Mr. Appleseed. Even planting one tree that you'll look after and care for is a meaningful act. But if you or your kids do feel like extending your reach, a little money can sometimes achieve a lot. When Willie Turkle of Groton, Massachusetts was in third grade, his class decided to see what they could accomplish for the environment just by collecting pennies. They enlisted other third grade classes in the effort, and within a month, they were "ready to deal." "With the money we raised, we bought several acres in the rain forest," Willie brags. They even had enough left over to purchase memorial trees at the school.

Chapter 9 Resources

General

50 Simple Things Kids Can Do to Save the Earth by The Earthworks Group (Andrews and McMeel, 1990).
    The best starter book for children's environmentalism. Brimming with simple see-for-yourself projects (take lid off the toilet tank and see how it works), boiled-down environmental information on why it matters, beginning kid activist steps such as writing to world leaders, and even ways to poke Mom and Dad into being better environmental role models. Written in kid-friendly language.
50 Simple Things You Can Do to Save the Earth by The Earthworks Group (Earthworks Press, 1989).
    A quick-reading bestseller packed with easy-to-do environmental actions, resources, and facts. See also *The Next Step: 50 More Things You Can Do to Save the Earth* by The Earthworks Group (Andrews and McMeel, 1991).

Teaching Your Children to Appreciate the Wisdom of Nature

How the Environment Works by Preston Gralla (Ziff-Davis, 1994).
    Not really a children's book but its rich illustrations and simple prose make it a valuable resource for all ages. A great resource for helping your children understand how what they see and hear in nature, including the impact of humans, interrelates.

Talking to Fireflies, Shrinking to the Moon: A Parent's Guide to Nature Activities by Edward Duensing (Plume, 1990).

Describes in friendly detail dozens of nature discovery activities you can undertake with your kids. Duensing's own childlike fascination with nature's wonders and weirdnesses animates every page.

Teaching Kids to Love the Earth by Marina Lachecki Herman, Joseph F. Passineau, Ann L. Schimpf, and Paul Treuer (Duluth, MN: Pfeifer-Hamilton, 1991).

A grab bag of activities, resource lists, related stories, and "Did You Know?" information sections. Also available: a second volume entitled *More Teaching Kids to Love the Earth.*

ORGANIZATIONS

National Audubon Society, 700 Broadway, New York, NY 10003, (212) 979–3000
website: www.audubon.org

Write to this organization or check out their website for information on bird feeding.

Helping Your Children Develop a Sense of Place

The "Celebrate the States" book series (Benchmark Books, 1997).

Series includes one volume for each state. These books give only a very introductory sense of natural features of a state, mainly in the Geography chapter, but other chapters— History, Government and Economy, People, Achievements, Landmarks—work together to give a good overall sense of place from a state perspective. Each volume also lists en- dangered animals and plants and other prominent species, as well as manufactured prod- ucts, agricultural products, and natural resources for that state.

The Golden Field Guides series (Golden Press, New York).

Well-designed, no page-flipping required to match pictures, maps, and text. The series includes *Birds of North America, Trees of North America, Rocks and Minerals, Seashells of North America,* and *Amphibians of North America.*

Teaching Your Children to Conserve

BOOKS

Consumer Guide to Home Energy Savings by Alex Wilson and John Morrill (Washington, DC and Berkeley, CA: American Council for an Energy-Efficient Economy, 1995).

Guide to the best energy-efficient products and how to use them, plus other energy- saving strategies.

See also books reviewed under "General" above.

ORGANIZATIONS

Most local utilities will provide energy audits and easy-to-follow written guides for free. Many also offer free items such as water heater blankets. Call your local utility to see what as- sistance they can offer.

Teaching Your Children About Simple Living

The Simple Living Guide by Janet Luhrs (Broadway Books, 1997).

Living a life that is more sustainable—psychologically, bodily, and financially—by making careful choices. By the founder/editor of *The Simple Living Journal.*

Voluntary Simplicity: Toward a Way of Life That Is Outwardly Simple, Inwardly Rich by Duane Elgin (Morrow, 1981).

A bible of the simplicity movement, along with the book reviewed below.

Your Money or Your Life by Joe Dominguez and Vicki Robin (Viking, 1992).

The title of this book says it all about what our possessions and shopping addiction cost us in real happiness and satisfaction. The environmental significance of this book for a sustainable society is profound.

Family Tree-Planting

BOOK

Taking Care of the Earth—Kids in Action by Laurence Pringle (Honesdale, PA: Caroline House, 1997).

Pringle describes numerous kid- and earth-friendly projects.

ORGANIZATIONS

Global ReLeaf 2000, American Forestery Association, P.O. Box 2000, Washington, DC 20013, (800) 873–5323
website: www.amfor.org

Project aimed at planting twenty million trees by the year 2000.

For information on tree planting groups in your area, contact your state urban forest coordinator, local extension agent, or the National Alliance for Community Trees at (800) 228–8886.

10

a sense of community

hildren grow up as members of several communities at once, as if at the center of concentric ripples when a stone is tossed into a pond. Most immediately, children belong to a family. That basic unit is in turn linked to a larger, extended group of relatives, some of whom may live as far away as the other side of the world. Kids also live in a neighborhood, a community of people with geographical ties and interests both intertwined and diverse. The neighborhood exists within a larger, local entity—a town or city or county—again made up of people with both shared and competing concerns. Children belong to a cultural community as well—this may be more obvious with ethnic cultures that cultivate consciousness of their heritage, such as Jews, African Americans, Latinos, or Asian cultures, but it is no less true for others. And, of course, all children are part of the planet's human family, itself a strand in the web of all living things.

But none of this is obvious to a child. Unless their parents encourage and celebrate the loving, communal aspects of family, children are likely to take their immediate family for granted. Unless parents and relatives emphasize it, children won't experience the affections and support of an active extended family or cultural community, either. If the family lives in isolation from its neighbors, the child won't understand community at that level. Nor are children likely to get their human and ecological family connections without their parents' help because this is a society that emphasizes achievements of the individual, not the collective welfare of the many.

Fostering an experience of community in your child fits into Whole Parenting in several ways. For one thing, a sense of community in the different dimensions we've mentioned helps a child know herself in a deeper way: I am a Jefferson or a Levy, I'm an African American or an Irish American, I'm a San Franciscan or a Bostonian, and so on. Community consciousness grows familial love, compassion, and social responsibility. And it expands children spiritually by expanding their awareness of both self and others including, potentially, other species.

The topics in this chapter will aid you in teaching your child about community from several angles, starting with her community of family relations. The community value of being of service, which we cover in our section on volunteerism, activism, and charity, demonstrates to children that giving to others or to the planet as a whole is really giving to oneself, experientially and otherwise. Family vacations can also incorporate community values, as the section on volunteer and homestay vacations reveals.

Parents hunger for community, too. Many hope to network with other moms and dads, to meet both practical and emotional needs. In the following pages, we'll show you how.

JUMPING IN THE GENE POOL—CULTIVATING RELATIONSHIPS WITH EXTENDED FAMILY

Just a few generations ago, the term "extended family" and the single word "family" meant much the same thing. A widowed grandmother might make her home in an upstairs guest room, aunts and uncles and cousins lived just blocks away, and regular gatherings of the whole brood kept the extra leaf of the dining-room table in constant use.

Over the last few decades, the shift in family composition has been so dramatic that even the so-called nuclear unit is becoming the exception. Nowadays, extended family as likely refers to ex-spouses, stepchildren, and multiple sets of grandparents, while work demands and after-school activities make it a challenge to get even one household to the table for dinner. Chances are that in the course of chasing job opportunities and independent lifestyles, your family of origin has scattered to all parts of the country. For many of us, catching up with relatives at an annual holiday bash is as close as we get to true family togetherness.

In her 1997 book, First Lady Hillary Rodham Clinton popularized the African proverb "It takes a village to raise a child," which emphasizes communal responsibility for the care of our children. Lost in the translation, however, is the likelihood that the "village" of the saying was actually an extended family network—aunts, uncles, grandparents, and others with strong biological, emotional, and spiritual ties. Not that building community beyond family isn't valuable, as we discuss elsewhere in this chapter, but we're intrigued by the tribal origins from which community springs, a concept of clan that lingers in the collective unconscious. As our culture's definition of family grows increasingly amorphous, it's not hard to understand why many of us seek to forge closer links with those we can call kin.

Perhaps new parents feel this urge most keenly. With families living far apart, we're far less likely than previous generations to have built-in caretakers. Yet we're much more in need of them because of modern financial pressures that make it harder for parents to stay home with the kids. For those able to turn to extended family for child care, the benefits can be incalculable. Michael Daley—an Irish American whose wife, Tushalini, is from an East Indian family—discovered this even before their son, Connor, was born. "Tusha comes from an extended-family culture, and she's always been close to her cousins," Michael says. "They all live either in one house or within five minutes of each other. That support structure and closeness they have, it's not something they need to rekindle—it's always there." When Connor entered the picture, Tusha's mother moved into their Boston home to care for her grandson, and other family members took over on days when she couldn't be there. "Knowing they were going to be taking care of Connor made for a lot less worry in our lives," says Michael.

Then a job transfer led the Daleys to relocate to San Francisco, where they had no relatives nearby. While they hope to network with other parents in their new neighborhood, Michael feels that leaving his son with friends will always be "more of a request" than it would be with family. He also fears that the distance will slacken the family's emotional ties. And so it goes in America, where geographic mobility makes experiencing a sense of community one of the greatest challenges for American families to overcome. And working parents like the Daleys feel it most of all.

The Grandparent Connection

For many of us who rebelled against our own folks, the experience of becoming a parent has been chastening—especially when we find ourselves seeking support from *our* moms and dads. But fostering such a cross-generational connection is also vital to the health of the family, some experts say. According to family psychiatrist Arthur Kornhaber, M.D., known as the "Dr. Spock of grandparenting," the grandparent/grandchild bond is second in emotional importance only to the bond between parent and child.

MICHAEL ALLEN JONES

Nurturing grandparents offer a young child a brand of unconditional love and support rarely found anywhere else, playing roles as varied as mentor, spiritual teacher, family historian, and co-conspirator. This connection continues to be valuable into the turbulent adolescent years: While parent/teen interactions may be fraught with tensions, adolescents usually feel less need to assert their separateness from grandparents, who can provide an important emotional sanctuary. Indeed, it's been said, only half-jokingly, that grandparents and grandchildren get along so well "because they have the same enemies."

While most children today do not live with—or even nearby—their grandparents, short periods of intimate contact can go a long way toward cementing a bond that will withstand time and distance. To this end, Dr. Kornhaber has set up a weeklong Grandparent/Grandchild Camp in the Adirondacks, offering one-on-one activities for grandparents and grandchildren who may live thousands of miles apart (see the Resources at the end of this chapter). Periodic visits to one home or the other (scheduled off-season for the best discounts) or trips taken together can also fulfill this goal.

Meanwhile, it's important for grandparents and grandchildren to stay in touch when they're *not* together. Here are some suggestions, many of which can also be applied to other relatives who live far away:

Telephone time. To avoid having the phone ring during dinner- or bath-time chaos, parents and grandparents might want to agree on a mutually convenient calling time that grandchildren can look forward to.

Video visits. Family camcorders make it a cinch to record special occasions—birthdays, holidays, school performances—for the benefit of absentee grandparents. Even more touching are the everyday moments captured in between. On their end, grandparents might tape themselves telling anecdotes, planting spring bulbs, or baking a favorite recipe.

Audio action. Dr. Kornhaber tells of one family that flips on the tape recorder at dinnertime, letting the grandparents in on the way they *really* interact. Gramps and grandma may want to tape-record themselves reading bedtime stories. Or try this variation: Start a suspenseful story that stops at the cliffhanger point—and invite the grandchild to add the next chapter.

It's in the mail. Sent by snail mail, e-mail, or fax machine, letters between grandchildren and grandparents create a stack of keepsakes that grow more poignant with every passing year. Flourishes such as funny little drawings or photographs make them all the more memorable.

Getting the Whole Clan Together

Even when extended family live nearby, it can take a major production to gather the entire tribe—not counting weddings, anniversaries, bar mitzvahs, and other formal affairs, that is. As a result, some families aren't able to see each other as often as they'd like, despite their best intentions. To overcome this hurdle, some families set up their own standing organizations to manage the details. Alan's family on his father's side has met regularly as "The Cousins Club" since 1958. The group is tightly structured in some respects (members pay dues, for example) because it has to be: Events such as the annual Passover seder can draw over one hundred people from all over the country. But that's where the formality ends. "This is one big, happy, funky bunch," says Alan. "First cousin, fifth cousin, blood relative, married-in—doesn't matter. You decide if you belong. No one else makes any distinctions."

This special dynamic has made the idea of family-as-community immediate and direct, not abstract, for Cousins Club members. Realizing that what they have created is rare, Alan and the other parents in every generation of the clan have striven not only to preserve family closeness, but also to reinforce its value in their children. Not every family enjoys the type of camaraderie that lends itself to a Cousins Club. But when affectionate relationships do exist naturally among extended-family members, they are an invaluable resource to pass along to kids. Family is always there for you in a way that friends may not be. And friendships between relatives, when they form, tend to be especially deep, because of shared genes and histories.

Shared history helped inspire the formation of another family club, Cousins, Inc., which has been meeting monthly in Oakland, California since 1981. "As kids we used to all go to my great-grandmother's house on holidays for family dinners," says founding member Barbara Gordon. "As we got older, my kids and other peoples' kids weren't close, so we thought if we started meeting, it would bring the family together."

Pulling the tribe back together is an urge more and more families feel today, regardless of family configuration. For those whose family is geographically dispersed, bonds among extended kin may often be forged with the help of an old-fashioned family reunion. According to the San Francisco-based company Reunion Research, Americans throw more than 200,000 family reunions a year. The trend is particularly strong among African Americans, for whom the concept of family-as-community tends to be deeply held. Whether acknowledged officially at big reunion bashes or played out privately (adopting children from troubled families within the clan, for example), African Americans honor a long tradition of extended-family loyalty as do many other ethnic and cultural groups in America.

A successful gathering of extended family depends on thoughtful organization. You don't need to establish your own Cousins, Inc., but it's still advisable to form planning committees. The brunt of the labor may ultimately fall to one or two people who have the time and passion, but that's okay if it's a labor of love—especially when children can join in the process. Here are some ideas from seasoned reunion planners (see the Resources at the end of this chapter for more ideas):

Start planning well in advance. You may want to send out that initial flyer as much as a year ahead of time. Involving your children in its design will not only get them excited about the event, but will no doubt charm both adults and kids on your mailing list.

Cook up a theme. Some family reunions go all out on concept—a costume party geared to a certain era, say, or a potluck menu linked to each family member's ethnic heritage. Engage your kids in brainstorming a theme with which every family member can connect.

Schedule activities to appeal to all ages. Some standards are perennial hits such as having each attendee bring a baby picture and awarding prizes to anyone who can guess who's who. But to keep everyone happy, your best bet is to appoint separate "activity committees" run by members of each age group.

Make a family "documentary." Start by transferring old 8-millimeter movies and even family photographs and slides onto video, which is easily edited these days. The family reunion offers the perfect occasion to take new footage to add to your ever-expanding story. Keep in mind, however, that videos and audiotapes are not permanent records. Tapes deteriorate over time, and may be unusable in under ten years, although periodic copying will prolong the life of the images and sounds.

Start a family newsletter. Even before the reunion, you can whet people's appetites with snippets of news—college acceptances, pending marriages, babies born— that will make for instant conversation on the big day. You might also include a calendar featuring family birthdays and anniversaries.

a community of parents

My husband Carl and I have found it possible to build community with other parents in our area while simultaneously improving our parenting knowledge and meeting our child care needs. All three aspects were incorporated into a parenting book club we recently organized at our local Unitarian church. Here's how the logistics work:

We know how hard it is for many families to find baby-sitting so they can attend church functions because of the time of the evening they are usually offered. We purposely set our club meetings early in the evening (5:30 P.M.) on Saturday so that families can bring their children. In one room, we have a baby-sitting service complete with a potluck dinner that includes the kids. It gives the children a chance to build community amongst themselves while the adults are doing the same. Each month, one family chooses a parenting book they would like the group to discuss and acts as moderator when the discussion occurs. Another family handles finding baby-sitters and organizes a simple, kid-friendly meal.

The results have been wonderful. Books we've read include *The Wonder of Boys* by Michael Gurian, *The One-Minute Mother* and *The One-Minute Father* by Spencer Johnson, *Emotional Intelligence* by Daniel Goleman, and *The Seven Spiritual Laws for Parents* by Deepak Chopra. This group is serving our family well in bringing my husband and I together to discuss our parenting skills in a community of other families who are similar in their thinking about family values. Often, families have to deal with whatever crisis is at hand and don't have the luxury of taking some time to be deliberate in their approach to parenting. We have both read many books on parenting, but this forum gives us a chance to pick and choose and really give our approach some thought. I also feel much closer to my husband because of the class. I feel hopeful about our ability to co-parent in the future in a way that will be both beneficial to our children and a pleasure for us.

We belong to a neighborhood baby-sitting co-op, too, and that has bonded us to like-minded families as well. I am very concerned with giving my children the attention they need and not subjecting them to undue stress from having to be on my schedule. As a stay-at-home mom, I'm able to devote myself to this more than many parents can. Still, the co-op gives me the flexibility to drop my children off at a friend's while I do errands that are difficult to do with kids. A lot of community building comes from this and the small-town neighborly feeling that I miss from my own childhood is starting to emerge from this group. I don't panic when things come up at the last minute because I have thirty families I can call on to help me out and they know I can return the favor for them.

JEANINE CALABRIA, Indianapolis, IN

Use the occasion to learn more about family history. Some families appoint a griot, or storyteller, to collect and tell family stories to the rapt reunion audience. Having the clan together creates a perfect opportunity to go around and gather some individual oral history, especially from your family's elders. Pack along a tape recorder, notepad, and video camera, and be sure to take some black-and-white pictures—they'll last longer than color and will be treasured for generations to come.

HELPING OUT—VOLUNTEERISM, ACTIVISM, AND CHARITY FOR KIDS AND FAMILIES

How many parents think, "If only my kids could stop being so selfish and do something for somebody else?" However, those involved in volunteer work and activism soon find out that giving to others or working for social change are the ultimate selfish acts. When others are helped, the biggest thrills go to the giver. That will be tough to get across to your kids until they experience it for themselves. But once they do, they may want to keep going back for more.

In many ways, kids make the perfect troops and even leaders for service activities. For one thing, kids have more time and energy to spend. For another, they have the motivation, thanks to their straightforward sense of right and wrong. With activism in particular, kids possess "the power of being underestimated by adults," notes Phillip Hoose in his book on kids' activism, *It's Our World, Too!*. For example, they have an easier time attracting the media because kids always make good copy, and they have the advantage of being in school, an ideal place to do organizing. They can recruit other students and, with teachers' or administrators' cooperation, utilize meeting rooms, copy machines, bulletin boards, and student newspapers. For the right cause, a teacher or administrator may even help guide the activity or line up community sponsors.

In addition, kids can gain some tangible benefits from being involved in community activities. For example, a volunteer or activist assignment can provide teens valuable job experience in managing an event, doing office work, or raising funds. They may even learn tradeable job skills—for example, learning to utilize computer databases or helping to construct a house for Habitat for Humanity. A volunteer activity may help build a resume or fulfill a school requirement. And what better way to meet new friends with shared interests?

The intangible benefits of service may be just as enticing. Children feel powerless in much of their lives. Service shows them that they can make a difference to an individual or the community. Clearly, service also builds self-esteem—knowing that they have helped makes kids feel better about themselves.

Thus, kids should expect to get every bit as much out of service as they give to it. In fact, only when kids approach service with at least some selfish ends in mind is it likely to succeed long term.

Service As a Family Activity

Your kids don't necessarily need you by their sides when they venture into the world of community service. But volunteering and activism can make a spectacular family experience, especially if you follow the same advice we just gave for your children—make sure your chosen activity meets your needs as well as the community's. Assisting an environmental group in getting out a mailing, gathering firewood for a needy family, or painting an elderly person's house may well fit your kids' idea of a perfect family weekend.

Some families take volunteering further still, making it as integral a part of family life as dinners together. Lynn Willeford was raised in a neighborhood where community service "wasn't even called volunteering . . . it was just what you did." So, when she became a parent, involving son Brook was a given:

"Brook has come along with us on all the work parties we've been to, and has seen for himself how much fun it can be to work together. And there's usually very good food as well! He's also been involved in all the sorts of volunteer activities we do as neighbors . . . When our friend Judy, a single woman, got cancer and things became all too much for her to handle, Brook chipped in with the rest of us. He'd cook her dinner on Monday nights—whatever she wanted—and take great joy when his garlic mashed potatoes or homemade macaroni and cheese tempted her to eat seconds.

"I've started several charities here on the island, so Brook has grown up with phone calls from people who need a leaky roof replaced or help paying their medical bills—I think he thinks it's normal. He takes part as his school schedule allows. He clearly understands the caring and commitment that underpin community."

The key to making service a successful family undertaking is to pick carefully. Choose an activity that interests all of you, both in its intended goal and the work itself. But keep your commitment to it limited. Begin with the idea that you're going to just try it at first. If your kids decide that the reality is much less wonderful than they imagined it would be, don't force them to continue. Don't force yourself to do something that disappoints you, either. You can't model the joy of giving when you're giving without joy.

Because enjoyment and interest is so important, consider an animal-based project for your child's first volunteer experience—for instance, raising guide dogs for the blind or people with other disabilities. Rhonda Stebbins of Shady Cove, Oregon has supported her children in raising four dogs, which were placed with the family as puppies and raised with much care, love, and handling, as required by the program, until they were ready for more intensive schooling and placement with a blind partner. "I was looking for a way for my children to begin to learn to give back, and to begin to recognize that there are people in this world who have bigger needs than they do," says Rhonda. She also wanted her kids to experience the thrill produced by contributing to others.

Raising the dogs and then letting them go so they could be matched with a blind person imparted all that and more, says Rhonda. By speaking and giving demonstrations about the program at service organizations, her children have become more poised and self-confident. In caring so completely for the dogs, her children learned basic parenting skills, a goal of their school district. And, of course, they are now more compassionate about people with disabilities. The hardest part of the program is letting go of animals that have lived in your home for a year to eighteen months. But kids—and their parents—adjust, especially when they realize they have just provided a blind person with a new pair of "eyes."

Charity: Showing Your Kids the Power of "Green Energy"

For so many kids, an allowance just speeds their entry into consumerism. They get to buy what they want because they have their own money. But it's also possible to teach larger lessons with an allowance, as the Willefords did with Brook:

"We have always talked with Brook about our charitable contributions—why we support certain groups, how much of our income we dedicate to this purpose, why we do it," says Lynn. "When we first began giving him an allowance, we told him that 10 percent was to go to charity, 10 percent to savings—for some long-term purpose like an expensive toy or sports equipment—and the rest for whatever. He was also expected to put away 20 percent of monetary gifts for the same purposes.

"Brook had two plastic cups on his bureau for his two tithes. Whenever the charity jar got full, he'd decide where to give the money. I remember once he chose the Cousteau Society, and was he ever thrilled when he got in the return mail an autographed picture of Cousteau himself! He took it to school and showed it off—in fact it's still on his wall a decade later . . .

"Now that Brook's in high school and has more expenses, as well as college to think of, he's been released from both his charitable and his long-term savings tithes. He saves well on his own now, and he donates labor rather than dollars."

As with volunteering, charity need not—and shouldn't—be approached as sacrifice. Remember to ask your kids which dollars have given them the greatest satisfaction—those spent on an impulse purchase or those thoughtfully directed to a cause.

VOLUNTEER VACATIONS AND HOMESTAYS

Vacation time finally comes, you've saved money, and you need the break. But you also know that family vacations have a way of turning into no vacation at all, at least in some respects. That much-dreamt-about getaway can become a chaotic schlepp-fest focused on the same interactions that seemed so much easier at home.

Some people have transcended this pitfall by expanding the very notion of what "vacation" means. What they seek is not so much a break from work but rather an escape from ordinariness itself, even if some work is involved. Thus, the advent of "challenging" vacations, which include such things as study tours, adventure travel à la Outward Bound, spiritual retreats, acting and dance programs, survival skills training, volunteer vacations, and "homestays" with families in other cultures. Those who take this route have discovered that shattering the mold of their life often reinvigorates them far more thoroughly than lying on a beach somewhere with the same old worries crowding their thoughts.

Of all these unusual vacation ideas, volunteer vacations and homestays in particular offer intriguing benefits to kids: education, the satisfaction of making a contribution to others, immersion in diverse cultures, and widened perspectives. We cover each of these vacation types separately below because they can be quite different in their aims, although as you'll see, they can also overlap.

Volunteer Vacations

On the face of it, volunteer vacations are the height of silliness—you take your hard-earned vacation time to work for someone else, and pay them for the privilege. But testimonies from volunteering families prove that there's more than a little method to this "madness."

The general term "volunteer vacations" describes trips to unfamiliar places where spending your money and your time gives as much to a worthy cause as it does to your family. This is truly an example of getting by giving. You help pay for and implement much-needed work that can include anything from cleaning up a public space to assisting in science projects or helping people in need.

Volunteer vacations vary widely in how the "volunteer" part of the equation works. Some are quite labor intensive. Others put the emphasis on adventure but there's a secondary agenda of giving back to the area you visit. As an example of the latter, the travel company Journeys International incorporates a service aspect in its trips which may range from cleaning up after trekkers in Nepal to helping repair a temple prayer wheel in Ladakh.

KRYSTA MORGENTHALER, EAST BAY HABITAT FOR HUMANITY

You may also want to consider volunteer science for your family getaway. This subcategory of volunteer vacations began in the 1970s when the government cut funding for scientific fieldwork and scientists suddenly needed both short-term labor gangs and money. Traditionally, archaeologists have hired local labor to help with excavations and scientists have taken students with them to do on-site work. Few precedents existed for interested amateur volunteers who wanted to come along, and there were no precedents for volunteers who were willing to pay for the privilege. Volunteer science solved the problem in a way that met scientists' needs, too.

For families with science- or animal-loving teens especially, volunteer science can make for a spectacular holiday. Science vacations range from digging for artifacts of the ancient Anasazi in the American Southwest, to tracking hamsters in Siberia, to listening for volcanoes in Costa Rica, to counting elephants in Mali, to bird-watching in China, to helping to build a city of the future (Paulo Soleri's Arcosanti) in the Arizona desert. And the list grows and changes daily.

However, volunteer science—or virtually any volunteer vacation—is not for the Sheraton set. Bear in mind that on many volunteer outings, families will get to bunk with strangers, cook their own food, and use a latrine. The temperature might be 105 degrees Fahrenheit all day every day and the person in charge will in no way resemble a cruise director.

Perhaps the common denominator in a good vacation is being in the presence of that which makes us feel small. Like trips to the ocean and the mountains, these unconventional vacations put us in touch with the awesomeness of being a part of something enormous and complex. When the setting matches the intangibles, it's just a bonus.

By the way, since you will be paying for your volunteer science or other volunteer vacation, you may wonder where the money goes. Some pays for organization, administrative costs, recruiting, advertising, and fund-raising. With science vacations, a slice of your money goes to the scientist for his research grant. But keep in mind too that unlike the usual family trip, volunteer vacations are often tax deductible.

When planning such a journey, consider that not all available projects will be appropriate for younger or immature children. It's important to ask for feedback from the trip organizers about your children's ages and other limitations.

Homestays

If exposing your kids to other cultures means far more to you than taking them to some theme park's international village, a homestay may be just what you're looking for. During homestays, you live with a family and pitch in by becoming a part of their community. These vacations plunge the family into other worlds where all of you can explore the language, customs, problems, and joys of indigenous life in a foreign place. And unlike volunteer vacations, which are often best-suited to families with teens, children of all ages can find a fit in homestay situations.

Homestay agencies, educational institutions, and language schools in the United States and abroad can all make arrangements for you to be hosted by a local person in Europe, Latin America, or Asia, or even in another part of the U.S. The people you stay with are regular folks, not professional innkeepers jaded by a sea of faces, and you are generally treated like family, sharing meals and conversation. In return for this hospitality, you must be willing to give up some privacy and share your life, as well as be open to experiencing the life of your host family.

But these are all plusses, in Lynn Willeford's eyes: "These sorts of experiences—learning the ground-level truth of situations, seeing things through other people's eyes—cause [my son] Brook to question assumptions and statements made about the working poor, and give him empathy toward those who have less than he . . .

"Next September, Brook will be eighteen and starting his first year at college. He's far enough along in the maturation process for us to see what's worked. I'd say he's certainly more aware of the realities of the rest of the world than most of his friends, and far more forgiving of the foibles of others."

One bit of advice about homestays: It's wise to choose organizations that maintain local staff. That way, they can resolve problems or provide alternative arrangements if the chemistry between you and the host family just doesn't work.

CHAPTER 10 RESOURCES

General

ORGANIZATION

The Power of Hope c/o The Whidbey Institute, P.O. Box 57, Clinton, WA 98236, (360) 341–4828

Offers summer retreats for teens ages thirteen through eighteen, held at an ecological retreat center on Whidbey Island, near Seattle. The retreats combine creative arts, leadership activities, self-exploration, outdoor adventures, and environmental education; their purpose is to motivate teens "to live fully engaged lives in which they draw on their deepest resources to work for a positive future." Co-director is *New Age Journal* cofounder Peggy Taylor.

Jumping in the Gene Pool—Cultivating Relationships with Extended Family

BOOKS

The Family Reunion Planner by Donna Beasley and Donna Carter (Macmillan, 1997).

Geared largely to African-American families but useful to everyone, this book covers all the bases, from fund-raising to follow-up.

Fun & Games for Family Gatherings by Adrienne E. Anderson (San Francisco, CA: Reunion Research, 1996).

A lively potpourri of tips and activities for family gatherings.

ORGANIZATIONS

The Foundation for Grandparenting, 7 Avenida Vista Grande, Suite B7–160, Santa Fe, NM 87505

website: www.grandparenting.org

A nonprofit organization founded by family psychiatrist Arthur Kornhaber, M.D., coauthor of *Grandparent Power!* and other books, the organization publishes a quarterly newsletter, "Vital Connections," engages in intergenerational research projects, and operates a summer camp for grandparents and grandchildren in the Adirondacks.

MISCELLANEOUS

The "Gift of Heritage" video. Order it from Mary Lou Peterson, P.O. Box 17233, Minneapolis, MN 55417, (800) 774–8511

website: www.giftofheritage.com

Compiled by veteran reunion planner (and grandmother) Mary Lou Peterson, explains how to create your own family video keepsake.

Helping Out—Volunteerism, Activism, and Charity for Kids and Families

BOOKS

160 Ways to Help the World: Community Service Projects for Young People by Linda Leeb Duper (New York, NY: Facts on File, 1996).

This is the best book we've seen for youth on volunteering. It includes lists of organizations categorized by issue.

The Good Heart Book: A Guide to Volunteering by David E. Driver (Chicago, IL: Noble Press, 1989).

Written for both adult and teen volunteers in simple, clear prose. A particular strength of this guide is its discussion of the social issues for which people volunteer: illiteracy, AIDS, help for people with disabilities, domestic violence, abandonment of the elderly, and so on. Focused almost exclusively on social service issues.

It's Our World, Too by Phillip Hoose (Little, Brown & Co., 1993).

Part I includes stories of young activists throughout American history as well as contemporary stories. Part II is a feisty handbook for young activists, teaching readers everything from how to get research money to how to plan boycotts and demonstrations. It also discusses such essential skills as negotiation and working with media.

A Student's Guide to Volunteering by Theresa Foy Digeronimo (Franklin Lake, NY: Career Press, 1995).

Emphasizes the tangible benefits of volunteering: career experience, building a resume, meeting people with similar interests, fulfilling school requirements, and so on. Also useful is a chapter on doing it yourself when no organization exists to fulfill a need you want addressed, and a directory of organizations including general volunteer organizations listed by state.

The Student Environmental Action Guide: 25 Simple Things We Can Do by The Student Environmental Action Coalition (New York, NY: HarperCollins and the EarthWorks Group, 1991).

Written by college students for college students. Most of the suggested projects involve the school itself—getting credit for environmental research, donating leftover cafeteria food to homeless shelters, and so on. It also covers personal environmental behavior and community actions.

Volunteer Vacations and Homestays

ORGANIZATIONS

Earthwatch, 680 Mt. Auburn Street, Watertown, MA 02272, (800) 776–0188

website: www.earthwatch.org

Earthwatch puts out an annual expedition guide and updates its list of current and upcoming expeditions. The guide includes complete trip-by-trip descriptions with color photos and charts detailing costs, rendezvous sites, and accommodations, along with information on the degree of physical challenge involved in each trip, and generally, what to expect. Also available at many public libraries.

Global Volunteers, 375 East Little Canada Road, St. Paul, MN 55117, (800) 482–1074
website: www.globalvlntrs.org

In addition to answering questions about your "Adventure in Service," recruiters will put you in touch with previous volunteers and send you journals kept by previous teams. After you sign up, a notebook with the Global Volunteers policies and philosophy, cultural information, emergency contact numbers, and some language basics is sent to you, and the program director will phone to answer any final pre-trip questions.

International Summerstays, 620 S.W. Fifth Avenue, Suite 400, Portland, OR 97204, (800) 274–6007

This group sets up homestays in France, Germany, Mexico, Russia, Poland, Spain, and Japan for individuals, couples, and families.

Journeys International, 4011 Jackson Road, Ann Arbor, MI 48103, (800) 255–8735
website: www.journeys-intl.com

Organizes adventure travel to Africa, Asia, Latin America, and the Pacific that includes some service activities in the area visited.

LEX American, 68 Leonard Street, Belmont, MA 02178, (617) 489–5800
website: www.lexlrf.com

Arranges homestays in Japan, Korea, Mexico, France, and Germany for adult individuals, couples, and families.

family means

As we noted in the opening to this book, nearly all the choices we make in our parenting have effects that reverberate far beyond the well-being of our families. Some of the most wide-ranging effects come from the choices we make involving money and the work we do to earn it. For instance, the simple act of filling up our shopping carts at the supermarket will affect our local communities, the society-at-large including other children, people in other countries, and both the local and planetary environment, depending on which items we purchase.

How we handle work and money in our lives also teaches important lessons to our children, some of which we intend, some of which we don't. Most of us try to teach our children moral and ethical values that we emphasize to them as being important to us. But do we try to incorporate those same values in our purchases, banking, and investments? Does our work reflect our values? Remember that children are far more impressed by what we do than what we say. In addition, the choices we make about money in our lives have a dramatic impact, when combined with those of other consumers and investors, on the world in which our children are growing up.

Our purpose in this chapter isn't to castigate you for any of your choices. It's simply to offer information and insights so you can make your choices more conscientiously. Many of us feel helpless to change aspects of our society that we don't like. But if more people viewed their purchasing, banking, and investing dollars as votes for a world they want to create, they just might "elect" the world of their dreams.

In the same way, we suggest to you perspectives about the world of work that you might not have considered before. All of us who work struggle with the balance between the demands of work and family. But there are value choices here too that you might not have figured into the equation. If yours is a two-worker household, we also give you a tool for reconsidering whether that second income is really contributing—financially and emotionally—all that you think it is to your family's stability. And we take up the topic of "Right Livelihood" (appropriate work) in an unusual light—not from the standpoint of judging your current occupation as "right" or "wrong" but from the angle of encouraging your children to "follow their bliss."

SOCIALLY RESPONSIBLE INVESTING FOR YOUR CHILDREN'S COLLEGE EDUCATION AND YOUR FAMILY'S SECURITY

Financial gurus promise that with proper planning, anyone of ordinary means can put their kids through a good college, secure the family's monetary future, and retire to a life of independent wealth and comfort. So why isn't this a reality for more of us? Lack of data, for one thing—few people have been taught even the most basic concepts of personal finance. Which brings up another point—a goodly number of us lack drive as well as information. In the back of our minds, we know we should be taking steps to provide for our family's future security and our children's college education. But money makes us uncomfortable. Investing in particular seems impossibly complex, or we figure we could never find the extra dollars for it, or we tell ourselves we're still too young to worry about it.

If the above describes you in any way, be assured that you are not a "terminal case." Turning yourself around on family investing is often no more complex than disabusing yourself of some mistaken notions. First off, ordinary investing need be no more complex than finding a trust-worthy, competent financial advisor and following her advice. Nor does investing take a vast amount of money, just some degree of disposable income—the marketplace overflows with investment products tailored to people of modest means. As for putting it off until later in life, later has arrived. Most experts feel that parents should start investing for their children's college education while the kids are still in diapers, because it will take most parents that long to build up enough capital to pay tomorrow's tuition rates.

You may also have avoided investing up to now because you feel that any dollars you make will be dirty money—profits generated by polluting the environment, exploiting workers, hawking weapons, and the like. We're not going to be so glib as to promise you invest-ment returns that are ethically spotless. It would take a sea change of social progress for that to happen. But we can show you how to earn returns that are far clean-er than, say, the interest you make on your bank ac-counts, or the endeavors you support with your ordinary purchases of products made and sold by mainstream corporations.

MIRIAM JACOBS

We can also lead you to investments that will fur-ther some of the very things you may believe in most, such as affordable housing for the poor and small-business loans for women and minorities, while pay-ing you an acceptable return. Do keep in mind that the investing world is not a hospitable place for ethical purists. Nevertheless, if you want to know how to combine your financial and social goals, you've come to the right place.

As with other sections of this book, it would take a book of its own to give you all the information you should have before setting up invest-ment accounts for college tuition and other family needs. But we'll get you started down the path, and our Resources section at the end of this chapter can take you the rest of the way.

Why You Should Invest for Your Family and Why You Should Start Now

We've already mentioned two vital reasons for a family investing program: paying the soaring costs for your kids' college expenses and providing financial security for your family. Even if the current inflation rate is modest when you read this, the rate at which college costs are increasing is not. College costs have been significantly outstripping the broader cost-of-living index seemingly forever. The problem plagues families sending kids to both private and public institutions. For example, in several states, tax-limitation voter initiatives have led states to cut funds for their public university system. To compensate, the colleges have had to radically increase tuition.

As for family security, are you prepared financially if a medical or other emergency forces your family's main wage earner out of work for a while? What if your kids need a little financial help early in their adulthood? And although you may think it's too soon to be thinking about the estate you leave to your heirs, there likely won't be much estate to leave unless you start building it when you are relatively young.

The urgency to invest now has to do with the mechanism that fuels middle-class investing, compound returns. Investing is most likely to succeed when you invest steadily and patiently over a period of many years, don't take undue risk, and simply allow the mathematics of compound returns to work in your favor. Here's how compounding works: Suppose you invest $1,000 (called your *principal,* which means the amount invested) in an account earning 10 percent per year and commit yourself to reinvesting your earnings. At the end of the first year, you will have $1,100—your original $1,000 plus the $100 the investment yielded. (For simplicity's sake, we're assuming yearly compounding, although bank accounts often compound daily.) In the second year, you will be earning your 10 percent on $1,100, yielding a return of $110. In the third year, your principal will be $1,210 and the amount earned $121.

Do you see what's happening? Your account is actually growing at a greater rate than 10 percent a year because you earn returns on your reinvested earnings as well as your original thousand bucks. And with each passing year, the account grows faster and faster. At the end of ten years, you will have $2,594 even though you haven't added another penny of cash.

Now suppose instead that you invest $100 per month, a more likely scenario if you're investing for college tuition. At the end of ten years, you'll have $19,128, assuming a 10 percent annual return and reinvestment of earnings. Not bad for a total cash contribution of $12,000. And if you start earlier and invest for fifteen years, your account will nearly double again to $38,124.

The key ingredient here is time. Compounding can't work its magic without it. Remember that compounding gathers more and more steam with every year your money is left in the account to grow. That's why you have to start investing as early as possible, particularly with the large sums needed to get your kids through even a modestly priced four-year school.

Other Important Investing Concepts

You don't need to know anything to invest, but that means leaving everything in the hands of an outsider, your financial advisor. Your investing experience will be far more satisfying personally if you're able to hold an intelligent conversation with her. And a little knowledge may increase your chance for financial success, too. Here are a few terms to understand:

- *Investing.* Investing means either 1) lending money to an entity that will pay you interest on it until the original amount, your principal, is returned to you, or 2) buying something that you expect to grow in value. Examples of (1) include bank accounts, certificates of deposit, and government bonds. Examples of (2) include stocks and real estate. Lending investments produce income (the interest) but the principal never increases in value (although you can reinvest interest to increase the principal). On the other hand, you buy stocks or real estate with the hope that your principal will grow in value, i.e. "appreciate." Some ownership investments also produce income. For example, some stocks pay dividends and some real estate produces rental income. As a rule, ownership investments will produce greater returns than lending investments. They are also riskier, which goes with the territory.

- *Risk.* You may find the occasional free lunch in life, but not in investing. No one gives away money, so the rule in investing is that the higher return you seek, the more risk you'll have to take. Conversely, the safer the investment, the smaller the return.

- *Real return.* Inflation is always eroding the value of your money. If the inflation rate is 3 percent in a given year, your money is worth only 97 cents on the dollar at that year's end. To get anywhere in investing, you have to outstrip the rate of inflation; otherwise, you are just running in place financially. Investors use the term "real return" to refer to the difference between the investment's actual return and the rate of inflation. For example, if the inflation rate is 3 percent and the investment returns 8 percent, the real return is 5 percent. Experts generally figure that a real return of less than 3 to 4 percent is a waste of time and money. Throughout much of the 1990s, bank savings accounts paid only about as much as the inflation rate, roughly 3 percent. In times of high inflation, savings account interest rates usually trail the cost of living. In other words, money kept in a bank gains nothing in real terms and may even lose value. Now you know why savvy financial types keep only as much money in the bank as they need to pay daily bills, and invest the rest.

· *Liquidity.* The ease with which you can unload an investment is called its liquidity. If you have a financial emergency, you may want to cash in your investment sooner than you had planned. Bank accounts are highly liquid—you can withdraw your money at any time. Stocks are considered liquid, easily sold through stock exchanges, although you may get back less than you put in if you are forced to sell when the stock price is down. Real estate is not liquid—you have to find a buyer and go through a lengthy and complicated escrow procedure to get your money.

· *Stocks and stock mutual funds.* Shares of what are called common stocks represent ownership shares in a corporation. Financial advisors almost universally agree that for the average middle-class investor, stock investments are the best way to build wealth for college or retirement. No other investment gives you such a good mix of reward, risk, and liquidity. And most middle-class people can afford the price of admission, particularly if they buy stocks through stock mutual funds, which are diverse portfolios of stocks managed by investment professionals. Note that our examples above were based on a hypothetical rate of return of 10 percent, a realistic number for the long-term investor. Over the last seventy years, the average share of common stock traded on the New York Stock Exchange has grown in value at a compound annual rate (assuming reinvested dividends) of between 10 and 11 percent, and that's with serious market crashes such as the one in 1987 figured in. During that same seventy-year period, the compound inflation rate has been about 3 percent, so stocks have produced a real return of about 7 percent—hard to beat, especially for the price.

· *Long-term investing.* Any honest advisor will tell you that the secret to success in the stock market is patience. The big losers in stocks tend to be speculators trying to squeeze every last buck out of the market or novices frantic to sell every time the market takes a little dip. If you can avoid both of these extremes, history is very much on your side. The growth in the market over the long term is likely to carry you up with it as long as you've selected your investments wisely. There are no guarantees here, just as in life in general. But consider that people who fear the risks of stocks tend to leave their money in the bank, where inflation will eat away at its worth. You can't escape financial risk so you might as well pick risks that are most in your favor.

Socially Responsible Investing for Families

We can hear your thoughts already: "Let me get this straight. I open an investment account so I can afford to send my kids to college. The funds are invested in stocks. The stocks finance companies that are wrecking the world into which my kids graduate. Gee, any more nifty ideas?"

We don't have a perfect answer for your concerns. It's not a perfect world. But with socially responsible investing, you may feel good enough about what your money is doing—or in the case of stocks you avoid, not doing—to open that account.

Socially responsible investing (SRI) means investing in a way that's consistent with your personal ethics and social concerns. For example, many families object to investing in the stocks of tobacco companies, whose success is predicated on hooking young people on an addictive, dangerous product. Others object to investing in the stocks of companies that are major contributors to environmental pollution, ozone depletion, or global warming, all of which threaten their children's current and future health and well-being. Many investors object to holding the stock of companies that do business in repressive regimes such as Burma, or companies doing business with sweatshop factories or factories that employ child labor.

The social investment industry addresses such issues. In general, it is oriented toward promoting peace; expanding opportunities for women and minorities; providing good conditions for workers; pressuring governments that abuse human rights; improving company relations with communities; safeguarding consumers; not profiting off the abuse of alcohol and gambling; and "no nukes." To serve the expanding SRI marketplace, dozens of mutual funds now screen their stock and bond investments for companies with more favorable records in these areas. In addition, the investment profession now abounds with brokers, many of them former and current activists, who specialize in SRI. Even the mainstream brand-name brokerages will usually have several such specialists on board.

Social investors tend to fall into two camps: those who want to avoid the guilt of profiting from activities they consider unethical, and those who want to wield their money more proactively, as a tool for building a better world. Can socially responsible investing really accomplish these things? The answers aren't simple. If you invest in stocks, which we believe is the best way for you to *financially* accomplish your goals, you will probably have to accept some compromise of your values.

For example, if the CEO of Saint Geraldine's Clothiers looks up one day and finds that all her competitors are having their products made overseas at factories paying people two dollars a day, there is no way she can compete by hiring only Americans and paying them eight dollars an hour plus benefits. In this circumstance, ethical businesspeople will usually resign themselves to shipping work overseas but try to ensure that conditions at the factories they work with are as humane as possible. When you invest in stocks, you too will have to accept such compromises.

Still, SRI can and is making an impact on the world your children are inheriting. During the 1980s, many individual investors and, even more importantly, large institutions withdrew investment money from South Africa because of its racist and brutally maintained apartheid system. The so-called divestment effort contributed to that country's snowballing economic woes and almost certainly hastened the end of its pro-segregation government. South Africa is SRI's greatest success story and a powerful example of its potential.

Of course, apartheid represented a unique situation which most people outside South Africa opposed. Most issues that social investors care about are at least somewhat more controversial in society and that makes it harder to achieve reforms. Still, SRI has had some notable successes, particularly when it has been able to combine its voice with those of socially responsible consumers, activist groups, other concerned citizens, and government regulators. For example, in the environmental arena, such coalitions have convinced large corporations such as Monsanto and DuPont to adopt more environmentally friendly policies. In addition, retailers have reduced packaging and increased the recycled content in their packaging and products under pressure from social investors and others.

Such gains may seem modest compared to the enormity of the social problems SRI tries to address, but you should realize that SRI represents only a tiny portion of the investment marketplace here and worldwide.

As more and more dollars are piled on its table, SRI will grow in clout—another reason to consider putting your dollars there, too.

As Ben Cohen of Ben & Jerry's once noted, business has helped create many of the social and environmental problems that threaten your children's world: "If business were instead trying to solve these problems, they would be solved in short order." By investing in stocks, particularly if you do it as we advise below, you can have a least a small say about the future direction that business takes.

Show Me the Money—Do Social Investments Perform?

Here are some of the things you'll hear from friends and relatives and even so-called "experts" when you mention that you're considering socially responsible investing:

"Why don't you just make as much money as you can with regular investing and then give some to your favorite causes?"

"You can't possibly make enough money if you're going to reject good stocks just because a company doesn't meet your social standards."

"Socially responsible mutual funds don't do as well as regular funds."

The fact is that you needn't sacrifice a penny in profits to invest according to your values. While it is true that many socially responsible mutual funds have not performed impressively, several others have for periods of time been among the country's most outstanding funds of their investment type (that is, funds pursuing a similar investment strategy—large company stocks, small company stocks, etc.). For example, as of this writing, the Domini Social Equity fund has outperformed the market, as well as most other funds of its investment type, for all seven years of its existence. Many SRI professionals who manage individual accounts have also produced above-average returns (and in investing, above-average is considered excellent).

Publications such as *Business Week* magazine have also studied the performance of socially screened funds and concluded that screening does not hurt performance. Indeed, the professionals who manage the massive California state pension fund would argue that one can improve investment performance by applying social criteria. The pension fund's managers prefer to invest in companies that treat their employees well, because happy employees do better work and are more loyal to their employer.

Nor do you have to look hard to see through the argument that rejecting stocks for social reasons hurts investment performance. Yes, the stocks of tobacco companies have turned in some pretty fancy earnings throughout much of their history. But so have the stocks of plenty of other companies whose businesses aren't nearly so ethically compromised. Besides, as the questionable practices of tobacco companies began to catch up with them in the late 1990s, their stocks began to look far less attractive, particularly for long-term investors. The bottom line is that socially responsible investors have no shortage of solid-performing stocks to choose from, and their refusal to invest in corporate "bad guys" offers some investment protection, as well. For instance, companies in trouble with environmental regulatory agencies often take a hit in their stock prices because investors know that environmental problems are generally expensive to clean up.

In certain instances not having to do with stocks, social investors will in fact accept smaller returns to further worthy social goals. We cover those circumstances below. Such investments may not play a prominent role in the investing you do to get your kids to college, but you should know about them so you can make that decision for yourself.

The Range of Social Investments—from "Guilt-Free" to High-Social-Impact

The type of social impact you make as an ethical investor will be determined by the interplay of two factors, what investments you choose and with whom you conduct the transaction, as the following indicates:

Mainstream brokers. You will make the least impact—in fact, virtually no impact at all—if you work with a mainstream broker and simply instruct her to invest in individual stocks that conform with your values. Stock investments made in this private manner may permit you to sleep easier at night, knowing the bad guys don't have any of *your* money. But that's where the impact ends.

SRI specialists. Companies will get the message that you are selecting or rejecting their stocks for social reasons if the stocks are purchased through people known for representing socially responsible investors exclusively. If you are investing in individual stocks or other individual investments (i.e., not mutual funds), working with a socially responsible investment specialist, particularly one linked with a larger organization associated with SRI, helps ensure that this message is sent.

SRI investment products. Investing in products created for social investors—for instance, screened mutual funds—also sends a direct message to companies that their social behavior matters, even if the fund shares are purchased through mainstream brokers. In addition, many of the SRI mutual funds give you even more social bang for your buck because they engage in some direct social activism of their own. SRI funds have been independently rated for their social commitments. The A-rated funds consistently engage in what is called shareholder activism and/or use their influence to dialogue with company executives about how to improve their corporate citizenship. Shareholder activists are stockholders who exercise their ownership rights by directly pressuring companies in which they own shares to change. For example, Calvert Group, a well-known socially responsible mutual fund company, has pushed companies in which it owns shares to improve hiring practices and include women and minorities on the board. Many of the A-rated funds, including many Calvert funds, also invest some of their money in high-impact community investments such as community loan funds (see below). Some of the A-rated fund management companies donate substantial portions of their own profits to address targeted social problems.

High-social-impact investments. For all its promise, investing in socially screened stocks is still a relatively indirect way to produce social change. For that reason, many social investors prefer to invest at least a portion of their capital in what are variously called community, direct, targeted, or high-social-impact investments. Such investments include loans to what are called community loan funds and deposits in financial institutions such as community development credit unions and banks. For example, a "development deposit" made to Chicago's South Shore Bank helps fund loans to create affordable housing and jobs in a low-income Chicago neighborhood. A deposit made to Vermont National Bank's Socially Responsible Banking (SRB) Fund supports loans for affordable housing, environmental projects, small business development, agriculture, and education. In addition, since bank funds are invested when they're not being loaned, the SRB Fund's money is managed according to social screens that reflect the progressive values of its depositors.

Many high-social-impact investments pay market- or near-market rates compared to banking or other lending investments. However, such investments by themselves won't accumulate money rapidly enough to finance a middle-class child's college education. We still feel stocks are your best bet for this purpose, but you may want to apportion a small amount of your investment capital for community investments, just as some SRI mutual funds do.

SOCIALLY RESPONSIBLE CONSUMING FOR PARENTS AND KIDS

You may not think of yourself or your kids as activists. And you may consider your family powerless to affect improper behavior by huge multinational corporations. But corporate executives realize that if you and enough others like you make principled decisions when you shop, you can bring a Fortune 500 giant to its knees.

That may go double for kids. In the 1980s, teenagers led a boycott of tuna companies that were catching and killing dolphins in their nets. The companies were also barraged with letters from protesting customers, many of them children. They quickly got the message and changed their fishing methods so that dolphins were better protected.

How can companies worth billions be so vulnerable to ordinary consumers like you and me and even our kids? Quite simply, their billions come from us. Two thirds of the American economy is fueled by ordinary consumer purchases. A popular boycott can cost a company millions of dollars in sales, which not only slices its income but drops its stock price. The latter in turn hurts its ability to borrow money to expand its business. Even better, it doesn't take anywhere near a majority of consumers to affect a company's thinking. The loss of a few percentage points of "market share" will usually send executives scrambling for answers. In short, business can only get away with socially destructive behavior if its customers don't pay attention.

The accessibility and power of socially responsible consuming makes it an ideal way to involve your children in changing their world. Kids affect, directly or indirectly, a considerable portion of the consumer economy. As of 1997, kids fourteen and under were directly spending $20 billion per year. Children also influence the money their parents spend—from fad snack foods to the choice of the new family car—to the tune of $200 billion per year. For instance, knowing that kids' opinions can make the critical difference when parents are choosing between several models of cars, Chevrolet placed a two-page ad for its Venture minivan on the inside cover of the May, 1997 issue of *Sports Illustrated for Kids,* targeted mainly to eight- to fourteen-year-old boys.

When children understand the social implications of the purchases they request you to make, or make themselves, they are more likely to make responsible choices. To them, a wrong is a wrong and must be addressed. You are probably the only one in your children's lives who can teach them about the social impact of consuming, because their other potential sources of such information, such as schools and the media, are too beholden to corporations to do the job. For instance, the media live off of corporate advertising and increasingly do whatever their sponsors ask. (CBS sports announcers have even worn Nike "swooshes" on camera.) Corporations have become so aggressive in influencing media content that some now demand to review magazine or program content before deciding whether to run ads.

Nor are your children likely to learn about corporate misdeeds in their schools. Desperate for financial support, many schools carry corporate ads of their own—for soft drinks and snack foods, for example. Schools have also become more and more dependent on corporate gifts of computers and other equipment. They will not be anxious to bite the hands that feed them, and many companies perceive any negative coverage of business as a direct affront. This disturbing interference by business in the day-to-day flow of information to citizens makes it more crucial than ever that parents inform themselves about social issues— preferably getting information from alternative, noncommercial sources— and pass their knowledge to their kids.

At the same time, you don't want your kids to become jaded. Help them understand that only a minority of corporations misbehave out of sheer ill will. When they're old enough, kids should learn that business pressures sometimes push companies to do things that under better circumstances, they would not do. The point of socially responsible consuming is to create conditions in which companies will do the right thing because it is in their best interest. For example, many companies have modified their products to be more environmentally friendly because consumers have made it known that this is what they prefer.

To look at it another way, it takes consumer responsibility to create business responsibility just as it takes citizen responsibility to create good government. That's the message we think children should be taught instead of "it's all business' fault."

Teaching Your Kids to Be True Smart Shoppers

Socially responsible consuming takes many forms. The following actions all make a substantial impact. Most can be performed by kids on their own or by you and your children together. Others are actions that teach socially responsible consuming to your children through your good example:

Write the company. Your decision to buy or not buy a product for social reasons instantly multiplies in significance many, many times over if you accompany it with a short note penned to the CEO of the company. The CEO may not personally read it, but someone who reports to him or her will and it will probably be taken quite seriously. Companies figure that for every person who bothers to write, hundreds or even thousands more feel the same way. Thus, it may only take a handful of letters to turn a company around on an issue. By the way, consumer letters helped convince McDonalds to switch from plastic foam food containers to a more planet-friendly material several years ago.

When you or your kids do write, communicate only one issue per letter. Summarize your position in your first sentence, in case that's all the company staff has time to read. Briefly explain your reasoning after that first sentence.

Phone the company. Depending on the company, phone calls may or may not be as effective as letters, but they do take less time. Many companies list toll-free phone numbers right on their packaging, in which case they may be receptive to consumer feedback. If you wish to call a company but can't find a toll-free number for it, call toll-free information at 1–800–555–1212. When your kids want to make the call, assist them to make sure the message gets through.

Don't buy logo clothing. Sports heroes are paid millions to be walking billboards for companies like Nike. How much do your kids and you get for doing the same? Clue: rhymes with "hero." In fact, most companies charge far more for logo products than the price of a similar plain, non-logo item. We have so uncritically accepted the corporate dominance of our culture that it has actually become fashionable to brand ourselves. Note also that the same companies draping their ads all over our family's willing bodies may be paying foreign workers mere pennies an hour to make the clothing, which is often assembled under deplorable working conditions as well.

Buy environmentally positive products. For example, low- or no-phosphate laundry detergent; unbleached toilet paper; cloth napkins; natural household cleansers such as Bon Ami; and energy- and water-saving appliances and fixtures. Your local natural foods store and companies such as Harmony (formerly Seventh Generation, available by mail-order and in many regular supermarkets) carry conscientious household products.

Don't buy environmentally destructive or wasteful products. For example, conventional lawn and garden chemicals, plastic trash bags, paper towels, caustic cleansers, and so on. In some cases that may mean accepting modest compromises—for instance, most green laundry detergents aren't quite as potent as the best "brown" ones. But in other cases, substitute products—cloth towels instead of paper, say—shouldn't make much of a ripple in your lives.

Consume less. Anything we can do to cut our consumption of products, raw materials, and energy directly benefits the planet and helps reverse a dangerous trend.

Buy recycled products. Start with paper for your children's school binder and your own paper needs around the house. As more and more consumers buy these products, the prices will drop until they equal or better products made from virgin materials.

Don't buy products made from endangered species of plants or animals. Items made from large animal pelts, tortoise shell, coral, ivory, and reptile skins come from endangered species. In many cases, it is consumer demand that caused the species' numbers to dwindle in the first place. If enough people refuse to buy these products, the situation can be reversed.

Don't buy products that destroy rain forests. Rain forests are being cut down for many reasons, but primary among them is the demand by consumers in the U.S. and other wealthy countries for rain forest woods and fast-food beef. You should refuse to purchase products made from woods such as rosewood, mahogany, teak, and ebony. And inform your kids that many fast-food corporations buy their beef from cattle ranches that were carved out of rain forest land. Before buying fast-food burgers, you and they should ask the store manager if the company buys meat from rain forest cattle.

Reward good corporate citizenship. Companies that try to be good corporate citizens or who have reformed objectionable practices should be rewarded every bit as much as bad citizens should be punished. Point out "good" companies to your children and select their products when possible. A note or phone call to let them know they are appreciated helps, too.

APPROPRIATE AND LIFE-AFFIRMING WORK

Perhaps you never expected to hear this in a parenting book, but we'll ask anyway: What do you do for a living?

Do you consider your work meaningful? Does it make particular use of your talents, gifts, and skills? Do you feel fulfilled at the end of the work day, content in the knowledge that you've made a contribution? Or do you feel drained, frustrated, questioning the point of it all?

We don't mean to plunge you into an existential crisis, but we do want to urge parents to consider how what they do for a living affects their children, by virtue of how it influences their parenting. For one thing, people who experience frustration or boredom at work, spend too many hours on the job, or face long commutes every day, are not likely to come home energized for the demands of being a parent. What's more, the attitudes we model about our work influence our kids' expectations about *their* careers.

Our aim here is to encourage you to believe that you can find work fulfilling and urge you to inspire your children to chase their dreams, as they're figuring out "what I wanna be when I grow up."

"That's Why They Call It 'Work' "

One of the age-old myths we carry with us into the workplace is the no-tion that what we do to pay the bills is a necessary evil, tolerated because it allows us to feed and shelter our families. To be sure, any of us with steady work have reason to be glad, even if we don't have the job of our dreams. But we go too far when we believe that, as many of us were told growing up, "You're not *supposed* to like it—that's why they call it 'work.'" This kind of reasoning has doomed millions of people to a lifetime of drudgery and dissatisfaction when they might experience creativity, chal-lenge, and accomplishment.

As an alternative, we offer the views of Matthew Fox, author of *The Reinvention of Work.* Fox argues that work "has to include our deepest values and passions and feelings and commitments, or it's not work, it's just a job. A job is something to pay our bills with. Work is something that touches our heart and expresses our being."

Finding that kind of work may seem impossible. And with a family, there are always mouths to feed and bills to pay, which will not wait while a parent sets off on a quest for the perfect profession. But every parent would do well to reexamine his or her line of work in the light of how decently it not only sustains the family materially, but also how it nurtures them as people.

Doing What You Love and Loving What You Do

"I have a great job that supports me as a parent and gives me great satisfaction," says Ralph Silber, uttering words any parent would love to repeat. Silber and his wife Robin Baker, of Berkeley, both work in jobs related to health policy: He heads an association of nonprofit health centers in the county where they live, and she directs the Labor Occupational Health Program at the UC-Berkeley School of Public Health.

Both Ralph and Robin consider it a "privilege" to have work that is intellectually rewarding, makes an important social contribution, *and* supports their family materially. But privilege is too modest a term because they both figured out what they were interested in and went after it. That meant long years of education but the result, says Ralph, is that "our sons have two parents who have really satisfying jobs that make them feel really good about themselves, and I think that's an incredibly important factor in being a good parent: being a happy person."

Across town, Karen Burks and her husband Marc Toma, who run their own firm, Burks Toma Architects, derive much the same set of benefits, personally and as a family, from their vocation. They design facilities such as wastewater treatment plants, municipal recreation centers, and Forest Service fire stations. The making of things, says Karen, is what is so gratifying: "You create something in the world . . . When something is done, it's wonderful to go see a place that didn't used to exist—and does something good."

Like Daniel and David Silber-Baker, Karen and Marc's two sons, Matthew, fourteen, and Walker, twelve, are also learning from their parents that meaningful work can be theirs as adults. "They both think liking what you do is more important than how much you earn," Karen says with obvious pride. Both boys, she adds, "see themselves as successful people. No one's ever told them, 'You can't do that.' . . . They see you can be good at all these things you like."

Guiding Your Kids to "Follow Their Bliss"

Matthew and Walker are learning something that has evidently eluded many of today's youth—the idea that there's more to life than the acquisition of material wealth. Indeed, young people not only get society's message that materialism is a worthwhile pursuit, most embrace it wholeheartedly. A huge annual survey by the Higher Education Research Institute at UCLA found that the number of college freshmen who said it was essential or very important to be very well off grew from 41 percent in 1968 to 74 percent in 1995. Over that same span, the percentage of freshmen who agreed that "developing a meaningful philosophy of life" was a top priority dropped from 83 percent to 41 percent.

In a high-tech, knowledge-based economy, there would seem to be more opportunities than ever for our children to achieve wealth and success. But to make sure they also factor personal satisfaction into the equation, do the following:

- *Talk about your work.* Assuming you like your job (if you don't, see the next page), make sure your kids know that, and have a good sense of what you do and why you like it. Explain why and how you chose your profession. Take them to visit your workplace, if you can. Discuss some especially interesting challenges or projects.

- *"Interview" your kids.* To start them thinking about work in a positive way, ask them about the kinds of activities they really enjoy—e.g., art, music, nature, science, sports—and find out if they enjoy them so much that they'd like to do them all the time. Then, visit the library together, to find out more about career opportunities in those fields and how to prepare for them.

- *Scope out unusually interesting professions.* On a trip to the zoo, see if your kids can talk with an animal keeper. Stop by an adventure-travel company so they can "interview" an expedition leader. Have fun with this!

- *Acknowledge your kids' "work."* Children are naturally interested in a wide range of subjects and activities. Acknowledging those interests—and your kids' accomplishments, however modest or fitful—is key to fostering confidence and aspiration. "Value everything your kid does," advises Karen Burks, "so they come to understand that everything they do is valuable. If they see that, they should grow into the kind of people who will seek out those things that give them satisfaction, as opposed to what's *expected* of them." Not surprisingly, both Karen and

Marc got that kind of encouragement from their parents, as did Ralph and Robin.

From Here to There: How to Pursue Meaningful Work

If you'd like to redirect your career toward greater satisfaction, here are a few tips to get you started:

- *If you hate your job, don't hate yourself.* Instead, do what you can to make your job better. For one thing, you can join or help form a union in an effort to improve working conditions. Robin Baker advocates "union activism as a form of mental health," and calls union involvement life-affirming in its own right. Organized labor, she says, "is you and me getting together and saying, 'Let's see what we can do to make this the best possible job it could be.' " If your job isn't conducive to union organizing, talk with your employer and/or fellow workers to seek improvements to the way things are.

- *Cultivate professional and personal pride.* Take satisfaction in doing your job well, whatever it is. Acknowledge yourself for having gainful employment, for supporting your family, for being knowledgeable in your profession.

- *Develop yourself.* Moving toward a more rewarding position may require additional training, credentials, or knowledge, and that can take some time, so start now. Take other courses that interest you, too—keeping yourself intellectually stimulated is one of the keys to a fulfilling *life,* not just fulfilling work.

- *Volunteer.* One option to pursuing the perfect job is finding rewarding *volunteer* work. Many people find themselves profoundly energized and gratified by spending a few (or many) hours each week performing some vital social service, such as helping at a senior center, participating in an amateur theatrical troupe, or coaching in a youth sports program. Many volunteers find themselves soon viewing their volunteering as their "real" work, and their job as something they do in their "free" time!

BALANCING WORK AND FAMILY—THE INCOME ANGLE

For single-parent Monica DeFries, finding that tricky middle ground between work and family meant scaling down a high-paying career. For Lynn and Blake Willeford, the answer lay in never scaling up. And so it goes on this rocky road to quality kid time. It's still fashionable here to tout the American Dream and celebrate family values. But we're only beginning to recognize that they can't always occupy the same space at the same time.

For some families, conflicts between work and family can't be avoided. Every able-bodied adult must hold down a job and bosses decide if parents even get home in time for dinner. Kids are entrusted to day care, school, other family members, or a latchkey and a TV—and the hope that they'll do okay.

However, in other homes, the compromises are made voluntarily, even if they don't appear so at first, as the following tales illustrate:

Monica's Story—When "Work/Family" Programs Don't Work

Monica learned the hard way that having it all sometimes means redefining "all." For nearly a decade before becoming an adoptive parent, she had made good money selling equipment for one of America's largest corporations. This Fortune 500 company has been widely recognized for its programs that help working parents meet their family needs. But as with most companies, large and small, the work/family reality doesn't always match the organization's commitments on paper. Employees at Monica's level—those earning over $50,000 per year and paid by salary, commissions, and bonuses instead of hourly wages—are allowed to set their own hours to a large extent, crucial for making those parent/teacher meetings and soccer games. But the company expects so much from its salaried people that everyone, caring parents or not, must work a fifty-five- to sixty-hour week to meet the goals the company sets for them.

"I see people working on weekends, working late into the evening," says Monica. "There is so much emphasis here on productivity and maximizing profitability that I see people's lives revolving around work. The family gets some quality time on the weekends and maybe a bedtime story, and that's about it. People who are in commissionable jobs here—who are managers, who are supervisors—they share stories with me of how their children have suffered. I've watched numerous marriages go on the rocks."

None of this affected Monica's circumstances at first. Divorced and childless, she wanted what those long hours could buy. Then, while doing volunteer work for an organization that serves abused children in foster care, Monica decided to foster an abused infant herself. Won over by Michael, she soon applied to adopt him. But lingering developmental problems from a troubled beginning—his mother was homeless and undernourished—left Michael frequently ill and needing extra care, especially in his first two years. It proved to be more than Monica could handle, at least with her job configured as it was. The daily strain of dropping Michael off at day care, commuting a long way to the job, and doing all the parenting by herself began to affect her sales numbers.

Monica did eventually win a transfer to a company site closer to her house, which boosted her performance briefly. But then a mountain of new pressures hit: Financial strain, in part from the company changing the way it paid salespeople. A serious health condition that went undiagnosed for a long time, affecting Monica's memory. Plus, Michael's continuing health problems. Monica's sales plunged again. After first trying to fire her, her supervisors had her demoted to a less demanding but lower-paying position. Ironically, the change produced a revelation:

"As painful as all this has been, I've learned a wonderful lesson," Monica says glowingly. "The balance between work and home is about right now. I work eight-to-five. I don't work nights. I don't work weekends. I'm focused at work on my job. The rest of the time, I'm focused on my family.

"I wouldn't have done it if my life hadn't gone into crisis . . . I had to learn how to go to work and come home and just be with my child and not go to the mall and go on expensive vacations and drive a sports car. I feel so fortunate because I would have just kept on that treadmill and this little boy would have just gotten lost."

The Willefords' Story—Small Is Beautiful

Although they walked a far different path from Monica's, Lynn and Blake Willeford also discovered that the secret to balancing work and family was keeping their personal ambitions in check. "We are workers, both of us, and I expect we will work until we die," says Lynn, "either for money or for love or a combination of the two. . . . We have always tried to work on projects or for businesses that we can feel proud of." But never so much that son Brook got pushed to the side.

a second income—what it buys and what it costs

If you're a single parent or your financial circumstances *demand* that both you and your spouse work, the following won't apply. But two-parent, middle-class families, listen up—that second income you're considering or already earning to make your life easier may cost you almost as much as you pull in.

In a 1997 *Business Week* article that focused on the financial aspects of second incomes, Barbara Hetzer analyzed the case of a hypothetical couple that lived in the suburbs and worked in New York City. In this example, Dad made $80,000. A second income earned by Mom would have added $70,000 for a total family income of $150,000—hardly a typical American family although perhaps a typical *Business Week* family. Nevertheless, the analysis produced an astounding result. Considering the costs of working (taxes on Mom's income, child care, commuting, meals out, housekeeping, and so on), the family only loses about $4500—not $70,000—by Mom staying home!

As Hetzer herself acknowledged, such a study makes all sorts of assumptions that affect the outcome—differences in family spending habits, cost of living (New York's costs certainly far exceed those in, say, Billings, Montana), and such. Still, the main point stands—it costs a lot of money for a spouse to work, particularly when small children are involved.

The emotional side of the decision of whether or not to work is also complicated because for many parents, there are compelling factors on both sides of the equation. Some parents will always forego the second income because they feel that staying home is better for the kids, but that's certainly not to say that parents who choose to maintain their careers care

(continued on next page)

When Brook was born, Lynn stopped working outside the home until Brook began elementary school. With a nudge from Lynn, Blake pared his five-day-a-week carpentry job to four days so he had more time to be with his son and help Lynn out at home. "I'm pretty self-disciplined about not taking on too much work myself," Lynn says, "but Blake sometimes needs to be reminded—'we only have Brook for "x" more years.' "

Today, the Willefords earn most of their income from the town movie theater they own and operate on Washington's Whidbey Island. Running the business takes only thirty to forty hours between them, and contributes to family recreation time, as well. "Most of the time we're watching a movie, after all," Lynn notes. In addition, Lynn takes assignments as a freelance writer and Blake still takes on construction projects about half the year. "Neither of us has a career," Lynn says. "We both have useful work we enjoy, work that is generally flexible enough for us to see school plays, sports competitions, etcetera."

Obviously, taming their ambitions has cost them income. Has it cost them in other ways? "Sure, neither of us is president of the U.S. today," Lynn shrugs. "But we've been very successful at maintaining a balance between work and family, family and individual, money and happiness. . . . I can't see that we've lost anything of value by insisting on balance in our lives."

The Big Picture—
Tough Choices but
Choices Still

No one who has studied work/ family conflicts in America has come up with easy answers to the question of balancing income and family needs. But choices do exist beyond the trade of ambition for family time illustrated in the above stories. For instance, in two-worker households especially, kids get more of both parents when dads take on a greater share of the workload at home.

For many parents, trimming back their careers is not a realistic option because the self-esteem and intellectual satisfaction their careers bring them is crucial to their being good with their children. An active career reduces the available choices but it doesn't eliminate them. For some careerist families who can

(continued from previous page)

less about their children. Some people do a better job of parenting if they're able to maintain a substantial professional life outside the home.

We can't make the very personal decision about a second income for you. But we can help you by listing all of the common factors, financial and emotional, to make sure you've considered everything.

PROS OF A SECOND INCOME

Emotional—Maintaining your identity and self-esteem as a professional. Maintaining stimulating work relationships and activity. Day care can improve children's social skills, help prepare them for school, and get them used to schedules.

Financial—Salary and benefits, including any contributions your employer makes to a 401(k) or other pension plan. Maintaining your position and progress on the career ladder.

CONS OF A SECOND INCOME

Emotional—Much less time with your children. Difficulty of finding quality day care that's affordable; illnesses passed to children in day care; any emotional distress children feel as a result of being in day care.

Financial—Day care costs; federal, FICA, state, and local taxes paid on the second income; costs of a professional wardrobe including drycleaning costs; transportation costs including parking; meal and snack costs if you eat out.

afford it, high-quality, intellectually stimulating day care does seem to be a reasonable compromise. Others fit their work around their family needs—by telecommuting, starting a home-based business, starting a business in which their kids can help out, or homeschooling their kids in their office. When family truly does come first, the rest of the picture tends to paint itself.

The above covers only the barest introduction to the complex subject of balancing work and family. For sources that can help you identify quality day care facilities, handle child care when work emergencies come up, reconnect with your children after work, and so on, see Resources.

CHAPTER 11 RESOURCES

**Socially Responsible Investing for Your Children's
College Education and Your Family's Security**

BOOKS AND PUBLICATIONS

Business Ethics magazine, P.O. Box 8439, Minneapolis, MN 55408, (612) 879–0695
e-mail: Bizethics@aol.com

> Excellent columns, features, and interviews on the moral complexities of business ethics
> and social responsibility. It often includes features and performance data on socially re-
> sponsible investing.

Clean Yield, P.O. Box 117, Garvin Hill Road, Greensboro Bend, VT 05841, (800) 809–6439

> A newsletter for socially responsible investors. Especially appropriate for those who are
> picking their own stocks without an advisor.

The Greenmoney Journal, 608 West Glass Avenue, Spokane, WA 99205, (509) 328–1741
website: www.greenmoney.com

> Covers SRI issues and lists performance data. A good gateway to brokers, mutual funds,
> organizations, publications, and other resources in the field.

Investing for Good: Making Money While Being Socially Responsible by Peter D. Kinder, Steven D. Lyden-
berg, and Amy L. Domini (HarperBusiness, 1993).

> This book is an introduction to socially responsible investing with a focus on the envi-
> ronment, labor, diversity, communities, consumer issues, and so on.

Investing from the Heart: The Guide to Socially Responsible Investments and Money Management by Jack A. Brill
and Alan Reder (Crown, 1992).

> Covers the basics of both investing and money management and shows readers socially re-
> sponsible options in every money category.

INVESTMENT ADVISORS

First Affirmative Financial Network, 1040 South Eighth Street, Suite 200, Colorado
Springs, CO 80906, (800) 422–7284
website: www.firstaffirmative.com

> Nationwide network of socially responsible investment advisors which can help you find
> a representative in your area.

Franklin Research & Development, 711 Atlantic Avenue, Boston, MA 02111, (800)
548–5684
website: www.frdc.com

> Large, established socially responsible firm that actively influences corporate policies re-
> garding the environment, human rights, employee safety, diversity, and animal rights.

Progressive Asset Management, Inc., 1814 Franklin Street, Suite 710, Oakland, CA 94612,
(800) 786–2998

> This nationwide network of socially responsible investment advisors can refer you to a
> nearby advisor.

Social Investment Forum, 1612 K Street, NW, Suite 650, Washington, DC 20006, (800)
58–GREEN
website: www.socialinvest.org

> This national network of social investment professionals, including investment advisors,
> researchers, and so on, can refer you to a nearby advisor.

Appropriate and Life-Affirming Work

BOOKS

Making a Living While Making a Difference: A Guide to Creating Careers with a Conscience by Melissa Everett (Bantam, 1995).

Perhaps the most practical, useful tool-in-book-form for making the transition to life-affirming work.

True Work: The Sacred Dimension of Earning a Living by Justine Willis Toms and Michael Toms (Bell Tower, 1998).

A relentlessly upbeat discussion of the quest for soul-nurturing work, and your chances of finding it, by the cofounders of New Dimensions Radio. Includes advice on how to deal with "toxic work."

Balancing Work and Family—The Income Angle

The Working Parents Handbook by June Solnit Sale and Kit Kollenberg with Ellen Melinkoff (Fireside, 1996).

Practical advice on balancing work and family. Child care, before- and after-school routines, after-work vegging, pregnancy and new motherhood in the workplace, and more.

Your Money or Your Life by Joe Dominguez and Vicki Robin (Viking, 1992).

Not a family life book per se, but a crucial resource for examining what your income costs you in "life energy," and what to do about it.

12

family spirituality

Few parents would argue with the proposition that parenting is at root a spiritual experience. From the moment we first hold our newborn, we are nose-to-nose with the Mystery, with something much bigger and deeper than anything we've ever known. Of course, parenting also includes plenty of moments devoid of awe and wonder, but when you catch a moment to watch your children sleep, or as you see them develop before your very eyes, you'd probably agree that "rapture" speaks to what you're feeling.

The spiritual rapture of parenting also has its flipside, a kind of spiritual angst—about your child's future, about your ability to handle the responsibilities of parenthood, about where your family fits in the grand scheme of things. The rapture and angst are not just sideshows of parenthood. They take center stage much of the time alongside the diapers, day care hassles, and homework crises.

But spirituality truly becomes Family Spirituality when your children join you on the journey, starting when their personalities begin to emerge in toddlerhood. Although parents expect to have to meet their children's material needs, they are often blindsided by their child's first spiritual inquiries, like "Where do we come from?" and "Where do we go when we die?" Or a beloved relative or pet passes on and we find ourselves struggling for something to say. We may utter something we think will help, but we soon end up scrutinizing our own beliefs. We find ourselves wondering, "Is there anything I was taught as a child that I can use here? Do any of the stories from my own religious background still make sense to me? Have I really put enough thought and meditation into my own understanding of the Universe to have anything useful to pass on to my kids?"

As we sort through the various teachings we learned long ago, and revisit how our beliefs may have changed, we're not only trying to find answers for our children, we're really resuming our own spiritual quest, something we may have neglected until now because of the serenity-challenged condition of our adult lives. In addition, many of us don't easily accept pat or dogmatic answers to our own questions. Nor do some of us feel comfortable passing along to our kids religious doctrines we may have disavowed ourselves. As a result of all these things, it can take years to fully integrate the spiritual dimension into family life. In the following pages, we offer you tools and perspectives to ease the process—the final piece in the puzzle of raising the Whole Person and the place where body, mind, and heart meet.

CREATING YOUR OWN FAMILY SPIRITUALITY

A few generations ago, most Americans spent their entire religious lives in one spiritual "house," adhering to the faith of their parents. People were commonly born into, married at, and buried in the same parish or congregation. But no longer. Not only do people migrate to other towns or states in pursuit of education and careers, they also emigrate from the faith traditions into which they were born. Some remain spiritual expatriates for the rest of their lives.

Of all the dramatic changes in our society over the past half century, perhaps none is more striking than the fact that religion has become a matter of choice—including the choice not to practice a religion at all. A study by sociologist Wade Clark Roof, detailed in his book *A Generation of Seekers,* showed that fully two thirds of the seventy-five million baby boomers had left the religion of their parents by their early adult years.

About half that number "return to the fold" at some point, usually after marrying and/or starting a family. Some find another denomination, or even a radically different tradition such as Buddhism or Hinduism. Millions more either concoct their own personal spiritual practice or are . . . still searching.

KURT BUSER

To many of us in this state of perpetual searching, the adventurousness and iconoclasm that led us to question our own spiritual traditions can lead to one of the biggest and most surprising challenges of our parenting careers. It's one thing to evolve your own spiritual beliefs gradually, over years of study and exploration. It's quite another when your little ones start biting your ankles with cosmic questions for which you don't have—and may not want to have—ready answers. As parents, we're programmed to dispense information, and not being able to offer any can make us feel inadequate, or worry about confusing our kids.

Many of today's parents have spent years undoing what they considered were the harmful effects of their own religious upbringing. For them, the ill effects they associate with religion—repression of individuality, guilt, racism, sexism, atrocities against indigenous peoples, and antienvironmentalism, for starters—make it hard to consider religion's possible benefits.

Nevertheless, many parents who have rejected religion as part of their family lifestyle still feel an intense longing for "something." They cherish the deep mystery of their children's birth and development. They want their children to embrace the vitality and wonder of the natural world. They hope to see their children become strong, ethical, responsible people. They yearn for their family to feel part of a soulful community and of the eternal continuum of life. And without religion, they're still grasping for a context in which all this can be explained, understood, and fully experienced.

If you feel marginalized by your own spiritual idiosyncrasies, if you want to nurture your children's spiritual growth without falling back on dogmas you disavowed long ago, take heart. There remains much you can do—from the general to the very particular—to help your family's spiritual life flower, while maintaining your spiritual autonomy.

General Approaches: Starting Where You Are

Setting out to add a spiritual dimension to your family life doesn't require you to have Absolute Truth tucked securely in your pocket—quite the opposite, in fact. Your own questions and doubts are your spiritual "work." Likewise, your kids' questions and insights will help guide you toward the resources, rituals, and teachings that will best suit your family. With that in mind, here are a few tips on beginning that journey:

"Church" is where you live. Do you and your spouse treat each other with respect? Do you honor the food you eat as well as the Earth which produced it? Do you model reverence for your children? Even if you haven't settled the question of whether or not there is a God, you can still cultivate a sense of the sacred, and pass it on to your children.

For instance, you may find the sacred in nature. Phil's family, which does not attend church regularly, experienced that on an Easter Sunday when they were planning to take in services at a local church. When the day dawned sunny and bright, full of spring's blooming, they elected to go on a hike instead. Their rationale: "Why not visit God where 'He' lives?" They came home full of appreciation for the elegance of creation. You'd have a hard time convincing them that their hike didn't pass muster as a worship service. Not that you need live near a mountain or forest—if you're capable of experiencing awe and expressing reverence, you can find the sacred everywhere you go.

Keep family traditions alive. Although you may no longer practice the faith of your childhood, odds are you have countless memories—not all of them unpleasant!—of meals, holidays, prayers, celebrations, and other details of your family's traditions. You may not want to light the Sabbath candles every Friday night, for instance, but your children will be fascinated to see the ritual, and to hear about its origins.

If all the trappings of conventional family religion make you uncomfortable, ask yourself: Which of the other elements from my family's religious tradition might still be valuable for me and my kids? For example, Jews have a long heritage of involvement in movements for social justice. Those of Jewish descent might ask how they can keep that spirit alive in their family. Alan says he most feels his Judaism not in a synagogue but when he is acting as an activist or volunteer and working with others similarly engaged. He and Hyiah convey this aspect of Judaism to their kids, as well as their personal interpretations of other aspects of their families' traditions that still have meaning for them.

What meal blessings, Sunday school teachers, baptisms, weddings, confirmations, holidays, special meals, songs, dances, or other customs do you remember with particular fondness? If these memories are mostly unhappy ones, don't let it go at that. Even things you may remember bitterly can provide fertile ground for you and your kids to plow together. Talk about the customs or teachings, about what good they taught you, what you felt uncomfortable with, and so on. The important thing is for your children to know about your family's customs and to learn about what made you who you are. In that way, your family's traditions will remain "alive" even if you don't observe them faithfully.

Start early. From the time your children are infants and toddlers, they should begin to notice that periodic reverence, spiritual seeking, thankfulness, excursions into nature, or time set aside for quiet or quiet prayer (more on these later) are all part of what it means to be a family. If you wait too long to start spiritual practices, youngsters may rebel or resist what they take as sudden efforts to "find God" or "get religion."

Explore the unfamiliar. Even if you're not "in the market" for a congregation to join, visit a variety of churches and temples. You'll be surprised at what you learn, what you may wish to adapt for your own purposes, and what tickles your kids' fancy. For instance, houses of worship incorporate a "technology" of sacred experience. The sunlight streaming through stained glass in a church; the incense and otherworldly music of an ashram; the joyous, body-swaying beat of a black gospel choir—these are designed to transport worshippers beyond their earthly concerns. Somewhere here may be elements you can adapt to your personal spirituality, especially if you eventually develop a home-based practice or self-defined worship service.

Weave. Where is it written that Hindu prayers can't be said beside Buddhist ones, Native American chants sung along with Christian hymns or Jewish psalms? Islam recognizes biblical prophets, but how many of us who were raised as Jews or Christians have ever examined the Koran, let alone shared any of it with our children? Endless treasures await those who are willing to look in unexpected places.

When you find a prayer or story or passage from scripture that inspires you, share it with your family, perhaps over a meal. You might start with some that you remember from your own childhood—you'll probably be better able to explain and discuss those than ones you discovered recently. But whatever you like, and wherever you find it, blend it into your family's spiritual tapestry. Don't worry about how well the pattern is taking shape. It will emerge in its own good time.

Be creative. "There are a thousand ways to kneel and kiss the ground," said the medieval Islamic mystic Rumi. Sometimes cooking a meal can be a prayer. An art project done with your child can be an act of worship. Planting a tree or doing some other work in the garden can yield an epiphany. If you don't like any of the meal blessings or bedtime prayers you come across, *make up your own.* And encourage your kids to do likewise. In fact, if you have a hard time improvising, ask for their help. Val Schultz and her children came up with the following song that serves as a meal-time grace in their home: *Earth who gives to us this food/Sun who makes it ripe and good/Dearest Earth and dearest Sun/Many thanks for what you've done/Blessings on the meal.*

Create a "sanctuary" at home. Look for a place at home that seems to invite reflection and silence—your back porch, a corner of your study. If space allows, it can be an entire room, patio, or side of the yard. Whatever its dimensions, you and your kids can decorate it to personalize it as much as possible. Allow your kids to contribute ideas and artifacts, especially if you want them to regard this as a special space. You needn't set up any elaborate paraphernalia there, a simple shrine with a candle, some offering from nature—fruit, a twig, or a stone—and perhaps a spiritual book should create enough of a welcome setting to inspire regular visits.

Margaret Birdlebough of Syracuse, New York, built a small shrine to Mary, mother-symbol of life and earth. "The kids have helped me arrange it with a statue of Mary, some flowers, and fake snow," Margaret says. "But I was so moved when I got up one morning and saw that Andre [then six] and Delia Rose [then three] had opened a jar of bay leaves and arranged them nicely all over the altar."

ANSWERING CHILDREN'S SPIRITUAL QUESTIONS

Few parents—avid churchgoers or decided agnostics—ever escape the challenge of discussing some notion of God, as well as other spiritual matters, with their children. For instance, in our society and culture, the references to a single, all-powerful—and usually Judeo-Christian—deity are so pervasive that they can't be ignored. So it's better that children's earliest ideas on the subject come from you. Obviously, we can't offer you one, singular, perfect way to discuss creation or other spiritual topics, but we can suggest these three tips:

- Avoid telling your child anything that you yourself don't believe—unless you introduce the idea as something that other people hold as true. And even talks about other people's beliefs are better reserved for children old enough—seven and up—to understand that beliefs in themselves are not right or wrong.

- When your best and most honest answer to a question is that you don't know, say so.

- And in the next breath, consider mentioning that many spiritual tenets are based on faith, not knowledge. That way, when you do outline a very specific spiritual viewpoint, you can speak of it in terms of what feels right, what resonates with you, or what makes sense to you, while leaving the door open for the fact that other people may believe differently.

Culled from the work of experts on children and spirituality, as well as our own interviews with parents in a variety of religious denominations or states of seeking, here's a short list of the kinds of questions your children might eventually ask.

What Does God Look Like?

In order to reasonably prepare yourself to answer this question—which, in our culture, is hardly an unusual one—you'll have to do some soul searching. Many of us who try to raise our children holistically find ourselves fending off the classic Western image of God (courtesy of Michelangelo) as an elderly white man with a beard. But how do we replace this image without substituting our own form of propaganda?

Several years ago, Stephanie was reading a kid-friendly version of an Old Testament tale from Madeleine L'Engle's *Ladder of Angels* to her children. When she happened upon the phrase "the Lord," she instinctively substituted "Mother/Father God" for the more medieval-sounding L-word. "But my daughter Tulani was hip to me instantly and she asked, 'Mom, does the book really say that?' "

Well no, Stephanie admitted, and before she could remind her kids that she believed God most likely has male and female qualities, Tulani and her brother burst out laughing. "I chuckled too, but I remember feeling uncomfortable with Tulani's idea that 'the Lord God' might be the real thing while my own phrase of choice was some New Age-ish construct," Stephanie recalls. "Even at such a young age [the children were then six and eight], the outside world had already gotten its Euro- and male-centered mitts all over their psyche. And maybe I let this happen by taking too long to bring up the subject."

In answering questions about God, it helps to fine tune your own image of the Almighty. Is this Presence flesh or spirit or simply Nature itself? Is this Higher Power loving, laissez-faire, or vengeful? Does it have a divine purpose for all people, animals, and things? Is it endowed with male traits, female traits, both, or neither? Is your best answer to these questions that you simply don't know? As you discuss God with your child, you might want to point out to her that your concept of God may change and grow just as you and she will change and grow.

Some months after your initial talks about God, invite your child to draw his impression of the deity. This emphasizes the point, through art, that discovering God can be an ongoing and creative process, and that anyone can bring a valid idea of God to the table. A few years ago, editors at *Parenting* magazine asked several second-and third grade classes—mostly in San Jose, California—to draw their image of God and explain their artwork in a sentence or two. One seven-year-old, Carey, combined abstract and realist painting to render a picture of a mountain and three star-like structures floating above it. "God's face is in the sky," Carey explained, "and the mountain is for people to climb and see God better." Eight-year-old Ahmad's depiction of a supreme being may well have been a picture of himself as a grown-up. In his pencil and crayon sketch, God was big, brown, and buff with dark, serious eyes, and a flat-top haircut—a man, Ahmad wrote, "who is always nice to his mother and father."

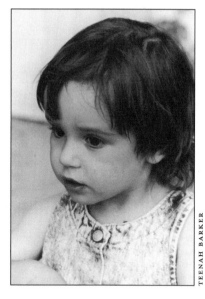

TEENAH BARKER

Despite our very Western tendency to depict God as a single person or thing, more and more parents subscribe to mystical beliefs in which God is described as a presence too vast to be confined to any one particular form. In some Native American and West African traditions, for example, God is many things at once, a central force with numerous side deities, often represented by forces of nature that are simultaneously aspects of the Supreme. Don't assume that such ideas are too complicated for your kids since they're clearly transmitted to kids in cultures holding these beliefs.

How Did We Get Here, or How Did Grandma's Grandma's Grandma First Get to Be Born?

Despite the claims of traditional religious people on one side and many scientists on the other, creation remains one of the great mysteries of existence. So we advise treating this question with the flexibility it deserves. Tell your children that different people believe different things and the universe is a complex enough place that several of these beliefs could be true at the same time. They may not find this very satisfying, because they came to you for The Answer, but shouldn't spiritual upbringing include becoming more comfortable with the enigma of it all?

When children ask about creation, take the occasion to introduce them to myths from other cultures besides our own. Reading these to your children makes for some spectacular storytimes and gives them even more fodder for their imaginations on this perplexing subject.

What Happens to Us After We Die?

Since the answer to this also depends on your beliefs, it's worthwhile to have articulated your ideas—at least to yourself—before this question arises. Some parents have a fairly short answer about burial or cremation, but even they should be prepared for any follow-up questions their kids have. They may, for example, be asked to elaborate on decomposing.

Many parents also use this query as an opportunity to elaborate on their beliefs about the eternal life of the soul. "We tell our son Julian that when we die, our consciousness lives on and comes back in another body," says Stephanie Gelfan of Amherst, Massachusetts. "But we also talk about how, when we die, we go into the ground and eventually become part of the grass, so we humans feed those same animals that we eat by becoming part of the grass."

Is There a Heaven?

Obviously, your answer to this question will depend on your own beliefs. Parents who don't believe in a celestial hereafter with billowy clouds and harp-playing angels may want to emphasize aspects of life on earth. Moms and dads who see heaven more as a metaphor for a state of bliss or a moment of joy, for instance, will probably have much to say about the feelings of connectedness, love, and understanding that are part of a state of being that could be called heaven.

Whether couching your response as your own beliefs or other people's, you may also want to discuss heaven's southerly counterpart. Take extra care with the scarier aspects of describing hell, though. Children of all ages need the hope and reassurance that come with knowing that redemption is possible no matter how badly a person behaves.

Why Does God Let Bad Things Happen?

Few children, or adults for that matter, are ever completely satisfied with the possible answers to this age-old question, no matter how wise or understanding some responses sound. One fairly common explanation is that seemingly unfair events are part of a divine plan that's beyond human comprehension, and that there's always a lesson embedded in the tragedies we face. Again, this explanation may be believable, and even acceptable, on some level, but not always comforting.

Perhaps the real reason this question is so sticky is because it just opens the door to other mysteries. Is the Universal Intelligence all-powerful but not completely good or is Spirit all good but not completely powerful? If either perception of God is true, how can we go on revering this Force? One answer that many children can grasp is that even though God created the universe, this Higher Power doesn't have time to attend to all the little details and inner workings of the universe. A variation on this theme is that even though everything in nature is the work of the Almighty, nature has its own laws that may not seem fair. When it comes to human tragedies such as violence and cruelty, one explanation is that humans were given the freedom to choose between good and evil and God can't force people to behave without taking away their freedom.

Other valid answers are more Hindu-inspired. You might say, "Life is about learning from bad events and learning how powerful we are to be able to overcome them," or "The difficulties on earth require the very best from us to triumph over them, and that's the point."

Again, as you frame your answers to these tough questions, be mindful of how mysterious these topics are, and try to convey to your children that you, like them, may still be searching. And always be willing to point out that others may feel differently. In the end, you may want to simply congratulate your children for asking such profound questions and note that you and they may be asking the same questions and refining the answers your entire lives.

FAMILY MEDITATION AND PRAYER

A late friend of Phil and Alan's, John Holewinski, once came to a profound realization while cleaning his apartment. A bachelor living alone with typical bachelor habits, he had let his household chores go until he couldn't stand it any longer. Attacking the place with a vengeance one Saturday afternoon, he restored it to some semblance of order and then invited his two buddies over to observe his handiwork. John, a sort of Zen monk in hiding, then told them how profoundly the scrubbing, vacuuming, and straightening had transformed him. "I realized," he said in wide-eyed seriousness, still in the throes of rapture, "that your place doesn't get clean unless you clean it!"

That's the dumb thing about spirituality, too. Like more material endeavors (vacations, exercise, and, yep, housework), we have to make a little space for it in our day to have it in our lives. Thus, the beauty of meditation and prayer. Both are entirely portable, are easy to do, can be accomplished in a few focused minutes, and provide a spiritual connection as direct and accessible as making a phone call.

They're also suitable for children. In the case of meditation, that may surprise us at first because most of us who meditate started as adults and think of it as a private, subtle art. The fact is, though, that while many of the subtleties of meditation may be lost on kids, the form—observing or counting breaths and such—could hardly be simpler. Prayer, of course, has been practiced by children in many families for generations. Whichever of these practices you choose will serve the purpose of grounding your children in spirituality. Your kids will see the importance of spirituality to you because time is set aside for it regularly. What's more, completely by themselves, both prayer and meditation constitute a satisfying approach to the sacred.

How Meditation and Prayer Are Alike and How They're Not

Prayer and meditation have so much in common that the distinctions between them are more a matter of emphasis and nuance than substance. In the broadest sense, prayer is any act of communion with a higher presence, including our highest selves. In fact, it could be said that being kind to others, forgiving someone else's trespasses, cultivating a garden, carving a sculpture, walking around a lake, and so on are also prayer. In a sense, any act performed with humility, reverence, or reflection counts.

Meditation is also a kind of communion, though it involves a quieter, more receptive, more single-tasked posture. When we pray, we keep many balls in the air—our emotions, our yearnings, our goals, and often our actions. When we meditate, we have only one ball aloft—sometimes something as simple as the sensation of our breath—and we follow its trajectory until our minds are still. In prayer, we petition or offer thanks or praise. In meditation, we ask nothing and give nothing but our attention. In prayer we speak and God or the universe—we fervently hope—listens. In meditation, God or the universe speaks, and *we* listen. In prayer, we supplicate. In meditation, we surrender.

Prayer or meditation with our children can yield positive and inspiring results or it can disappoint. Yet even if it falls short of expectations at your house, you've still made the point to your kids that spirituality matters. Again, both prayer and meditation are best practiced regularly—weekly at least, and daily is better. Doing it at the same time of day helps ritualize it which may make it more meaningful for all of you. Here's a closer look at both prayer and meditation so you can try them on for fit:

Why Pray?

Teaching children to pray trains them to tune in to their spiritual lives and to notice the many ways in which they are blessed. When we teach our children thankful prayers, for instance, we are reminding them that they are not alone, that nothing should be taken for granted, and that gratitude is an appropriate response to the gifts of life. One way to help our children develop a fully-rounded spiritual life is to encourage them to perform a variety of prayers. Here are several that may work for your family:

Grace. In saying grace before a meal, it's fairly obvious to remember to thank the Universe, the cook, and the farmers. Families might also fashion prayers that thank the earth for providing the soil, the winds for spreading the seeds, the sun for warming and nourishing the plants, the water for hosting the fish, and any other elements or beings that played a part in putting the food on your table. Such graces foster a keen awareness of our connection to nature and our world.

Other forms of thanks. Besides gratitude for food, try teaching kids to come up with their own reasons to be thankful: for love, for grandparents, for health, for getting a good grade, for shelter, for clothing.

Forgiveness. Family prayer time can also be a time when you ask to be forgiven for any wrong you've done. Of course, such prayers shouldn't be held in place of apologies to the one actually wronged, but they are a way of letting children know that your conscience doesn't shut down the moment you say "I'm sorry." Some families take their requests a step further by also asking for the strength or presence of mind to avoid repeating the mistake.

How can we serve?   Older children can benefit by listening to their parents ask questions like, "The world needs different things from each of us—what does it need from me?" This prayer also models a willingness to work for goals beyond satisfying our material wants and desires.

Petitions.   Children shouldn't be made to feel guilty when they ask for very concrete things—a new bike, a popular doll, or a different teacher. They're only expressing their yearnings and family prayer should be liberating enough to allow them to do just that. If we feel that our children's desires are not selfless or evolved enough, we should keep that judgment to ourselves. But if you want to suggest to kids that some requests are more attainable than others, you might shape your own prayers accordingly for them to see. For instance, instead of asking for a good grade for the course you are taking, you might instead pray out loud for all the things— perseverance, understanding, stamina, the ability to concentrate—that might lead to this result. In such prayers, you demonstrate to children how it's possible to give of yourself even as you receive.

Praise.   Consider teaching your kids to honor the moment—not just the birthdays, the holidays, the vacations, but also the wow-did-you-see-that-pretty-bird-on-the-way-to-the-store times, the did-you-notice-the-way-that-lady-smiled-at-us occasions.

Prayers for departed ones.   In many religions, those who came before us are as important as the living and are often asked through prayers for guidance through life's challenges. But even if they're not consulted, relatives who have died can be included in family prayers to recall their goodness and their input in our lives.

Why Meditate?

We exercise to tune and train our bodies. We meditate to tune and train our minds and souls. The ultimate purpose of meditation will vary with what you believe. For some people, the goal is to discover their highest selves. For others, it's to reach their fullest potential. For others still, it's no less than to merge their own soul with the Soul of Creation. On the practical plane, meditation also enhances our perceptions, sheds layers of stress, increases our capacity to love, and "gets us here" in the present moment.

None of this is particularly enticing to children, so they may instead prefer to goof off, play, or otherwise disrupt the process. But what they *will* notice and hopefully remember is that, once again, the family is doing some spiritual work together.

For all of the following family meditation techniques, you'll want to rid yourselves of as many distractions as possible: Turn off the phone ringer and turn on the answering machine, turn off the stereo and television, move to a quieter part of your home. You'll also want to sit or stand together, in as comfortable a position as possible. Lying down is not a good idea—it's too easy to fall asleep. It's also not advisable to sit in an upholstered chair, for the same reason. Better instead to sit on the floor or on a chair with no armrests, so that it takes a slight effort to hold yourself erect and be alert. As you sit, rest your hands on your thighs, palms up—in Eastern religions, this is the traditional posture of being receptive. Experiment with keeping lights on or off and keeping eyes open or closed.

You might want to try all three of the meditation techniques below before deciding which one works for your family—or you might want to consult our resources for books that offer a wider range of techniques. Whichever method you chose, give yourselves a full fifteen to twenty minutes for each session. Veteran meditators agree that few are able to reach a true meditative state in less time than that.

Counting your breath. "Let's see how well we can all do one thing and one thing only," you might announce once everyone seems settled into position. "The only two things we're trying to do for the next fifteen minutes are closing our eyes and counting our breath. The first time you breathe out, count silently 'one.' Then after breathing out again, say to yourself 'two' and so on until you get to 'four.' On the next out breath, go back to 'one,' and then on the next three breaths, count 'two,' 'three,' 'four.' We'll keep counting to 'four' this way until the time is up. Don't change the way you breathe or speed it up or slow it down. Just notice your breath and count it."

At this point, your competitive young participants may well ask, "Why not count to ten or as high as we can go? Anyone can count to four!" Answer: because by the time most people get to seven or eight, they're worrying about whether they'll remember to start all over again instead of just observing their breathing. The idea here is to think as little as possible and just be aware. Let your kids know that if other thoughts besides counting their breath come into their minds—and they will—they should silently tell themselves that's okay and get back to the counting task at hand.

Candle meditation. This meditation is great for families who are more visually oriented. In the middle of your family circle, place a lit candle and dim or turn off all other lights. Ask your family to focus on the tip

of the wick or flame. Suggest to them that even though they will have many thoughts as they watch the flame, their goal is simply to keep their eyes on the flame. Warn them that because this meditation is highly visual, other senses may interrupt the flow. They may notice the sounds of crickets chirping or pots banging in the apartment next door. They may feel an itch that they need to scratch. But after noticing these things, they should get right back to the task at hand, just focusing on the flame.

As they watch the candle, they may notice a slight halo emanating outward from the flame and may feel themselves to be part of the halo and part of the flame. That's all well and good, so long as they stay with the activity, watching the flame for as long as possible.

Chanting a mantra. In Eastern religions such as Hinduism, mantras are used in a couple different ways. In sitting meditation, they're repeated silently while observing the breath—for example, in place of the numbers in our counting meditation above. They can also be repeated vocally—that is, chanted. Chanting is designed to be performed like meditation—with complete attention on the act itself, without indulging in daydreams or other thinking. And it produces a similar effect, quieting the mind to a state of profound stillness and awareness.

Traditionally, a mantra—essentially, the word or phrase that is repeated in silent meditation or chanting—is supposed to have spiritual significance in and of itself. For instance, in several Eastern traditions, the mantra OM or AUM is considered to be the most sacred of spiritual sounds. Certain Sanskrit mantra syllables are also said to vibrationally hum in ways that stimulate certain organs, or otherwise spiritually benefit the meditator. But here in America, meditators have taken to using English words and phrases, too. For instance, some families use the mantras "Love," "Peace," "God is love," and "All is One."

Here's a chanting meditation you can try with your family: With mantra meditation, it's especially important that you avoid slouching to prevent constricting the chest and throat. Many kids will want to shout their mantras at the top of their lungs, and that may evoke some laughter. Let it be. You don't want to trounce on children's natural urges to giggle and have fun. But once everybody's settled back in, tell them that their goal is to keep chanting and to be focused on it exclusively. Then coach them to chant without straining their voices or using up too much breath. As you repeat the mantra, find a rhythm that everyone can stick with, then stay with it. For some families, fifteen minutes of chanting may be too long to start with, so begin with five minutes' worth. As always, remain attuned to how this activity is going for the group—you can always go longer if it's going well.

To make your chant more interesting and fun for all of you, you might invent a short, simple, positive melody that everyone can sing the mantra to. The melody, like the mantra itself, should be repeated over and over and not be so complex that it distracts. For a model, think "Row, row, row your boat."

Dealing with a Spiritual Crisis

No matter how well we perform our other parenting roles, shepherding our family through a crisis with a family member can make us feel inadequate and even incompetent. Our children look to us to be sturdy and able navigators, but it's hard to be a source of strength when the threat of losing a loved one leaves us distressed, saddened, or frightened. The following tactics can help you handle your own emotional turmoil and find support as well as give your children what they need during a difficult period of family life:

Expect to go through a period of feeling lost. And accept it. After all, when a loved one is seriously ill, it is as if the entire family is under siege. Many parents report feeling completely estranged from the fabric of everyday life. The usual challenges of keeping food on the table, paying the bills, and staying on top of everyone's schedule are now compounded by hospital visits, medical procedures, mounting healthcare bills, and all the new anxieties, tensions, and stress attendant with this illness. Accept that things will fall apart and your ability to focus will slip away. In time, you'll be able to at least try to refocus. And that's where others can help.

Call on extended family and your network of friends. In times of great stress, it is not only okay to accept help, it is absolutely vital to seek it. So don't hesitate to ask. Your family still needs nutritious meals, the clothes still need laundering, the garbage will still pile up if it isn't dumped. Also, children still need help with their homework and reassurance that they are loved and will continue to be cared for. Requests for assistance with all these things are fair game. Keep in mind that relatives and friends are looking for concrete and discrete ways to help.

Sometimes a crisis can help bring together people who haven't spoken to one another in years. If you have any hesitation about calling someone you've had a falling out with, weigh the consequences of not getting in touch: Would continued silence be even more painful for you both in the long run? Would it mean a great deal to you to reconcile or at least accept the comfort of this person? Perhaps healing and transformation can come from this otherwise unwelcome event. Think through what's best for everyone, sort through your needs, and act accordingly.

Be prepared to talk about the crisis. The earlier you talk about what is happening to you as a family, the easier (and somewhat less shocking) it will be to discuss later on should things take a turn for the worst. Try to level with your children as honestly, and comfortably, as possible, using phrases like "very sick" or "we're not sure what's going to happen next." Children, particularly younger ones, are often startled to see adults cry, so you might warn them at a time when you can be matter-of-fact about it, that sometimes even grown-ups break down, and that weeping is an expression of adult feelings, too.

Be mindful of siblings. If it's a child with brothers or sisters who is sick, the first things the siblings might want to know are when the ailing child will be home, if he or she will be okay, if they will also become sick, and whether or not they had anything to do with the illness. Moms and dads will need to be alert to signs of emotional wear and tear on the siblings. Younger siblings might, for instance, regress to such earlier activities as bed-wetting, thumb sucking, whining, and tantrum-throwing in their fervent need for attention. Or they may take on psychosomatic illnesses themselves. It's important for parents to try to reassure them both emotionally and physically, with hugs, back rubs, holding hands, or other forms of soothing, affectionate touching.

When Ann and Russ Albano's daughter Kari was first diagnosed with acute lymphocytic leukemia, the couple took several steps so that their other child, Manny, then four, wouldn't feel abandoned. Once, when Kari had to go back in the hospital, Russ, a fireman, took Manny on an overnight at the firehouse during one of his shifts. Not surprisingly, Manny thought this outing was cool and, Russ says, it helped appease his feelings of being left behind while his sister was always getting to "go somewhere."

Over time, though, it was clear to Ann and Russ that Manny was also having trouble with this crisis: "He started keeping everything inside," says Russ. "So I concocted this idea where I'd keep a journal about every-thing that was going on—'Kari's hair fell out today, or Manny did this today'—and I'd ask him if that's really what happened." After a while, he says, Manny would participate in the readings and correct him, saying things like "No, that's not the way I felt." It got to the point, Russ says, "where he would tell me 'Read me the Manny book,' and we'd pull it out and add something to it."

When the siblings of an ailing child are much older—say, teenagers—the issues are often different altogether. Many mothers and fathers find themselves short on patience with adolescent siblings because they need older kids to pick up the slack around the house. It's important to make sure these expectations are realistic and age appropriate. If your young-sters were too self-involved to do the laundry before the family was in crisis mode, how practical is it to demand they do it now? Sometimes supportive friends and relatives can get better results from teens than Mom or Dad can. In the end, remember, even adolescents who act cool, independent, or flip are still in need of comfort, reassurance, and TLC themselves.

Set aside quiet time for soulwork, alone. If the family is to remain stable and whole, the grown-ups must do what they can to find some balance. Med-itation is an ideal centering activity, but since it's hard to let go of wor-rying and quiet the mind during a crisis, you might prefer prayer in-stead. While no one can prove that prayer "works" or even helps, many a parent in crisis can attest to feeling empowered once they've asked the Universe for help. Others draw strength from having faith that things will get better. Phil and his wife, Michelle, had a number of intense ex-periences with crisis and prayer during their middle child Gabriel's battle with leukemia. Once, three years after Gabe was initially diagnosed, Phil was sitting on an outdoor bench just outside the hospital where Gabe was undergoing a battery of tests to see if his illness had returned. Phil remembers offering a prayer, the ferocity of which took him deeper inside his own heart and soul than he had ever gone before. The gist of the prayer: "O Mother and Father of All Things, thank you for blessing us with this boy. We place him now in your loving arms. Guide the surgeon's hands. Let them find what they must to make possible his healing. We ask only for mercy. He has suffered so much, and has so much to give. We beg you, let him live that he may glorify your Creation. Amen."

No one, says Phil, was more surprised than he that his words poured out in so focused a manner from such a despairing state. "But I found that when the fires of your own personal hell threaten to consume you," he recalls, "the mere act of petitioning the Universe offers a kind of salvation."

Form healing circles to visualize wellness. This is a concrete, unifying exercise that you can do as a family or as a community—of coworkers, fellow worshippers, neighbors, friends, or even online users. Whether you hold hands in a circle and wish your loved one a good recovery in unison or sit separately and visualize him or her swathed in light, using such guided imagery can feel powerful, focused, and right. Quakers call their version of this exercise "holding one in the light." Practitioners of Mahikari meditation (a Japanese practice) refer to their method as "giving light." During the course of the Catalfos' crisis with Gabriel, Phil gathered an extensive online network of friends and even well-wishing strangers— mostly people in the electronic community known as The WELL— who consciously prayed for Gabe and sent e-mails with impassioned wishes for his recovery. Phil, in return, would send out messages to the network containing updated reports and heartfelt thanks.

Take care of yourself. Often, tending to your most basic needs is the first thing to go in times of family crisis. But the basics like eating nutritiously, getting some form of exercise, and getting plenty of rest are all the more critical now. You'll need to do these things in order to feel recharged and renewed for any coming tribulations.

Be willing to seek counseling—or a support group. When a family member's illness turns out to be prolonged, some families, couples, or individual parents find that their need to unburden themselves increases just as help from their usual network of family and friends is waning. A professional therapist, particularly one trained in crisis or grief counseling (and/or spiritual healing) may prove helpful.

Attending a facilitated family support group can be more comforting still: "In these groups, everyone there understands what it's like to live in constant fear of a life-threatening illness, and in most families, nobody else can give them that understanding," says Gary Pelzner, an acupuncturist, registered nurse, and facilitator of a support group for families of children with cancer in San Francisco. Many such groups are run by foundations that not only serve as clearing houses for up-to-date medical information, but bring families in touch with all sorts of free or low-cost resources. Many also hold separate meetings for the children themselves who are ill, as well as for the parents.

Be there (for one another) now. There is no time but the present to be with—and to enjoy—the ones you love. Instead of spending all your visiting time nagging your ailing relative about diet or pain management, think of ways to bring a smile to his or her face. And instead of begrudging your healthy family members the chance to go sailing or enjoy a concert, see if you can join them. Whenever and wherever possible, seek and find the glimpses of lightness and joy between darker moments of the crisis, both with the loved one who is ill and those who are well.

Spiritually Integrating Grieving and Death

As anyone who has lost a close family member knows, grief can be an all-consuming, overwhelming process, compounded by the sight of seeing other loved ones in distress. Experts have identified several stages of the grieving process.

Numbness/denial: This is the shock stage, the sensation of emptiness. It's as if the psyche were buying time to make the enormity of the loss more bearable. Living family members may tell themselves "Maybe she really didn't die."

Anger: As survivors come to grips with the fact of a particular death, feelings of hostility may ensue. "What kind of God would let this happen?"

Guilt: Even if surviving family members don't blame themselves for the death, they may be angst-ridden about not having been sweeter, kinder, more patient with the deceased.

Depression: The sadness and intense feelings of loss during this stage can be quite intense. And while this grief may never be completely overcome, it does, over time, become less pronounced.

Acceptance During this latter stage of grieving, the bereaved may actively detach themselves from the reality of the death. Some people resume normal social activities or throw themselves into work or volunteering. Others simply withdraw, even as they accept their loss.

Not everyone goes through these stages in exactly this order. Nor does everyone successfully "pass" through each stage and on to the next. Certainly the relationship of the deceased to the survivors, and the way he or she died, will affect the way they grieve. Nevertheless, recognizing these stages can be a useful guide in such difficult times. In addition, some of the following activities can invite meaning, closure, and a comforting salve for the entire family's pain.

Find several ways to say good-bye. Your first opportunity to begin a personal, profoundly felt farewell comes long before the departed is sent to a mortician. It arrives in the minutes and hours after death—right there in the presence of the deceased's body. When the deceased person was an ailing grandparent, some children have been known to request that they see the body. Parents will have to use their intuition and discretion in deciding whether or not a surviving child should see their loved one so soon after death. However, children as young as five have been brought into the presence of a recently deceased family member (who had a long, lingering illness) without "freaking out," says Stephen Levine, counselor for the terminally ill and author of *Who Dies?* (see the Resources at the end of this chapter). Although a parent's first impulse might be to spare their child the sight of a dead relative, allowing such close and personal involvement in the hours after death may encourage a child to accept death as a part of life.

Later, more opportunities to say good-bye will come. Although the larger, well-attended services certainly provide an important outlet for mourning and connecting with family and friends, some people—particularly children—don't feel comfortable paying their respects so publicly. So try setting up a time when just immediate family members can talk, tell stories, reminisce, play the deceased's favorite music, look over old photos or add related mementos to the family scrapbook. Initially, such informal memorials may seem too painful to go through, but they have a way of empowering those who are nearly overcome with grief. In storytelling especially, the experience of the deceased can live on through the power of words, memory, and imagery. Consider, also, speaking *to* the deceased in a way that acknowledges not only how much you miss him, but how open you are to the possibility of communing with him, even though his body is no longer living.

Go forth into nature. Many a grieving family has found solace in natural and even seemingly supernatural moments that evoke the memory of the deceased—a seagull or sparrow that seems to follow a sibling around, a sudden rain shower, the benevolent covenant of a rainbow, a scattering of wildflowers that have sprouted suddenly where none had been before. So go out and embrace all the incidents and incidentals of nature, whether you interpret them as signs from the departed or the simple, vibrant comforts of the great outdoors.

Consider dedicating a seedling to the deceased. A fruit tree seedling, committed to the earth in a small planting ceremony, allows participants to talk about being nourished by the deceased after death, just as they were beforehand. Such a ritual also provides a perfect springboard for parents to discuss the cycle of life. Remind kids that they can visit with this newly planted tree at any time.

Be prepared for the inevitable life-after-death questions and discussions. Although adults may feel cynicism and pessimism setting in during times of grief, it's better for the sake of surviving children to accent whatever you can find that's positive and hopeful. For instance, you might want to share such comforting thoughts as "she's no longer suffering" or "he's always with us in our hearts." Be willing to explore and discuss what this second thought might mean to you and your loved ones. Also be sensitive to what your grieving children are ready to hear, temperamentally and developmentally. If you sense your child will find your views on death too stark or final, you might want to discuss the spiritual beliefs of the deceased or others instead.

Permit yourself to laugh and be happy again. Whether it's inspired by the deceased's past jokes or some retold memories, go with the laughter and the joy whenever you're able, and don't feel guilty about it—there will be time enough again for the sadder feelings that accompany your loss.

Sometimes, unexpectedly humorous moments can happen surprisingly soon after the loved one's death, perhaps while preparing the home for guests or making arrangements at the funeral home. If you find yourself feeling irreverently amused, take comfort in the idea that your dearly departed would have thought it was funny, too. And in general, remember that he or she would have wanted you and yours to enjoy life again.

Although no one would ever volunteer for the experience, there are abundant lessons to be learned from losing a family member—about love, caring, courage, perseverance, sacrifice, letting go, and healing. Welcome or not, such trying times can help you and your family figure out in a hurry what *is* important in life, and what is not.

TEACHING AND MODELING RELIGIOUS FREEDOM AND TOLERANCE

Children learn early in their school years that freedom of religion was a founding American ideal. Reality, of course, has followed a rockier path.

The Pilgrims, after all, were an extremist religious cult with no patience for dissenting views. So were the Puritans of Massachusetts Bay, who only allowed fellow believers to vote, even though nonbelievers were subjected to the same laws and taxes. To this day, powerful religious organizations relentlessly campaign to impose their religious ideas on the rest of the population in such areas as prayer in the schools, abortion, and censorship of the arts.

But never mind all that. It's the *idea* of religious freedom that counts to kids because it makes so much sense to them. Their beliefs change all the time as they learn more and more. The idea of accepting something on faith, religious or otherwise, goes against the very grain of their existence. Try to force your family religion or personal spirituality on them and you'll discover exactly what we're saying. Rebellion may not show up until their teen years, but when it does, it can show with a vengeance.

The idea of religious tolerance flows from the value of religious freedom. In the family context, religious freedom means giving your children the freedom to hold and express spiritual beliefs that are different from yours. Religious tolerance in this context means teaching your children to acknowledge the right of people outside your family to believe something different than you and your children do. Religious tolerance doesn't come nearly as easily to people—children or adults—as does religious freedom, for reasons we'll examine below. Still, it's just as important to teach it to your kids if we're all going to get along in a world that is increasingly diverse, both culturally and spiritually.

Modeling Religious Freedom, or How to Give Your Kids Space for Their Own Beliefs When Your Mind Is Already Made Up

Many of our readers will find the notion of modeling religious freedom a no-brainer. Of course, their kids should be free to believe whatever is true for them in their experience. But the task is tougher for parents who have already committed themselves to a faith or who are atheists, for that matter, since atheists are as firmly committed to their beliefs as any fundamentalist.

When you feel that your own spiritual questions have been answered, it isn't always obvious that you should encourage your children to do their own seeking. "Adults often act as if children are empty vessels into which religion must be poured," note parenting authors Sheila and Celia Kitzinger. But the fact is that children possess the ability to draw their own religious conclusions and have profound religious experiences, even as early as the preschool years. They may even come up with insights that will inspire *you.*

Here are a few other things to think about before presenting your spiritual answers to your kids:

Modeling critical thinking. Who's a better student? The one who simply memorizes material and accepts everything he reads as fact? Or the one who actually thinks about a subject and asks probing questions? The answer is obvious, so why would we want a child who is learning spirituality to be less curious than one learning, say, biology?

Acknowledging your child's intelligence and wisdom. If your children don't learn that their opinions and beliefs count, too, how will they ever develop a sense of self?

Teaching the value of spiritual experience. If you believe that a truth can't be known until it is experienced, grant your child the freedom to have his own experience, which may well differ from yours.

Acknowledging the mystery of it all. Spirituality addresses the greatest questions of human existence: How did the universe start? What happens to us after death? In such a complex universe, why isn't life more chaotic? You may think your particular system of belief provides some pretty good answers to those questions, but let's be honest, how do you really know that your answers are right and all others are wrong?

Encouraging imagination. Religious faith appeals to many adults precisely because of its certainty, because it leaves nothing to the individual to decide. But is certainty of this type really healthy for children? Their minds develop and grow through the exercise of their imaginations, and nothing is more challenging to the imagination than questions of spirit. Is it really wise to try to curtail this at an early age?

None of this is to suggest that you shouldn't *share* your faith with your children. Just don't insist that they agree with you. If you have found deep meaning or satisfaction in a set of spiritual beliefs or practices, your kids will appreciate hearing about that from you—if it comes with no strings attached. They want to hear about your life and understand why you do and feel the things you do. But they want to have their own lives, too. Repeating things that you tell them are true won't feel right to them if they don't have the understanding or experience to support those beliefs.

We also don't want to suggest that you shouldn't pass on the family religion to your kids, particularly in the case of a traditional religion that has been handed down in your family for generations. But it's just as appropriate that you eventually give your children the freedom to break from the family tradition if they so choose. The early teen years, when kids are beginning to establish their identities and lives separate from their families—a necessary and crucial stage—may be the perfect time for this. Besides, they'll pull away from the family religion if they want to anyway. If you don't allow it in their behavior, they'll just do it secretly, in their own minds.

Ultimately, kids are going to follow whatever spiritual path beckons them. The best you can hope for is that they will choose freely rather than out of angry rejection of your beliefs.

Modeling Religious Tolerance

Religious tolerance may be a cherished American value but that doesn't make it any easier to teach it to our kids. The reason has to do with our own unresolved issues about it and also the nature of religion itself. Tolerance is not something that religions do well. How many religions do you know that teach that maybe the other guy is right, after all?

Which leads to the next challenge: being tolerant of religions that are intolerant of you. Not everyone can feel warm and fuzzy about those who regard them as sinners, heathens, or at best, little lost sheep. The intolerance of some religions toward even some of their own followers—for example, women and homosexuals—also makes them hard for some of us to take. Your children are learning democratic values in school and presumably at home. It may seem strange to them at first that they should open their arms to people who appear to threaten those values.

Of course, it is precisely because our society and world is so divided and conten-tious on spiritual matters that we need to, as they say, agree to disagree. Here are some tips that will help you get this point across to your kids:

Help your kids learn about other religions. Your children will better appreciate their friends and classmates of other faiths when they know more about their spiritual beliefs and practices. Both your library and quality bookstores have many excellent books—both in the adult and children's sections—that can assist in this process. Local churches, synagogues, and organizations of clergy may also sponsor activities designed to promote understanding between faiths.

Understand and root out the intolerance in your own spirituality. Major religions are infamous for their intolerance, and it is a tragedy when religious prejudices—whether against nonbelievers, women, homosexuals, or ethnic populations—are taught to children in the guise of faith. But those of us who have rejected the faith traditions we grew up with and adopted more personal beliefs aren't necessarily any less guilty of spiritual biases. A smug feeling that we are smarter and wiser than those walking the more traditional path leads to its own subtle form of intolerance, one that we may overlook but that our children will recognize in a quick minute. (Children have an unerring eye for democracy, since most of them consider themselves unjustly ruled in their own homes!) We have to recognize the intolerance in our own hearts and do our best to eliminate it if we expect to have any credibility with our children on the subject.

Help your children understand fundamentalism. The toughest part of learning, and teaching, tolerance may be accepting those who don't accept you, meaning fundamentalists in almost any religion. So it may be useful to show your children why fundamentalists feel as they do. As Middlebury College professor of religion Steven Rockefeller explains, many religions teach that your salvation depends on obedience to God's will, which is expressed in the religion's doctrines and laws. People who don't follow those doctrines and laws are your enemy because they might lure you away from your source of salvation. Show your kids that the best way to practice tolerance with fundamentalists is simply to make room in your hearts for them to have those beliefs and realize that they are just trying to be the best people they can be.

Teach that God has many faces. By the time children reach school age, they are old enough to understand that everyone is different. By then, they may also be old enough to understand that a single truth—including spiritual truth—can take on many different appearances. Metaphors are a powerful teaching tool to get this point across. Try the old one that God has many faces and that the one you see isn't necessarily better or more true than the one your neighbor does. You might also compare spirituality to tastes in food. A child who likes chocolate ice cream isn't better than one who likes strawberry—it's just a matter of taste. The same goes for religion—it, too, is a matter of personal taste.

Go beyond tolerance to deep respect. Professor Rockefeller suggests that the basic American value of tolerating others of different races, religions, ethnic origins, and nationalities doesn't really go far enough. If we expect to get along, we have to regard others with positive respect. Citing a Jewish teaching, he notes that a wise man is someone who learns from everyone. "That is, a Christian can learn from the Jews and the Buddhists and vice versa. There has to be an openness to others, without surrendering the uniqueness of one's own tradition." This is not at all difficult for children to understand, if their folks get it first.

CHAPTER 12 RESOURCES

General

BOOKS AND PUBLICATIONS

Inquiring Mind: A Semi-Annual Journal of the Vipassana Community, P.O. Box 9999, North Berkeley Station, Berkeley, CA 94709

> Published by the Vipassana Buddhist meditation community, but it has evolved into one of the most interesting and valuable periodicals of any spiritual stripe.

New Age: The Journal for Holistic Living, P.O. Box 1949, Marion, OH 43305, (800) 755–1178 (subscriptions only)

website: www.newage.com

> This is one of the oldest (founded in 1974), most independent-minded, and creative of the many periodicals spawned in recent decades to chronicle the spiritual and political quests of the post–World War II generations.

Raising Spiritual Children in a Material World by Phil Catalfo (New York, NY: Berkley, 1997).

> This book explores many of the themes of this chapter in depth, and presents a series of families walking different spiritual paths, working out their own solutions to the same dilemmas many Whole Parenting families face as they try to define their families' spiritual practices.

Sojourners, 2401 15th Street, NW, Washington, DC 20009, (800) 714–7474 or (202) 328–8842

website: www.sojourners.com

> With an editorial viewpoint based where fervent Christianity meets progressive social activism, this bimonthly offers unflinchingly challenging and passionate discussions of "Faith, Politics, and Culture."

Yoga Journal, P.O. Box 469088, Escondido, CA 92046-9624, (800) 600–9642

website: www.yogajournal.com

> Originally aimed at yoga teachers, this lively bimonthly is now a direct competitor to *New Age* in both quality and content.

OTHER MEDIA

New Dimensions Tapes, New Dimensions Radio, P.O. Box 569, Ukiah, CA 95482–0569, (800) 935–8273

website: www.newdimensions.org

> *New Dimensions* offers cassettes of nearly two thousand interviews with many of the leading philosophers, psychologists, artists, and authors of the last three decades, from the acclaimed radio series *New Dimensions.* Contact them for a free newsletter or catalog and listen for the radio show, available on many public stations nationwide.

Creating Your Own Family Spirituality

BOOKS AND PUBLICATIONS

Celebrating the Great Mother: A Handbook of Earth-Honoring Activities for Parents and Children by Gail Johnson and Maura D. Shaw (Rochester, VT: Destiny/Inner Traditions, 1995).

> An outstanding guide to creating an earth-based family spirituality.

Creation Spirituality Network Newsletter/Original Blessing, 2141 Broadway, Oakland, CA 94612, (800) 973–2228

website: www.csnet.org

> This bimonthly newsletter, the successor to the quarterly magazine, is the best place to keep updated on the eco-feminist spiritual philosophy and cultural work of "maverick

theologian" Matthew Fox, author of *The Coming of the Cosmic Christ, Original Blessing* and many other provocative books, and the main agitator for reclaiming the celebratory, "creation-centered" spirit within the Christian tradition. Each issue also includes articles by other eco-spiritual thinkers and rituals readers can adapt in their own lives. This newsletter is on the cutting edge of contemporary spirituality.

Gently Lead: How to Teach Your Children About God While Finding Out for Yourself by Polly Berrien Berends. (HarperCollins, 1991).

> *Gently Lead* is a splendid, lyrical meditation on the subtle, challenging parental task of awakening one's own spirituality while cultivating it in one's children.

God Is Red: A Native View of Religion by Vine Deloria, Jr. (Fulcrum, 1994).

> A dense but comprehensive and authoritative overview of Native American spirituality, which is usually underappreciated, sometimes romanticized, and often misunderstood by European-American culture.

Jewish Renewal: A Path to Healing and Transformation by Michael Lerner (Grosset/Putnam, 1994).

> A bold vision of Judaism that blends its historical concern with social justice with a contemporary, almost mystical spirituality, and attempts to apply that blend hopefully to the world of the coming decades. The author is the founder-editor of *Tikkun* magazine.

Of Water and the Spirit: Ritual, Magic, and Initiation in the Life of an African Shaman by Malidoma Patrice Somé (New York, NY: Tarcher, 1994).

> A fascinating autobiographical account by a West African shaman who also holds three master's degrees and two Ph.D.s, thus bridging the worlds of the West and "the village." A good companion to *God Is Red* (above), and an illuminating expression of the worldview and spirituality of indigenous peoples.

Answering Children's Spiritual Questions

Small Wonder: How to Answer Your Child's Impossible Questions about Life by Jean Grasso Fitzpatrick (Penguin, 1994).

> Explores the reasons behind many kids' questions and suggests meaningful answers that encourage critical thinking, social responsibility, and creativity. See also her *Something More: Nurturing Your Child's Spiritual Growth* (New York, NY: Viking, 1991).

Talking to Your Child About God by David Heller, Ph.D. (Bantam, 1988).

> A crisp, lucid guide to cultivating dialogue with your little ones about the biggest, most elusive topic the human mind can confront. Heller is especially good at urging parents to be sensitive to kids' own ideas and feelings, and the different ages at which they're developmentally ready to handle deeper, more complex aspects of The God Question.

Family Meditation and Prayer

Seven Times the Sun: Guiding Your Child Through the Rhythms of the Day by Shea Darian (LuraMedia/ Innisfree Press, 1994).

> This ordained Methodist minister, Waldorf school administrator, and mother of two offers practical, playful advice for establishing stimulating yet harmonious rhythms to daily life in the home, from quiet morning rituals to creative afternoon play to bedtime transitions.

Dealing with a Spiritual Crisis

What Helped Me When My Loved One Died by Earl A. Grollman, ed. (Beacon, 1982).

> Many varieties of death are explored in this anthology edited by rabbi, author, and grief counselor Grollman, who has written over ten books on loss and death.

When a Friend Dies by Marilyn E. Gootman, Ed.D. (Minneapolis, MN: Free Spirit Publishing, 1994).

Addressed mainly to teens but also useful to their parents, this book offers smart, wise, grounding advice delivered in spare, accessible format that invites the reader to pick this slender volume up whenever one is feeling troubled.

When Bad Things Happen to Good People by Harold S. Kushner (Schocken, 1981).

Kushner takes the view that humans should accept the notion that God is good but is powerless to prevent tragedy from happening. He counsels survivors not to spend time finding fault but to seek out the many ways to rediscover the Creator's benevolence.

Who Dies? by Stephen Levine (Anchor, 1982).

An eloquent, spiritual exploration of death, grieving, and dying that stands apart from most of the books of the genre. The title refers to the author's point that we are not our bodies, nor are we our pain.

Teaching and Modeling Religious Freedom and Tolerance

BOOKS

The Illustrated World's Religions by Huston Smith (HarperSanFrancisco, 1994).

A useful reference for adults in explaining diverse religious traditions to their children. One of the world's best recognized authorities on religion and spirituality, Smith is unusually sensitive to mystical traditions.

Sacred Scriptures edited by Jaroslav Pelikan (available through the Quality Paperback Book Club, Camp Hill, PA 17012, 800/998–1979).

This is an elegant, affordable, seven-volume collection of many of the world's most important religious scriptures, including Buddhism's *Dhammapada*, Christianity's Old and New Testaments, Hinduism's *Rig Veda*, Islam's *Koran*, Judaism's *Tanakh*, and more.

The World's Religions edited by Peter B. Clarke (Pleasantville, NY: Reader's Digest Books, 1993).

Like other recent *Reader's Digest* projects, this impressive, coffee-table book is a lucid, comprehensive, and exceptionally reader-friendly introduction to its subject. Young children won't follow the text but they'll love the photos in this outstanding family reference book.

ORGANIZATION

The Interfaith Alliance, 1012 14th Street, NW, Suite 700, Washington, DC 20005, (202) 639–6370

website: www.tialliance.org

A nonpartisan, national network of clergy and lay citizens across a diverse array of religious traditions. It strives to provide a progressive, unifying voice within the faith community.

index